THE
CANADIAN POLITY

A Comparative Introduction

Ronald G. Landes
St. Mary's University

Prentice-Hall Canada Inc., Scarborough, Ontario

To my wife, Peggy,
and our children,
Megan and Donny

Canadian Cataloguing in Publication Data

Landes, Ronald G., 1945–
   The Canadian polity : a comparative introduction

Bibliography: p.
Includes index.
ISBN 0-13-114116-3

1. Canada — Politics and government.   I. Title

JL65 1983.L36   320.971   C82-095310-5

Prentice-Hall, Inc., Englewood Cliffs, New Jersey
Prentice-Hall International, Inc., London
Prentice-Hall of Australia, Pty., Ltd., Sydney
Prentice-Hall of India Pvt., Ltd., New Delhi
Prentice-Hall of Japan, Inc., Tokyo
Prentice-Hall of Southeast Asia (Pte.) Ltd., Singapore
Editora Prentice-Hall do Brasil Ltda., Rio de Janeiro

ISBN 0-13-114116-3

Production Editor: Charles Macli
Design: Joe Chin
Compositor: Compositor Associates Limited
Production: Alan Terakawa

Printed and bound in Canada by John Deyell Company

1 2 3 4 5   JD   87 86 85 84 83

Contents

PART FOUR: EVALUATING THE CANADIAN POLITICAL
EXPERIMENT

List of Tables and Figures

Preface for Students

Studying the politics of one's own country should be an exciting experience, for politics and government determine not only our present condition, but our future survival. To that end we have sought to provide an interesting examination of how the Canadian political system operates. We begin with an overview of the nature of government and politics (Part One), proceed to a consideration of basic political institutions (Part Two), investigate political processes and political behaviour (Part Three), and conclude with an assessment of the workings of the Canadian polity (Part Four). In considering such topics, we seek to introduce the student to three main areas of investigation: first, the nature of political analysis; second, the fundamentals of Canadian government; and third, the study of comparative government. These three goals are intertwined throughout the text and should be borne in mind by students as they read the various chapters.

Several suggestions concerning the use of this text may be helpful before proceeding. Each title page presents one or more quotations, which express that chapter's main theme. Upon completion of each unit, the student should return to these opening ideas and reflect upon them. Second, at the end of each chapter we have provided a list of recommended readings. These items include several of the most important historical works on each topic, along with more current publications. Except in a few cases, these works should be accessible in most university libraries and intellectually rewarding for the beginning student. Finally, a different footnote style than usual is employed throughout the text. Instead of footnote numbers with references at the bottom of the page or at the end of the chapter or book, relevant bibliographical information is included in the body of the text itself. The first item refers to the author's last name, the second to the year of the publication of the work cited, and the third to the page number, if the reference is to a particular passage. This format does not break the reader's train of thought, but allows him or her to see immediately whose work is being quoted. Full reference information for each item cited is contained in the bibliography at the end of the book. For major historical works, the original date of publication is given in the text, with both the original and later edition dates included in the bibliography.

Since the text is written for undergraduate students, the author encourages you to write to him with your comments or suggestions for improvement. Please send your views to the Political Science Department, Saint Mary's University, Halifax, Nova Scotia, Canada, B3H 3C3.

Preface for Teachers

Many teachers approach the introductory course in political science with a considerable amount of apprehension. Too often the initial politics course at the university level is seen as either a burden to be endured or an affliction to be assiduously avoided in the future. This reaction is unfortunately a fairly typical one: we are socialized in graduate school to be specialists in ever-narrowing subfields of increasing irrelevance. Not surprising, then, is the negative reaction to the task of giving a "general overview" of the discipline to beginning students.

This pattern, to put it bluntly, is a mistake. For one thing, it deprives the student of a chance to learn from those who should know the most about the discipline. Too often it is forgotten that probably half of all the students ever enrolled in political science courses across the country take only the beginning political science option. If we do not teach them an understanding of politics at that level, we never will. Avoidance of the introductory course is also a mistake from the professor's perspective, for it relieves him or her of the responsibility to teach the most difficult of all courses. Contrary to a myth of the profession, we would contend that the easiest courses to teach are the advanced ones, for the quite simple reason that students will learn in spite of what we do. In the introductory course we have the opportunity to motivate people to learn about politics, at least in part, because of what we do. If we cannot communicate effectively with beginning university students, it is doubtful that we can do so with our colleagues either.

The downplaying of the introductory course is clearly evident in the available teaching materials – few, if any, works are designed with the beginning Canadian politics student in mind. The purpose of this book is to fill this gap by providing a readable and informative text that introduces students to both the Canadian and Comparative Politics areas. While the major emphasis is on an introduction to Canadian politics (approximately 60 percent of the material), included as well are detailed analyses of the politics of Britain and the United States and general concepts from the field of Comparative Politics (approximately 40 percent). Thus, the text has three basic goals: first, to serve as an introduction to the craft of political analysis; second, to provide an introduction to the study of Canadian government; and third, to offer students a look at the practice of comparing political systems. Part One introduces students to the nature of government (Chapter 1) and to the basic concepts and principles of political analysis (Chapter 2). Quite likely, students will find Chapter 2 the most difficult one in the book. As a result, if it is to be successful, Chapter 2 may require particular attention from the teacher. Chapter 2 is significant because it lays the basis for the way the various political institutions and processes are analyzed in Parts Two and Three.

The basic institutions of Canadian government (constitution, executives, legislatures, and judiciaries) are analyzed in Chapters 3 through 6. Having set the institutional context of government, we then proceed to an analysis of political processes and political behaviour in Part Three. Chapter 7 expands the context of politics by introducing the student to the concept of political culture. Chapter 8 investigates the nature of political parties and party systems. The electoral process is dealt with in the next three units: Chapter 9 looks at the nature of elections and political recruitment; Chapter 10 discusses the topic of electoral systems; and Chapter 11 considers how the individual learns to participate and does participate in the political process.

Part Four of the text seeks to place the nature of Canadian government in sharper focus by analyzing how it works in practice (Chapter 12) and how it relates to the concept of classical democracy (Chapter 13), which then serves as a basis for recommending some needed areas of political reform. Chapter 12 tries to connect the various topics together by analyzing the content and passage of the 1982 Canada Act. Although the Canada Act has technically changed the name of the BNA Act of 1867 to the Constitution Act of 1867, we have used the older term, so as to avoid unnecessary confusion for the students.

Since each teacher probably has a particular way of structuring the introductory course, no order of chapters is likely to satisfy everyone. We have tried to make each chapter a self-contained unit, so that the teacher might rearrange their order in Parts Two and Three without seriously undercutting the flow of analysis. Each chapter in Parts Two and Three begins with a brief introduction and consideration of basic concepts relating to the specific topic, applies these ideas to the Canadian, British, and American polities, and ends with a look at the key areas for comparing how the various political institutions and processes operate. A point-form summary and list of recommended readings is also provided for Chapters 1 through 11. This chapter structure should allow the smooth incorporation of a discussion of any other countries of particular interest through the use of lecture material. While aimed at the introductory level, this text may also be of use as required reading in second and third year Canadian government courses.

The ideological bias of the author is that of a liberal-democrat. A variety of approaches are utilized throughout the text, including the historical, institutional, and behavioural perspectives.

Any suggestions or comments concerning this text would be most appreciated by the author, especially those that might be incorporated into future editions. Please send your views to the following address: Political Science Department, Saint Mary's University, Halifax, Nova Scotia, Canada, B3H 3C3.

Acknowledgments

In writing a textbook, an author quickly realizes how much he depends on others. Over the years, numerous teachers, students, and researchers have contributed in their own way to this final product – such help is hereby gratefully acknowledged.

Others have also been essential in the development of this work. Saint Mary's University aided in a number of ways, in particular, by granting me a sabbatical leave in 1979-1980, during which time this book began to take shape. Ms. Laurie Wheeler, political science secretary, managed to turn handwritten scrawls into a first-draft manuscript. The wizardry of Miss Shirley Buckler and Miss Sharon Whitefield on the word processor artfully transformed numerous revisions into a finished manuscript. Finally, two friends provided helpful comments and encouragement throughout: Dr. Peter Dale and Professor Edward J. McBride.

Various individuals at Prentice-Hall have been essential to the completion of this project. Along with Prentice-Hall's local representative, Don Blair, the late Frank Hintenberger signed the book in December of 1980. Cliff Newman and Marta Tomins have guided the manuscript throughout its various stages. To these people and their staffs, more than a word of thanks is due.

Finally, recognition must be given to my loving family, without whose cooperation this project would not have been possible. Somehow, my family managed to endure this book – to them it is lovingly dedicated.

PART ONE

The Nature of Government and Politics

1 THE COMPARATIVE STUDY OF CANADIAN GOVERNMENT

The study of comparative politics, to borrow a phrase from Guys and Dolls, *is the "oldest established permanent floating crap game" in the social sciences. It moves freely across the boundaries of academic disciplines as well as nation-states. The pioneers of comparative politics, from Aristotle to Alexis de Tocqueville, were born too long ago to have had their thoughts confined by the narrow boundaries of a single academic discipline, or by a single national culture (Rose and Peters, 1978: xi).*

CONSIDER FOR A MOMENT the following events from the past decade and a half of Canadian politics:

1. *October 1970*: Canada is shocked when the FLQ abducts and later releases British Trade Commissioner James Cross and then kidnaps and later murders Pierre Laporte, Quebec Minister of Labour, House Leader of the Quebec Government, and senior colleague of Premier Bourassa. Apprehending an insurrection, the federal cabinet, at the request of the Montreal and Quebec governments, imposes the War Measures Act. For nearly two months the federal government exercises a vast arsenal of emergency powers and for an additional five months utilizes slightly less power under the Public Order Temporary Measures Act. The police forces conduct 5000 raids and arrest 465 people, many in the middle of the night. Included in the roundup are mainly separatist sympathizers in Quebec, among them many academics and artists.

2. *November 15, 1976*: Nine years after resigning as a provincial Liberal cabinet minister and eight years after the founding of the Parti Québécois, René Lévesque, in his third try for elective office as leader of the Parti Québécois, gathers 41 percent of the popular vote and 69 of the 110 seats in the Quebec National Assembly. For the first time in Canadian history, a major provincial government is controlled by an avowedly separatist political party. As a prelude to Quebec's possible secession from the century-old Canadian Confederation, the Parti Québécois promises a future referendum in Quebec on Lévesque's blueprint for "sovereignty-association."

3. *January 30, 1978*: Francis Fox, age 38, Solicitor General and Member of Parliament from Quebec, a possible future leader of the Liberal party, rises in the House of Commons and in an emotional and tearful speech announces his resignation from the Trudeau cabinet. Fox admits that, before entering the government, he had an affair with a married woman who became pregnant. In order to expedite her legal abortion, Fox forged her husband's name to the hospital consent form. One of Canada's highest law enforcement officers stands liable for criminal prosecution; his political career appears finished.

4. *May 22, 1979*: Prime Minister Pierre Elliott Trudeau, Canada's leader for 11 years and survivor of three previous general elections, is defeated by Joe Clark, a result that leads the *Toronto Star* to proclaim, "Now Joe Who really is a somebody!" At age 39, Canada's youngest Prime Minister, Clark ends 16 years of Liberal government

in Ottawa. Gaining only 36 percent of the popular vote (4 percent less than the defeated Liberals on a national basis) and 136 seats in the House of Commons (6 short of a majority government), Clark, with minimal representation from Quebec, is faced with the task of forming Canada's fourth minority government in 17 years.

5. *December 13, 1979*: After only six months in office and two days after presenting its first budget, the new Tory government faces an NDP non-confidence motion in the House of Commons. With the small Social Credit caucus abstaining, and with the combined opposition of the Liberal and NDP caucuses, the Conservatives are defeated by a vote of 139 to 133. A dissolution of Parliament is granted by the Governor General on December 14, with the election writs issued for February 18, 1980. Canada's thirty-second general election aborts the nine-month old minority Tory government and reestablishes a majority Liberal government under the resurrected tutelage of Pierre Trudeau. Joe Clark becomes Canada's youngest former prime minister.

6. *May 20, 1980*: The Parti Québécois, in an attempt to gain public support for negotiating sovereignty-association with Ottawa, holds its long-awaited referendum. After an extremely hard-fought, emotional, and at times bitter campaign, 60 percent of the Quebec electorate refuse to grant the Parti Québécois its desired mandate. The federal Liberal government, in an attempt to seize the political initiative, quickly begins another round of constitutional talks, with new constitutional proposals to be ready by September 1980. René Lévesque postpones calling a provincial election in Quebec and indicates his willingness to participate in the new series of constitutional deliberations.

7. *February 17, 1982*: In the Olds-Didsbury riding for the Alberta legislature, Gordon Kesler, running as a separatist under the Western Canada Concept label, sweeps to victory in a by-election. The country faces the threat of a growing separatist movement in Western Canada, in addition to the existing one in Quebec.

8. *April 17, 1982*: After two years of intense political conflict between the federal and provincial governments and 115 years after Confederation, Canada becomes, in all respects, an independent country. The proclamation of the 1982 Constitution Act by Queen Elizabeth II in Ottawa adds a Charter of Rights and a series of amending formulas to the existing Canadian Constitution.

The above examples tend to belie the often-made charge that Canadian government and politics are uninteresting. One reason students have found Canadian politics less than exciting is that many introductory textbooks place a great, if not exclusive, emphasis on the analysis of political structures and institutions. Much time is spent on the "nuts and bolts" of governmental structure and organization (e.g. how many senators there are from each province, their method of appointment, their length of tenure). Therefore, there is often a neglect of political processes (e.g., elections, federal-provincial relations).

A Canadian attempting to understand the debates surrounding the reform of the Canadian Constitution, for example, would see the importance of both political structures and political processes. Before one could understand the significance of proposed constitutional changes, it would be necessary to have a knowledge of the components of the current constitutional system. An historical perspective on how the Canadian Constitution has evolved from 1867 to the present would provide additional insights into the need for various constitutional reform proposals. However, to know what the Constitution is and to comprehend the nature of the proposed changes would still leave much unsaid. An appreciation of the amendment process (i.e., how amendments are proposed and adopted) would also be crucial. As is so often the case in politics, these two factors of structure and process intermingle and influence each other. An understanding of Canadian politics requires knowledge and insight into both political institutions and political processes.

A second reason why students often seem bored by Canadian government is that our system is treated in relative isolation from other political systems. Yet the injunction "to know ourselves" (Symons, 1978) should be a call for understanding, not parochialism. A fundamental assumption of the analysis in this book is that Canadian government and politics can be best understood and appreciated in a comparative context. The problems encountered by the Canadian system are not necessarily unique, and in most cases are not. Many countries face problems of regionalism, secessionist threats, minority governments, and constitutional change. Not only do comparisons with other countries teach us about other political systems, but they provide us with a basis for assessing the strengths and weaknesses, advantages and disadvantages of the Canadian political experiment.

THE NATURE OF GOVERNMENT

In beginning our analysis of the Canadian polity or political system, we will first consider the nature of government. Much of what political science knows about the nature of government that is worth knowing can be summarized as follows: government is ubiquitous, multiple, expansive, necessary, and varied.

WICKS

7/20

"It must be some form of government. You can tell by the direction that they are travelling."

Government is *ubiquitous* in both geographical and practical terms. Territorially the world is divided among governmental units called nation-states (over 150 of them). All earthly domain is claimed by these nation-states – there is literally no place on earth that one can go to get away from governing authority. If people emigrate from one country to another, they do not rid themselves of government, but merely exchange one governing authority for another. Attempts to create utopias of one kind or another may seek to do away with government, but they do so on territory claimed by the government of a nation-state and are usually allowed to exist only as long as they present no immediate threat to existing political institutions. Even the possible escape to outer space appears to be unlikely without the monetary and technological support of an existing government.

Government is also ubiquitous in practical terms: little we do in life is free from government control and regulation. The extent of governmental regulation in Canada was summarized by then Justice

Minister Jacques Flynn in August 1979, in a speech to the Canadian Bar Association, in which he pointed out that a listing of federal regulations came to over 15 000 pages. In addition, the Law Reform Commission of Canada has found that federal laws have created 30 000 offences, while provincial laws have added another 20 000. Given these numbers, it is little wonder that most aspects of our lives are touched by governmental authority. The taxes we pay, the conditions of our workplaces, the nature of the products we buy, our medical treatment, the procedures of birth, marriage, and death are all regulated by government. On a larger scale, governments decide questions of war, peace, and environmental protection, the consequences of which determine whether we live or die, as individuals and as a planet.

Although government is ubiquitous, it is difficult to define. This difficulty stems from the fact that government is a summary concept that organizes our perception of reality: we usually see the manifestations or results of government (e.g., taxes, laws), not government itself. One can physically see governmental buildings (such as the Parliament buildings in Ottawa), governmental personnel (cabinet officers, civil servants such as deputy ministers), and governmental processes (passage of a piece of legislation through Parliament, a federal-provincial First Ministers' Conference). Yet there is no single place where one can go to see the government in total: government resides in many places. However, the varied perceptions of governing activity are likely to contain a common theme: we propose to define this common theme of government as the institutional organization of political power within a given territory.

A second characteristic of government is that it is *multiple*: each citizen is subject to a number of governments and governmental units. A common view is to perceive government as a cohesive organization, united in its goals, coherent in its programs, and consistent in the implementation of its policies. It is typical in political analysis to find phrases such as "the government decided." However, political reality suggests an alternative view: government is a plural, rather than a singular phenomena. For example, all people in Canada are subject to at least three levels of government: the federal government in Ottawa, the government of the province in which they reside, and their local government. All three levels have the power to tax and to otherwise regulate our behaviour. Some citizens in the major metropolitan areas are faced with an additional layer of government, as are those residents subject to various regional governmental units. Both metropolitan and regional governments interpose an additional layer of government between the local and provincial units of organization. An extreme example of the multiplicity of governments can be found in the array of governing authorities that control our nation's capital.

> Canada, it is said, is the most over-governed country in the world. If the complaint is valid, surely no corner of the land suffers more from a surfeit of government than the national capital. On top we have the federal Government; it owns the place, or, at least, 16 000 acres of it. It owns outright 470 buildings (ranging from the barns at the Central Experimental Farm to skyscrapers in downtown Ottawa and Hull to the official residence of the Prime Minister).
>
> Next we have the National Capital Commission, a quasi-autonomous and, at times, dictatorial federal agency. Next, the Ontario Government. Next, the regional municipality of Ottawa-Carleton (under the chairmanship of a former suburban reeve). Fifth, the generally ineffectual administration of the City of Ottawa. To complete (and further complicate) the picture, add, for the Quebec side, a provincial, regional, and municipal administration (Stevens, November 30, 1979).

The complexity of government is further enhanced if we also remember that each governmental level (federal, provincial, local) is composed of numerous governmental units. Governmental units refer to such institutions and political structures as the executive, legislative, and judicial branches of government, as well as to various government departments and agencies. For example, there is a federal cabinet as well as ten provincial cabinets, and a national Parliament as well as ten legislative assemblies at the provincial level. One study of local government in the late 1960s in Metropolitan Toronto discovered a total of 101 governmental units (del Guidice and Zachs, 1976). The multiplication of governmental units within each governmental level has developed to such an extent that it would be difficult to make an accurate count of them. Thus, it is not surprising to find that one writer has insisted that "governments are like bees, birds, fish, cattle, or wolves; they come in swarms, flocks, schools, herds, or packs, but never alone" (Schattschneider, 1969: 12).

The number of governments imposed on the citizen by the state varies among political systems. In unitary political structures, such as Britain and France, the central government in the national capital governs, while local governmental structures are used primarily as a means for administering policies determined by that central government. In contrast, Canada, as a federal political structure, interposes an intermediate level of government (e.g., the provincial level) between the central government and the citizen, while local government is also more independent in Canada than it is in either Britain or France. Thus, the Canadian citizen deals with more governments than do citizens in unitary political systems. The multiplication of governments has proceeded the furthest in the United States. As a federal political system, the United States has 50 state governments (compared to 10 provincial governments in Canada), in addition to the national government in Washington. However, it is at the local level where the multiplication of government occurs most dramatically: if one counts all units with the power to tax (federal, state, and local governments, as well as school districts and special districts), there are today nearly 80 000 governmental units in the United States, a reduction from the 155 000 such units that existed in the early 1940s.

Recognizing the multiplicity of governments helps us to understand how governments actually operate. If governments are multiple, then it stands to reason that each governmental level or unit may have different goals or purposes. As a result, governmental actions often appear contradictory or lacking in consistency for the quite simple reason that they are contradictory and inconsistent. Understanding the multiplicity of governing authorities allows us to see why such a pattern develops: different government levels and units with varying goals rarely act with unanimity in the making of public policy. For example, the Canadian federal political system, which divides political authority between a central government and various provincial governments, ensures conflict over major policy decisions. Setting the price of oil in Canada provides an illustration of this point: the federal government's goals (to achieve a rough equality of energy costs to all Canadians and to gain additional tax revenues for Ottawa) are at odds with the Alberta government's goals (to move Canadian domestic oil prices to the world price for oil and to build up the Alberta Heritage Trust Fund as a means of compensating future generations of Albertans when the province's natural resources are depleted).

The same type of conflict and contradictory policy occurs between governmental units within the same level of government. For example, within the federal government, one department, National Health and Welfare, spends time and money trying to convince us of the harmful effects of alcohol, while other departments rely on the tax money raised by the sale of liquor to support their programs. The height of absurdity is probably reached in the Department of Consumer and Corporate Affairs: within a single department, two competing and often contradictory interests are joined in an uneasy marriage of convenience. Only through recognizing the multiplicity of governmental levels and units, and the political conflict that results from their contradictory policy objectives, can we understand the nature of the political process.

A third characteristic of government is that it is *expansive*: the functions, costs, and personnel of government are ever-increasing. Although conservatives argue for a slower expansion of government than do their opponents, they do not believe in, nor do they implement in office, an actual reduction in the absolute size of government.

> Government, it seems safe to say, is one thing that has been growing rapidly in the West. Wherever governments were once small they have become big, and wherever they were big they have become bigger. Nothing is so rare as a shrinking government (Nutter, 1978: 1).

The growth of government in the 20th century, particularly evident in the rise of government expenditures in the decades since World War II, has occurred for a number of reasons. Perhaps most importantly in democratic political systems, people have simply demanded that their governments provide them with a greater range of benefits and services (e.g., medical care, pensions, unemployment insurance, consumer protection). Politicians and political parties have responded to these demands, which they have themselves helped to create, as a means of winning political power. Politicians prefer to run on platforms that offer more, not less to the average voter: the promise of mortgage interest deductibility by the Conservatives in the 1979 campaign in Canada exemplifies this point. Likewise, the defeat on December 13, 1979 of the Clark budget and his government's ensuing loss in the February 18, 1980 election can also be viewed in this light. The Conservative budget sought to slow the expansion of government expenditures and to substantially raise energy costs as a means of both forcing a conservation of scarce natural resources and of increasing government revenues. As Finance Minister John Crosbie phrased it, Canadians were being asked to bear "short-term pain for long-term gain." The short-term pain was borne, however, by the Conservatives rather than by the Canadian electorate. The Liberals returned to power after only nine months in opposition by promising not to impose the Tory's 18-cent-a-gallon excise tax on gasoline and by suggesting that their energy cost increases would be based on a "blended, Canadian-made price," far below those predicted by the Conservatives.

If a political party does advocate a withdrawal or tightening of government services, it does so in relation to those segments of the electorate that would not vote for the party anyway. The Conservative party's proposals in the 1979 campaign to make drastic cuts in the size of the Ottawa bureaucracy and to further tighten the eligibility rules for Canada's unemployment insurance program probably cost the party few votes, since the two groups affected by these changes were not likely supporters of the Conservatives anyway. These examples seem to confirm the view that in democracies "the bias in the electoral cycle favors increased spending. Rightly or wrongly, politicians consistently calculate that voters want more, and so, they promise more" (Rose and Peters, 1978: 112-113).

A second important cause of the expansion of government is simply increased population, also a significant factor in the initial development of government in society: "Governments were instituted among men not because men are bad but because there are too many of them'' (Schattschneider, 1969: 119). Government will cost more in absolute terms if the number of people governed increases: providing government for 24 million Canadians in the 1980s will require larger expenditures than providing services for only 10 million people, as there were in 1930. More significant than their numbers is the age distribution of this increasing population. The baby boom of the postwar years meant that government expenditures on family allowances increased dramatically. Likewise, as the baby boom generation moved through the school system, governments were required to provide for the rapid expansion of educational facilities. When this generation reaches retirement age in the early 21st century, it will create additional government expenditures on such items as old age pensions, medical care, and housing. Moreover, it is important to remember that because people now live longer than in the past, governments are required to provide services to each individual for a greater number of years.

A third reason for governmental growth is that society itself, through such developments as urbanization and industrialization, has become more complex, necessitating a corresponding development of government services and regulations. The invention of the automobile at the beginning of the 20th century is one indication of why government has expanded. With this new form of transportation, government became involved in the building of highways and their maintenance (the cost of snow removal alone in Canada runs into millions of dollars each year), with regulations concerning the proper use of highways (speed limits, weight limits, traffic signals), with the regulation of the building of automobiles (including safety features, emission controls) and at times direct financial support for the automotive industry (aid to a nearly bankrupt Chrysler Corporation in 1980), and with the development of consumer protection (rust prevention, safety checks, licensing, seat-belt legislation, mandatory insurance requirements). In return, governments receive a considerable amount of tax revenue from the automotive industry through such mechanisms as a sales tax on the purchase of new cars, taxes on the sale of gasoline, and various required fees such as the issuance of individual driver licences.

Thus, governments have been drawn into new policy areas as a result of the nature of modern society. Governments in earlier times did not have to deal with such problems as the ongoing energy crisis, environmental protection, the regulation of air travel, and the production, control, and sale of atomic power. Similarly, governments have become involved in such concerns as garbage. Major metropolitan areas in Canada have passed bylaws respecting the collection and disposal of solid wastes that specify in detail the amount and type of garbage a householder may leave for pickup, the time of day for placement and collection of garbage, the number of bags that can be disposed of at any one time, the type of containers that may be used, and the weights allowed for any single item of garbage. It is this area of regulation that "has emerged in recent years to rival taxing and spending as a primary means by which governments seek to influence, direct and control social and economic behaviour" (Schultz, 1981: 313).

A fourth reason for government expansion relates not to developments in society, but to the nature of bureaucratic institutions. For personal and organizational reasons, bureaucrats seek to increase their staffs, budgets, and functions.

> Internal influences and patterns of behaviour characteristic of bureaucratic organizations tend to promote a constant increase in the scope of activities undertaken by component agencies and, in doing so, expand the possibilities of greater monetary and non-monetary rewards for the bureaucrats themselves (Butler and Macnaughton, 1981: 99).

Once a program or agency is established, it usually expands. Bureaucratic success is often measured in terms of budget appropriations. Those organizations that gain more one year are in a better position to acquire even greater rewards the following year. More government today leads inexorably to even more government tomorrow. This organizational explanation zeros "in on the motivational structure of the governmental bureaucracy as the primary source" for the expansive nature of government (Buchanan, 1977: 18).

The expansion of governmental activity in the 20th century is a reflection, then, of four primary causes: first, there are more people for which governments must provide basic services; second, citizens, particularly in democratic systems, have demanded more from government; third, the complexity of modern society has drawn government into an ever-increasing array of new policy areas; and fourth, once established, bureaucratic institutions have a tendency for growth. The result has been a tremendous expansion in the scope of governmental activity: governments today perform many functions that in the past have not concerned the governing authorities. While there are some obvious differences between Western nations, it is generally true to say that in previous centuries government was perceived by most people, the public as well as leaders, as playing a limited role within a restricted political sphere. Today, government plays an expanding role within an expanded political sphere.

The growth of governmental activity is a trend as applicable to Canada as to other Western nations. The data in Table 1.1 reveal a dramatic increase in total government expenditures and revenues during the last 50 years, especially noticeable in the past several decades. For example, between 1926 and 1950, total government expenditures, as a percentage of the Gross National Product, only increased by 6 percent (from 16 to 22 percent), but in the quarter-century between 1950 and 1976, they nearly doubled (from 22 to 42 percent). While government spent $4 billion in 1950, by 1976 all governments were spending nearly $55 billion or 51 percent of the country's total National Income. As Section B of Table 1.1 demonstrates, government expansion slowed in Canada in the early 1960s, but between 1965 and 1975 it rose again, from 40 to 51 percent of the country's National Income. Indicative of this latest round of government expansion is the fact that the total federal government expenditures in 1968 when Pierre Trudeau first became Prime Minister were less than the federal government's deficit for the year he first left office a decade later in 1979. Estimates tabled in the House of Commons (February 1982) projected total federal government spending to be more than $76 billion in 1982-83, with that figure expected to rise to over $100 billion by the mid-1980s. If more evidence is needed to support the claim about the expansive nature of government, then the burden of taxation would surely provide it. For example, by 1980, the average Canadian family was paying 46 percent of the family's total cash income in all kinds of taxes (Pipes and Walker, 1982: 36).

Although they are dramatic, the figures in Table 1.1 underestimate the extent of government expansion in Canada: many actual costs of government are not included in government budgets. For example, since tax expenditures do not involve a direct outlay of public funds, they are not included as a government expenditure in Canada. Tax expenditures refer to the various deductions allowed by the government before arriving at a person's or corporation's taxable income: such items as the personal and married exemptions, registered retirement savings plan contributions, registered home ownership savings plan contributions, and the employment expense deduction. A study by the federal Finance Department discovered 190 such tax exemptions, write-offs, and deductions in effect for the 1979 tax year. These tax expenditures amounted to $32 billion in

TABLE 1.1   *The Growth of Government in Canada*

SECTION A: TOTAL GOVERNMENT EXPENDITURES AND REVENUES

Year	Total Government Expenditures as a percentage of the Gross National Product	Total Government Revenues as a percentage of the Gross National Product
1926	16	17
1950	22	25
1960	30	28
1970	36	37
1976	42	39

Source: Marsha A. Chandler and William M. Chandler, *Public Policy and Provincial Politics* (Toronto: McGraw-Hill Ryerson, 1979), pp. 9–10.

SECTION B: GOVERNMENT SPENDING RELATED TO CANADA'S NATIONAL INCOME

Year	National Income million dollars	Total Government Expenditures million dollars	Government Expenditures as a percentage of National Income
1950	14 128	4001	28
1955	20 690	7275	35
1960	27 380	11 261	41
1965	40 875	16 431	40
1970	63 618	30 982	49
1975	106 748	54 726	51

Source: G. Warren Nutter, *Growth of Government in the West* (Washington, D.C.: American Enterprise Institute, 1978), adapted from pp. 36–37, 60–61.

"lost" revenue for the federal government. The difference between a budget expenditure and a tax expenditure sometimes helps to shape, as well as to explain, government policy. The move by the federal Liberal government in 1979 to shift from a focus on family allowances (a budget expenditure) to a child tax credit scheme (a tax expenditure) can be seen in this light: on paper the federal government appears to be restraining its level of spending, while in fact it is spending more.

The pattern of government expansion is also evident in other Western nations. A study of 16 Western democracies over a 25-year period (1950-74) found a clear increase in the total amount of governmental expenditures (Nutter, 1978: 1-18). Government expenditures rose from a third of National Income in the early 1950s to more than one-half of a country's National Income by the early 1970s. More significant is the finding that the major cause of government expansion was domestic spending requirements (e.g., welfare programs, medical care) rather than external ones (e.g., defence and foreign affairs). This conclusion is consistent with our earlier discussion of why government has expanded: internal domestic pressures, rather than external international factors, are the primary cause of the extensive nature of government in modern society. In Table 1.2 we see that these basic patterns are true for Canada, Great Britain, and the United States. Such data demonstrate that the "growth of government seems universal in the West" (Nutter, 1978: 18).

The expansive nature of government is perhaps best illustrated by the actions governments take to control their own size: more government is created in order to reduce the size of the present government. For example, in its attempt to convince the Canadian public that it seriously wanted to slow government's growth, the Trudeau administration in the late 1970s created the Office of Paperwork Burden. The task of this new bureaucracy was to reduce the duplication of forms and information requests that citizens and businesses were required to submit to various governmental authorities. Even more revealing is the dramatic growth in the expenditures of the auditor general. The job of the auditor general is to examine or post-audit all government expenditures as one means of helping to keep government spending in check. The cost of this service rose from $4 million in the fiscal year 1972-73 to $26 million in 1978-79: a six-fold increase in just six years. As in other countries, the attempt in Canada to control government's size has simply produced more government.

The fact that government is ubiquitous, multiple, and expansive creates the impression that government is also *necessary*: governments exist because of the functions they perform, that is, because of what they do for society.

Governments carry out many different tasks or jobs: that is, they have many consequences for and effects on society. Governments are required as the institutional means for controlling and regulating conflict within society. Any society is composed of many individuals, groups, classes, parties, interest groups, and regions, each of which typically desires a competitive advantage over the

TABLE 1.2   *Government Expenditures as a Percentage of National Income (1950–1974) for Three Western Democracies*

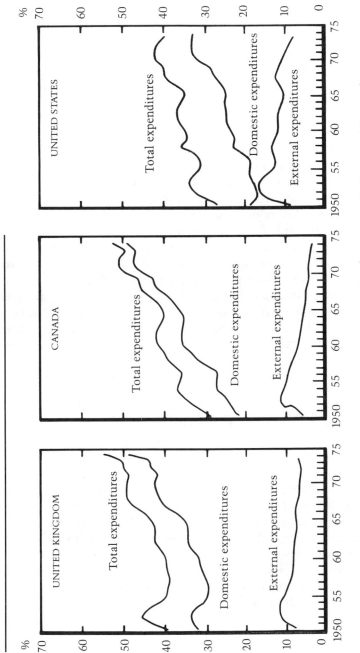

Source: G. Warren Nutter, *Growth of Government in the West* (Washington, D.C.: American Enterprise Institute, 1978), adapted from pp. 8, 11.

others. In Canada, with 24 million people, 10 provinces, many regions, and at least several social classes, to name only a few of the more obvious divisions in Canadian society, some mechanism is required to ensure social order. Government is just such a structure: it is a "central function of political processes to control conflict in organized society" (Pirages, 1976: 5).

Conflict develops in society primarily because of one fundamental fact of life: scarcity. Whether it is scarcity of wealth (gold, money, standard of living), natural resources (oil, natural gas, food), or status, the result is the same: conflict over who will control and benefit from the limited but highly valued goods and services. Given the scarcity of resources and the ensuing conflict over their distribution, government becomes the means for resolving these conflicts by certain agreed upon rules of the political process. Political systems attempt to channel and transform conflict (including violence, coercion, and force) into peaceful competitive pursuits. For example, in liberal-democratic political systems election campaigns between competing political parties are one way of arriving at decisions about the goals and purposes of the government. Elections determine which party will control the government, and thus, as a consequence, who will decide the allocation of scarce resources. Government budgets, for example, specify which groups, regions, or individuals receive the benefits of government, and which sectors of society bear the costs of these allocative decisions.

A second cause of social conflict is diversity. Linguistic, ethnic, economic, regional, and religious differences may all become linked to political concerns: in Canada, such sociopolitical cleavages have an important impact on the structure, operation, and future of the political system. Likewise, differences in values, that is, what people want and expect from government, may lead to conflict. In liberal-democratic political systems, governments seek to harmonize these divergent interests, not to eliminate them. Moreover, in most political systems, these two causes of conflict reinforce each other. For example, minority groups based on religious, regional, or ethnic differences are usually the same groups that receive the least in terms of the society's allocation of scarce resources. The combination of scarcity and diversity produces difficult challenges to any polity: in Canada, it is just such a pattern that continually challenges the wisdom of our leaders, if not the very existence of our political system.

In viewing government as the institutional means for the settlement of conflict resulting from both scarcity and diversity, we have emphasized the negative side of government: its role in mediating, reducing, and avoiding conflict. However, government can also be creative, or at least attempts to be. Government's second major function is positive in the sense of being purposive, of wanting to achieve certain desired goals. For example, Pierre Trudeau's promise of a Just Society in the 1968 federal election, although it turned out to be just another example of campaign rhetoric, illustrates that politicians may often have goals or objectives other than simply winning power and maintaining themselves in office. Likewise, the Conservative's 1979 election promise of mortgage interest deductibility could be seen, in its most favourable light, as an attempt to use government to achieve a desired end: namely, to encourage home ownership and family life in Canada. Governments seek to be creative mechanisms when they promote our health and welfare (e.g., medical care, dental care, consumer and environmental protection), when they attempt to alleviate the negative economic results of a capitalistic system (e.g., unemployment insurance, manpower retraining programs, disability and pension plans), when they promote widespread educational opportunity through financial aid to education and vocational training programs, and when they seek to develop a sense of national unity (e.g., the adoption of ''O Canada'' as the official national anthem in time for the 1980 Dominion Day celebration).

The utilization of government as both a regulator of conflict and creator of values helps to explain the previously cited characteristics of government. The ubiquitous and multiple nature of government stems, in part, from government's attempt to regulate an ever-increasing number of policy areas in an ever expanding political sphere. The use of government as a creative instrument is directly linked to the expansive nature of government. If more and more individuals and groups seek to use government to achieve an increasing range of goals and purposes, then the size, cost, and scope of government is bound to grow. Finally, we should realize that the use of government as a creative mechanism leads to political conflict: given the value differences among individuals, groups, or regions, it is not surprising that many political battles concern the goals and future direction of public policy.

In utilizing government in both its regulative and creative capacities, numerous types of governmental structures have been devised: in other words, government is *varied*. In some ways, of course, each government is unique: no two governments are identical in all respects. However, it would be an impossible task to describe in detail the historical and present array of governments if we assumed the absolute uniqueness of each political system. Instead, one of the significant tasks of political science is to look for patterns of similarities and differences among political systems so that various typologies or classifications of governments can be developed.

Although political science has produced a prolific number of classifications, we should keep in mind that there is no right or wrong way of classifying governmental types. Classifications should be developed and used with a specific goal in mind, which thus allows for the selection of the appropriate criteria on which the typology is to be constructed. Since we are primarily concerned with comparing the political systems of Canada, Britain, and the United States, we have chosen for consideration several typologies that highlight their similarities and differences. In order to show something of the diversity of people's political experience and to set the Canadian, American, and British pattern within the world context, we begin with a general classification of governments. This first typology emphasizes the similarities among the Canadian, American, and British forms of government. The second and third typologies to be discussed, namely the distinctions between federal or unitary and presidential or parliamentary forms of government, focus on the differences in governmental structure among these three liberal-democratic political systems.

After surveying the historical development of governmental types, British political scientist Bernard Crick (1973: 69-73) concluded that three basic forms could be identified: autocratic, republican, and totalitarian.

> Autocracy ... is the form of government which attempts to solve the basic problem of the adjustment of order to diversity by the authoritative enforcement of one of the diverse interests (whether seen as material or moral – almost always, in fact, both) as an officially sponsored and static ideology.

> Republican government ... is the attempt to solve the basic problem of the adjustment to diversity by conciliating different interests by letting them share in government or in the competitive choosing of the government.

> Totalitarian government ... is the attempt to solve the basic problem of the adjustment of order to diversity by creating a completely new society such that conflict would no longer arise: it attempts to do this by means

of guidance and enforcement of a revolutionary ideology which claims to be scientific, thus comprehensive and necessary, both for knowledge and allegiance.

The advantage of Crick's classification is that the form of government (i.e., autocratic, republican, or totalitarian) is related to the functions of government (i.e., how government performs its regulative and creative tasks in reconciling diversity with political order). An autocratic system imposes one divergent interest over all others; a republican system conciliates competing interests; while a totalitarian system creates a new political society in which competing interests have been eliminated. Examples of autocratic governments would include the monarchies in Europe through the 18th century, Czarist Russia, and Iran under both the Pahlavi dynasty and the Ayatollah Khomeini; republican governments would include the current liberal-democratic systems of Europe and North America, along with Israel and Japan; totalitarian governments would be exemplified by Nazi Germany and Soviet Russia under Stalin and his successors.

In addition to handling conflict and diversity by different means, these three basic forms of government also diverge on a number of more specific criteria. An autocratic government is characterized by an agrarian economy, a self-perpetuating elite group, a highly stratified social structure, an official doctrine typically based on religion, and a political system from which the ordinary citizen is normally excluded. A totalitarian government is characterized by an industrializing and planned economy, an elite group based on a single ideology, a social structure which in theory is based on equality but in practice is highly stratified around a sole political party, a revolutionary ideology, and a political structure based on mass participation but not mass control. Finally, a republican system centres on a capitalistic or market economy, an elite which is relatively open to new participants, a stratification system based on a large middle class, a mix of ideologies, and a political system based on competitive parties and elections.

Although the term republican has been utilized for several centuries within the field of comparative politics, in more recent times the concept of liberal-democracy has become more commonly used. In order to avoid any possible confusion, we will employ the term liberal-democracy – or just simply democracy – to refer to the type of government classified as republican by Crick. A liberal-democratic system "is one in which public policies are made, on a majority basis, by representatives subject to effective popular control at periodic elections which are conducted on the principle of political equality and under conditions of political freedom'' (Mayo, 1960: 70).

The construction of any typology forces political analysts to specify the criteria which they feel are the most significant for investigating the similarities and differences among political systems. A classification scheme also produces an either/or decision by the political scientist: for example, Crick's classification results in the placement of any specific government in one of three possible categories. As a result, few political scientists would disagree that the Soviet Union under Stalin belonged in the totalitarian category. By contrast, under Nikita Khrushchev's leadership, the extent of state control and political repression in the Soviet Union receded, however modestly, while crackdowns on political dissent under Leonid Brezhnev indicated a return to a more Stalinist approach by the leadership in Moscow. Such internal changes have led some observers to claim that the Soviet Union no longer exemplified the characteristics of a totalitarian government. However, if one considers all of its governmental characteristics, the Soviet Union clearly belongs in the totalitarian category, both in the past and under present Soviet leadership.

In addition to forcing either/or decisions on the political analyst, a second problem associated with the use of classifications is the assumption that a specific government exhibits all the characteristics of a particular category. For example, with respect to the control of property, the Soviet Union, as a pure totalitarian government, would not allow the existence of private property. In fact, however, private property has not only been allowed to exist, but at times, has even been encouraged by the Soviet leadership, particularly with respect to private agricultural plots. Thus, no specific government exhibits, in all respects, every single characteristic of a particular classification scheme.

A good way of perceiving governmental types, therefore, is to see the classification as a continuum, with a specific government showing more or less of a particular characteristic. Such a procedure is especially useful when comparing governments within a particular category. For example, if we compare Canada, the United States, and Britain in terms of political participation with respect to the percentage of voting turnout in national elections, we would rank Britain as the most participatory (79 percent in February 1974 and 73 percent in October 1974), with Canada a close second (71 percent in

July 1974), and the United States a distant third (56 percent in 1972 and 54 percent in 1976). However, if we use a criteria other than voting turnout – such as the number of opportunities for political participation offered the average citizen in each country – a very different ordering of these three countries emerges. Given, in the U.S., the number of political offices filled through elections, the frequency of elections, the openness of the political recruitment process through the use of direct primaries, and the opportunities for utilizing the recall, initiative, and referendum techniques at the state and local levels, it would be classified as the most participatory. Canada, which gives the average citizen the right to vote in national, provincial, and municipal elections and also allows for limited participation in the leadership selection process through the national party leadership convention, would rank second in terms of opportunities for political participation. In such a comparison Britain would rank third, because of its closed recruitment process, the selection of the party leader by the party caucus, and the use of only national and local election campaigns. These examples demonstrate an important aspect of comparative political analysis: the conclusions reached in any comparison depend to a large extent on the aspect of the political process being considered.

Finally, with respect to classifications, we should remember that, since political systems change through time, so does their placement in any typology. For example, Germany has moved from autocracy in the 19th century to a democratic form of government during the Weimar Republic in the 1920s, to a totalitarian variety under Hitler and the Nazis, and back to a democratic form in West Germany and a totalitarian version in East Germany since World War II. Similarly, any particular government changes through time even within the same category: for example, Canada, Britain, and the United States are all more participatory today than they were 50 years ago. This problem of political change emphasizes an additional consideration in comparative political analysis: the conclusions reached depend on the historical period of the comparisons.

In addition to classifications that compare governments in total, more limited typologies, which focus on a particular aspect, may also prove useful, especially for comparing governments within a specific category. Two such limited typologies will be considered: first, the distinction between federal and unitary forms of government and second, the differences between presidential and parliamentary governmental structures.

The classification of governments into federal or unitary systems is based on the structure of the central or national government and the resulting way in which political power is shared with the constituent political units (i.e., provinces in Canada, states in the United States). A *federal* form of government is constructed on the principle of the division of powers between levels of government: in other words, in Canada, governmental power is shared between the national government in Ottawa and the 10 provincial governments, while in the United States governmental power is divided between the national government in Washington and the 50 state governments. The organization of the political units in a federal nation-state is on a geographical basis (i.e., provinces or states) and represents an attempt to incorporate diversity (economic, cultural, linguistic, ethnic, regional) within an overall unifying framework.

In such a system, each level of government can act directly on the citizen (e.g., taxation) and also independently exercise certain governmental powers, which are usually specified in the country's constitution. Generally, some responsibilities are shared between the levels of government. As a result, federalism creates a structure of government as well as a process of governing: after the initial design of a federal system, the continuing distribution and sharing of powers becomes a primary political issue. When jurisdictional disputes arise in a federal system, the judiciary is often called upon to act as an arbitrator of the precise role of each level of government. In other words, we can say that the essence of a federal system is the division of power between a national government and various constituent units. Political systems which are federal in structure include Canada, the United States, Australia, and West Germany.

A *unitary* government consists of a national or central government and local governmental units: in other words, in contrast to a federal structure, the intermediate level of government (provinces or states) is missing. More importantly, the central government monopolizes political power and determines which powers it will allow the local government to use. Local government does not exercise power independently of the central government and the powers, structure, and boundaries of the local units can be changed by the central government acting on its own initiative. Examples of unitary systems include Great Britain, Sweden, and France.

A third alternative, although rarely tried in the 20th century, is that of a confederal structure. In such a system the constituent units create the national or central government, which then governs only with the consent of the constituent units. The central government's authority is not independent: it acts on behalf of its creators.

Such a system was tried in the United States after the American Revolution with the Articles of Confederation: its failure led to the adoption of a federal system under the present American Constitution. In Canada, some proponents of provincial rights come close to advocating a confederal form of government under a revised Canadian Constitution. The Premier of Newfoundland, Brian Peckford, asserted on the night of the Quebec referendum on independence (May 20, 1980) that the national government was a creation of the provinces. While such statements may be politically advantageous in Newfoundland, they are incorrect from both an historical and theoretical perspective. Although Canada is called a confederation, what was intended and created by the British North America Act in 1867 was a federal political structure, and a highly centralized one at that.

Our third classification, that of presidential or parliamentary systems, focuses on the structure of the executive (single or dual) and its relation (separation or fusion of powers) to the legislature within a single governmental level. A *parliamentary system* has a split executive: that is, a head of state or *formal executive* with relatively limited political power (e.g., the British monarch, in Canada, at the federal level the governor general, and in the provinces the lieutenant governors) and a *political executive*, which is the repository of extensive political power (e.g., the British and Canadian prime ministers, the premiers of the 10 Canadian provinces). The formal executive performs primarily symbolic and ceremonial functions, while the political executive exercises effective political power. A second characteristic of a parliamentary system is the executive's relation to the legislature: a parliamentary system is based on the principle of the fusion of executive and legislative power. Whichever party has a majority of seats in the legislature also controls the executive branch; in other words, the same group of political leaders operate both the executive and legislative institutions of government. This fusion of executive and legislative power is accomplished through the cabinet, described in the British context by Walter Bagehot (1867: 68) as ''a hyphen which joins, a buckle which fastens, the legislative part of the State to the executive part of the State.'' In turn, the cabinet is collectively responsible to the legislature for its actions and retains office only so long as it receives majority support in the legislature. A third characteristic of parliamentary government is that a maximum time limit, usually five years, is set for how long a government can stay in office without returning to the people through an election to renew its mandate. Within this maximum time limit, however, elections are held at varying intervals: for example, federal elections in Canada occurred in 1957, 1958, 1962, 1963, 1965, 1968, 1972, 1974, 1979 and 1980. The timing of elections is generally within the powers of the political executive to decide.

In contrast, each of these three characteristics of executive structure, executive-legislative relations, and the calling of elections operates differently in a presidential system. First, a *presidential system* operates with a unified or single executive. In the United States, the American president performs both the formal and political executive functions of government. Second, the relation of the executive and legislature in a presidential system is based on the principle of the *separation of powers* (i.e., that each branch of government operates independently from the others). This separation of powers principle is maintained through a series of *checks and balances*, which are the specific constitutional powers granted each branch to control, in some respects, the operation of the other branches of government. For example, in the American system the legislature may pass a law, but the president may veto it. A countercheck is given to the legislature in that it may override a presidential veto by a two-thirds vote in both the House of Representatives and the Senate. A presidential system is also characterized by elections at set intervals: there is no leeway when an election will be held, because the dates are mandated by law. An American presidential election is held in November every four years: such elections are automatic and will be held in 1984, 1988, 1992, 1996, and 2000. The executive in the American presidential system has no power to determine when to seek a renewal of the mandate to govern. These various characteristics of parliamentary and presidential governments are summarized in Table 1.3.

In beginning our discussion of the presidential/parliamentary distinction, we indicated that these forms operated within a particular level of government. However, the presidential/parliamentary classification can be joined with the federal/unitary distinction to produce a combined classification of governmental forms. In Table 1.4 we present such a typology for various democratic governments. (A combination classification for other types of government could also be developed: for example, the Soviet Union is a totalitarian government which in theory has a federal political structure, but in practice a unitary system of government). Canada is parliamentary and federal in structure, Britain is parliamentary and unitary, the United States is presidential and federal, and France is presidential and unitary. All of these designations are clearcut except perhaps the case of France, which is usually labeled "quasi-presidential." The Fifth French Republic combines both parliamentary and presidential patterns, but since the presidential aspects tend to dominate, it is classified in the presidential category.

TABLE 1.3   *Parliamentary and Presidential Governments*

	STRUCTURE OF GOVERNMENT	
Characteristic	*Parliamentary*	*Presidential*
1. structure of the executive	*dual*: both a formal and a political executive	*singular*: formal and political executive combined in a single office
2. executive–legislative relationship	*fusion of powers*: achieved primarily through the cabinet and based on the principle of collective responsibility	*separation of powers*: based on independent branches of government, maintained by a system of checks and balances; no collective responsibility of the executive to the legislature
3. elections	*maximum time period* fixed, with varying election periods within the maximum determined primarily by the political executive	*set time period* for elections, with the political executive playing no role in determining when elections will be called

TABLE 1.4   *A Combined Classification of Democratic Governments*

	LEVELS OF GOVERNMENT	
Executive–Legislative Relationship	*Federal*	*Unitary*
Parliamentary	Canada	Britain
Presidential	United States	France

Our consideration of three basic classifications of government (autocratic, democratic, totalitarian; federal, unitary; presidential, parliamentary) demonstrates the useful nature of typologies in political analysis. Beginning with a criterion that appears to be an important point for comparing political systems (e.g., the structure of the executive, executive-legislative relationships), a typology groups various systems in terms of their similarities within categories (e.g., all federal states share certain characteristics) and differences between categories (e.g., democratic governments vary from totalitarian governments in many ways). Thus, the classification of governments is a shorthand or summary method for describing their organizational structure and operating principles. For example, Canada's government is democratic, federal, and parliamentary in nature; Britain is democratic, unitary, and parliamentary; while the United States is democratic, federal, and presidential. To make such a description summarizes in three words a wealth of pertinent information concerning the operation and structure of these political systems. Therefore, classification is not merely an idle academic exercise – it is a particularly useful starting point for comparing political systems.

A COMPARATIVE PERSPECTIVE ON CANADIAN GOVERNMENT

In analyzing the nature of government as ubiquitous, multiple, expansive, necessary, and varied, we have suggested the need for viewing any particular political system from a comparative perspective. The importance of bringing just such a comparative focus to the study of Canadian government can be justified on several grounds. First, people's political experience, both historical and contemporary, has produced an array of possible political systems. Only a comparative approach can begin to introduce students to this diversity of political institutions and processes. Second, in learning about other political systems, students can overcome the parochialism of their own limited political experience. Few people directly experience different forms of government. Knowledge of alternative political arrangements can thus broaden one's intellectual perspective. Third, the increasingly complex interdependence of nations means that it has become impossible to isolate domestic from foreign politics. Other political systems directly affect the internal politics of Canada. For example, decisions by OPEC to increase world oil prices underlie the recurring confrontations between

Ottawa and the Western oil-producing provinces concerning the domestic price of oil and the distribution of the resulting tax revenues between the federal and provincial governments.

In addition to recognizing the diversity of political experience, overcoming the parochialism of a single system focus, and emphasizing the interdependence of political systems, a comparative approach to politics seeks to develop generalizations or hypotheses that explain the similarities and differences among political systems.

> Comparative analysis is an integral part of the study of politics. The comparative study of politics suggests immediately the laboratory of the scientist. It provides us with the opportunity to discuss specific phenomena in the light of different historical and social backgrounds.... More specifically, however, the function of comparative study is to identify uniformities and differences and to explain them (Macridis, 1955: 1).

It is this search for similarities and differences between political systems, and an explanation of such patterns, which has been described as the "highest objective of comparative analysis" (Scarrow, 1969: 8). However, before explanations can be developed, one must start with description, that is, a knowledge of what exists. After an understanding of the workings of several particular political systems has been developed, then the student can begin to focus on the explanation of important patterns of political phenomena.

The reasons for utilizing a comparative approach in studying any particular political system are as applicable to Canada as to any other country. For example, the decade of the 1970s saw a much needed focus among Canadian political scientists on an analysis of our own political system. However, as a consequence, an older tradition has been downplayed, if not entirely forgotten: that is, the explicit, comparative analysis of Canadian politics (Bryce, 1921; Corry, 1947; Brady, 1947). A comparative approach can widen our intellectual horizons and, at the same time, allow for a fuller understanding of our own political system. A comparative perspective is an aid, not a hindrance or substitute, for understanding the Canadian political experiment. Similarly, the interdependence of the modern world has particularly affected Canada. It is often forgotten that Canada is the only country in the world that borders on both superpowers. Likewise, Canada's economic interdependence with other countries, particularly with the United States, is extensive.

A comparative approach is also useful because Canada's polity embodies an interesting combination of political principles. For example, Canada was the first political system to counterpose federal and parliamentary institutions within a single government.

> The Canadian constitution at the time of its creation presented to the world of political science a novel combination of constitutional principles. England's great contribution had been parliamentary and responsible government; the United States had shown that federalism was the system best adapted to a disunited people scattered over wide areas. Canada was the first nation to weld these conceptions into a new whole... (Scott, 1977: 35).

As a result, Canada provides an interesting case study for comparing these principles with other possible variations. To date, however, the Canadian political system has often been neglected within the field of comparative politics.

Although we have argued for the need to compare Canada with other political systems, we have not yet justified the selection of countries to be used in our comparative analysis. While other political systems may be utilized on specific points, most comparisons will centre on Britain and the United States. Our choice is based on both historical and theoretical criteria. Historically, Britain and the United States have exercised the greatest impact on the evolution, development, and structure of the Canadian polity. In fact, Canada is often viewed as a mix of the political principles and practices of these two countries. Until World War II, England was the dominant influence on Canada, a position since relinquished to the United States in both domestic and foreign affairs. Both political systems continue, however, to be an important influence on Canadian politics.

SUMMARY

1. To understand Canadian politics properly requires a focus on two essentials: first, the importance of and difference between political structures and political processes and second, the significance of seeing the Canadian polity from a comparative point of view.
2. The nature of government can be described by five key attributes: government is ubiquitous, multiple, expansive, necessary, and varied. Each of these characteristics points to a significant element of government in the modern era.

3. Classifications of different types of government can focus on broad comparisons – such as the typology of autocratic, democratic, and totalitarian systems – or on more limited criteria – such as the differences between federal and unitary or presidential and parliamentary systems.
4. The Canadian polity is democratic, federal, and parliamentary. Britain is democratic, unitary, and parliamentary. The United States is democratic, federal, and presidential. Such classifications are an important tool in comparing the various institutions and processes of a polity.

RECOMMENDED READINGS

The Nature of Government

CRICK, BERNARD (1973) *Basic Forms of Government: A Sketch and a Model.* London: Macmillan Press.

ELLUL, JACQUES (1972) *The Political Illusion.* New York: Vintage.

GORDON, MARSHA (1981) *Government in Business.* Montreal: C.D. Howe Institute.

NUTTER, G. WARREN (1978) *Growth of Government in the West.* Washington, D.C.: American Enterprise Institute for Public Policy Research.

PIPES, SALLY and MICHAEL WALKER (1982) *Tax Facts 3: The Canadian Consumer Tax Index and You.* Vancouver, B.C.: The Fraser Institute, 3rd ed.

ROSE, RICHARD (1978) *What is Governing? Purpose and Policy in Washington.* Englewood Cliffs, N.J.: Prentice-Hall.

_____ and GUY PETERS (1978) *Can Government Go Bankrupt?* New York: Basic Books.

SHARKANSKY, IRA (1979) *Wither the State? Politics and Public Enterprise in Three Countries.* Chatham, N.J.: Chatham House Publishers.

2 POLITICAL ANALYSIS: CONCEPTS AND PRINCIPLES

Politics is a strong and slow boring of hard boards. It takes both passion and perspective. Certainly all historical experience confirms the truth – that man would not have attained the possible unless time and again he had reached for the impossible.... Only he has the calling for politics who is sure that he shall not crumble when the world from his point of view is too stupid or too base for what he wants to offer. Only he who in the face of all this can say "In spite of all!" has the calling for politics (Max Weber in Gerth and Mills, 1958: 128).

It would clear the air of a good deal of cant if instead of assuming that politics is a normal and natural concern of human beings, one were to make the contrary assumption that whatever lip service citizens may pay to conventional attitudes, politics is a remote, alien, and unrewarding activity.... In liberal societies, politics is a sideshow in the great circus of life (Dahl, 1961: 279, 304).

LIKE IT OR NOT, politics is a fact of human existence. One can detest it, ignore it, or attempt to change it, but the pervasiveness of politics remains. Human behaviour occurs in the context of political communities organized in modern times on the basis of nation-states. As with birth itself, initial membership in a political system gives one little freedom of choice – it is a nonvoluntary option. We are automatically members of a political system at birth and are subject to the consequences of such membership throughout our lives. If government is ubiquitous, then politics is more so, for government constitutes only a portion of the broader process of politics. If government is the institutional organization of political power, politics can be defined as the exercise of power and influence on matters that affect the community.

While pervasive, politics is not found in every facet of human existence, although many actions have potential political implications. Matters which for the ordinary citizen may be considered private and nonpolitical can for a politician quickly generate potent political ramifications. For example, one's personal sexual behaviour and sexual preferences, including events that may have happened long before the individual entered the political arena, can have an impact on one's later political power and influence. While it may be true, as Pierre Trudeau said in 1967 (Gwyn, 1980: 64), that in a liberal-democratic society "the state has no business in the bedrooms of the nation," the converse of that is not evident: the people often demand to know about the sexual behaviour and preferences of their leaders.

If politics is the exercise of power and influence on matters that affect the community, then political analysis is the attempt to explain why a specific pattern of power and influence emerges, how power is gained and lost, and why certain political events occurred. Thus, what we call political analysis is simply one approach used in answering that basic question of all the sciences, both natural and social: why? Political analysis is the exercise of imposing conceptual order on an apparently incoherent political process. The political analyst assumes that things rarely happen by chance in politics. Even those events which appear at first glance to be part of a mysterious process are, upon closer inspection, understandable and explainable in light of certain regularities of human behaviour. For example, although it may be difficult to explain why a particular individual voted for a specific candidate in a single election campaign, the political analyst can make general explanations of Canadian voting behaviour based on socioeconomic factors such as class, occupation, region, religion, and ethnicity. One of the tasks of the political analyst is to search for such general patterns as a foundation for explaining what has happened.

The analyst is often called on to make predictions about future political events. Those who pretend to know the future in politics, as in other areas, are usually very brave or very foolish, or both. The political landscape is littered with the decaying remains of political prophecies. For example, numerous pundits suggested that the Liberal party would not bring down the Clark government in December 1979. Even a person as close to Pierre Trudeau as Arnie Patterson, who had served as communications advisor for the 1979 federal Liberal campaign, predicted that the defeat of the Clark administration was highly unlikely – a prediction published two days after the event had actually occurred (Patterson, 1979). Such a well-known and respected political columnist as Peter C. Newman, then editor of *Maclean's*, can have his views falsified by events: in a November 26, 1979 editorial, Newman (1979) prophesized that the Liberal party could never again win with Pierre Trudeau as its leader. Less than three months later, in February 1980, Trudeau won a solid majority victory. As these examples indicate, political predictions are, at the best of times, risky, even though they are often politically necessary. Much of what occurs in the political process is based on the perception of future developments held by political leaders. For example, it is highly unlikely that the Liberal party would have defeated the Clark government if they had not been working on the prediction, subsequently proven correct, that they could regain power in the next election. Often, however, politicians' predictions fare as badly as those of the political pundits: the defeat of the Parti Québécois in the May 1980 referendum is a case in point.

The political analyst frequently enters the treacherous arena of prediction when discussing the topics of political reform and change. The analyst is asked to predict the consequences of specific reforms. For example, what will be the impact of changing Canada's plurality electoral system to a proportional representation scheme? (See Chapter 10 for a detailed discussion of this issue.) Political debate often centres on the expected consequences of proposed courses of action. For example, much of the response to Trudeau's patriation proposal in the Fall of 1980 focused on just such a problem: how would the amendment formula and the Charter of Rights affect the power of the provincial governments in the years to come? Once changes have been implemented, the political analyst is also concerned with evaluating such reforms. The question asked then is the following: have the changes produced the desired effects and, if not, what effects have they brought about? For example, did the 1974 change in the financing of the federal political parties disturb the traditional pattern of party finance, or did this reform fail to produce the desired results?

The inability of politicians and political analysts alike to predict accurately events even in the immediate political future reveals a fundamental point about the nature of politics: that is, the human basis of the polity. As a result, politics itself is an art, a way of organizing varieties of individual uniqueness into patterns of collective purpose. The political analyst must thus accept the fact that the political process is not a mechanical one that can be dissected once and for all: if it were, a description of it would be as interesting as repeated explanations of the workings of the internal combustion engine. By contrast, the political process is always changing, developing, and adapting to new concerns and problems. A person who is trained in political analysis knows what to look for. For example, to know the names, portfolios, and dates of appointment of current cabinet ministers is a meaningless exercise of one's memory. The political analyst will more properly ask: what are the functions or jobs of the cabinet, why have certain ministerial appointments been made, and how does the cabinet arrive at collective decisions under various prime ministers?

THE NATURE OF POLITICS

Having lived in a political system for a number of years, most people, if they were asked to define what politics is all about, would likely respond with several basic ideas, which might include some of the following concepts: conflict, power, government, influence, the state, violence, decisions, patronage, laws, and corruption. Some people would see politics in a very favourable light, while others might view it as a "dirty business." Some would perceive politics as involving almost all areas of social and economic life, while others would want to restrict the political sphere to rather narrow limits. One would quickly realize that not only do definitions diverge widely among individuals, they also differ extensively in various historical periods and between types of political systems. For example, people within a democratic system conceive of the political sphere in much different terms than those who live in an autocratic or totalitarian system. Although individuals and societies may differ in their definitions of politics, a common theme is a concern with order, or its lack thereof:

> I had learned the first real lesson of politics, government and history: governments are instituted among men in the first instance, and accepted by men gratefully, to protect them from random violence and killing. . . . They offered protection. Many other lessons in politics and government were to follow over the years, but none more important than that (White, 1978: 101).

The reason for the emphasis in various definitions of politics on the theme of order, which can be labeled as the "godfather function" of politics, can only be appreciated in the context of how the political sphere initially developed as a distinct part of society in the Western world.

Development of the Political Sphere in Western Society

Early history was prepolitical: that is, the political system was not yet differentiated from other social systems. What we would now interpret as political power and influence were part of an integrated whole – human beings were a part of nature, not distinct from it. Speculative thought based on myth, rather than the rational and scientific approach of modern times, prevailed. However, such initial speculative thought served a similar function with later political thought: it sought to underpin "the chaos of experience" so that it might "reveal the features of a structure – order, coherence, and meaning" (Frankfort et al., 1949: 11).

The development of a political sphere was a long and complex process, which involved the basic step of separating human beings from nature. Nature became an inanimate object to be understood, manipulated, and controlled. Divorcing humans from nature meant that they had to find a rationale for this separate organization – nature could no longer be depended on to provide it. As a result of this redefinition, which occurred during the 5th and 6th centuries B.C. in Greece, political thought replaced speculative thought and thus assumed the function of providing order, coherence and meaning. The task of the political philosopher was to "fashion a political cosmos out of political chaos" (Wolin, 1960: 8).

If the function of political thought is to develop a pattern from political chaos, then it is not surprising to find that most definitions of politics focus on the concept of order. Given this perspective, we can now expand our initial definition of politics to the following statement: politics is the exercise of power and influence concerning the establishment, maintenance, and breakdown of order in the community. The different types of political systems (autocratic, democratic, or totalitarian) establish different kinds of political institutions, with differing relationships between those institutions, in attempting to achieve order in the political community. One way of categorizing these numerous approaches to politics is to group them on the basis of whether or not they provide a normative or an empirical definition of the political sphere.

Normative versus Empirical Definitions of Politics

A comparison of normative and empirical interpretations reveals one basic difference: a *normative* view is concerned with "what ought to be," while an *empirical* definition deals with "what is." A normative conception of politics develops a desired or a preferred pattern of political organization, while an empirical approach is based on existing political reality. The perspective of this book is heavily cast in light of the second alternative: that is, an empirical assessment of the Canadian polity.

An example may help to explain the difference between the empirical and normative approaches. The statement that "All men are equal" may reflect a normative judgment that all "men" should be equal; as an empirical observation the assertion is simply false. An empirical approach would need to specify "equal" according to which characteristics: sex, height, weight, intelligence, educational training, or social class? Does equality refer to equality of condition (i.e., money, economic rewards) or to equality of opportunity (i.e., the right to become unequal by earning more money or completing more education than other people)? Thus, the statement that "All men are equal" may be proposed or accepted as a normative view of how society should be structured; as an empirical statement it must be rejected. No political system, ancient or modern, of whatever type has ever produced equality of social, economic, or political condition. No existing polity seems destined to change this historical assessment.

A normative statement cannot be disproven, while an empirical statement may be. A normative statement is neither true nor false, while an empirical statement may be either. A comparison of the view of politics held by Aristotle, one of the first practitioners of comparative political analysis, with that of Robert A. Dahl, a past-president of the American Political Science Association, should help to delineate the difference between a normative and an empirical approach to political experience.

The view of politics held by Aristotle is positive: politics is a worthwhile and noble activity – in fact, politics is the master science on which all else is founded. The polis or political association – in modern terminology, the political system – is the final and most perfect type of human association. In contrast to the lower forms of human organization – the household and the village – only the polis is a self-sufficient association and thus, only it can provide justice for its members. For Aristotle, "man's" full moral and psychological development can only be achieved by participation in the political community. Individual maturity requires participation in the polis: "man," by definition, was a political being.

> The man who is isolated – who is unable to share in the benefits of political association, or has no need to share because he is already self-sufficient – is not part of the polis, and must therefore be either a beast or a god (Aristotle, trans. Barker, 1962: 6-7).

Thus, the polis existed for the moral development and perfection of the individual. Within the polis "man" was the best of animals; outside of it, he was the worst of all. Aristotle's normative conception of politics thus included a very positive view of political activity, of the polis and its benefits, and of the perfectibility of "man" in conjunction with a political association. Politics was a salient feature of the human condition. By contrast, recent empirical definitions of politics stand in stark disagreement on each of these major aspects.

In investigating how the American political system actually worked in New Haven, Connecticut, Robert Dahl (1961), in his now classic study entitled *Who Governs?*, discovered that for most citizens politics was not a particularly salient activity. Politics was an area of limited concern and interest for the average individual.

> At the focus of most men's lives are primary activities involving food, sex, love, family, work, play, shelter, comfort, friendship, social esteem, and the like. Activities like these – not politics – are the primary concerns of most men and women.... Since the primary activities are voracious in their demands for time, political activity must enter into competition with them. For most people it is evidently a weak competitor (Dahl, 1961: 279-280).

Politics is not a particularly salient focus for most individuals, and is seen by these same people as a "remote, alien, and unrewarding activity." By implication, the empirical approach also tends to view politics in a negative way: it may be important to some, but it is not a significant activity for most individuals. For Aristotle, political involvement was a precondition for individual fulfillment; for Dahl, political involvement rarely leads to such a result.

This brief comparison of the view of politics held by Aristotle and Dahl shows that they differ on a number of key features: what is meant by the word political, whether what is political is a positive or negative force in the community, and whether most people gain individual maturity and growth from political activity. It is on these kinds of indicators that most normative and empirical definitions of politics vary. Thus, the distinction between an empirical and normative definition of politics is not a trivial one, because each approach consequently differs on the subject matter to be studied, how one should investigate the area, and what one should do with the knowledge so gained. Given such profound differences, it is not surprising that there is sometimes considerable animosity between the practitioners of the normative and empirical approaches.

Ideological Definitions of Politics
A second way of categorizing the multitude of possible definitions is on an ideological basis. An *ideology* itself can be described as "a set of ideas held by a number of people: it spells out what is valued and what is not; what must be maintained and what must be changed; it shapes accordingly the attitudes of those who share it" (Macridis, 1980: 6). Different political ideologies project various conceptions of people's political experience.

Three basic ideological definitions of politics will be considered: conservative, liberal and Marxian. These perspectives correspond to status quo, reformist, and revolutionary approaches. A *conservative or status quo* definition of politics is one that defends and rationalizes "the existing economic, social, and political order"; a *radical or revolutionary* approach, such as Marxism, advocates "far-reaching changes in the existing social, economic, and political order"; a *reformist perspective*, exemplified by liberal theorists, falls somewhere between these two extremes by favouring gradual or modest change in the existing system (Macridis, 1980: 9). The various political ideologies and their views of politics differ most significantly with respect to the idea of political change: for a conservative, change is always suspect, if not downright detrimental; for a revolutionary, change, including the use of violence, is mandatory and often a desired state of affairs; for a liberal, incremental change (slow, modest change) is preferred: change if necessary, but not necessarily change.

Our example of a conservative view of politics will be the

writings of Professor Michael Oakeshott of the London School of Economics and Political Science. Oakeshott (1962: 168) is explicitly conservative, defining it as a disposition to think and act in certain ways: ''a propensity to use and enjoy what is available rather than to wish for or to look for something else; to delight in what is present rather than what was or what may be.'' Thus, a conservative favours tradition over innovation: the imperfections of the present are preferable to the unknown possibilities of the future. As a conservative, Oakeshott is opposed to many elements of modern political thought, which he labels as Rationalism. Rather than emerging from a people's tradition and accumulated experience, Rationalism, which he equates with modern political ideologies, attempts to structure the polity on the basis of preconceived principles. Oakeshott's (1962: 112) view of conservatism and his resulting critique of Rationalism is linked specifically to his definition of politics and political activity: ''Politics I take to be the activity of attending to the general arrangements of a set of people whom chance or choice have brought together.'' Politics is not the pursuit of dreams or goals, but, instead, is a tradition of behaviour.

We have classified Oakeshott's view of politics as conservative because he prefers what exists to what might be: people are not only imperfect, but, quite likely, imperfectible. Politics and government are limited and specific types of activity that should not be confused with, or replaced by, rationalist thought. These themes are well expressed in the following metaphor:

> In political activity, then, men sail a boundless and bottomless sea; there is neither harbour for shelter nor floor for anchorage, neither starting-place nor appointed destination. The enterprise is to keep afloat on an even keel; the sea is both friend and enemy; and the seamanship consists in using the resources of a traditional manner of behaviour in order to make a friend of every hostile occasion (Oakeshott, 1962: 127).

If a conservative views politics as a tradition of behaviour, a liberal definition focuses instead on the individual's rights and responsibilities. A liberal philosophy argues for both the existence and expansion of basic human rights, such as the right to vote, and for the limitation of the state's role in interfering with these rights. Thus, liberalism has traditionally argued for limited government, with constitutional protection for fundamental political and civil liberties. The political system must be structured or organized in a manner that maximizes the rights and freedoms of the individual: the state exists to serve and to protect the individual. An interesting variation of what we would classify as a liberal view of politics can be found in British political scientist Bernard Crick's famous essay, *In Defence of Politics*.

Politics is defined by Crick (1964: 21) as the "activity by which differing interests within a given unit of rule are conciliated by giving them a share in power in proportion to their importance to the welfare and survival of the whole community." This perspective sees "politics as conciliation," as a process for accommodating diversity within the political order. The unique aspect of Crick's analysis is that he argues that the acceptance of diversity is the basis of politics, and since the value of diversity is only accepted in free societies, then politics can only occur in such a context. For Crick (1964: 18, 20), "politics are the public actions of free men," and the "unique character of political activity lies, quite literally, in its publicity."

Several important implications flow from this particular definition of politics. First, politics is not a universal phenomenon that occurs in all societies. For example, politics and its corresponding pattern of governance, which is labeled political rule, does not exist in totalitarian systems. Since totalitarian governments seek to eliminate diversity, they also at the same time eradicate politics. Second, Crick's definition takes a narrow view of politics. Basic arenas of social interaction, such as art, education, and beliefs are not inherently political: the attempt to make them so results in the demise of politics. Third, politics is anti-ideological – politics cannot exist where one ideology becomes dominant and eliminates all of its competitors. The diversity of political ideologies helps to sustain political rule, while the dominance of a single political ideology results in the demise of politics. Fourth, politics is a valued activity because the conciliation of divergent interests is a better alternative than the use of violence and coercion in the making and implementation of public decisions. Finally, Crick explicitly rejects both the conservative and revolutionary approaches to politics.

Crick's analysis of politics as a worthwhile endeavour contrasts sharply with the negative view of politics and politicians currently dominant in many Western political systems. For Crick, politics is not only a virtuous activity, but the essence of freedom itself.

Politics, then, is civilizing. It rescues mankind from the morbid dilemmas in which the state is always seen as a ship threatened by a hostile environment of cruel seas, and enables us, instead, to see the state as a city settled on the firm and fertile ground of mother earth. It can offer us no guarantees against storms encroaching from the sea, but it can offer us something worth defending in times of emergency and amid threats of disaster (Crick, 1964: 140).

Our third ideological definition of politics is an example of a revolutionary conception: namely, a Marxian view of the political sphere. Marx viewed politics in an extremely negative light: politics was a mechanism for the exploitation of people by people, the means by which the dominant class ruled over other classes. Since politics represented class domination, in the final stage of history, when class conflict was eliminated, politics would also disappear – there would be a "withering away of the state." In order to understand this perspective, a few essential aspects of Marxism must be discussed.

Three basic themes of Marxism can be identified: first, history operates through a recognizable series of economic laws, what is called dialectical materialism; second, history moves through various stages of development, culminating in a communist society; and third, the moving force of history is the class struggle or class conflict. Underlying these themes is a basic assumption that relates political development and organization to the economic sphere: for Marx, economics largely determines and controls politics. History evolves as people's relationship to the means of production shifts. The various stages of history (primitive society, feudalism, capitalism, communism) reflect differences in the basis and ownership of the means of production. For example, under capitalism, the capitalist class or bourgeoisie, operating under the principle of private property, owns the means of production, while under communism, the proletariat or working class acquires such control. The dominant class in each historical period is the class that owns the productive capacity of society. As a result, the political system is one means of institutionalizing and perpetuating the dominance of the ruling class. Thus, at the base of all societal relationships lies economic reality (i.e., ownership of the means of production), which can be labeled the economic base or substructure; all else, including politics, art, law, and religion, are elements of the superstructure. If, for Marx, "politics is superstructure," then it is not surprising that he had a negative view of politics and felt that it would be and should be eliminated in the final stage of history.

Since the class structure at any given historical moment represents a pattern of domination by the ruling class and a pattern of subordination for those excluded from the ownership of productive forces, the classes of society find themselves in an antagonistic and possibly violent relationship with each other. This adversarial pattern is magnified as the substructure of economic relationships changes from one type of economic system of production to another (e.g., from a feudal pattern of production based on the landed aristocracy to a capitalist mode of production based on commerce and manufacturing). At some historical juncture the class struggle will reach a boiling point of frustration, the exploited class will rise up and in a revolution overthrow the previously dominant class, and a new pattern of dominance and subordination, based on a new series of economic relationships, will emerge. In the final stage of history, this class struggle will abate, because in a communist society, classes, and the dominance-subordination syndrome, will have disappeared.

The Marxian view of politics stands in sharp contrast to both the conservative and liberal definitions with respect to two essential aspects: the nature of political change and the relationship between the economic and political sectors of society. Given the nature of class conflict, the antagonistic relationship between social classes, and the use of the political system by the dominant class to ensure the continuation of the existing system of exploitation, political change can only be achieved through revolution. Revolution is a tidal wave of political change that crashes onto the shore of earth, sweeping it clean, and thus creating the conditions for the restructuring and rebuilding of economic and political relationships. This emphasis on revolutionary change in Marxism is diametrically opposed to the conservative's view of "politics as tradition" and the liberal's perspective of "politics as conciliation."

A second distinctive aspect of Marxism is its view of the relationship between economics and politics, with the former controlling the latter. The causal arrow runs from the economic structure to the political structure. By contrast, conservative and liberal theories reverse the Marxian pattern of causation: that is, politics determines economic relationships. In Marxism, economics is the substructure and politics the superstructure, while in conservative and liberal views, politics is the substructure and economics the superstructure. A liberal argues that "political life, then, is far more than an occasional random shock to a self-contained, isolated economic system; rather, economic life vibrates with the rhythms of politics" (Tufte, 1978: 173).

The above consideration of three ideologically-based views of politics (conservative, liberal, and Marxian) should amply demonstrate the array and complexity of such definitions. While numerous other perspectives are possible, these three illustrate that definitions of politics vary with respect to their image of politics (whether it is a positive or negative activity), to the scope of politics (conservative and liberal approaches define politics more narrowly than Marxism or other revolutionary doctrines), to the type of political change allowed or desired (a conservative defends the existing order, a liberal favours change on an incremental basis, a revolutionary argues for radical change in the existing order), and finally, to the relationship between the economic and political spheres (liberal and conservatives assert the dominance of politics over economics, while Marxists argue the contrary position). Whatever their nature, however, all such definitions deal with the crucial problem of establishing order for the political community.

BASIC CONCEPTS OF POLITICAL ANALYSIS

If politics is the exercise of power and influence concerning the establishment, maintenance, and breakdown of order in the community, then power and influence are two essential concepts that must be defined as precisely as possible. Power and influence share several common attributes. First, both concepts deal with human behaviour and human relationships. If a dog chased a cat up a tree, we would not say that the cat had been influenced by the dog (scared perhaps, but not influenced). However, if one person's behaviour is modified or changed as a result of another person's behaviour, then we can speak of influence or power. Not only do the concepts of power and influence concern people, but more significant is the point that they are the result of a relationship or pattern of behaviour. In other words, a power or influence relationship involves interaction between two or more people. If there is no such interaction, there is no relationship, and hence influence or power could not have been exercised. For example, if after attending a political rally and listening to a speech by a political candidate, a person decides to vote for that candidate, then we can say that the candidate has influenced how that person would vote. However, if another person attended the same rally and listened to the same candidate, but had already decided to vote for the candidate, then no influence was exercised. Although power and influence are based on human relationships between two or more people, such interaction need not be direct or on a face-to-face basis. A voter may watch a political advertisement on television for a particular candidate and decide to vote on that basis. In such a case, the interaction or relationship is indirect, but influence has still been exercised.

In emphasizing that power and influence are evident in the pattern of human interactions, we are also implying a second common attribute of both concepts; namely, the idea of causation. We cannot directly observe power and influence, but we can assess their presence in light of events. For example, we say a candidate influenced voters because they behaved in a different way than they would have otherwise. Likewise, politicians are judged to be powerful or not on the basis of their ability to influence or direct people's actions. A prime minister is seen as more powerful and influential than an ordinary citizen because a prime minister can make cabinet appointments, is a key participant in the legislative process, and can change the direction of public policy. In other words, power and influence are not directly observable, but the results of power and influence are. In saying that power and influence deal with causal relationships, we are also asserting that they are exercised before the change of behaviour is observed. For Factor A to cause Event B, it must occur prior to Event B: causation is thus antecedent to its behavioural result. In our previous illustration, a speech by a candidate was deemed to have influenced the behaviour of the voter because it occurred before the voter had decided how to vote; in the other example, the candidate's speech did not influence the individual's voting intention because it was presented after the voter had already made a decision on how to vote.

A third characteristic of power and influence is that, when we use these terms in political analysis, we are obviously speaking of political power and political influence. Power and influence are political when they affect the operation of the wider community or society, which thus distinguishes political power and influence from other forms such as religious influence or economic power. For example, a clergyman who changes an atheist into a regular church attender may have exercised religious influence, but few would say he had also exercised political influence. However, if a preacher delivers a sermon on the evils of capital punishment to a congregation, which includes a politician, and that politician, because of that sermon, introduces a bill to outlaw capital punishment, then the preacher has exercised political influence. In this example, political influence has not been exercised simply because the person affected was a politician, but because the bill to abolish capital punishment is an action that affects the decision-making structure and concerns of society. For similar reasons, patterns of influence and power within the family are not normally considered political in form. Given these considerations, we can say that political power and influence are concepts that describe human relationships that are causal in nature and public in their import.

Although political power and influence share several attributes, these concepts describe somewhat different aspects of human inter-action. Generally speaking, influence is the broader term, with power seen as a specific type of influence. People exercise influence when they change another person's attitudes or behaviour: "A influences B to the extent that he changes B's actions or predisposi-tions in some way" (Dahl, 1976: 29). Individuals have been influ-enced when their attitudes and behaviour have been modified from what they would otherwise have been. In our previous example, a candidate influenced a voter as a result of a speech because the voter's later behaviour was modified. Power, likewise, represents a change in a person's behaviour, but for a different reason: namely, the use of sanctions:

> It is the threat of sanctions which differentiates power from influence in general. Power is a special case of the exercise of influence: it is the process of affecting policies of others with the help of (actual or threatened) severe deprivations for nonconformity with the policies intended (Lasswell and Kaplan, 1950: 76).

For example, if a candidate says to an elector, vote for me or you will lose your job, and the elector votes for the candidate because of the promised sanction, then the candidate has exercised power over the elector. Sanctions are usually more effective as threats than as actual acts. People over whom power is being exercised must, however, believe that the threat will be subsequently carried out if their behaviour is not modified.

Having delineated the basic meaning of influence and power, our next concern is with what makes an individual or group influential. People are influential to the extent that they both control political resources and are willing to exercise the control necessary to translate potential influence into actual influence. Although politi-cal resources may vary from one political system to another and from one historical period to the next, the following definition should adequately illustrate the nature of *political resources*:

> A political resource is a means by which one person can influence the behaviour of other persons; political resources therefore include money, information, food, the threat of force, jobs, friendship, social standing, the right to make laws, votes, as well as a great variety of other things (Dahl, 1976: 37).

The transformation of political resources into political influence is at least a two-stage process: first, a person must have control of resources, either directly, such as by being personally wealthy, or indirectly, such as by having wealthy political supporters; second, a person must have the willingness and ability to translate control of resources into actual influence. For example, wealth does not, in and of itself, generate political influence. A few people are able to translate wealth into power and influence, as the political success of Pierre Trudeau in Canada and John F. Kennedy in the United States demonstrate. But many wealthy individuals abstain from political activity or involvement. Other individuals may try to convert wealth into power and influence, but may lack the necessary skills and expertise to successfully effect the transformation. Wealth in no way guarantees political success, although it certainly can facilitate one's climb up the political opportunity structure.

Another valuable political resource besides wealth is time. Some occupations are structured so that an employee may be able to take a leave of absence to run for political office, while in other occupations (e.g., self-employed and manual workers) no such possibility exists. For example, one reason the legal profession dominates the political process in North America (more so in the United States than in Canada) is the generous number of resources, such as time, which lawyers possess and ordinary citizens lack. By contrast to the legal profession, Canadian academics are increasingly discouraged from seeking political office: several recent contracts between university administrations and faculty unions have included provisions limiting a leave of absence to one term in office. With the vagaries of political life and the bleak prospects of university employment, few professors seem likely to trade economic security for possible political success. Thus, combined with political skills, political resources such as wealth and time are the tools needed for obtaining political influence.

Given the fact that in all political systems the control of political resources is unequally distributed and that various political actors differ in their willingness and ability to translate their potential for influence into actual influence, all political systems end up with some people and groups having more influence and power than others. If political influence is unequally allocated, the question becomes one of explaining why people accept such a pattern. A differential distribution of influence is permissible as long as it is seen as legitimate, as long as it is accepted by the people as a justifiable, if not a preferred, state of affairs. When an individual's influence is perceived as legitimate, it is usually referred to as *authority*.

Numerous ways of legitimating influence have been used historically, including racial, religious, and ethnic bases. Perhaps the best-known classification of the means of legitimating influence is Max Weber's typology of traditional, legal-rational, and charismatic modes of authority (Gerth and Mills, 1958: 294-301). The *traditional basis of authority* is a justification of influence which claims that the way things have been done in the past is the reason why they should be continued in the same manner in the future. An example of a traditional basis of authority is the existence of a monarch as head of state, typified by the Queen in Britain and Canada.

In contrast, the *legal-rational basis of authority* asserts that a distribution of influence is accepted because certain procedures or "rules of the game" have been followed in acquiring it. For example, if a political party wins an election by gaining a majority of seats in the legislature, it is accepted as the legitimate government with the right to run the country until the next election campaign. In a legal-rational system of authority, individuals do not necessarily like the result, in that they may have voted for a different party in the election. However, the results of the election are accepted as granting legitimacy to the winning party because certain well-established procedures were followed. One accepts the authority of Pierre Trudeau because he occupies the Office of Prime Minister of Canada. Authority resides with the office (i.e., prime minister, premier, mayor, president, senator) and not with the individual who happens to occupy that office at any particular time.

Weber's third basis of authority is what he labeled charisma or "gift of grace." *Charismatic authority* refers to rule over people in "which the governed submit because of their belief in the extraordinary quality of the specific *person*" (Gerth and Mills, 1958: 295). The individual leader is seen as being more than human, or having powers and capabilities well beyond those of most mortals. Historical examples would likely include Christ, Hitler, and Ghandi. Unfortunately, the utility of the concept of charisma in political analysis has been greatly weakened in recent decades, since it has become a common theme of journalistic portrayals of the political process. Popularity, in terms of winning elections, is often equated with charisma; in political analysis, the two are not necessarily synonymous. For example, Bill Davis won a majority of seats in the 1981 Ontario provincial election – few would describe him as being charismatic. Similarly, Pierre Trudeau is not a charismatic figure on a national basis in Canada, although he may be with respect to his standing in Quebec. An individual who has never won a majority of the popular vote in Canada in five election campaigns and who, in

Robert Stanfield
The Gazette

the so-called charismatic campaign of 1968, won only five percent more of the national vote than Lester Pearson had gained three years earlier, is a considerable distance from exemplifying the concept of charismatic authority as defined by Max Weber. Although relatively infrequent, charismatic leaders have appeared in Canada, perhaps best illustrated by John Diefenbaker in the 1958 campaign or by Réal Caouette as leader of the Social Credit party in rural Quebec in the 1962 election. Typically, democratic political systems, such as Canada, the United States, and Britain, are more often characterized by leaders who lack, rather than exemplify, charismatic qualities.

Although political systems vary in the emphasis given to each method of legitimating authority, these three bases are usually present, in differing degrees, in any particular political system. As a general comparison, legal-rational authority predominates as the basic mode of legitimation in Canada, Britain and the United States; charismatic authority is only rarely present; traditional authority is primarily used to reinforce legal-rational authority, especially in Britain and Canada. For example, although the prime minister of Canada prepares the Speech from the Throne, it is read and presented by the governor general. Similarly, although the governor general may have no alternative but to ask the leader of the party with a majority of seats in the legislature to form a government, no government is formed until the governor general so acts.

Even though such actions are symbolic, they nevertheless reinforce the legitimacy of those who have acquired political influence on a legal-rational basis. An important form of traditional authority in Canada, which is often overlooked, is the role that custom and convention plays in the operation of the political system (e.g., that a member of the Canadian cabinet is expected to also be a member of the House of Commons). Many key aspects of Canadian politics are based on "the practice," that is, on tradition. As a result, traditional authority is a significant, if secondary base of political influence.

Even in the United States, where legal-rational authority prevails, there are elements of traditional authority. For example, the 130-year dominance of the Republican and Democratic parties has established a "tradition" against new parties or third parties in presidential election campaigns, illustrated by John Anderson's dismal failure in the 1980 contest. Traditional authority is probably the strongest among our three countries of comparison in Britain, best typified perhaps by the deference toward political authority and political institutions such as the monarchy. The outpouring of emotion over the marriage of Prince Charles and Lady Diana Spencer in July 1981 reveals much about the continuing importance of traditional authority in the British polity. Custom and convention plays a significant role in the operation of the British political system, because Britain lacks a comprehensive, written constitution, preferring instead to rely on traditional modes of behaviour. As these examples illustrate, each political system is first of all a mixture or combination of the various bases of authority and second, the strength of the differing bases of legitimation change from one political system to the next.

If political systems seek to legitimate their distribution of influence through traditional, legal-rational, or charismatic means, then one can properly ask that basic question of political analysis: why? The answer is relatively straightforward:

> Authority is a highly efficient form of influence. It is not only more reliable and durable than naked coercion, but it also enables a ruler to govern with a minimum of political resources (Dahl, 1976: 60).

No political system could long endure which rested on the sole use of sanctions and coercion to maintain a particular pattern of influence. People are taught to obey, to accept the legitimacy of particular political institutions and political processes, thus making coercion unnecessary: the "vast majority of men have the habit of law-abidingness" (MacIver, 1965: 58).

When a particular distribution of influence loses its legitimacy, assuming it was accepted as legitimate in the first place, and when a new distribution of influence is sought, then coercion and violence may become important aspects of the political process. Both those who wish to continue the existing arrangements and those seeking a new pattern of influence may turn to coercion and violence to accomplish their ends. No political system is immune from such a development: "In politics we are always living on volcanic soil. We must be prepared for abrupt convulsions and eruptions" (Cassirer, 1946: 280). In Canada the willingness of the FLQ in the late 1960s to use violence (bombings, kidnappings, and murder) to overthrow the existing political system, led to the use of coercion (the War Measures Act) by the political leadership. Similarly, Britain's continuing problem in dealing with the conflict in Northern Ireland shows that no system can entirely avoid such phenomena. However, a legitimate distribution of influence reduces the likelihood of such conflicts.

Having defined the key concepts of political power, influence, and authority, we can now ask how it is that they are carried out. The answer is that if politics describes patterns of human interaction, then such relationships involve a process of communication, or as one writer described it, "politics is talk" (Bell, 1975: 10). Political communication, including the development of political concepts, their changes in meaning through time, and the control of political language by agencies of the political system, reveals a lot about the distribution and nature of political influence in any particular polity.

The importance of political language can be seen in the political controversies that have faced the Canadian system over the years. Concepts describing the federal structure of the country have included classical federalism, executive federalism, dual federalism, cooperative federalism, among a host of others. Perhaps more revealing about the significance of language than any other term is the concept of Confederation itself. If one assumes that Canada is a confederal system, then a totally incorrect view is the result: Canada may be a confederation, but it is not a confederal form of government. As well, a related battle over Quebec's role in the federal system has been in part a conflict over language and its meaning: will Quebec remain in the federal system as a result of a "renewed federalism," will it obtain greater autonomy under a "special status" option, or will it acquire "sovereignty-association"?

Not only do political concepts differ in their explicit meanings (i.e., their denotative aspects), but also with regard to what they imply (i.e., their connotative aspects). For example, René Lévesque has insisted that the Parti Québécois use the term "independence" rather than "separation" to describe its political objectives. While the final product of independence and separation may be identical, the connotative aspects of both words are not: independence has positive connotations, while separation has negative connotations, conjuring up an image of secession and political strife, even violence. Similarly, during the 1976 American presidential election campaign, Gerald Ford announced that he would no longer use the word détente to describe Soviet-American relations. The reason for such a declaration was simply that détente was beginning to be critically viewed as an international balance-of-power system weighted in favour of the Soviet Union, and no president of the United States, especially a non-elected incumbent president in the midst of a primary election battle, could accept such a situation. A further example of the connotative aspects of political communication was the assertion by then American Secretary of State Alexander Haig in March 1981, that those individuals and groups in the

THE OUTCASTS

international system who used violence to achieve their ends were considered by the United States government to be "terrorists" backed by the Soviet Union, not "freedom fighters." The connotative difference between "terrorist" and "freedom fighter" is considerable. Such controversies as these over the denotative and connotative aspects of political language demonstrate that the political communication process is significant because it helps to structure how we perceive, think, and act politically.

The importance of political language is reflected in the extensive efforts political systems make to control or at least to regulate and influence various aspects of the political communication process. Generally speaking, the extent of control is greatest in totalitarian systems, least in democratic systems, and moderate to widespread in autocratic polities. One way of controlling language is to have a single, state-run communications network which can then be used to ensure conformity of political discourse, as in the Soviet Union. One of the most disturbing aspects of the growth of the Solidarity Union in Poland, from the Soviet Union's perspective, was the demand that this group be given access to and the right to appear on the state-run television system. The temporary acceptance of this demand, as a result of the strikes in the Fall of 1980 and Winter of 1981, indicated to the Soviet Union that the Polish Communist Party was losing control of the overall political situation. State control of the political communication process can sometimes produce ludicrous results, as when Afghanistan's state radio announced that "President Noor Mohammed Taraki had resigned 'for reasons of ill health'; it turned out his health was affected by 12 bullet holes in his body" (Safire, 1980: 213).

Perhaps the most notorious use of political language in recent history was the direct control exercised by the state in Germany under Hitler (Mueller, 1973: 24-42). Through the Office of the Press, for example, Language Regulations were issued, as on December 13, 1937, when the order was given that the term "League of Nations" could no longer be used: "This word no longer exists." Under the Nazis new terms were created: for example, "Rassenschande," which meant marriage to or intimate relations with a non-Aryan, equivalent to "blemishing one's race." Old words acquired new meanings, as was the case for "Intellect," which in the Weimar Republic meant "creative capacity," but under Hitler was "a term denoting a critical, subversive, and destructive quality." The extent of state control over the political communication process in totalitarian systems is based on the explicit recognition of the fact that "language and political consciousness are elements that go hand in hand and that determine the way in which the individual relates to his environment" (Mueller, 1973: 19).

In democratic political systems like Canada, the United States, and Britain, such extensive control of the political communications network is limited. However, issues do arise on a fairly regular basis that provoke debate over the legitimate role of the state in the political discourse of the nation. For example, in the Fall of 1980, the federal government ran a series of ads in support of its constitutional renewal efforts, ads that featured idyllic scenes of the Canadian landscape and talked generally of the need for political change. Opposition parties rightly attacked such advertising as an example of how the Liberal party was using public money to build support for its own purposes. After viewing the constitutional ads, which featured Canadian wildlife, then NDP finance critic Bob Rae asserted, "I'll never look at a beaver or a Canada goose in the same way again. I'll see them as Liberals in disguise."

The significant issue raised by government advertising is the proper role of government agencies in controlling the nature of and access to the political communication process. Democratic political systems have tended to refrain from state control, and if state-supported communications systems are created, such as the CBC in Canada or the BBC in Britain, then provisions are made to try to ensure the political neutrality or nonpartisanship of such an effort. The recurring charges of a supposedly "separatist" bias in the French CBC network are a case in point. The blatant use in the 1970s of the state-run network in France by the political executive illustrates the danger, even in a democratic political system, of involving the state directly in the political communication process.

The ability to use language has had an impact on the success of various political leaders in Canada. The dominance of Pierre Trudeau over both Robert Stanfield and Joe Clark was due in no small measure to his greater effectiveness as a political communicator. Inability to communicate is seen by the Canadian voter, rightly or wrongly, as reflecting an inability to lead the country, or as Allan Fotheringham (1981: 60) wrote, "the real reason why Joe Clark has trouble grasping the nerve ends of the nation is that he does not talk like a normal 41 year-old male North American." For example, I have often suggested that Joe Clark might define an examination as the students' opportunity to explicate the totality of the specificity of their ignorance. Effectiveness of political communication and the ability to use political language is an important political resource, therefore, in gaining influence in the political system.

BASIC PRINCIPLES OF POLITICAL ANALYSIS

The concepts of political influence, power, authority, resources, and language are the basic building blocks of political analysis. However, they only provide a starting place, not our final destination. In using these basic concepts, we must also be familiar with a number of more general items, what we have called basic principles of political analysis. Each of these principles focuses on how we study and analyze political phenomena.

Principle One – Political Theory versus Political Practice
In the sphere of politics, considerable distance separates the practices or reality of the political process from the way that process was designed to operate. The political analyst is particularly concerned with the discrepancy between intent and practice.

A classic example of the difference between theory and practice concerns the respective roles of the governor general and prime minister in the Canadian system. While the British North America Act contains an extensive description of the duties of the governor general, no mention is made of the prime minister. However, no political analyst would seriously argue, as a result, that the governor general is more influential and powerful than the prime minister. To assume that the governor general's role is the same as that described in the British North America Act would give one a totally fallacious perspective of the political influence of Canada's formal executive (Dawson, 1970: 59).

An analogous argument could be made about the respective powers of the monarch and prime minister in British politics: the monarch reigns, the prime minister governs. What has happened is that the political executive in both Canada and Britain has followed "the technique of the hermit crab, the crustacean that destroys a mollusk in order to set up housekeeping in its shell. The outer appearance is scarcely altered but the interior is completely changed" (Duverger, 1974: 51-52). In other words, the governor general has retained some of the trappings of power in the Canadian system, while the prime minister has acquired its substance.

Any political system provides numerous instances of the differences between theory and practice. In the United States, for example, the Vietnam war created a major constitutional debate over which branch of government (executive or legislative) had the right to commit American power and prestige to a foreign conflict. Although the United States Constitution is explicit in granting Congress the power to "declare war" (Article 1, Section 8), in practice the president has acquired, particularly in the 20th century, the power to "make war." The president, as Commander in Chief of the Armed Forces, can commit troops or take other actions to involve the United States in a war. As a result, although the legislative prerogative to declare war remains, in current circumstances it is largely a formality. In France, the Constitution of the Fifth Republic (1958 to the present) envisages the role of the president as an arbitrator of the constitutional system: however, under Charles de Gaulle, the president quickly became the chief politician and policy-maker. In theory, the Soviet Union is a federal political structure; in practice it is more unitary than federal. What these examples show is the importance of recognizing in political analysis the difference between how a political system was theoretically designed to operate and how it works in fact. The political analyst usually begins with a consideration of intent and concludes with a focus on actual political practice.

Principle Two – Political Custom and Convention

The emphasis on actual political practices brings us to our second principle of political analysis, which stresses the role of custom in any political system. In many respects this principle is an outgrowth of Oakeshott's argument that politics in any country represents a "tradition of behaviour." Some of that tradition may be embodied in law; much of it, however, reposes in the custom of the polity. Political custom and convention fills in the interstices of the political structure, turning abstract principles into working institutions. For example, if a constitution provides a structural skeleton for the political system, custom and convention fleshes out the body politic.

In Canada, the role of custom and convention is particularly significant. Many of the most important aspects of the Canadian political system are nowhere written down. For example, the notion of responsible government, that a government must have the support and confidence of the House of Commons in order to remain in power, is based on political tradition, not law. The need for a cabinet minister either to have a seat in the House of Commons or to be appointed to the Senate is similarly undefined. Custom requires ministers to seek a seat at the earliest reasonable opportunity, but if they lose in the first election bid, they can remain in the cabinet and try again later. The composition of the cabinet is likewise based on custom. The working of the representation principle, that all provinces and major groups, whenever possible, be given cabinet portfolios, which has been the basis of cabinet selection since John A. Macdonald, has become a "rigid convention" of the Canadian political process (Matheson, 1976: 27).

Custom and convention may even modify those aspects of the political process which have been defined in law. For example, the legal right of the federal government to disallow any piece of provincial legislation within one year of its passage has been greatly restricted in actual practice. The last time a provincial act was disallowed was 1943. The federal government, because of the convention of only considering disallowance if the provincial legislation usurps federal jurisdiction or powers, has allowed its legal power to fall into nonuse. The legal basis for disallowance remains; the political will to exercise it has been circumscribed by custom. In some cases, a specific custom or convention may be recognized as so important that it is later incorporated into law. For example, until 1940 in the United States, no individual had ever served for more than two terms as president of the United States. However, when Democrat Franklin Roosevelt broke this tradition with his four presidential election victories (1932, 1936, 1940, 1944), the Republicans, when they won office, secured the Twenty-Second Amendment to the American Constitution, which limited all future presidents to two terms. Thus did a 150-year-old custom become law in 1951.

Although custom and convention fill in the details of a political structure, too heavy a reliance on tradition can create some difficult political conflicts. If everyone, or at least all major political actors, are agreed on what the convention is and how it operates, few problems arise. However, when there are differing interpretations of a political custom, controversy may result. A good example of this is the Canadian Constitutional Crisis of 1968: a Liberal government, defeated on a tax measure, refused to resign, claiming that its defeat did not constitute a motion of non-confidence. So much for the convention that a defeat of a government's legislation constitutes a defeat of the government itself.

Custom and convention pervade all aspects of the political process, as the polity accommodates itself to its political environment. Custom and convention, then, flesh out the workings of the body politic. In particular, custom and convention are adaptive mechanisms for reconciling the political structure to changed circumstances. As such, they point to the importance of our third principle of political analysis – namely, the significance of political change.

Principle Three – Time and Political Change
Time is probably the most overlooked element in political analysis. More often than not political analysis has ignored the historical dimension, concentrating instead on the problems of the present. However, "without knowledge of the details and patterns of the past, a student of politics is like a man without a memory" (McNaught, 1978: 103). The political patterns of the present are the children and grandchildren of the political battles of the past. One cannot adequately understand the present polity without some understanding of how we got here.

Every major issue facing the Canadian system has been influenced by how that issue was dealt with previously. The move by Pierre Trudeau to patriate the Constitution unilaterally in the Fall of 1980 was justified, in part, by the federal government on historical reasons: half a century of attempts to acquire unanimous provincial consent for such a move was seen as sufficient provocation to act. Likewise, Canadian-American relations must be seen in an historical context, otherwise more current problems, such as the failure of the United States Senate to ratify the fishing treaty in the Fall of 1980 or the dispute between North Dakota and Manitoba over the Garrison Dam Project, appear to be unintelligible. Similarly, the way particular institutions such as Parliament have evolved can only be appreciated in their historical context.

Time, then, is the context of history, which provides the setting for the drama of politics. Time is also involved in the process of political change for the simple reason that birth is highly correlated with death: no political leader can last forever (even those, like Mackenzie King, with extensive contacts in the spirit world). When Pierre Trudeau became Prime Minister in 1968, he was the youngest member at any First Ministers' Conference; at the point of the 1979 election, he was the oldest. Trudeau's reincarnation less than a year later as Prime Minister, and his subsequent move to patriate the British North America Act, were greatly influenced by historical considerations: he viewed giving Canada a new Constitution as possibly his last political contribution before retirement. Time is also a direct influence on the polity because many basic political events are conditioned by when they occur. For example, timing of a budget, a cabinet shuffle, or an election call can have an important bearing on the distribution of influence in a political system. While our analysis will centre on present political practices in Canada, Britain, and the United States, we will attempt to show how these current patterns have evolved historically.

Principle Four – Legal versus Political Decisions
Our fourth principle of political analysis focuses on the differences
between a legal decision or action and a political decision or action.
We use legal in the sense of pertaining to the law: a legal decision is
based on the law and constitution, or one that is assumed to be
consistent with the law, even though it may not be specifically dealt
with in a particular statute. A political decision is one based on
considerations of influence and power. While we would expect that
political decisions would also be legal ones, especially in democratic systems, such a congruence need not be the case. The
legitimacy of government is certainly enhanced when legal and
political decisions mesh, and undercut when they do not.

The difference between a legal and a political decision is well
illustrated by the federal government's reaction to the passage of
Bill 101 in Quebec by the Parti Québécois after their 1976 provincial
election victory. There was no doubt that certain aspects of Bill 101,
which moved Quebec towards being a unilingual province, infringed on the language rights guaranteed by the British North
America Act. In particular, Section 133 of the Constitution, which
gave protection to both the English and French languages in the
Quebec provincial legislature and the federal and provincial courts
in Quebec, was explicitly disregarded by Bill 101, as subsequent
court rulings made clear. Why then did the Quebec government pass
the legislation in the first place and why did the federal government,
in response, not disallow such a measure? The answer to both
questions should be obvious: the provincial and federal governments were making political, not legal, decisions.

Having won their first provincial victory on a "nationalist"
program designed to protect the French language and culture in
Quebec, the Parti Québécois had little to lose and much to gain by
being seen as the only political party with the will to take strong
action to protect French interests in the province. With 80 percent
of the population French-speaking, being in favour of the linguistic
rights for that sector could only be politically rewarding, particularly in light of the party's 41 percent popular vote in the election.
An emotive issue like language rights was being used to appeal to
those members of the public who had not voted for the party in
1976. Moreover, vigorous action in promotion of the French language undercut the political base of the opposition parties, particularly the Liberals, who were labeled by the government as the party
defending English interests in Quebec. No party could survive such
an image, since it would be impossible to win power in any future

election on the basis of the English sector alone. Thus, certain provisions of Bill 101 were known in advance to be contrary to Section 133 of the British North American Act – a fact that did nothing to deter the provincial government's passage of the legislation. The possibility of Bill 101 being disallowed by the federal government was also a political plus for the Parti Québécois: such a move by Ottawa could then be seen as further proof that the French culture would survive only through independence.

The federal government's response to Bill 101 was political, rather than legal, in form. Even though Prime Minister Trudeau repeatedly condemned the legislation, Ottawa decided not to use its power of disallowance against Bill 101, because of the political repercussions such an action might precipitate in Quebec. The federal Liberals took a hands-off attitude, while at the same time they encouraged private groups and individuals to challenge the legislation in the courts. It must also be remembered that the Liberal party was in a majority position in the national legislature, making it most unlikely that their stance on this issue could bring about their defeat, and second, that the Liberal party's dominance in national politics resides in their Quebec stronghold. No federal party based in Quebec could use the power of disallowance against their "home" province on a piece of legislation designed to protect the French language and culture in Quebec. Hence, for political reasons, the federal Liberal party did not invoke the disallowance power against Bill 101: legally it could have done so, but the political judgment was contrary, and it prevailed.

Many events in the political process can be understood only if the distinction between legal and political actions are kept in mind. For example, the formal executive in Canada, the governor general, has the legal basis for refusing a request coming from the prime minister for a dissolution of Parliament. Politically, however, such an action by the governor general is unlikely, except in the most extreme circumstances. Such an argument could be made about other aspects of the formal executive's role in Canada as well: as one writer asserted, the governor general is "a legal survivor who has contrived to remain a political necessity" (Dawson, 1970: 143).

While the governor general's role illustrates the pattern of having a legal basis for decisions, even though such action is rarely taken for political reasons, governments also find that political decisions are made without having a legal foundation for them. For example, considerable evidence presented to the McDonald Royal Commission on RCMP Activities showed political actions being taken that were clearly illegal. The most notorious situation involved the burning down of a barn in Quebec so that a group of political radicals could not hold their meeting. One wonders whether the Forum in Montreal might also have been torched if the radicals had decided to meet at a hockey game. Other actions were also clearly illegal, but seen as politically necessary, as when the computer tapes containing the membership files of the Parti Québécois were stolen, copied, and then returned.

If too many such examples come to light, they might undercut the legitimacy of the government. As a result, governments may make legal actions they consider to be politically necessary. The federal government's move in the mid-1970s to provide a legal basis for wiretapping is a case in point. Similarly, in response to the RCMP wrongdoings revealed before the McDonald Royal Commission in the late 1970s, both major parties, when in office, took the view that the way to handle the situation was to make whatever the RCMP was doing legal in the future. Even if political actions are challenged in court and ruled illegal, the government can always call the legislature into session and, in most cases, pass what is known as retroactive legislation. Such legislation changes the law so that previously illegal actions are declared legal after they have occurred – a convenient weapon in the arsenal of government power. A citizen may also find that a previously legal action can be declared illegal by the government, with penalties imposed retroactively. For example, with the imposition of the War Measures Act in 1970, it became a crime, retroactively, to have ever been a member of the FLQ, even though being an FLQ member in the 1960s was not illegal (Stewart, 1971: 59)! Such examples demonstrate the importance of our fourth principle of political analysis.

Principle Five – Political Structures and Political Functions
Our final principle of political analysis looks at the difference between political structures and political functions. *A political structure*, such as the House of Commons or the cabinet, is composed of a set of political roles or expected patterns of behaviour. No matter which party or individual happens to fill these roles, certain behavioural patterns can be discerned. For example, the House of Commons will be presided over by the speaker or deputy speaker, the government will sit on the speaker's right-hand side and the opposition on his or her left, and legislation will be passed after proceeding through First, Second, and Third Readings. In other words, the House of Commons is a structure composed of regular and recurrent patterns of action. Political analysis usually begins with a look at political structures, presenting a description of

the framework or institutional context of the political process.

Political functions refer to the consequences or results of the various political structures: the jobs or tasks the structures perform for the political system. To describe the structure of the Canadian cabinet, a political analyst would discuss its size, how its members are selected, how it arrives at decisions, and how it is internally composed of various cabinet committees. In describing the function of the Canadian cabinet, the political analyst would look at its effects on the political process in terms of a policy-making function (i.e., it is the primary policy-making institution) and possibly a representation-symbolic function (i.e., it represents the various groups in the Canadian parliamentary system).

Any political structure can perform one or more political functions and any political function can be carried out by one or more political structures. A structure such as a political party provides several functions, including the recruitment of candidates to run for office, the organization of the electorate around certain policies and programs, and, if it wins the election, the provision of people to occupy the top political positions in the country. An example of a function being performed by several structures would be the policy-making function, exercised by the cabinet, the prime minister's office, and the civil service. Thus, in political analysis we must distinguish between structures and functions and deal with both topics in examining any particular political system.

The above five principles of political analysis, as well as the basic concepts, will serve as our guide in investigating the political process in Canada, Britain, and the United States. These principles and concepts reflect a combination of the basic ways through which we study political phenomena.

COMPARATIVE POLITICAL ANALYSIS

Several basic approaches can be used to make a comparative analysis of the political process. After discussing these approaches, we will consider the goals and purposes of comparative political analysis.

Approaches to Political Analysis

There are three basic approaches to political analysis: historical, institutional, and behavioural. Each approach focuses on somewhat different aspects of the political process, but each adds to our understanding of the polity.

The *historical approach* stresses the development and evolution of the political system, rightly arguing that in order to understand the present and future, we must know something about our past. Every political institution and political practice has been molded and refined by history and each political system has had a different history. For example, to speak of the monarchy in Canada is to discuss a very different institution from the monarchy in Britain. History has given each polity certain unique characteristics and practices.

The second approach to political analysis focuses on political institutions and political structures. The *institutional approach* describes and explains the basic political structures and how they were designed to operate. Political institutions and structures reflect and create a distribution of power and influence in any political system, for "government institutions consist of those structures whose incumbents actually or potentially regulate all other power centers or institutions within that country" (Redekop, 1978: 156). Thus, political institutions provide the framework within which the struggle for power and influence takes place. An institutional approach will therefore discuss such factors as a country's constitution and the structure of the various branches of government (legislative, executive, and judicial). Since politics occurs within a particular institutional context, the student of politics must have a firm grasp of political structures in order to achieve an understanding of politics in a specific country.

Although the historical and institutional approaches contribute valuable insights into the political process, an additional perspective is also needed. The *behavioural approach* focuses specifically on how individuals, groups, and institutions actually behave and operate in the political process. For example, knowing the institutional structure of the polity will not tell us how that institution operates in practice. As James Bryce (1888: 159) observed, "Institutions are said to form men, but it is no less true that men give to institutions their colour and tendency." The presidency of the United States was a very different institution under John F. Kennedy than under any of his successors. The office of prime minister in Britain operates differently with Margaret Thatcher as its occupant than with James Callaghan or Edward Heath. The impact of the behavioural approach has been to expand our attention from institutions and their development to a concern with actual behaviour. The result has been a focus on such topics as voting behaviour and political parties. The behavioural persuasion in politics has as its goal the "explanation of why people behave politically as they do, and why,

as a result, political processes and systems function as they do"
(Eulau, 1963: 24).

An approach to political analysis, then, is a "way of looking at
and explaining politics" (Redekop, 1978: ix). The historical, institutional, and behavioural perspectives each provide insight into different aspects of the political process. No single approach can adequately describe and explain the workings of the polity. Our five
principles of political analysis reflect the wisdom of integrating the
historical, institutional, and behavioural perspectives.

Comparative Political Analysis

To this point, we have dealt with the nature of politics, the basic
concepts of political analysis, the key principles of political analysis, and the various approaches to political phenomena. However,
we have also indicated that the overall goal of our study is to make a
comparative analysis of the political process in Canada, Britain, and
the United States. Such a view implies that there is something
distinctive about both the subfield of comparative politics and its
method of analysis.

At its most basic level comparative politics is focused, obviously,
on politics in two or more countries.

> Comparative politics is concerned with behaviour, institutions, proc-
> esses, ideas, and values present in more than one country. It searches for
> those regularities and patterns, those similarities and differences be-
> tween more than one nation-state that help to clarify the basic nature,
> working, and beliefs of regimes (Curtis, 1978: 1).

Comparative politics, then, analyzes political phenomena in several
countries as a way of describing and explaining the nature of the
political process. Hence, comparative political analysis refers to the
method used in making such comparative descriptions and explanations.

> The comparative study of politics suggests immediately the laboratory
> of a scientist. It provides us with the opportunity to discuss specific
> phenomena in the light of different historical and social backgrounds....
> More specifically, however, the function of comparative study is to
> identify uniformities and differences and to explain them (Macridis,
> 1955: 1).

Comparative political analysis is significant because of the understanding of politics it can provide. It not only overcomes the

parochialism of simply dealing with one's own country, but it also allows us to develop a better appreciation of that system, including both its strengths and weaknesses. For example, the immediate reaction to the victory of the Party Québécois in the 1976 provincial election was one of disbelief, bordering on panic, among some English-Canadians. However, a comparative perspective on Canadian politics might suggest that the opposite response would have been more appropriate. Few countries in the world would even permit a separatist party to develop in the first place, let alone allow it to contest for office through the electoral process. Such parties are regularly banned, even in democratic systems, and if they are not made illegal, they are discriminated against directly or indirectly. The Canadian polity not only allowed a separatist party to peacefully win power in a major province, but further allowed it to later hold a referendum on its platform of independence. A comparative assessment of the Canadian polity leads this author to contend that the political system is much stronger and more vibrant than most gloom-and-doom pundits and politicians can bring themselves to admit.

A comparative analysis of Canadian politics greatly enhances our knowledge of how the political process operates and pinpoints needed areas of reform. The expansion of the political executive's role in Canada, for example, is not an isolated development – similar trends have occurred in Britain and the United States. Only a comparative approach can make such a Canadian development explicable in terms of similar processes elsewhere. Likewise, political reform in Canada has often been inspired by events abroad. The Watergate scandal in the United States in the early 1970s helped to create a climate favourable for the adoption in 1974 of public financing of election campaigns in Canada. The existence of a freedom of information law in the United States has helped to spur the demand for such legislation in Canada. Viewing a country's political system from a comparative perspective thus expands our knowledge of our own and other systems, and produces explanations for the patterns of politics that are discovered. Comparing political systems, however, creates a number of problems for the political analyst.

Problems of Comparing Political Systems
While the following concerns are relevant to any political analysis, their importance is enhanced when we compare political systems with each other. The first problem is the selection of countries to be compared. The subject of comparison should be chosen to increase

the likelihood of being able to identify similarities and differences between them. For that reason, since we seek to understand Canadian politics from a comparative perspective, we will primarily compare it with British and American politics, the two systems that have had the greatest historical impact on the development of the Canadian system. Moreover, these two systems, given their particular composition of various types of political structures, should highlight key aspects of the political process in Canada.

The second problem concerns which aspects of those systems to compare. At the most general level, we are interested in cross-national comparisons, that is, comparing Canadian politics with the British and American patterns. However, in order to make our comparisons more manageable, we will most often compare various subunits of each system. For example, in Chapter 10 we compare the electoral systems used in the three countries, investigating both the types utilized and their effects. Comparisons of electoral systems, legislatures, or parties are examples of structural or institutional comparisons. However, we will also consider functional comparisons, that is, how the tasks carried out by an institution, such as the legislature, vary between political systems.

A third problem relates to the question of time: which historical periods should serve as the basis for the comparison? The use of different historical periods would greatly change the nature and conclusions of our comparisons. For example, a comparison of Canadian and American politics in the 1880s would produce very different results than such a study of a century later, because both systems have changed drastically in the past 100 years. The time frame for our comparison will thus be the current political practices in Canada, Britain, and the United States.

While problems such as these increase the difficulty of comparing political systems, if they can be overcome the results can be most rewarding, for comparisons help us answer that basic question of political analysis: why? In this sense, political analysis has an analogous objective to that of political philosophy, namely, the search for order.

SUMMARY

1. Politics can be defined as the exercise of power and influence on matters that affect the community, while political analysis is the attempt to explain why a specific pattern of power and influence emerges, how power is gained and lost, and why certain political events occur.

2. Politics can be defined in numerous ways, with normative approaches stressing "what ought to be" and empirical ones focusing on "what is." Politics can also be defined in ideological terms, with a conservative definition seeing "politics as tradition," a liberal one viewing "politics as conciliation," and a revolutionary perspective, such as Marxism, perceiving "politics as superstructure."

3. Political power and influence are concepts that describe human relationships that are causal in nature and public in their import. People exercise influence when they change other people's attitudes or behaviour and power when such changes are accomplished by the use of sanctions, real or apprehended. Authority is legitimate influence, and can be based on tradition, charisma, or legal-rational norms. Political communication is the means of carrying out influence and power relationships, with political language structuring how we perceive, think, and feel about politics.

4. In analyzing politics, five principles should be kept in mind: first, the difference between political theory and political practice; second, the importance of political custom and convention; third, the historical dimension and political change; fourth, the difference between legal and political decisions; and fifth, the difference between political structures and political functions.

5. Approaches to political analysis include the historical (a focus on the development and evolution of political institutions and processes), the institutional (a look at political structures and how they were designed to operate), and the behavioural (a focus on how individuals, groups, and institutions actually operate).

6. Comparative political analysis, which is based on a consideration of politics in two or more countries, helps to overcome the parochialism of only dealing with one's own country, while at the same time it aids in a recognition of the strengths and weaknesses of various kinds of political institutions and political systems.

RECOMMENDED READINGS

The Nature of Politics

BARKER, ERNEST, ed. (1962) *The Politics of Aristotle*. New York: Oxford University Press.

MACIVER, R. M. (1965) *The Web of Government*. New York: The Free Press, rev. ed.

MACRIDIS, ROY C. (1980) *Contemporary Political Ideologies: Movements and Regimes*. Cambridge, Mass.: Winthrop Publishers.

TAYLOR, CHARLES (1970) *The Pattern of Politics*. Toronto: McClelland and Stewart.

WOLIN, SHELDON S. (1960) *Politics and Vision: Continuity and Innovation in Western Political Thought*. Boston: Little, Brown and Co.

Basic Concepts of Political Analysis

BELL, DAVID V. J. (1975) *Power, Influence, and Authority: An Essay in Political Linguistics*. New York: Oxford University Press.

DE JOUVENEL, BERTRAND (1962) *On Power: Its Nature and the History of its Growth*. Boston: Beacon Press.

LASSWELL, HAROLD D. and ABRAHAM KAPLAN (1950) *Power and Society: A Framework for Political Inquiry*. New Haven: Yale University Press.

MERRIAM, CHARLES E. (1964) *Political Power*. New York: Collier Books.

Basic Principles of Political Analysis

DAHL, ROBERT A. (1976) *Modern Political Analysis*. Englewood Cliffs, N.J.: Prentice-Hall, 3rd ed.

EULAU, HEINZ (1963) *The Behavioral Persuasion in Politics*. New York: Random House.

REDEKOP, JOHN H., ed. (1978) *Approaches to Canadian Politics*. Scarborough, Ont.: Prentice-Hall Canada Inc.

Comparative Political Analysis

ALMOND, GABRIEL A. and G. BINGHAM POWELL (1978) *Comparative Politics: System, Process, and Policy*. Boston: Little, Brown and Co., 2nd ed.

ROBERTS, GEOFFREY K. (1972) *What is Comparative Politics?* London: Macmillan.

SCARROW, HOWARD A. (1969) *Comparative Political Analysis: An Introduction*. New York: Harper and Row.

PART TWO

The Political Structure of the Canadian Polity

3 THE CONSTITUTION AND FEDERALISM: OPERATION AND REFORM

A constitution establishes a structure and framework for a country based on certain values. If, like ours, it is largely a written constitution for a federal state, it is a law for making laws, looking to the future exercise of the powers distributed for the attainment of the desired ends (Scott, 1977: 392).

What it adds up to is that a constitution, any constitution, is not a panacea but an experimental attempt of arriving at a viable and legitimate government (Friedrich, 1974: 11).

SOMEWHERE IN THE WORLD TODAY there is bound to be a busy group of constitution writers scribbling out their design for either a new or a reformed political system. Although we live in an era of constitution-making, we do not, at the same time, exist in an age of constitutional government. Constitutionalism is an unrealized ideal for the vast majority of nation-states in the international system, while in others it is no longer even a goal to be sought. Nonetheless, political systems continue to produce constitutions, even when they may not be operative for any great length of time, because constitutions render important political functions.

Constitutions structure the polity by establishing the boundaries of political action, that is, they outline the basic rules of the political game. For example, when a new political system is being established, such as after a revolution, the first task to be faced is the form the desired polity will be given. Constitutional design, therefore, is an act of political creation, an attempt to translate political principles into actual institutions of government: "A 'constitution' is a matter of purest politics, a structure of power" (Black, 1963: 1). The daily workings of the political process take place within these rules of the game, with constitutional matters usually becoming salient only during times of crisis. For example, the federal government's imposition of the War Measures Act in Canada during the October Crisis of 1970 sent concerned members of the public and constitutional scholars scurrying to the textbooks to brush up on the Act's provisions, since the last time it had been imposed was in 1939.

By establishing some of the key rules of the political game, constitutions not only structure power, but they do so in a way that helps some groups gain power and influence, while limiting the political significance of others. The rules of the political system are never neutral in their effects, although their legitimacy is certainly enhanced when they are so perceived by the public. Constitutional rules protect the interests of the people who write them: the "final, finely chiseled product then reflects the way in which the ruling elite desires its national community to be governed for its own good – and for the elite's good" (Duchacek, 1973: 9). By bestowing political advantages to some groups and disadvantages to others, constitutional rules not only structure the polity, but determine the kinds of issues and concerns likely to be dealt with in the political process. Although all kinds of systems typically utilize constitutions as a way of outlining the key features of the political regime, only in a small group of political systems does having a constitution also mean having a constitutional form of government.

CHARACTERISTICS OF CONSTITUTIONAL GOVERNMENT

In the current international system, there is not a strong correlation between having a piece of paper called a constitution and actually running the polity on constitutional principles. A constitution may aid in the creation of a constitutional government, but it certainly does not guarantee it. Almost all countries have constitutions, but few embody the principle of constitutionalism. A *constitutional government* is one wherein the constitution effectively limits the power of the political elite. Thus, in a constitutional polity the "constitution organizes, but also restrains" (Friedrich, 1968: 133). The key idea of constitutional government is the effective restraint of power, not simply whether such theoretical limitations are specified in a constitutional document. Although the Soviet Union's Constitution (e.g., both the Stalinist Constitution of 1936 and the revised Constitution or fundamental law of 1977) grants each Union Republic the "right freely to secede from the USSR," no such right exists in fact. While other examples could be cited, the Soviet Union's use of a constitution illustrates that constitutional government is ultimately dependent on political restraints and political forces, not constitutional niceties. A constitutional format does not lead inexorably to constitutional substance. Constitutionalism is dependent on appropriate belief and behaviour patterns to buttress an initial constitutional structure. Such a pattern of constitutional forms, reinforced by appropriate beliefs and political activity, is found in democratic systems, while autocratic and totalitarian polities may have constitutions, but not systems of constitutional government.

Particularly in those countries with constitutional government, the constitution usually contains four basic elements: a preamble, an organizational chart, an amending clause, and a bill of rights (Duchacek, 1973: 25-38). The preamble serves as a political manifesto, setting out the goals and priorities of the polity. Most manifestoes are nationalistic in outlook and emotional in content, a summary statement of political idealism. Once the broad goals are defined, the rest of the constitution usually outlines the basic structures of government. In effect, constitutions provide an organizational chart or power map of the polity. In so doing, the constitution delineates whether the political institutions are to be federal or unitary, presidential or parliamentary in nature. For example, if a federal structure is created, then the constitution attempts to specify which level of government can exercise which political functions, which tasks are exclusive to a single level, and which functions can be performed by both levels. Since political goals and functions change over time, constitutions may also incorporate a procedure for their own future revision, that is, an amending clause. Amending clauses are often made difficult to use, on the assumption that the "supreme law of the land" should not be routinely changed or manipulated. An amending clause attempts to specify who is involved, the nature and kinds of amendments allowed, and the procedures to be utilized. Finally, constitutions are likely to incorporate a bill of rights, based on the assumption that individuals need extra protection from their own government, as well as from the actions of their fellow citizens. Certain liberties, such as freedom of speech and freedom of assembly, are so fundamental to a democratic polity that they must be made immune to attack, no matter what the size of the government's majority or the state of public opinion. Unfortunately, it is often forgotten that popularity has nothing necessarily to do with constitutionality. In fact, it is when what is constitutional is also unpopular that the real mettle of constitutional government becomes apparent.

If constitutions outline the ingredients of the political structure and the basic rules of the political game, then they are inherently political by their very nature, for they help to determine the distribution of influence and power in the polity. The notion of constitutional impartiality is a myth, because constitutions are political documents with significant political consequences. Although constitutions are often valued as somehow being "above mere politics," such a belief has to be interpreted as a means of legitimating the constitution, rather than a description of its role in the political process. Constitutions are political mechanisms of considerable import because they deal "with the hard core of all politics, namely who leads whom, with what intent, for what purpose, by what means, and with what restraints" (Duchacek, 1973: 9). Constitutions are also political in the sense that they may become symbols of national unity or disunity. In many countries, especially in those which have thrown off a colonial power, a constitution is an initial symbol of sovereignty, of political independence in the international arena. Constitution-making is, therefore, an ingredient of nation-building, of creating a national identity where none may have existed before.

Reforming a constitution or writing a new one is a reflection of a changing distribution of influence and power. For example, after the death of Mao Zedong in China, the constitution was revised to reflect the evolving patterns of influence and power within both the state and party structures. However, because the process of constitutional reform is often difficult, political practices simply evolve. Thus, there is often a considerable discrepancy between the political process envisaged in the constitution and the realities of current practice. Political systems modify constitutional intent through such devices as judicial interpretation, custom and convention, and changing public beliefs. As a result, a constitution must be interpreted not only with respect to its initial design, but also in light of its adaptation to present circumstances.

THE CANADIAN CONSTITUTION

While the Canadian polity is an example of constitutional government, the nature and specifics of that constitutional system are complex. Much of its intricacy stems from the difficulty of delineating exactly what is included in Canada's Constitution. For example, while the British North America Act of 1867 is certainly the basic constitutional document, it is not the only one. Other documents of constitutional consequence would include the Bill of Rights, the War Measures Act, the Statute of Westminster, the Supreme Court Act, and the various acts which have added new provinces since 1867. Thus, while Canada is usually classified as having a written constitution (i.e., the BNA Act of 1867), it has more than one written constitutional document. Moreover, it is often a surprise to learn that Canada has had, in fact, a series of BNA Acts. The major revisions to the initial act were entitled BNA Acts as well. For example, the BNA Act (Number Two) of 1949 empowered the federal government to amend its own structure and operation without resort to the British Parliament. Thus, the Canadian constitutional system includes all BNA Acts from 1867 to the present, plus the various constitutional documents such as the War Measures Act. The most recent addition to this series would be the Constitution Act of 1982, which brings the amending power to Canada from Britain, as well as adding a Charter of Rights, which applies to both the federal and provincial governments.

The complexity of constitutional government is further enhanced by the importance of custom and convention in the Canadian context. Some of the most essential aspects of the polity are nowhere written down. For example, the two key ingredients of the political process, the prime minister and the cabinet, are not mentioned in the BNA Act of 1867. The principle of the collective responsibility of the cabinet to the House of Commons, the necessity of a cabinet minister to hold a seat in the Commons, the relationship between the formal and political executives, and the practice that a defeat on a major piece of government legislation is also a defeat of the government are all examples of crucial customs of parliamentary government that are constitutional in import but unspecified in law. Thus, when we speak of constitutional government in Canada, we include such constitutional practices, in addition to the series of constitutional documents.

Constitutional Structure

The British North America Act of 1867 created a political structure based on the principles of parliamentary sovereignty and federalism. As set forth in the Preamble, the provinces of Canada, Nova Scotia, and New Brunswick desired to be "federally united" in a new political structure, "with a Constitution similar in Principle to that of the United Kingdom." The "similar in principle" phrase, in effect, designated a parliamentary structure for Canada; at the same time, it enshrined an important role for custom and convention in the Canadian polity. Unfortunately, the principles of parliamentary sovereignty and federalism are potentially contradictory in operation, especially in a decentralized federal system. However, the highly centralized federation outlined in 1867 did not bring the potential discrepancies between federalism and parliamentary sovereignty immediately into the open.

The initial structure of power provided for in the BNA Act strongly favoured the federal government over the provinces. This highly centralized federalism, which seemed almost unitary in design, is well-illustrated with respect to the following areas: the initial allocation of federal and provincial powers outlined, for the most part, in Sections 91 and 92; the residual power clause; the declaratory power; and the powers of disallowance and reservation.

The principle of *federalism*, that is, the division of powers between levels of government, created two layers of government in Canada: the national or federal government in Ottawa and the various provincial governments. The allocation of powers to these respective levels could theoretically range from a highly centralized federal system (i.e., most of the power retained by Ottawa) to a highly decentralized one (i.e., most of the power retained by the constituent units or provinces), with numerous variations between them. The intent of the Fathers of Confederation clearly placed Canada in the first category, as witnessed by the political functions assigned to each level.

In Section 91, the federal government was granted a list of 29 classes of subjects, ranging from several minor functions (Section 9:

Beacons, Buoys, Lighthouses, and Sable Island; Section 11: establishment and maintenance of Marine Hospitals) to major ones (Section 2: Regulation of Trade and Commerce; Section 3: any Mode or System of Taxation; Section 7: Militia, Military and Naval Service, and Defence; Section 14: Currency and Coinage). It must be remembered that government itself in the mid 19th century was limited, but of the political functions performed at the time, the federal government received the vast majority. In addition to the powers already mentioned, the federal government was given control over the public debt and property, public credit, the postal service, navigation and shipping, banking, Indians and their lands, marriage and divorce, and criminal law. In contrast, the remaining political functions allocated to the provinces were mostly minor ones, perhaps best stated in Section 92(16) as "Generally all Matters of a merely local or private Nature in the Province." Such powers included prisons in and for the province, the borrowing of money on the sole credit of the province, licences for the raising of provincial revenue, and the administration of justice in the province. While limited in their initial effect, several classes of subjects in Section 92 would later become significant, particularly the control of public lands, property and civil rights, and municipal institutions. Moreover, Section 92(7) laid the basis for provincial control over health and welfare, although such powers did not emerge as major ones until well into the 20th century.

Provincial control of municipal institutions in Section 92(8) means that the federal system created in 1867 was composed of two levels of government, not three as popularly perceived. The constitutional position of local government is subservient to the provincial level, and no relationship at all is established by the BNA Act between local government and the national government in Ottawa. For example, a provincial government can legally rearrange local government, setting up regional or metropolitan governments as it desires. A provincial government can cause two towns or cities to merge or it can impose spending restrictions on the municipal units. Local governments are typically forced by their provinces to balance their budgets, a restriction which is obviously inapplicable to the provinces themselves.

In addition, the power of the provinces over local government is seen with respect to the process of constitutional reform and federal-provincial agreements. Local government representatives may be included for political reasons as part of a province's delegation, but they have no legal right to participate or even to have their views presented. In recent years, the Canadian Federation of Municipalities has several times requested that the municipalities be recognized as a separate level of government within a revised constitutional structure, and just as regularly have the provinces ignored their pleas. While the provinces demand more power from the federal government, they have obstinately refused to give up any of their own power to local government. In an attempt to make an end run around provincial control of the municipalities, the federal government created the Department of Urban Affairs in 1971. However, the outcry from the provinces was such that this experiment was largely unsuccessful and the department was disbanded in 1978. The result is that when the federal government deals with the municipalities, it does so through their respective provincial governments. For example, in the early 1970s, the federal government sought to reduce the tax strain on municipal budgets by granting the provinces money for their urban areas. However, several provincial governments siphoned off part of this money for their own purposes and legally the municipalities could do nothing to stop it.

In addition to the powers already mentioned with respect to Sections 91 and 92, an important one is the area of taxation. The federal level was given the superior taxing power in Section 91(3), since it could raise "Money by any Mode or System of Taxation," while the provinces were limited by Section 92(2) to "Direct Taxation within the Province in order to the raising of a Revenue for Provincial Purposes." The consequence of this inequity has meant that throughout Canadian history the federal level has more easily raised revenue than the provinces. As a result, the provinces have legally given up portions of their power by agreeing to amendments to the BNA Act that have allowed the federal government to pay for social programs technically within areas of provincial jurisdiction. For example, a 1940 amendment added Section 91(2a) to the list of federal powers, giving Ottawa the legal basis for providing unemployment insurance. The superiority of the federal taxing power is one reason why the initial expansion of government in Canada was an expansion of the national government.

The allocation of powers and functions between the two levels of government in Sections 91 and 92 was predicated on the assumption that the tasks of government could be neatly delineated and given to one or the other level. For example, if the provinces were given control of municipal institutions, then the federal government was excluded from that area of activity. Similarly, federal jurisdiction over defence, the money supply, and the post office meant lack of provincial participation in such concerns. Thus, by and large, Sections 91 and 92 delineate areas of *exclusive jurisdiction*. Another example can be found in Section 93, which gives the provinces control over education, although the federal government was granted the task of protecting religious minority educational rights. Thus, exclusive control was limited by exceptions to exclusivity.

A second type of jurisdiction is also apparent in federal constitutions, namely, the idea of shared or *concurrent jurisdiction*. In these areas of activity, both levels of government may legislate: for example, in Section 95, both the national and provincial governments may regulate with respect to agriculture and immigration. If both levels can legislate in areas of concurrent jurisdiction, then a means must be established for deciding questions of precedence when federal and provincial laws conflict. Such a provision in a federal constitution is known as the *supremacy clause*. In Canada, supremacy in areas of concurrent jurisdiction is given to the Parliament of Canada. However, the supremacy clause does not apply to the division of powers in Sections 91 and 92, because that allocation was seen as exclusive in nature, and hence no supremacy clause was logically needed.

Once matters of exclusive and concurrent jurisdiction are designated, the drafters of a federal constitution face an additional problem: which level of government is given control over the present or future activities of government not explicitly dealt with in the allocation of the exclusive and concurrent powers? Not everything can be specified in the constitution, so a *residual power clause* is included, which allocates those powers not dealt with to one or the other levels of government. Typically, the residual power clause is given to that level of government that the constitution writers want to be paramount. In Canada, the residual power was granted to the federal government in the opening sentence of Section 91, which empowers Parliament to make laws for the "Peace, Order, and Good Government of Canada." The residual power or POGG clause is a potentially sweeping grant of power to the national government. It takes little mental agility to be able to justify any government action under it, for what Peace, Order, and Good Government means is defined by the federal government itself. For example, the POGG clause served as the justification for the federal government to pass and use the War Measures Act. In addition, the residual power clause was the cornerstone for legitimating the imposition of wage-and-price controls in 1975. A 1976 court challenge to the anti-inflation program was rejected by the Supreme Court on the grounds that, if the federal government perceived an economic emergency, then such a situation existed and could be dealt with under the residual power clause. While such powers are not invoked frequently, the POGG clause is an important reserve power retained by the federal government that allows it to become involved within areas of provincial jurisdiction.

In addition to the centralized allocation of governmental responsibilities and the residual power clause, a third aspect that sought to buttress the federal government's dominance over the provinces in 1867 was the declaratory power given the national government. The *declaratory power* contained in Section 92(10c) allows the federal government to usurp provincial powers if the federal Parliament asserts that such an action is "for the general Advantage of Canada or for the Advantage of Two or more of the Provinces." Significant is the placement of the declaratory power phrase in the BNA Act: within the list of powers given the provinces in Section 92 is a means by which any of them may be taken over by the federal government acting on its own initiative. It is difficult to conceive of a power or activity that could not be justified or rationalized as to the benefit of at least two provinces.

Although the declaratory power has been rarely used, it is not a dead issue in Canadian politics. In the constitutional bargaining of the mid-1970s, Premier Lougheed of Alberta asked for the dropping of the federal government's declaratory power as the price to be paid by Ottawa for a constitutional agreement. Alberta and the Western provinces were fearful that the declaratory power might be used to give Ottawa control over natural resources, such as oil and natural gas. As might be suspected, the federal government refused to give serious consideration to the suggestion. The potential use of the declaratory power is an important bargaining chip for the federal government. For example, during the Summer of 1981, when the energy-pricing talks between Ottawa and Alberta were deadlocked, Minister of Energy Marc Lalonde had his office issue a statement denying rumours that the federal government was contemplating breaking the impasse by invoking its declaratory power. It is highly unlikely that such a move was in fact being contemplated, but the rumoured possibility (probably started deliberately by Ottawa) of invoking Section 92(10c) served to remind Alberta of the need to reach an accord with Ottawa.

A fourth set of techniques through which the federal government could exert control over the provincial units in the BNA Act of 1867 concerns the national government's powers of disallowance and reservation. Although they differ in the details of their application, the effect of disallowance and reservation is to give the federal government a veto power over the provincial legislatures. *Disallowance* is the procedure by which the federal government rules a provincial law null-and-void within one year of its passage. In other words, a provincial legislature passes a law, it receives royal assent from the lieutenant governor, and it is enforced as a provincial law until the federal government decides otherwise. Provincial laws are sent to the minister of justice and, if he or she recommends that, within one year from the date of receiving a copy of the legislation from the province, the bill be rejected, then an order-in-council (i.e., a decision of the cabinet) is so issued. The grounds for disallowance need to be neither explained nor specific: they can be as vague as claiming that the provincial law runs counter to "sound principles of legislation." Under disallowance, the federal government can observe the implementation of a law before it decides whether or not to veto it.

Reservation is a procedure by which a provincial law is not applicable until the federal government reviews it. *Reservation* means that the bill has passed the provincial legislature, has been sent to the lieutenant governor for royal assent, but the lieutenant governor reserves the bill by neither granting assent nor refusing it. Such a bill is then sent to the federal government for a decision, wherein the governor-in-council (i.e., the cabinet) may or may not decide to allow the bill to become law. In the case of reservation, a provincial bill, in effect, is held in abeyance until the federal government has a chance to consider it. Thus, the national government's powers of disallowance and reservation placed the provinces in a situation of colonial subordination to the federal government, just as the federal government, itself, was so positioned with respect to Britain.

Given the original distribution of powers between the national and provincial governments, the granting of both the residual and declaratory powers to the federal level, and the national government's right to disallow or reserve provincial legislation, the intent of the Fathers of Confederation was clearly to establish a highly centralized federal system. The primary functions of government in 1867 went to the federal government, with those designated for provincial control able to be usurped by the national government acting on its own initiative. For such reasons, the BNA Act of 1867 has been classified as containing important "quasi-unitary" attributes (Smiley, 1980: 22-27).

Although the Fathers of Confederation felt that the allocation of powers in the new federal structure was clearcut, a federal political system inherently produces disputes and conflicts between the various levels of government over their respective powers. One way of settling such disputes is through a process of judicial review. On a general level, *judicial review* is the right of the courts to make judgments respecting the constitutionality of executive and legislative actions. In Canada, a restricted view of such a process has been used to settle jurisdictional disputes between the federal and provincial governments. In such a federal polity, the courts may be used in a pattern of *limited judicial review*, whereby they rule on which level of government can exercise what powers. In that sense, then, the courts are used as the referees of federalism: their task is not to stop the game by declaring an action unconstitutional, but to decide which team (the federal or provincial governments) has control of the ball so that the game can continue. For example, on November 30, 1978, the Supreme Court ruled that the federal government had exclusive jurisdiction over cable television, thus ending provincial hopes of controlling that new area of activity. Moreover, the practice of limited judicial review has meant that, as long as the federal and provincial governments legislate within their powers as allocated in the BNA Act, the courts will take a hands-off attitude toward the content of such legislation. By implication, such an approach favours the national government, since the courts are interpreting a document that created a highly centralized federal system.

The use in Canada of a pattern of limited, rather than full judicial review is a reflection of the principle of parliamentary sovereignty. If the courts were to exercise full judicial review, the result would be that a supposedly supreme legislature was subject to the interpretations of an outside body. However, a pattern of limited judicial review is consistent with a federal and parliamentary system, because the courts are merely interpreting which legislature has the right to exercise supremacy with respect to which powers. A movement in Canada from a pattern of limited to full judicial review would likely produce a clash between these two political principles.

In addition to the matters dealt with in the 1867 BNA Act, three major enactments since then have grafted important elements onto the constitutional structure. These include the War Measures Act in 1914, the Bill of Rights in 1960, and the Constitution Act of 1982. It is important to look at each of these modifications.

Although highly centralized in design, the BNA Act did not specifically deal with the means by which the federal government could act to meet either domestic or international crises. For 50 years it was assumed that the federal government's residual and declaratory powers were sufficient to counter any such threats. However, by the early 20th century the growing pattern of decentralization and the judicial restriction of the POGG clause, in conjunction with a world crisis, prompted the federal government to give itself emergency powers. Passed in 1914 as a federal statute, the War Measures Act sets up a system of "constitutional dictatorship" under the direction of the prime minister and cabinet. In effect, the federal government can rule by decree, usurping not only Parliament's powers, but that of the provinces as well. Moreover, penalties for failure to observe the new regulations can be imposed, with a fine of $5000 and/or five years in jail for each offence. A person can also be detained for a maximum period of 21 days, without being charged for a specific violation. Such regulations can be made retroactive: in the 1970 October Crisis it became illegal to ever have been a member of the FLQ! Under the War Measures Act, basic civil and political liberties can be suspended on the grounds that such actions are necessary to preserve the body politic.

The bringing into force of the War Measures Act is accomplished by a proclamation of the governor-in-council (i.e., the prime minister and cabinet) that there exists a situation of "war, invasion, or insurrection, real or apprehended." Of interest is the phrase "real or apprehended," which means that if the federal government perceives a crisis involving war, invasion, or insurrection, then a crisis exists. No evidence to support such a view needs to be presented. Once in place it is a prerogative of the federal government to decide how long it remains – there is no legal time limit on its application. The War Measures Act may last several months, as in 1970, or several years, as during the Second World War, from 1939 to 1945. The government may also wish to relax the extent of its control, once the immediate crisis is passed, but not to the position of returning to its normal powers. In this situation, it can impose a Public Order Temporary Measures Act, which limits some of its own arbitrary authority. This was used in both the 1970 crisis, when a public order temporary measures act was in place from December to April 1971, and after World War II from 1945 to 1954. The decisions about whether to use this procedure, the extent of the powers retained by the federal government, and the length of the application of a Public Order Act are all taken by the federal government itself. Although there is no legal restriction on how often such emergency powers can be used, for political reasons it is not likely to be resorted to often. Since its passage, the War Measures Act has been utilized on three occasions; during both world wars and the October Crisis in 1970. Even though it is a federal statute like any other law, the War Measures Act is a constitutional document with respect to both its content and its consequences for the political system.

The second major addition to Canada's constitutional structure came in 1960, with the passage of the Bill of Rights, although most of its provisions have now been superceded by the Charter of Rights contained in the 1982 Constitution Act. The basic assumption of a bill of rights is that the people need protection from their government, a view that challenges a core belief of parliamentary government. Historically, Parliament has been seen as the guarantor of people's freedoms, but a bill of rights asserts, in effect, that Parliament is not only incapable of continuing to protect the public, but also that the public needs a means of defence from its protector. A bill of rights is designed to establish a series of civil and political liberties, which no government can ignore or abuse. One way such protection is enhanced is to place the bill of rights explicitly in the constitution, a process known as *entrenchment*. Since constitutions are usually made difficult to change, having a bill of rights entrenched means it is less likely to be done away with or changed by the government of the day. An effective bill of rights stands, therefore, as a limit on parliamentary supremacy.

The late arrival of the Canadian Bill of Rights was a reflection of Parliament's belief that no such rights were needed as a protection against itself. However, public pressure and opinion was such that Parliament finally acquiesced and passed the legislation that created a potential check on its own power. The Bill of Rights was a normal piece of federal legislation that was not entrenched in the BNA Act. The Bill of Rights also reflected the impact of federalism, because it applied only to the federal level of government. However, by the mid-1970s, all provinces had enacted some type of "human rights" legislation, although most of these bills were not as comprehensive as their federal counterpart. The result of its lack of entrenchment and its applicability to only the federal level left the constitutional position of the Bill of Rights open to question. These concerns were reflected in the fact that it was nine years before the Supreme Court, in the *Drybones* decision of 1969, used the Bill of Rights to invalidate a section of federal law. However, in later decisions in the mid-1970s, the Supreme Court backed off from the full implications of such a stand and seemed reluctant to consider the Bill of Rights as a basis for challenging the legislative or executive actions of the federal government.

The provisions of the Bill of Rights were fairly typical in content, in that they protected a series of civil and political liberties. Unfortunately, these protections were not as effective as they appeared to be, because they could be bypassed by the federal government. By inserting the phrase "notwithstanding the Canadian Bill of Rights," any act of Parliament could be made immune from the application of these basic freedoms. Fundamental freedoms were simply not as fundamental as the principle of parliamentary supremacy.

A second limitation concerned the relationship between the Bill of Rights and the War Measures Act, with the latter taking precedence over the former. In times of crisis, when protection of basic civil and political liberties was most needed, fundamental human rights were held in abeyance. For example, the Bill of Rights in Part Two, Section 6(5), with reference to the War Measures Act, asserts that any action taken under the emergency powers provision "shall be deemed not to be an abrogation, abridgement or infringement of any right or freedom recognized by the Canadian Bill of Rights." Although the War Measures Act took precedence over the Bill of Rights, nevertheless, the Bill of Rights did modify the procedure for imposing emergency powers. Since 1960, any use of the War Measures Act must be accompanied by a notice to Parliament that a crisis exists. If Parliament is sitting, notification must be done "forthwith," that is, without undue delay. In a situation where Parliament is not in session when the emergency is declared, then it must be informed within the first 15 days of its next sitting. Within ten days of Parliament's notification, any ten members in either House can force a debate on the proclamation of the War Measures Act. If, at the conclusion of this debate, both Houses of Parliament "resolve that the proclamation be revoked, it shall cease to have effect." However, the government, if it felt it necessary, because of a continuing crisis or because of a new one, could legally invoke the War Measures Act a second time.

The lack of entrenchment, its application to only the federal level of government, the ability of the federal government to bypass it, and its inapplicability with respect to the imposition of the War Measures Act, were some of the major deficiencies of the Bill of Rights that led to a search for a more comprehensive and effective document. The result, in part, was the adoption of the Constitution Act of 1982, the third major addition to Canada's constitutional structure since 1867. While a detailed consideration will be given to the Constitution Act in Chapter 12, here we must indicate its two major modifications to the constitutional system: a Charter of Rights and amending formulas for future constitutional change. The Charter of Rights supplants the previous Bill of Rights, is more comprehensive in its powers, is entrenched, and applies to both levels of government. However, an override provision allows certain fundamental freedoms to be bypassed by the federal or provincial legislatures, although an override resolution would have to be renewed every five years. The second major change brought about by the Constitution Act concerns the amending formulas. Until 1982, the power to amend parts of the BNA Act remained with the British Parliament. The new amending formulas allow revisions to the Constitution as a result of agreements between the federal government and the provinces. As a consequence, Canada, for the first time, has the power to amend all aspects of its own Constitution.

This brief review of the key elements of Canada's constitutional structure in 1867 and the major additions since that time has stressed the idea of the almost unlimited power and influence of the national government in the affairs of the country. However, as in most countries, the intended constitutional structure may not be reflected in actual constitutional practice. The Canadian Constitution in the 1980s operates very differently than the above description would seem to indicate, a reflection, perhaps, of the view that a ''constitution that did not change would, by definition be nominal and not normative – an exercise in logic and not in life'' (McWhinney, 1979: 9).

The Evolving Constitutional Milieu
Before analyzing the major causes of its evolution, we must first begin with a description of how Canada's constitutional system has developed since the Confederation agreement. The general pattern of change can be summarized as follows: Canada has moved from the highly centralized political structure of 1867 to one of the most decentralized federal systems in the world in the 1980s. However, within this broad trend there have been alternating periods of centralization and decentralization. Canada was a centralized polity during both world wars, when the political system was run under the emergency powers legislation. Moreover, it is often forgotten that for 15 years, from 1939 to 1954, the polity was overwhelmingly Ottawa-directed. From this highly centralized system of the mid-1950s emerged a new round of provincial demands for greater autonomy, best symbolized by the Quiet Revolution in Quebec in the early 1960s. By the 1970s the provinces had gained a rough equality of power with the federal government, reflected in the Alberta-Ottawa battles over energy-pricing. This growing trend of decentralization was a prime motivation for Pierre Trudeau's entry into federal politics. One of the tenets of Trudeau's political

philosophy was that the decentralization of the early 1960s had gone too far and too fast and, as leader of the Liberal party and Prime Minister, he tried to reverse that pattern. Changes sought by Pierre Trudeau in the early 1980s with respect to limiting Ottawa's financial role in areas of provincial jurisdiction, a refusal to allow a further decline in Ottawa's constitutional powers in relation to the provinces (especially concerning Quebec), and the passage of the 1982 Constitution Act have all reflected a reassertion of the national government's role in the Canadian federal system. The basic equality of power between the two levels by the early 1980s means that any conflict is likely to resemble a 15-round, heavyweight championship match that ends in a draw. Neither level of government can govern effectively, for any extended period, without the cooperation of the other.

While the reasons for the change to a decentralized political system are complex, five interdependent causes seem to be important. First, the provinces quickly became dissatisfied with the highly centralized structure created in 1867 and began, by the last decades of the 19th century, to demand greater powers. One of the results of a federal system is to create a perception on the part of politicians in both levels of government that their level should be preeminent. Thus, the actual powers of each level of government in a federal system are always in a constant state of change.

A second cause of decentralization should perhaps be seen as a corollary of the first: as the provinces gained power, several of the key powers of the federal government became restricted. The legal basis for the exercise of these powers remained, but the federal government's political will to use them did not. Three important powers would fall into this category, namely, the declaratory power, disallowance, and reservation. Based on custom and convention, these powers of the federal government had become largely inoperative by the 1940s. For example, the declaratory power was last exercised in 1961 on a relatively minor matter, disallowance last occurred in 1943, and the power of reservation was last exercised by a lieutenant governor in 1961. However, these dates tend to hide the fact that the pattern of disuse had already been well-established. For example, while reservation occurred in 1961, it did so without the direction of the federal government, which then quickly moved to allow that piece of legislation to become law. Thus, the powers of disallowance, reservation, and declaration remain legally available to the federal government, but their exercise has been severely restricted by custom and convention. The use of these powers is still possible in a crisis situation, but their exercise is dependent on a political judgment by the federal government that they can get away with their implementation.

A third reason for enhanced provincial powers relates to a series of judicial decisions which began in the 1880s and continued into the early decades of the 20th century. Until the establishment of the Supreme Court of Canada in 1949 as the final court of appeal for Canadian cases, the highest court of appeal was the Judicial Committee of the British Privy Council (JCPC). Composed mainly of members of the British House of Lords, the JCPC rendered a series of decisions that had the effect of restricting federal powers and enhancing those of the provinces. For example, the broad grant of power to the federal government in the residual power clause was interpreted restrictively, that is, it was seen as only applying under special circumstances. In contrast, some of the powers of the provincial units, such as their control of property and civil rights, were generously applied by the JCPC. The result of such judicial decisions was to reinforce the evolving pattern of decentralization characteristic of the Canadian federal system in the 20th century.

A fourth contributing factor reflects the changing nature of society on the respective powers of the federal and provincial governments. Some of the activities granted the provinces in 1867, which were minor governmental functions in the 19th century, have since become major ones. For example, while the provinces obtained exclusive control of education in Section 93, few people received any such training, particularly in any kind of public school system. The acceptance of the notion of universal, public education through the high school years caused a massive expansion of this provincial government responsibility. A similar pattern has occurred with respect to the health and welfare functions. The result has been that provincial governments now spend about one-half of their entire budgets on these three concerns. Thus, minor provincial powers in 1867 have become major ones by the 1980s, and with that change has come more influence for the provincial units in the federal system.

A final reason for Canada's decentralized federalism is, perhaps, an outgrowth of the first four causes, that is, the emergence of a pattern of province-building. This concept stresses the development and significant role of the provincial governments in the federal structure (Hockin, 1976: 31). The growth of the provincial governments with respect to their size and areas of responsibility is both a cause and consequence of the enhanced power of the Canadian provinces. The trend of recent decades for the provinces to establish their own departments of intergovernmental affairs or, at least, to

have a provincial minister given responsibility for handling relations with the national government is an indication of this change.
In the past, the size and expertise of the Ottawa bureaucracy, in
comparison to their provincial counterparts, was one means of
federal government control of the provinces. How much this pattern
has changed was revealed in December 1981, when a meeting of
federal-provincial finance ministers ended in confusion because
Ottawa and the provinces could not agree on which set of financial
figures (Ottawa's or the provinces) were correct. Provincial bureau-
cracies and their expertise allow for such challenges to federal
government dominance.

The evolution of the Canadian system from a pattern of centralized to decentralized federalism has occurred, for the most part, as
the result of custom and convention rather than formal constitutional amendment. The lack of an explicit amending clause in the
BNA Act made the amending procedure difficult to use. In order to
adapt to a changing environment, the Canadian polity simply
changed the way it operated, without formally changing the rules of
the game. This pattern is one basic reason why custom and convention play such a significant role in the Canadian political experience. Although explicit amending formulas are now included in the
1982 Constitution Act, it is important to understand the amending
dilemma that confronted the political system from 1867-1982.

Constitutional Amendment 1867-1982

Two factors seem to account for the initial absence of an amending
clause in the BNA Act: first, because Canada was a colony, there
was no need for a specific amending procedure since any changes
would be made by the British Parliament, and second, the allocation of powers was seen as comprehensive by the Fathers of Confederation and, thus, no changes appeared to be needed in the
immediate future (Stevenson, 1979: 207-208). Such an optimistic
view appears shortsighted in retrospect. The lack of a specific
amending procedure created two obstacles, which had to be overcome whenever a change in the Constitution was proposed: agreement had to be reached on the amendment procedure and on the
content of the reform. However, questions of process and substance
could not be easily divorced.

Before delving into these intricacies further, we must first qualify
our assertion that Canada lacked an amending formula. In fact,
between 1867 and 1982, three different ways of formally changing
the constitutional structure existed (Mallory, 1971: 375-378). First,
from the very beginning, the provinces have been empowered to

THE OUTCASTS

change their own structure and operation. The BNA Act sets forth the structure of government for the four initial provinces, with the stipulation that such institutions would exist "until the provinces otherwise provide." For example, acting on this amending power, the provinces of Quebec (1968), Nova Scotia (1928), and New Brunswick (1892) all abolished their upper chambers or legislative councils. The second way of amending the Constitution was for the federal government to claim the same powers for changing its own structure and operation as that given the provinces. The BNA Act (Number Two) of 1949 formally established the federal government's legitimacy in this regard. For example, changes in the size of the House of Commons are made possible without a formal amendment, as long as the rules for the allocation of seats between the provinces specified in the BNA Act are not violated.

The real amending problem developed with respect to the third area, that is, the "safeguarded" portions of the BNA Act (i.e., federal and provincial powers in Sections 91 and 92, minority religious educational rights in Section 93, language protection in

Section 133). These responsibilities could only be altered by an amendment passed through the British Parliament at the request of the Canadian government. Several facets of Britain's power to amend the BNA Act must be kept in mind: first, no amendment was ever made except at the request of the Canadian government; second, no request from the Canadian government was ever refused; and third, the amending power remained in Britain because of the lack of an agreement within Canada itself on an amending formula. If points one and two, in particular, are kept in mind, then Canada has always had the *de facto* power to amend even the safeguarded portions of the BNA Act, if agreement on the content of such an amendment could be achieved.

Disputes about the content of such amendments to the safeguarded portions invariably raised concerns about procedure as well. Such amendments usually resulted after the federal Parliament passed a resolution outlining the contents of the changes proposed to Britain for implementation. The key procedural problem occurred prior to this resolution: if and when the provinces were to be consulted and, if consulted, the kind of consensus required before proceeding. From a narrow legal point of view, the federal government could act unilaterally. However, the custom and convention soon developed that the provinces should be consulted, or, at least, those provinces that were directly affected by the proposed amendments. If consultation did not lead to agreement between the federal governments and the provinces, then the federal government, on political grounds, would usually not proceed with the reforms. Thus, the content of the proposed amendment affected the procedure for its adoption, and both content and procedure limited the frequency of altering the BNA Act from 1867 to 1982.

Operating the Federal System

Difficulties of making formal amendments, a changing distribution of power between the federal and provincial levels, the impact of judicial decisions, and a changing political environment have all contributed to the complexity of the Canadian federal system. One result has been that both levels of government are involved in almost every major policy area. The exclusive powers of Sections 91 and 92 have, in many instances, become concurrent powers in practice. For example, the federal level's exclusive control of foreign affairs has been directly challenged since the 1960s by Quebec's insistence on its right to attend international conferences among French-speaking nations. Most other provinces now have the same kind of representation abroad, with Ontario having more than a dozen such offices. Similarly, the exclusive control of education given the provinces has not prevented the federal government's extensive participation in university and vocational education programs. Such complexity requires a constant process of negotiation between the two levels of government in order to keep the federal system functioning. This bargaining pattern between the elected and appointed officials of the two levels of government has been labeled *executive federalism* (Smiley, 1980: 91).

The pattern of negotiations is best symbolized by the Conference of First Ministers, which usually meets once a year, or sometimes more often, to handle special concerns such as economic problems or constitutional reform. Attended by the prime minister and the ten premiers, plus a retinue of other elected and appointed officials, these conferences resemble meetings between heads of state. This pattern is a reflection, perhaps, of the current powers of the provincial units, as well as the fact that the first such conference held in 1927 was organized along the lines of the Imperial Conference (i.e., an international meeting of nation-states in the British Commonwealth). The typical pattern of such meetings is for the first day of discussions to be held in public, before the full glare of the television cameras. The speeches by the prime minister and premiers are aimed at the folks back home, not towards each other. As in international diplomacy, the real bargaining goes on behind closed doors, away from the press and public, during the second or subsequent days of the conference. In addition to the First Ministers' Conference, the premiers, themselves, hold an annual meeting to discuss their common concerns. As well, the Western premiers meet annually, as do the Maritime premiers. Bilateral talks between two premiers are common, and Alberta and British Columbia even held a joint cabinet meeting in the Summer of 1981. More important, perhaps, are the almost daily contacts and discussions behind the scenes by various interprovincial and federal-provincial committees. Such constant contact, interaction, and bargaining have been important mechanisms for adapting an inflexible written constitution to a changing environment.

Financing Federalism
One of the key areas in the Canadian federal system is finance, the most complex aspect of federal-provincial relations. The basic conflict stems from the fact that each level of government wants credit for beneficial programs, yet at the same time it seeks to get the other level to pay the expenses. While the trend in recent decades has been for the provincial governments to seek financial

aid from Ottawa, the pattern is changing in the 1980s. Provincial reliance on federal largesse is well-illustrated by the equalization grants the poorer provinces receive from Ottawa, which mushroomed from $136 million in 1958 to $2.5 billion by the mid-1970s. By the early 1980s, as much as 40 to 50 percent of some provincial budgets were federal dollars.

Because the provinces spend the money, they receive credit for such programs as health, education, and medical care, while the federal government pays the bills. In renegotiating these financial arrangements for the 1982 fiscal year, the federal government insisted that it be given political credit for its good deeds – earthly rewards now, rather than heavenly ones later. A good example of the federal government's attitude took place in the Summer of 1981, when Pierre De Bané, Minister of Regional Economic Expansion, publicly refused to continue the financing of a joint Manitoba-Ottawa program because Ottawa was not gaining enough favourable publicity from its expenditures. Another example can be seen in the November 1981 budget, which sought to limit future federal government support in areas such as equalization payments and established program financing (EPF). By limiting its rate of growth in these areas, the federal government not only appears to be holding its expenditures in line, but also forces the provinces to assume more of the financial costs of these popular programs.

Conflicts between the federal and provincial governments over money are a result, in part, of their differential taxing powers. With the superior taxing power, the national government quickly became the financier of federalism, a source of revenue for tax-hungry, some would say greedy, provinces. The provinces have even been willing to give to Ottawa areas of provincial jurisdiction, such as old-age pensions, because the federal level has the tax sources to pay for such new activities. Against provincial opposition, the federal government has utilized its superior taxing power to become involved in other areas of provincial jurisdiction. For example, conditional grants, that is, federal money with strings attached, can be given to the provinces if they agree to spend it as the federal government desires. Provinces are often forced into cooperating because not to do so means the loss of millions of dollars for their citizens. Once such a program is established, the federal government may have second thoughts about it and later withdraw its funding, leaving the provinces either to pick up the tab or to face the political consequences of dismantling the program. For example, in October 1981, Prince Edward Island had to eliminate 161 civil service jobs because of federal government cutbacks in the province's economic development program. A further example of federal-provincial financial conflict was clearly evident in the 1981 Ottawa-Alberta energy-pricing dispute: the long delay was primarily the result of both levels wanting as large a share as possible of the increased tax revenues that would result from higher energy costs.

Although the traditional dispute in matters of finance has involved federal-provincial conflicts over who pays the costs and who receives the benefits from the federal system, a new financial concern came up in the early 1980s. This problem was a reflection of interprovincial financial arrangements, rather than a federal-provincial one, and was based on the Alberta Heritage Trust Fund. With its extensive revenues from oil and natural gas, Alberta decided to save a portion of these funds to use for long-term provincial undertakings. By 1982, the revenues had reached over $9 billion and, with the energy-pricing agreement of 1981, the trust fund was projected to climb to nearly $20 billion by the early 1990s. Thus, Alberta remained financially solvent, while the other provinces and the federal government faced problems of deficit financing in the 1980s. Alberta then proceeded to loan money at preferred interest rates to the other provinces, such as Quebec and Nova Scotia. These loans totaled nearly $2 billion by early 1982. The potential implications of such interprovincial loans are clear: one excessively wealthy province, which has loaned money to other provinces, might control or influence their policy stands at a First Ministers' Conference or in particular areas of federal-provincial conflict. While there is no clear evidence that such a tactic has been utilized so far by Alberta, the potential exists, even though the Alberta government announced in May 1982 that it intended to curtail future loans to the other provinces because of its own declining financial position.

Our survey of the constitutional structure of the Canadian polity has emphasized that there is considerably more to it than simply the BNA Act of 1867. Beginning with a highly centralized federal structure, the Canadian political system has evolved into a decentralized one, characterized by an intermingling of federal-provincial responsibilities and finance. This pattern reflects the needs of a changing society, as well as the impact of judicial decisions and evolving public beliefs about the role of the federal and provincial levels. Moreover, major additions to the initial constitutional structure, including the War Measures Act and the 1982 Constitution Act, have been effected. This series of reforms has filled in some of the interstices of constitutional government, so that in the 1980s, Canada has not only a series of written constitutional documents, but significant constitutional customs and conventions as well, both of which combine to produce a particular version of constitutional government.

BRITISH CONSTITUTIONAL PRACTICE

In describing the British system, one is faced with a problem: the British pattern of constitutional government is not outlined in a written constitution. Instead, as former Prime Minister Harold Wilson (1977: 208) put it, the British Constitution is "based on seven hundred years of mainly pragmatic experience." As a result, constitutional traditions are significantly embodied in the customs and conventions of the political process, although disagreements do exist over some of the specific ingredients of British constitutionalism.

> Thus, England ... has not felt the need to spell out for all time the principles of government in a single constitutional document. England's Constitution is not primarily a document distilling the abundant ... wisdom of an oppressed people, the inspired vision of revolutionaries and the common sense of contemporary politicians anxious to limit the sphere of government. It is a somewhat abstract and foggy notion which few people fully comprehend, but which most people dimly understand because of custom and convention (Verney, 1976: 37-38).

Although Britain is characteristically classified as lacking a written constitution, such a view must be modified, because Britain does have a series of written constitutional documents. What is missing is a single, written, and comprehensive constitutional statement. Such constitutional statutes would surely include the following: the Magna Carta (1215); the Petition of Rights (1628); the Habeas Corpus Act (1701); the Parliament Acts of 1911 and 1949; and the Representation of the People Acts (1948 and 1949). Also of constitutional import are the Reform Acts (1832, 1867, 1884), the Statute of Westminster (1931), the emergency powers legislation (1914, 1939), and the Peerage Act (1963). Each of these constitutional documents helps to delineate the workings and structure of major segments of the British constitutional system.

The second significant element of constitutionalism in Britain is custom and convention. Tradition establishes the relationship between the various governmental institutions that is indicated in the concept of the dual executive. The evolution of power from the formal to the political executive, and the present pattern of their interaction, is unspecified in any constitutional document. Similarly, notions of the collective responsibility of the government to the House of Commons, as well as the evolution of a system of party discipline and party government, both reflect custom rather than law. The lack of any comprehensive constitution has made the role of custom and convention even more significant in British politics than in the Canadian system.

A third aspect of constitutionalism concerns the role of the courts and the common law in Britain. Although the judiciary interprets the law in Britain, it in no sense takes an activist role in challenging Parliament's authority to define the law. Moreover, the concept of the common law, that is, the law based on custom and convention, has been an important ingredient of constitutionalism by establishing basic civil and political liberties, such as freedom of speech. Britain, for example, does not have a specific bill of rights to protect individual freedoms: instead, the Bill of Rights of 1689 established parliamentary control over the monarch. These ideas concerning judicial decisions and the common law are, perhaps, best summarized by the concept of the rule of law: "everybody, from the highest in rank to the lowest, is subject to the overriding claims of the law" (Wright, 1973: 10).

The various elements of British constitutionalism (i.e., the series of constitutional documents, customs and conventions, and the rule of law) are reflected in the major institutions and principles of government. Of paramount importance is the principle of parliamentary sovereignty, which is unlimited in Britain. The law is what Parliament says it is and there is no legal basis for challenging its authority, since Britain has never accepted the principle of judicial review or the need for a bill of rights to protect human liberties. Second, the structure of the polity is unitary in form, and, thus, the national government does not share power with other political units. Local government exists at the prerogative of the national government – it is not a separate level of government with independent authority. Third, Britain is a constitutional monarchy, that is, the Queen reigns, but the political executive, working through Parliament, governs. A monarchical form does not produce monarchical power, with the modern British monarch fulfilling primarily the symbolic and ceremonial tasks of the state. Fourth, cabinet government, centred around its collective responsibility to the House of Commons, has been combined with party discipline and unity to produce a pattern of governance classified as party government. Party government is the motor of the modern British parliamentary system, the key technique for the fusion of executive and legislative powers. Finally, explicit protection of civil and political liberties is not provided, nor thought to be needed, since Parliament itself will seek to guarantee their existence.

These five factors have created a political system strongly centralized in both theory and practice. From a legal point of view, there is very little that the government of the day could not achieve, including doing away with basic civil and political liberties. However, the customs and conventions of the polity limit the potential abuse of such a system of concentrated power, even if they do not eliminate such a possibility altogether. A political system of concentrated power is not inconsistent with constitutional government, as long as that power is constrained in use and effectively circumscribed by the customs and conventions of the polity.

The major advantage of the British constitutional system is its flexibility in reacting to changing public beliefs and circumstances. Since the basic constitutional documents are simply acts of Parliament like any other, they can be readily modified or replaced. Thus, there is no need for a specific amending procedure or a long, drawn-out debate about the content of the reforms, as there is in Canada. Moreover, since so much of British constitutionalism is dependent on custom and convention, its flexibility is further enhanced because the practices of politics are modified in the daily workings of the political institutions and processes of government. A final advantage of a British-style system is its ability to act, to get its legislative program passed, and to meet both domestic and international crises. Concentration of power has never been seen as automatically deleterious to constitutional government, but often in the modern era, as a prerequisite for its continuation. In contrast, the philosophical assumptions of constitutional government in the United States are based on the desire to limit any such concentrations of political authority:

> Lord Acton's famous phrase that "power tends to corrupt and absolute power corrupts absolutely," while that of an Englishman, has nevertheless found greater acceptance in the United States than in Great Britain itself (Mitchell, 1970: 109).

THE AMERICAN CONSTITUTIONAL EXPERIENCE

The nature of constitutional government in the United States has to be understood in the context of the American Revolution and its consequences. First, by achieving independence through the force of arms, the colonial leaders were confronted with the need to specify in a written, comprehensive document the structure of a new system of government. However, their initial attempt in the Articles of Confederation failed, which led ultimately to the present American Constitution. Second, the revolutionary context resulted in a revised philosophy of democratic government, which, in contrast to the British pattern of concentrated authority, emphasized the need to limit government. Finally, the people were made the basis of political authority: power flowed from the public to the government, that is, the idea of popular sovereignty. This outlook was summarized best in the words of the Declaration of Independence, which asserted that ''men'' were ''endowed by their Creator with certain unalienable rights, that among these are life, liberty, and the pursuit of happiness,'' and that to secure such rights, ''governments are instituted among men, deriving their just powers from the consent of the governed.'' The contrast of the liberal-based American perspective of ''life, liberty, and the pursuit of happiness'' with the British-based, conservative Canadian view of government's role as ''peace, order and good government'' is a remarkable one.

The essence of American constitutionalism, therefore, reflects the view that the people must be protected from government interference by producing a system of limited government. To achieve limited government, any undue concentration of political authority must be prevented. Such a philosophy of democratic government was explicitly argued in *The Federalist Papers*, a series of newspaper editorials written to convince the people of the need to adopt the new system of government. The best summary of the American political philosophy remains Federalist Paper Number 51, written by James Madison, who is often referred to as the Father of the American Constitution.

> But the great security against a gradual concentration of the several powers in the same department consists in giving to those who administer each department the necessary constitutional means and personal motives to resist encroachments of the others. The provision for defence must in this, as in all other cases, be made commensurate to the danger of attack. Ambition must be made to counteract ambition. The interest of the man must be connected with the constitutional rights of the place. It may be a reflection on human nature that such devices should be necessary to control the abuses of government. But what is government itself but the greatest of all reflections on human nature? If men

were angels, no government would be necessary. If angels were to govern men, neither external nor internal controls on government would be necessary. In framing a government which is to be administered by men over men, the great difficulty lies in this: you must first enable the government to control the governed; and in the next place oblige it to control itself. A dependence on the people is, no doubt, the primary control on the government; but experience has taught mankind the necessity of auxiliary precautions.

In addition to being the closest thing to poetry in the conversation of political analysts, this quotation stresses the need to limit government through the use of certain "auxiliary precautions," that is, those principles of government upon which the American system is founded. These auxiliary precautions are fourfold: separation of powers, checks and balances, federalism, and a bill of rights. The heart of American constitutionalism is reflected in the way the political structures embody these four principles, all of which seek to fragment and restrain the use and concentration of influence and power by the political elites.

The adoption and implementation of the separation of powers doctrine represents one of the unique contributions of American politics to the art of democratic government. *Separation of powers* refers to the establishment of several branches of government (executive, legislative, and judicial), the allocation of governmental powers among these three branches, and a pattern of political and constitutional independence of each branch of government from the other. The separation of powers principle is a reflection of the view that "ambition must be made to counteract ambition." Each branch of government is inherently in conflict with the others, as it jealously guards its own prerogatives and seeks to carry out the tasks assigned to it. Moreover, each branch must have the cooperation of the others in order to carry out these activities. Such cooperation among branches is essential in order for the American system to work, while such a pattern is made difficult by the structure of government so created. By fragmenting power among the several branches, cooperation among all three institutions was made improbable. In that sense, the American polity was created to prevent government activity – a goal that has, more often than not, been admirably achieved.

The political and constitutional independence of the three branches of government is explicitly provided for in the Constitution. For example, the officers in each institution are kept distinct, since no individual can serve in two branches of government at the same time. Thus, a separation of powers doctrine is implemented, in part, by a separation of personnel, in sharp contrast to the Canadian and British parliamentary systems. A further means of creating political independence for each branch is to have the executive, legislature, and judiciary responsive to varying political constituencies. Thus, the president and vice-president have a national constituency, members of the Senate a state-wide electorate, members in the House of Representatives a locally-based constituency, and judicial appointees a combination of such bases, depending on which court an individual serves. Moreover, members of each branch remain in office for differing time periods: the president serves a four-year term, with the possibility of being reelected once; Senators are chosen for a six-year period, with one-third elected every two years; all Representatives are voted on every two years; and judicial appointees generally serve for life. With each brand of government composed of different personnel, responsive to different constituencies, and staying in office for different time periods, individuals' outlooks and political interests rarely coalesce. The result is the prevention of undue concentration of political power.

In order to guarantee the continuation of the separation of powers principle once the political structure began operating, the second auxiliary precaution – namely, a series of checks and balances – was included in the Constitution. In other words, *checks and balances* are the constitutionally-specified mechanisms and powers designed to preserve the political independence of each branch of government. For example, the right of the executive branch not to turn over information to either the legislature or judiciary, what is known as executive privilege, is a major means for protecting its independence. Such a procedure is also a key defence against legislative supremacy, that is, the development of a parliamentary-style system. Numerous other such checks and balances could be cited. For example, Supreme Court appointments are recommended by the executive, but must be approved by the Senate. A treaty negotiated and signed by the president must be approved by a two-thirds vote in the Senate before becoming law. Any piece of legislation must be approved by both the executive and legislative branches of government, except when the legislature overrides a presidential veto. Even when approval by both branches is gained, the Supreme Court may rule such legislation null and void.

The result of the separation of powers principle and the series of checks and balances has been to create a governmental system "of separated institutions sharing power," a pattern of "mutually dependent relationships" (Neustadt, 1980: 26, 28). In such a system, every branch of government is given a certain portion of executive, legislative, and judicial power. For example, while the executive branch exercises most of the executive authority, both the legislature and judiciary are also given executive powers. The same argument holds true for the other branches. Thus, each "department is given a voice in the business of the others, and each is made dependent on the cooperation of the others in order to accomplish its own business" (Peltason, 1979: 24).

The third major restriction on the concentration of power is the principle of federalism, previously defined as the division of powers between levels of government. The division of powers and the separation of powers are principles that are not interchangeable in political analysis. In the American system, each level of government (i.e., national and state) is structured internally on the separation of powers principle. For example, the national government is composed of three branches of government, as are each of the 50 state governments. Thus, a federal structure is consistent with either a presidential system based on the separation of powers principle or a parliamentary system founded on a fusion of powers doctrine. Although both Canada and the United States are federal political systems, the federal principle was adopted for very different reasons in each country. Canadian federalism was a means primarily of handling ethnic diversity, while American federalism was designed to fragment and mitigate the concentration of political power. To enhance that fragmentation, the American federal system was initially decentralized. Although for generally similar reasons as in Canada, the evolution of American federalism runs counter to the Canadian experience: beginning with a largely decentralized federal structure, American federalism has become highly centralized, especially during the past 50 years.

The American Constitution allocated a series of explicit powers to the national government in Article One, Section 8, which included the right to collect taxes, provide for the common defence and general welfare, coin money, declare war, establish post offices, regulate commerce, and borrow money. Such functions are referred to as *enumerated powers*, with the national government also given the *implied powers* that might be needed to carry out the enumerated ones. Of interest is the fact that, after the list of powers given to the federal government, there followed a list of powers denied to Congress (Section 9) and a list of powers denied to the states

(Section 10). No specific allocation of powers was made to the states, because it was assumed that all powers not specifically granted the national government were retained by the states. A specific residual power clause was later added as the Tenth Amendment, to confirm the reserve power of the several states. However, within those powers granted to the national government, its laws would be supreme over those of the states (Article Six).

Local government was not recognized as a separate level, but was assumed to be under the powers retained by the states. Although local government was, therefore, in a unitary relationship with its respective state, over the years the municipalities have gained considerable independence. Despite considerable objections from the states, the national government has been able to deal directly with local governments, thus bypassing the intermediate state level. Such a development runs counter to the Canadian experience.

The American Constitution initially did not contain any provisions for emergency powers for the national government, nor have any such powers been added by the amendment process. However, the implied powers of the national government, with respect to defence and the general welfare functions, have been a sufficient basis for strong governmental action, when required. Finally, the American Constitution, unlike the Canadian, contained a specific amending clause (Article Five). Two ways of proposing amendments and two methods for ratifying such changes were outlined, thus producing four possible amending procedures. The usual method has been for an amendment to be proposed by a two-thirds vote in both Houses of Congress, followed by ratification by three-fourths of the state legislatures. However, such procedures are difficult to use, with the result that in almost 200 years, only 26 formal amendments have been made to the American Constitution.

Although the initial federal structure was decentralized, in the 1980s, the United States is an example of a strongly centralized federal system. Changes in society, governmental functions, and court interpretations have all contributed to such a pattern. For example, decisions of the American Supreme Court enhanced the powers of the national government with respect to three key areas: trade and commerce, taxation, and the war power (Burns et al., 1981: 60-63). Remember that in Canada, court decisions restricted the powers of the national government. Another cause of a centralized federalism in the United States can be seen in the responses to both domestic and international crises. Until the 1930s, American government remained decentralized, but in order to respond to the

Great Depression, the national government assumed many of the previous functions of the state and local units with respect to welfare, unemployment, and economic development. As in Canada, for example, the superior taxing power of the American national government eventually led to its participation in matters originally under state and local control. Through a series of financial mechanisms, such as the recent program of revenue-sharing, the federal government has become extensively involved in the financing of state and local government (Burns et al., 1981: 71-79). In addition, the Second World War and the emergence of the United States as a superpower in international affairs have greatly expanded the powers of the American presidency and, by implication, those of the national government. Such changes, more often than not, have been based on developing beliefs and conventions, rather than on explicit constitutional amendments. Finally, social changes, such as the civil rights movement of the 1960s and the urban crisis of the 1970s, have drawn governments, especially the national government, into new areas of activity. For these reasons, the national government has become the dominant level in the American federal system.

The final auxiliary precaution, a bill of rights, was not included in the original Constitution. However, in order to gain public support for its ratification, the backers of the Constitution promised that a bill of rights would be a priority of the new government. Thus, the first ten amendments to the Constitution were adopted in 1791 and they comprise the American Bill of Rights. Protections are given to basic civil and political liberties, including freedom of speech, religion, and assembly. Citizens are guarded against unreasonable searches and seizures by the government, granted the right of reasonable bail and the due process of law, prevented from self-incrimination, and guaranteed a trial by jury in common law cases. Although it was entrenched, the American Bill of Rights only applied initially to the national government. Beginning in the 1920s and continuing through the 1960s, a series of court decisions effectively "nationalized" the Bill of Rights, making it applicable to the states as well as to the federal government. This development was accomplished by judicial interpretation rather than by formal constitutional amendment.

The four auxiliary precautions of the separation of powers, checks and balances, federalism, and a bill of rights are the centrepieces of American constitutional practice. Based on the assumption of the inherently evil nature of political power, all four principles were designed to prevent its accumulation in the polity.

Concentration of power and by implication its misuse were made improbable by dividing political power between two levels of government (federalism); by splitting power within each level into executive, legislative, and judicial arenas (separation of powers); by structuring each department of government so that it would jealously guard its own powers and prerogatives (checks and balances); and by limiting the powers of any government through a series of civil and political liberties (a bill of rights). According to the American perspective, the way to create constitutional government is to structure a government of limited and circumscribed powers.

COMPARING CONSTITUTIONS

The most significant element in any political analysis of constitutions is determining whether or not they effectively restrain governmental power, that is, whether they produce, in fact, a pattern of constitutional government. Distinctions such as that between written and unwritten constitutions are secondary to questions of constitutionalism. However, to classify a polity as constitutional government, one has to go beyond the literal constitution to consider such things as whether or not a political system allows political dissent and political opposition. If a pattern of constitutional government does exist, then the way in which it is produced in different political systems becomes a significant basis for comparing political systems.

The structure of government itself may contribute to a system of constitutionalism. For example, some constitutional polities are presidential in format, while others are parliamentary. A presidential system, based on a separation of powers doctrine, seeks to constrain executive authority, while a parliamentary system concentrates power through the fusion of the executive and legislative branches of government. Some political systems are unitary in structure, while others are federal. If a polity is federal, then questions of how many levels of government have been created and their respective powers become significant. In analyzing federal systems, an important consideration is not only the initial distribution of powers outlined in the constitution, but the way in which those powers may have changed in practice. If there have been changes, then one must investigate how they have occurred and how the initial allocation of powers has been modified. The causes for the evolution and development of the pattern of power in a federal system are complex, but usually include a changing environment, the impact of judicial decisions, and modified public beliefs about the proper political role of each level of government. Changes in constitutional systems may be accomplished by a formal amending process, but, more often than not, are more typically produced by the evolving customs and conventions of the polity. These customs and conventions have a significant bearing on the existence and operation of constitutional government. The nature of these conventions, their strength, and the result of non-observance of them are all significant indicators for comparing the varieties of constitutional government.

A final point for the comparison of constitutions concerns their protection of civil and political liberties. A political analyst must consider what human freedoms are protected and how. The typical pattern in the modern era is to have some sort of bill of rights, which can be either entrenched in the constitution or passed in its own right. In federal systems, a key question is the application of such guarantees to each level of government: do human rights exist in relation to one or both levels of government? Moreover, in times of crisis, can a bill of rights be bypassed through the application of emergency powers and, if so, how long do such actions hold human freedom in limbo?

Three main areas, therefore, form the basis for any comparative analysis of constitutions: first, whether a constitution has helped to produce a constitutional government in practice; second, the kind of political structure that is outlined in the constitution (e.g., presidential or parliamentary, federal or unitary); and third, the mechanism, if any, that is used to protect basic human freedoms.

SUMMARY

1. A constitution is a political mechanism that structures the institutions of government; it is a power map of the polity. However, no such outline of the basic rules of the political game is ever neutral in its effects: constitution writers defend their own interests above all others. A country's constitution usually includes not only a written part, but significant political customs and conventions as well.

2. Having a piece of paper called a constitution and having a system of constitutional government are not necessarily synonymous

developments. Few constitutions produce constitutional government, that is, a polity that places effective limits on the powers and actions of its rulers.

3. The Canadian Constitution includes not only the BNA Act of 1867, but a series of constitutional documents as well. Moreover, political customs and conventions are significant elements in Canada's federal and parliamentary constitutional matrix. Beginning with a highly centralized federal structure, Canada has evolved to a decentralized federal pattern, with a rough equality between the provinces and Ottawa. Three major additions to the constitutional pattern have been added since Confederation: the War Measures Act, the Bill of Rights, and the Constitution Act. Although initially lacking an amending clause and a bill of rights, because of the Constitution Act, such discrepancies have now been rectified.

4. The British Constitution is unwritten in the sense of having a comprehensive constitutional statement. However, Britain does have a series of constitutional documents, plus an array of political customs and conventions, all of which produce a pattern of constitutionalism. Although political power is concentrated, as a result of its unitary and parliamentary structure, it is restricted in use, thus producing a unique example of constitutional government.

5. American constitutionalism is predicated on the view of the evil nature of political power and the need to restrict its concentration in the polity. Four basic techniques are used to achieve such a result: separation of powers, checks and balances, federalism, and protection for civil and political liberties. In contrast to the Canadian pattern, the United States has evolved from a decentralized to a centralized federal system. As a result of its revolutionary origins, the American Constitution was initially more comprehensive than the Canadian one, since it contained an amending formula, with an entrenched bill of rights soon added. Probably the unique contribution of the American example to the art of constitutional government is the principle of the separation of powers and its implementation through the various checks and balances. From the American perspective, the way to create constitutional government is to fragment and decentralize political power.

RECOMMENDED READINGS

Constitutional Government: General

DUCHACEK, IVO D. (1973) *Power Maps: Comparative Politics of Constitutions*. Santa Barbara, Calif.: ABC-CLIO Press.

_____ (1973) *Rights and Liberties in the World Today: Constitutional Promise and Reality*. Santa Barbara, Calif.: ABC-CLIO Press.

FRIEDRICH, CARL J. (1968) *Constitutional Government and Democracy: Theory and Practice in Europe and America*. Waltham, Mass.: Blaisdell Publishing Co., 4th ed.

_____ (1974) *Limited Government: A Comparison*. Englewood Cliffs, N.J.: Prentice-Hall.

ROSSITER, CLINTON (1963) *Constitutional Dictatorship: Crisis Government in the Modern Democracies*. New York: Harcourt, Brace and World.

The Canadian Constitution

FORSEY, EUGENE (1974) *Freedom and Order: Collected Essays*. Toronto: McClelland and Stewart.

MCWHINNEY, EDWARD (1979) *Quebec and the Constitution 1960-1978*. Toronto: University of Toronto Press.

SCOTT, FRANK R. (1977) *Essays on the Constitution: Aspects of Canadian law and politics*. Toronto: University of Toronto Press.

SMILEY, D.V. (1980) *Canada in Question: Federalism in the Eighties*. Toronto: McGraw-Hill Ryerson, 3rd ed.

STEVENSON, GARTH (1979) *Unfulfilled Union: Canadian Federalism and National Unity*. Toronto: Macmillan of Canada.

TARNOPOLSKY, WALTER SURMA (1975) *The Canadian Bill of Rights*. Toronto: McClelland and Stewart, 2nd rev. ed.

TRUDEAU, PIERRE ELLIOTT (1968) *Federalism and the French Canadians*. Toronto: Macmillan of Canada.

The British Constitution

BAGEHOT, WALTER (1867, 1963) *The English Constitution*. London: Collins, The Fontana Library.

PUNNETT, R.M. (1980) *British Government and Politics*. London: Heinemann, 4th ed. See Chapter Six, "The Constitution," pp. 163-193.

VERNEY, DOUGLAS V. (1976) *British Government and Politics: Life Without a Declaration of Independence*. New York: Harper and Row, 3rd ed. See Chapter Two, "Six Non-American Principles of Government," pp. 31-48.

The American Constitution

BLACK, CHARLES (1963) *Perspectives in Constitutional Law*. Englewood Cliffs, N.J.: Prentice-Hall.

PELTASON, J.W. (1979) *Corwin and Peltason's Understanding the Constitution*. New York: Holt, Rinehart and Winston, 8th ed.

REAGAN, MICHAEL D. (1972) *The New Federalism*. New York: Oxford University Press.

4 THE EXECUTIVE BRANCH OF GOVERNMENT: THE FACADE AND REALITY OF POLITICAL POWER

A constitutional monarch protects democracy from the results of the bends at the heights of political power (MacKinnon, 1973: 61).

In any sphere of action there can be no comparison between the positions of number one and numbers two, three and four (Winston Churchill).

THE CENTREPIECE of all forms of modern government – autocratic, democratic, or totalitarian – is the executive branch. The expansive nature of government in the 20th century has been both a cause and consequence of executive dominance. A combination of several factors has made the executive branch the engine of the political process, not the least of which has been the willingness of the political executives to provide leadership for the polity and to adapt themselves to a changing environment: "the birth of power presumes not merely a situation in which a form of arrangement and understanding is ripe for development, but likewise individuals or groups of individuals who are ready to utilize the opportunity afforded by the conjunction of circumstances" (Merriam, 1964: 45). Paralleling the growth of executive-centred government has been the phenomenal rise of bureaucratic government, the primary mechanism for implementing executive decisions.

THE NATURE AND GROWTH OF EXECUTIVE POWER

A frequent assertion of many analyses of the rise of executive government in the modern era is that executive power is a new trend. Unfortunately, the historical accuracy of such a conclusion is suspect, for few governments have ever been anything but executive-centred. The rise of executive government in the 20th century is a reassertion of the executive's traditional role, which was only temporarily lost to the legislature in democratic polities and never lost in autocratic and totalitarian systems. However, the reappearance of executive power has been accompanied by a change in the executor of that leadership from the formal to the political executive. The historical development of executive power has been from the king, to the king in Parliament, to a pattern of the prime minister in Parliament.

The characteristics of a *parliamentary executive* include its dual structure (i.e., both a formal and a political executive), its relationship with the legislature, which is based on the fusion of powers principle, and its term of office, which is variable within a maximum time limit. The *formal executive*, that is, the monarchical element, such as the queen or governor general, performs primarily symbolic and ceremonial functions for the polity. While an organizational chart of the executive branch would place the formal executive at its pinnacle, such a positioning represents the facade rather than the reality of political influence and power. The *political executive*, which includes the prime minister, cabinet, and bureaucracy, is the real locus of influence in modern parliamentary systems. Theoretically subservient to the formal executive, the political executive in fact controls the monarchical element. The formal executive reigns but does not govern, while the political executive governs but does not reign. This symbiotic relationship has always been an unequal one, with the formal executive initially controlling the political executive, while the reverse of this pattern is true in the reassertion of executive power in the modern age.

The connection between the political executive and the legislature in a parliamentary system is based on two principles: collective responsibility and ministerial responsibility. The concept of *collective responsibility* emphasizes the group basis of parliamentary government: as a team, the cabinet, that is, the government of the day, is sustained or defeated in Parliament. Individual government ministers cannot be rejected by Parliament. Moreover, unity of purpose is a necessary outgrowth of collective responsibility: the cabinet sings a common song, although some of its members may not always be in tune. Public disagreement with cabinet policy by a minister is rare. While initially developed as a means of legislative control over the executive, the combination of party discipline with collective responsibility has produced, in practice, executive control of the legislature.

In contrast to collective responsibility, the principle of *ministerial responsibility* emphasizes the individual responsibility of each cabinet member to Parliament. Individual ministers are responsible to the cabinet and the Commons for the conduct of their departments, including its finances, programs, and policies. Ministers must explain to the House any wrongdoing of officials under their jurisdiction, as well as justify to the public the direction of their department's major public policy decisions. Ministerial responsibility does not mean ministers are personally responsible for wrongdoings in their department, but it does mean they must answer questions and explain to Parliament what has happened, as well as be responsible for correcting present abuses and trying to prevent their reoccurrence. In modern parliamentary systems, the practice of ministerial responsibility can be circumvented (e.g., ministers refusing to take responsibility for wrongdoings in their departments), while that of collective responsibility remains largely, if not totally, in place (e.g., the Canadian Constitutional Crisis of 1968).

A *presidential executive* is characterized by the singular office of president, which combines the formal and political executive roles of a parliamentary system; by its relationship with the legislature, which is based on the separation of powers principle; and by its election periods, which are fixed by law. Because it has been rarely imitated, the American system remains the primary example of a presidential structure. As both the ceremonial and political leader, the American president has become the symbol of the nation. What has been created in the American presidential system is an executive office with the potential for leadership which, when combined with political skill and ambition, can make it the prime mover in the political process.

One of the most important distinctions between presidential and parliamentary government concerns the means of selecting the political executive. In a parliamentary system, the leader of the majority party is asked to form a government by the monarch. The prime minister is thus not technically elected by either the whole country (but is elected to the Commons from a single constituency, as is any other MP) or by Parliament. In contrast, presidential systems are based on a national constituency, which may select the president directly through popular election or indirectly through some sort of electoral college mechanism. This more direct relationship with the mass public has been an important reason for the enhancement of American presidential leadership in both domestic and international affairs. The dominance of the presidential office over the other political institutions is the basis for the idea of the *imperial presidency*, that is, an office that directs the course of events in the political process. Transferring this idea to a parliamentary context has resulted in the concept of *prime ministerial government*, where one individual, the prime minister, becomes the key actor in the parliamentary system. In such a system, cabinet government is superceded: the prime minister is no longer *primus inter pares* (first among equals) for the simple reason that he has no equals. The growth of prime ministerial power has often been labeled as the "presidentializing" of parliamentary government.

Whether of the presidential or parliamentary variety, the functions of the executive branch of government are similar in most political systems. There are three basic executive functions: leadership, policy-making, and the implementation of public policy. The leadership role focuses on the executive as the initiator of public policy, the branch of government given the responsibility for providing overall direction for the polity. In many cases, the leadership role of the executive branch is not constitutionally prescribed, but is based on custom and convention. A combination of circumstances, including the increasingly complex nature of both domestic society and the international system, the political will of the executive to exercise its powers, and the expansive nature of government in the modern era, has contributed to the leadership dominance of the executive branch of government. If the executive does not lead, then stalemate and confusion may characterize the polity. Neither constitutional prescription nor political custom can force or guarantee executive direction. However, one result is apparent: if the executive fails to lead, no other political institution appears, on a continuing basis, to be either adequately equipped or politically willing to assume the leadership function.

Executive direction is provided through the development of public policy. A *policy* is "an explicit set of preferences and plans drawn up in order to make the outcomes of a series of future decisions more nearly predictable and consistent" (Deutsch, 1968: 77). A *public policy* is a set of such preferences that has consequences for the community. Public policies would include examples such as a government's budget, taxation rules, or specific content areas such as economic development, immigration, culture, education, and foreign affairs. The initiation, development, and passage of public policy differs among political systems. The traditional makers of public policy in a parliamentary system have been the cabinet and the civil service, while prime ministerial government has shifted such power to appointed advisors. In a presidential system, the cabinet is rarely the centre of policy decisions: while individual cabinet members may play a significant role, the key decision-making power lies with the president and his advisors. On occasion, the legislature may assume the initiative for policy formulation. More often than not, the legislature's role is to legitimate the policy decisions of the executive branch of government.

Once a policy has been decided, the third function of the executive is to implement its provisions. The application and enforcement of public policy is the designated task of the bureaucracy, that portion of the executive branch referred to as the civil service. It is in the size of the bureaucracy that the real expansion of government has occurred in the 20th century. In addition to the factors that have contributed to the general growth of executive power, several others have enhanced bureaucratic powers. Most legislation is general in its provisions, leaving it up to the civil servants to fill in the details of how a policy will work in practice. The way a policy or law is implemented and applied is usually more significant than the generalized wording as approved by the legislature. In this sense, applying a general law to specific cases gives the bureaucracy, in effect, the power to make policy. Moreover, the bureaucratic role has been magnified by the expertise of its members. Knowledge and information are important political resources that the bureaucracy has often skillfully utilized to increase its own significance in the decision-making process. Modern government would quickly become inoperative without its bureaucratic component (or so the bureaucrats would like us to believe).

A *bureaucracy* is a hierarchically structured organization, which implements public policy on the basis of impartially applied rules. Comprised of appointed officials or civil servants who have been trained in the art of public service, the bureaucracy is the major point of contact between the individual and the political regime. In theory, the bureaucracy is designed to be free of political interference, applying set procedures to specific cases. Officials are paid from public funds and can be removed or fired for "cause," which means for incompetence rather than for holding specific political beliefs or for being associated with a particular political party. However, the view of the bureaucracy as impartial and outside of direct political involvement is wrong. Despite civil service examinations and appointments supposedly on the basis of merit, the bureaucracy remains a major bastion of partisanship and political patronage. Civil service regulations can often be circumvented. A party in power for any length of time can fashion the bureaucracy in its own image. Moreover, upon assuming office, parties usually demand the right to restructure at least the very top of the bureaucracy, that segment that plays a significant role in the policy-making process.

The role of the bureaucracy in implementing public policy and of the political executive in its initiation and development have made the executive branch of government the dominant force in the political process of autocratic, democratic, and totalitarian systems. The factors that have produced this pattern seem unlikely to recede in the decades ahead – if anything, these trends will become more pronounced. However, what is open to change is the evolving relationship between the various segments of the executive branch of government.

THE FORMAL EXECUTIVE IN CANADA

It would probably surprise many people to discover that executive authority is legally granted to the formal executive or head of state in the Canadian political system (BNA Act, Section 9). Moreover, that executive authority is vested in the Queen of Canada and exercised by her representatives (governor general and lieutenant governors) on a daily basis, a situation that has not been altered by the 1982 Constitution Act. The formal executive is surrounded and aided by a group of advisors known as the Queen's Privy Council for Canada (Section 11). Neither the prime minister nor the cabinet, the two key operative elements of the modern executive, are mentioned in the delineation of executive authority in the BNA Act. On the surface, therefore, the formal executive would appear to be preeminent. Consideration of the appointment of the formal executive and of the structure of the Privy Council should quickly dispel such an interpretation.

Since the day-to-day functions of the formal executive are performed by the governor general, he will be treated as Canada's head of state in the ensuing analysis. Although the governor general was initially selected by the British monarch, since 1926, the Canadian prime minister has recommended to the Queen the individual desired by the Canadian government. While still technically appointed by the Queen, for all practical purposes, such a procedure puts the appointment power in the hands of the Canadian political executive. Although it has never happened, it would also appear that the governor general could be removed on the advice of the prime minister to the Queen. Thus, while an organizational chart places the formal executive over the political executive, the appointment process demonstrates the contrary. The governor general's term of office is five years, although extensions of several months to several years have been granted. Since 1952, Canadians have been appointed, with the first four governor generals being Vincent Massey, Georges Vanier, Roland Michener, and Jules Léger. The appointment of Edward Schreyer as Governor General in 1978 produced a number of "firsts," probably the most significant being his youth and his Western Canadian background. At the provincial level the formal executive is appointed by the governor general, to whom the lieutenant governors are responsible. This selection procedure puts the effective appointment power for the provincial formal executives in the hands of the federal political executive. Usually, the provincial political executives are consulted by their federal counterpart before any appointment is made. Lieutenant governors have more often been selected on the basis of patronage than has the governor general. The term of office for the lieutenant governors is five years, with their salaries determined and paid for by the federal government.

If for some reason formal executives are unable to perform their duties (e.g., illness, travel outside of the country), the BNA Act makes provision for their replacement (Sections 10 and 67). At the federal level, the governor general can be replaced by a person appointed as the Administrator of Canada, who can exercise all of the formal executive's traditional powers and who serves until the governor general reassumes the duties of the position. In such a situation, the Chief Justice of the Canadian Supreme Court becomes the Administrator of Canada, as happened following Jules Léger's stroke in the mid–1970s and his temporary replacement by Chief Justice Bora Laskin. A similar procedure is followed for the replacement of a lieutenant governor at the provincial level.

The structure and workings of the Privy Council are a second clear indicator of the dominance of the political executive over the formal executive in Canada. The advisors to the governor general are selected by the prime minister and, in fact, advise the PM rather than the formal head of state. The operative or working part of the Privy Council is the cabinet. However, since the cabinet is not mentioned in the BNA Act, to acquire the right to exercise executive authority, its members are sworn into office as members of the Privy Council. Decisions of the cabinet are issued as decisions of the Privy Council (i.e., orders-in-council or minutes-in-council). While individuals are cabinet members only for the duration of their postings as determined by the prime minister, they continue as members of the Privy Council for life. Thus, in the late 1970s there were over a hundred members of the Privy Council, but the typical cabinet had only 30 to 35 people. Although former cabinet ministers remain privy councillors for life, they do not retain the right to advise the current government of the day. The cabinet meets frequently, but the full Privy Council rarely does so – only three times between 1945 and 1970 and nine times between 1900 and 1970. A Privy Council meeting is usually held when the Queen visits or on other special occasions (e.g., to receive the announcement from the Queen concerning the marriage of Prince Charles and Lady Diana). While most members of the Privy Council are there as the result of once being in the cabinet, other individuals may be appointed as well. In honour of the centennial celebration in 1967, the provincial premiers were named to the Privy Council. In January of 1982, Gordon Robertson, former Clerk of the Privy Council and senior cabinet advisor, was named by Prime Minister Trudeau to the body he had long served. In honour of the 1982 Constitution Act, all premiers were invited to join, with only Quebec Premier René Lévesque turning down the appointment. These considerations on the structure of the Privy Council emphasize that while the formal executive was granted executive authority, it is exercised in fact by the political executive. The formal executive retains the facade of power, while its substance has been coopted by the prime minister and cabinet.

The functions of the formal executive reflect this pattern as well. Two basic roles can be identified: a symbolic-ceremonial one and a political one. Most of a governor general's daily tasks fall into the symbolic-ceremonial category, which includes such duties as attending state dinners, receiving ambassadors, and officially granting memberships in the Order of Canada. As a symbol of national unity, the Office of Governor General has been used to stress the bilingual and diverse aspects of the Canadian nation. For example, the first four Canadian governor generals were from Ontario and Quebec, with an alternation between those who claimed English or French as their mother tongue. The fifth Canadian Governor General, Edward Schreyer, broke this tradition by being of non-French and non-British origin and by coming from Western Canada. Although often viewed as a unifying office, critics are apt to point out that, with its ties to the British Crown, the Canadian monarchy may be a symbol of subjugation for French Canadians. Moreover, more recent immigrant groups than either the French or English may feel no emotional ties to the Canadian Crown at all.

In its symbolic-ceremonial tasks, the formal executive exemplifies what Walter Bagehot described as the dignified elements of the constitution: "The duties of the Queen, Governor General, and Lieutenant Governors include the decorative functions to facilitate the conduct of public business" (MacKinnon, 1976: 136). These ceremonial or decorative tasks may not always be appreciated by either the public or the government of the day. For example, when the CCF (Cooperative Commonwealth Federation) became the government in Saskatchewan in 1945, the symbolic role of the lieutenant governor was greatly diminished, even to the extent of not providing him with an official residence, except for a three-room hotel suite. The initial Government House had its goods auctioned off and even though it had undergone a $4 million refurbishing in 1981, it remained a museum rather than the formal executive's residence. Such conditions must reduce the dignified and decorative tasks of the monarchy in Saskatchewan.

While the formal executive carries out a number of political tasks, most of these take place only under highly unusual circumstances. The key remaining political role of the formal executive is to select a prime minister, thus ensuring that there is always a government in office. However, even in this function, the governor general's leeway is greatly circumscribed by various political customs. If, after an election, a party has obtained a majority of seats in the House of Commons, then the governor general has no choice but to ask the leader of that party to form a government. Another party leader asked to form a government would surely be unable and, quite likely, unwilling to do so, since it would be an impossible undertaking to gain the confidence of the Commons. In a minority election result, the theoretical discretion of the formal executive is enhanced in choosing a prime minister, but in practice such discretion is rarely maximized. Since minority governments in Canada have usually been close to an actual majority of seats or for other reasons have been relatively stable, the governor general's leeway in naming a prime minister is limited. For example, while a coalition of the Liberal, NDP, and Social Credit parties could have governed after the 1979 election, its stability in office would have been weak. Moreover, since the Conservatives had a 22-seat margin over the Liberals, custom required that they be given the first chance to govern. In a minority election result, the parties sometimes act on their own to limit the formal executive's discretion. For example, after the Liberal minority victory in 1972, Liberal leader and Prime Minister Pierre Trudeau called a press conference to announce that his government would unofficially have the backing of the New Democratic Party. Trudeau was immediately followed to the microphone by NDP leader David Lewis, who confirmed the "working majority" between their two parties. Although either the Conservatives or Liberals could have governed with NDP support, the Liberal-NDP arrangement precluded a Conservative government. Thus, in the 1972 example, the formal executive's discretion to name a prime minister was circumvented by the actions of the parties; politically he could ask nobody else but Trudeau to form a government after the public news conference.

In addition to majority or minority election results, other scenarios are conceivable that might increase the discretion of the formal executive in naming a prime minister. For example, if a prime minister were to suddenly die in office and if there was either no obvious successor or if the governing party was divided on its choice, the governor general could name an "interim" prime minister until the governing party could hold a national party leadership convention. However, it is unlikely that the governing party would not agree on a successor. Another possible scenario would be a major political scandal involving the prime minister and key cabinet members. If those individuals resigned, the formal executive might be forced to ask another member of the cabinet or the full House of Commons to form a new government. Such a case is possible but not very probable; for all practical purposes, the formal executive has very minimal discretionary powers in naming the person who will become the prime minister.

The remaining political tasks of the formal executive are theoretically important and legally possible, but even more than with respect to selecting the prime minister, they rarely involve any real exercise of power. The various legislative tasks of the formal executive clearly demonstrate such a pattern. For example, while the governor general officially summons, prorogues, or dissolves Parliament, this is done on the initiative of the political executive. Similarily, the governor general delivers the Speech from the Throne to open Parliament but does not write it, even though phrases such as "my government will recommend" are liberally distributed throughout the address. The prime minister, in consultation with key advisors and ministers, determines the content of the throne speech. The formal executive may be consulted or the broad outline of government policy may be discussed with the political executive, but there is no legal requirement for this. A formal executive does not have the right, based on custom and convention, to make changes or additions to the throne speech.

A second legislative task, which has become a formality, is the granting of assent. When a bill has passed both the Commons and the Senate, the assent procedure is held in the upper chamber. In some provinces, the entire work of a legislative session is presented in total to the formal executive for approval at the end of a session. Such a process certainly eliminates any chance for the formal executive to give detailed thought to each item before granting assent. The formality of the assent procedure is illustrated by the fact that assent has never been refused a federal piece of legislation in Canada. The granting of assent by the formal executive is such a foregone conclusion that people rarely check to see if it has been carried out. For example, the passage of the language legislation (Bill 101) by the Quebec National Assembly in August 1977 only received assent in its French version. Lieutenant Governor Hugues Lapointe apparently refused to sign the English version into law, a fact that was not revealed until January 1978. At that point, the Lieutenant Governor was presented with another English copy of the law, which he signed in early February. The reason for Lapointe's refusal to sign the English version of Bill 101 the first time remains unexplained, but this incident illustrates the view that assent by the formal executive is assumed to be automatic. This example also reveals the irony that Bill 101, which was designed to make Quebec a unilingual French province, had to be passed in a bilingual format.

A final duty of the formal executive, which illustrates the difference between legal niceties and political reality, concerns the granting of dissolution when requested by the prime minister. If the political executive has been defeated on a non-confidence motion or if it desires a new election without having suffered such a defeat, it must obtain a dissolution of Parliament from the governor general. If the government has a majority or if it is the only party capable of forming a "working majority" even though it has only a minority of seats, the governor general has no leeway for refusing a dissolution request. However, if another party could form a government, then legally the governor general might not grant a dissolution, but instead ask another party leader to form a government. Such a situation did develop in the 1920s during the King-Byng Affair, when Governor General Lord Byng refused a dissolution request from Prime Minister Mackenzie King. Unfortunately for monarchists, this controversy ended up as an issue in the ensuing 1926 election campaign, with Mackenzie King vowing to prevent any future governor general from saying no to a dissolution request. When King won the election, he proceeded to undermine the power of the governor general, so that, since that time, the formal executive has, for all practical purposes, lost the ability to deny the political executive a dissolution of Parliament. A more recent example came to light in December 1979, with the defeat of the Joe Clark government. After his Thursday night defeat, Prime Minister Clark met with Governor General Schreyer on Friday morning to ask for a dissolution of Parliament. After nearly an hour's meeting, no dissolution was forthcoming; the Governor General made the Prime Minister return to his office before he was given his requested dissolution (Simpson, 1980: 38). In a later interview, Governor General Schreyer maintained that he had the right to consider the dissolution request without being simply a rubber stamp for the Prime Minister (Valpy, 1981: 10). However, such reflection lasted only an hour, demonstrating a more acute political judgment by Governor General Schreyer than by Lord Byng a half a century earlier. A political realist would seriously doubt whether the formal executive could have said no to Prime Minister Clark and gotten away with it. Governor General Schreyer was probably asserting his political independence in his recently acquired job, rather than attempting to enhance the formal executive's power in the Canadian polity of the 1980s.

In considering both the structure and functions of the formal executive in Canada, we have emphasized that the head of state embodies the facade, rather than the substance, of political influence and power. Most of the governor general's legal duties, such as opening Parliament or granting a dissolution, are exercised on the initiative of the political executive. Even those tasks in which some theoretical power remains, as in selecting a prime minister, are tightly circumscribed by custom and tradition. The formal executive's daily impact on the political system is thus modest, because the possible exercise of the position's potential powers becomes tenable only during the gravest of constitutional emergencies. As Governor General Schreyer put it, "Understanding this office in the full has to include some contemplation of worst-case scenarios and what is to be done" (Valpy, 1981: 10). Fortunately, such worst-case scenarios rarely develop, so that the potential influence of the formal executive is infrequently tested in the heat of political battle.

THE POLITICAL EXECUTIVE IN CANADA

In contrast to the office of the formal executive, that of the political executive occupies centre stage in the struggle for policy, power, and patronage. The public visibility of the formal and political executives reveals much about their relative influence in the Canadian political process. While the role of the formal executive is poorly understood or, for that matter, scarcely recognized, that of the political executive is the focus of public attention. For example, while the Queen is recognized by most Canadians, her representatives seem not to have made much of an impression on the ordinary citizen. One study of high school seniors found that 68 percent could not name the Governor General (Hurtig, 1975). If one proceeds past simple recognition of these leaders, the level of ignorance becomes overwhelming: considerable confusion surrounds their particular roles. For example, a national poll in 1977 discovered that more people chose the Prime Minister as Canada's head of state (42 percent) than those who named the Queen (37 percent) as the formal executive (*Weekend Magazine*, October 22, 1977). Such findings reveal much about the substance of influence in the Canadian polity, as does the fact that the first press conference ever held by a governor general took place on December 15, 1981.

This dominant role of the political executive is primarily a consequence of custom and convention, rather than a result of legal prescription. The prime minister and cabinet are not mentioned in the BNA Act, although the PM is named in other statutes. The evolution and development of the prime minister's tasks reflect an important mechanism of adaptation by the political system to a changing environment. Moreover, to a considerable extent, the role of the prime minister depends on the individual who occupies that office.

> Although Canada's political system culminates in this one man, and the arsenal of his authority is indeed huge, both the basis and the boundaries of that authority are ill-defined.... What the Prime Minister of Canada is not is established by legislative checks and the circumscribing realities of Canadian politics. What he is depends on him. The office is reconfigured by its occupant (Newman, 1973: 80–81).

Given such a context, the prime minister has come to be the key political actor of Canadian politics by combining political resources and skills with a political will so as to provide leadership on major questions of public policy. The preeminence of the prime minister is an outgrowth of the incumbent's relationship with the public, the formal executive, the party, and the cabinet.

With respect to the ordinary citizen, the prime minister is the most visible and salient symbol of political leadership in the country. Rarely will a prime minister escape or seek to escape the limelight – for visibility can be an important political resource of the office. It is not entirely coincidential that the growth of prime ministerial influence in the past few decades has occurred at the same time that television has become the essential political medium. The impact of television and its intimate relationship with the enhancement of the prime minister's role is clearly evident in recent election campaigns, which have become partisan-based media contests. Moreover, between election campaigns, the prime minister can clearly dominate the other party leaders with respect to news coverage: when the PM speaks, people listen, even if not always attentively or reverently.

The second basis of prime ministerial preeminence is the relationship between the formal and political executives. Once the governor general has named a prime minister by asking that individual to form a government, the PM is the sole link between these two parts of the executive. As the head of the political executive, the prime minister alone deals with the governor general. For example, only the prime minister – not the cabinet, personal aides, opposition parties, or even Parliament as a whole – can request a dissolution of Parliament from the formal executive. Although others may be consulted, it is the prime minister who recommends to the governor general those individuals who are to be named to the Privy Council, Senate, and other governmental institutions. Since much of the formal executive's role is only carried out on the initiative of the political executive and since the prime minister determines when those powers will be exercised, the PM's indirect control over the formal executive also enhances the direct control over the other elements of the political executive, such as the cabinet.

A third element of prime ministerial influence reflects the PM's role as a party leader: control of the party organization, when combined with the principle of party discipline within Parliament, gives the PM control of the legislative branch of government. Failure by the party leader to control the party makes it difficult to be elected prime minister, since the public probably perceives such an individual to be lacking in the necessary leadership qualities required by the job. Such a fate was that of Conservative leader Robert Stanfield. And those who gain the office of prime minister may lose it, at least in part, because of their difficulty in controlling their party caucus or organization (e.g., John Diefenbaker and Joe Clark). While the cabinet may help to impose a fusion of powers between the executive and legislature, it is embodied to an even greater extent in the role of the prime minister. Because the prime minister stands "at the apex of the party both within Parliament and outside", he is "by far the most powerful man in the Canadian system" (Matheson, 1976: 214).

The combination of these first three factors creates a fourth basis of prime ministerial leadership, namely, the PM's supremacy over the cabinet. Control over cabinet selection gives the prime minister the power to make or break the political careers of others. Talent, in and of itself, is not necessarily enough for cabinet promotion – that talent must be recognized by the prime minister.

Once a person has gained a cabinet nomination, a further prime ministerial prerogative becomes significant. The prime minister not only determines the number of cabinet members and the structure of departmental responsibilities, but the portfolios assigned to individual ministers. Federal cabinets under Pierre Trudeau have been unusually large – about 35 members. The smallest cabinet of recent times was that of the initial group selected by the new NDP Premier of Manitoba in December 1981 – it contained only 13 members. Once the question of size is determined, which itself sets limits on the allocation of departmental duties, then specific ministers for each department must be named. Political careers can be crushed or enhanced at this point, with probably more devastating effect than even with respect to cabinet elevation in the first place. It is difficult to become a national political figure when one is made Minister of State for Fitness and Amateur Sport. However, a high profile ministry, such as Justice, External Affairs, or Finance, need not be a political advantage. Much depends on what the individual makes of the assignment. Some portfolios are seen more as liabilities than as steppingstones to higher political office. In the last several decades, the position of Minister of Finance has become the suicide portfolio of Canadian politics, as the subsequent career patterns of Walter Gordon, Edgar Benson, and John Turner illustrate.

Once in the cabinet, a minister must also be concerned about *cabinet shuffles*, that is, a reallocation of ministerial responsibilities. Since the status or prestige of each portfolio is well-known, cabinet shuffles reveal who is on the "up" or "down" side of the political escalator, as well as the minister's current influence in Ottawa's political pecking order. Cabinet shuffles are a convenient means for the prime minister to help out ministers who are in political trouble in their current portfolios by moving them to a different posting. Sometimes the prime minister does not want to salvage a minister in trouble, as Lloyd Axworthy found out in 1981. As minister responsible for the Status of Women, Mr. Axworthy became involved in a highly publicized dispute with the Advisory Council on the Status of Women. At one point the minister sought to have Prime Minister Trudeau relieve him of his responsibility for this area of public policy, but the Prime Minister and his cabinet colleagues refused, until severe damage had already been done to his political career.

The extent of a prime minister's influence over the cabinet is also clear from the way ministers depart from the inner sanctum of power. For those loyal allies who have retained the prime minister's support, leaving the cabinet is made easier by appointment to the Senate or some other government institution. For those who have alienated their leader, a return to the backbenches may be their only reward for past service. There are few instances in which a minister who has been demoted from the cabinet has ever returned to it. A rare exception was the situation of Liberal Herb Gray, who asked so many questions of his own government from the backbenches that in order to silence him the prime minister brought him back into the cabinet. However, when ministers who are liked by the prime minister have been forced to leave the cabinet, the prime minister may resurrect their political careers by reappointing them. The careers of Francis Fox and André Ouellet are instructive on this point – a prime minister has the ability to breathe life back into apparently dead political careers.

In addition to being ousted by the prime minister, cabinet members may leave of their own accord, although not necessarily willingly. Resignations are often a symbol of protest against the prime minister's policies, but they also demonstrate that the minister who has resigned is an outcast in the cabinet and the governing party. Even when ministers have quit the cabinet, they have no right to explain in detail why they resigned, unless the prime minister releases them from the oath of secrecy they take upon being sworn into the cabinet. Ministers who have resigned rarely remain in the public eye for long – former Liberal Defence Minister James Richardson is a classic example of this point.

While it is a prime minister's prerogative to decide the size of the cabinet, its departmental structure, the frequency of cabinet shuffles, and the individuals to be named to this key decision-making body, some of the PM's leeway in these matters is circumscribed by political tradition. For example, each of the parties contain various ideological strands that insist on having representatives in cabinet. Likewise, a prominent party figure with a significant base of support in the country usually cannot be overlooked in the process of cabinet construction. At times, dissidents within the party are promoted to the cabinet to silence them by their cooptation into the party and governmental hierarchy; the selection of Liberal MP Serge Joyal to the Trudeau Cabinet in the Fall of 1981 could be seen in this perspective. Probably the most important restriction on cabinet composition, however, is the representation principle, a crucial convention of the Canadian political process.

The *representation principle* refers to the practice of naming representatives of the various regions, provinces, and major social and economic interests of Canadian society to the cabinet (Matheson, 1976: 22–46). This practice was instituted with respect to the composition of Canada's first federal cabinet by John A. Macdonald and has been followed ever since. The workings of the representation principle are embodied in a series of informal rules, which include the following. Where possible, each province should receive at least one cabinet appointment. In those cases where a province has not elected anyone to the governing party's caucus, then a prime minister may appoint a senator from that province to the cabinet. It would run counter to political custom to use senators from a province in the cabinet if the government had seats in the Commons from that same province. Minimal representation in Quebec for the Conservatives in the 1979 election and no representation in the Commons at all from British Columbia, Alberta, and Saskatchewan for the Liberals in the 1980 election forced both Joe Clark and Pierre Trudeau, respectively, to use several senators in putting

together a cabinet. Such a practice diminishes to the extent that the winning party in the general election gains seats from each province. This minimal rule of one cabinet position for each province means that the prime minister's leeway in choosing that representative may be narrow, especially for the smaller provinces, when only one or two government members are elected to the Commons.

More than one seat in the cabinet is allocated for the larger provinces. In recent years, Ontario and Quebec have typically been granted about 10 seats each in a 30-seat cabinet, with British Columbia receiving from 2 to 4 positions. The exact number of such portfolios for each province varies from one government to the next, but the general pattern remains: Ontario and Quebec, which have a majority of the population and a majority of seats in the Commons, also receive a majority (usually two-thirds) of the cabinet postings. The number of posts for the more populous provinces are distributed throughout that province, a pattern of regionalism within regionalism. For example, Northern Ontario usually receives one cabinet post, as do the major metropolitan areas. Major cities like Toronto and Montreal usually have more cabinet positions each than the Atlantic provinces in total.

Once the regional allocation has been made, other factors such as race, ethnicity, sex, and religion are considered. For example,

Quebec's cabinet representatives include French-speaking Catholics (a majority of posts) and English-speaking Protestants (usually several portfolios). On an ethnic basis, those of non-English or non-French origin have traditionally been underrepresented, although since World War II other ethnic groups are receiving greater attention (e.g., John Diefenbaker appointed the first minister of Ukrainian descent). Women are the most underrepresented group in the cabinet, a reflection of the fact that few women are candidates for office. In comparison to the "average Canadian," the cabinet, on factors such as age, sex, education, and occupation, is quite unrepresentative. In this regard it is well to keep in mind that the representation principle refers primarily to provincial and regional concerns, rather than to ethnic and religious ones, and only coincidently to such factors as sex, age, and occupation.

BEN WICKS

Whatever the reasons for their selection to the cabinet, once there, MPs are expected to speak for their province or region, irrespective of their specific portfolio. A Minister of External Affairs from Nova Scotia is Nova Scotia's cabinet representative. A Minister of Public Works from Ontario is expected to be a representative for Ontario in the cabinet's policy-making process. Ministers' portfolios may change, but their role as defender of provincial interests does not. However, based again on custom, certain portfolios have come to be associated with particular provinces. For example, Public Works, which is a key patronage department because of the number of jobs and contracts that it controls, is given to a minister from the governing party's "home" province or provinces. Responsibility for the Wheat Board is allocated to a minister from the West or perhaps rural Ontario, while Fisheries goes to a minister from the Atlantic Provinces (Roméo LeBlanc) or British Columbia (Jack Davis). Finance is typically granted to an English-Canadian, usually from Ontario, who has strong ties with the business community. Jean Chrétien's brief stint as Minister of Finance in the mid–1970s was the first time a French-Canadian had ever served in that post. The prime minister may assume the role of a minister with departmental responsibilities, such as that of External Affairs; however, the custom in recent decades has been not to do so. These traditional assignments of particular portfolios being granted to specific regions or interests is a reflection of the impact of the representation principle. Nothing legally prevents a Minister of Fisheries coming from a Metropolitan Toronto constituency; however, the political absurdity of such a move renders it highly unlikely.

In addition to circumscribing the leeway of the prime minister in forming a cabinet, the representation principle has had other significant effects on the political process. First, because it is designed to protect regional and provincial concerns, the cabinet has become the key decision-making body, as well as the primary defender of provincial interests, effectively usurping, in the process, the designated role of the Senate. Second, the size of the cabinet keeps increasing as more and more sectors of society demand representation. One internal cabinet result of this increasing size is a specialization of function, which has resulted in turning over a considerable amount of the effective decision-making power to a series of cabinet committees. Third, the cabinet is not necessarily composed of the most talented individuals available, for the most talented rarely have had the foresight to be elected to the Commons on a regional basis. Fourth, the cabinet, in its attempt to accommodate the various regions and interests, is not very efficient in its operation.

While the representation principle affects the allocation of the departmental portfolios, some cabinet members are also named as political ministers. *Political ministers* are cabinet members who are given the additional party responsibilities of party organization and patronage for the governing party within their province. These positions are allocated by the prime minister and reflect the political influence of the individual so named. To assess a minister's overall role in the cabinet, one needs to know his or her official responsibility and his or her party responsibility, if any. To be the political minister for a province is often more significant for one's political influence and power than an individual's departmental responsibilities. For the larger provinces several political ministers may be named (e.g., one for Northern Ontario, Southern Ontario, Metropolitan Toronto), while only one is typically selected for the smaller provinces.

Once the composition of the cabinet has been finalized, it is up to the prime minister to determine its uses and internal organization. Under the guidance of the prime minister, the cabinet determines its own structure and operation. The frequency of its meetings, the kinds of questions or issues it deals with, the decision-making procedure that it follows (i.e., majority vote or consensus) all emerge from the prime minister's intent, as well as from the evolving practice of the cabinet itself. Since the internal structure of the cabinet is undefined in law, its organization and role tend to reflect the prime minister's leadership qualities. Diefenbaker's demise as Prime Minister reflected the disintegration of his cabinet, while Trudeau's longevity is attributable, in part, to the restructuring of the cabinet decision-making process instituted on his becoming Prime Minister in 1968.

The revisions made in the cabinet decision-making process by Trudeau reflected two fundamental assumptons: first decision-making needed to be more rational, and second, the cabinet, rather than the traditional bureaucracy, had to become the effective decision-making centre. Two major structural innovations of the cabinet corresponded to these two goals: first, the cabinet, in order to become more efficient in its handling of issues and problems, greatly revised its committee structure, and second, in order to gain independent advice, the cabinet developed its own bureaucracy, which resulted in a significant expansion of its support staff in the Privy Council Office (PCO).

The use of cabinet committees reveals a specialization of function caused by the increasing size of the total cabinet and the complexity of modern legislation. Eight cabinet committees were set up, four dealing with broad policy areas and four others concerned with coordination of policy and purpose among the various departments and agencies. Each minister typically served on two committees, although under Trudeau the composition of these committees was not made public. It is doubtful that such secrecy kept the major interest groups or Ottawa's insiders from knowing their composition, but it did keep the public in the dark on this vital element of the political executive. As an issue was brought to the cabinet by a minister, the bureaucracy, or public protest, it would be referred to the appropriate cabinet committee for detailed consideration. After studying the problem and deciding how to act, the cabinet committee would report back to the full cabinet. Except on a highly controversial issues, the cabinet usually accepted the decision of the cabinet committee. For this reason, on many matters, real decision-making power has evolved to the cabinet committees acting in the name of the larger cabinet. Votes are rarely taken; instead, a consensus is sought, with the prime minister playing a critical role in its formation. Once the cabinet has settled on policy, it is communicated to the departments and bureaucracy for implementation.

The second major change instituted by Trudeau concerned the size and functions of the Prime Minister's Office (PMO) and the PCO, both of which were greatly enhanced. The PMO is composed of the PM's immediate aides and advisors, whose tasks range from the mundane ones, such as typing and airline scheduling, to policy-making ones, such as recommendations on the major political issues of the day (Radwanski, 1978: 133). The PCO is the support staff to the cabinet and its various committees and, as such, has become a most important actor in the political process (Campbell and Szablowski, 1979: 69). Even during the years when government restraint put a "freeze" on hiring personnel for government departments, the PMO and PCO were exempted. Together, the task of the PMO and PCO is to give the political executive advice and policy recommendations independent from that of the civil service. This counter-bureaucracy had the expertise and political clout to free the cabinet from its former dependence on the advice coming from the policy advisors at the departmental level. Some of the fiercest battles of the Trudeau years concerned the organization and role of the PMO and PCO structures. With the backing of Prime Minister Trudeau, the PMO and PCO, especially the latter, won a leading role in the policy-making process. Enhancement of the PMO and PCO and a revised cabinet committee structure were the major organizational changes implemented by Prime Minister Trudeau in order to make the decision-making role of the political executive more rational and efficient.

The flexibility of cabinet organization is illustrated by the fact that each new prime minister reorganizes it in some manner. The major innovation of the short-lived Clark government in 1979–80 concerned the first formal use of an inner and outer cabinet in Canadian history. Based on the British practice of making a distinction between all departmental ministers (the ministry) and the major departmental ministers [the cabinet], the inner-outer cabinet model sought to overcome the problem of the excessive size of federal cabinets; at the same time, it rationalized and made more efficient the decision-making process. From a cabinet of 29 members, ten were chosen for the inner cabinet. Although decisions from the inner cabinet could be appealed to the full cabinet, this was rarely the case in the Clark government. Besides setting up a highly visible caste system within the cabinet, the major flaw of the inner-outer cabinet structure in the Canadian context was its rigidity and inability to implement the representation principle. For example, the initial Clark inner cabinet contained no representative from British Columbia, so John Fraser (MP – Vancouver South) was added, while an individual as prominent as David Crombie, former Mayor of Toronto, was excluded (Simpson, 1980: 94–95). While all prime ministers have had an informal inner cabinet or "kitchen cabinet" composed of their most influential aides and ministers, to formally structure the cabinet along the same lines meant that the primary cabinet function of regional and provincial representation could not be sustained. An inner-outer cabinet structure can be justified by the need to make the decision-making process more efficient, but it failed in the Canadian context because it ignored the representation principle of cabinet composition.

Whatever its internal structure and operation, the key political functions of the cabinet are the initiation, development, and implementation of public policy under the direction of the prime minister. If the prime minister and cabinet fail to lead, there is little that can be done, except elect a new prime minister at the next election. Matters such as the representation principle are significant because they help to determine the quality of that leadership and the content and effectiveness of public policy.

Several aspects of the decision-making process characterize the nature of public policy in Canada. First, most policy is *incremental* in design, implementation, and effect; that is, change is slow, modest, and usually inefficient. Incrementalism means building on existing policy and practices, rather than starting over in a wholesale fashion. For example, tax reform in Canada involves tinkering with the existing structure, such as by raising taxes on some items, lowering it on others, or adding or deleting specific tax loopholes. A pattern of incremental decision-making reflects not only general bureaucratic tendencies, but certain elements of Canada's political culture (e.g., deference, elitism, and conservatism). (See Chapter 7 for detailed discussion of political culture.) A second characteristic of decision-making concerns the particular role of cabinet ministers as *generalists*, rather than as specialists. One of the assumptions of cabinet government, and one that is probably incorrect, is that a minister can adequately direct and control any department, irrespective of the content of that department's responsibilities. Cabinet shuffles specifically reflect such a view, since a minister may be in charge of Finance one day and External Affairs the next. If one is a competent administrator, then supposedly one can administer any department. Canadian cabinets are overwhelmingly composed of generalists – there are few specialists in the inner sanctum of power. In fact, sometimes competence in a particular policy area keeps a minister from being named to the most relevant cabinet post. Eric Kierans, with extensive business and financial expertise, became Postmaster General, instead of receiving a portfolio that dealt with economic matters. Mark MacGuigan's background as a constitutional lawyer reputedly kept him out of the cabinet for many years, until he ended up in the External Affairs portfolio. A more relevant initial post for Mark MacGuigan might have been as Minister of Justice, which he subsequently became in the September 1982 cabinet shuffle. Incremental public policy developed and administered by generalists is the context of the bureaucratic function and the most important source of the power of the civil service in the Canadian political process.

The theoretical or designed role of the bureaucracy is to implement the decisions regarding public policy that have been made by the political executive and authorized by the legislature. However, direction concerning the course of public policy may be vague, so that the act of implementation puts the bureaucracy in a policy-making role. To apply general policy to specific situations is neither easy nor neutral; it necessitates a decision-making function for the civil service. Considerable bureaucratic influence flows from its role as the interpreter of the meaning of the general law or what is called *delegated power*. For example, delegated legislative power means that the legislature has passed a bill that authorizes the executive and bureaucracy to flesh out the details of the bill's general provisions. A classic illustration of this pattern is demonstrated by the wage-and-price control legislation (Bill C–73), which passed the House of Commons on December 3, 1975. Section 3 of the Anti-Inflation Act provided the authority for the detailed specification by the civil service of how the wage-and-price restraint plan would work: "The Governor in Council may from time to time cause to be published and made known guidelines for the guidance of all Canadians in restraining profit margins, prices, dividends and compensation." The initial bureaucratic guidelines (many more were to follow later), known as the Anti-Inflation Act Regulations, were 60 pages long – four times the size of Bill C–73 itself!

A second basis of bureaucratic influence is the reputed expertise of the civil service with respect to the nature and content of public policy and of the government regulations based thereon. For example, there are probably very few civil servants in the entire country who can explain in detail the provisions of Canada's equalization formula. Moreover, because civil servants have long tenure in office (generally they can only be removed for "cause"), they have become significant participants in the decision-making process. Cabinet ministers come and go, while the bureaucracy remains in place. In a spirit of derision, bureaucrats often refer to their cabinet bosses as "our political masters." Often in Canadian history, the so-called political masters have been controlled by their servants, and not always in a civil fashion.

The bureaucracy is intimately involved not only in the implementation of public policy, but also in its initiation and formulation. The structure of the departments of government reflects this pattern. At the head of each department is a cabinet minister, surrounded by various aides and executive assistants who are directly responsible to him or her. Also included in this entourage are the *parliamentary secretaries*, who are MPs assigned to help the cabinet minister. Parliamentary secretaries are allocated to the major portfolios (Ministers of State usually receive no such help) on a regional basis according to the representation principle. Parliamentary secretaries are not members of the cabinet, but the position has been used as a training and testing ground to spot future cabinet material. These backbench MPs of the governing party often serve as stand-ins for the minister with respect to speaking engagements and as a "lightning rod" to attract any political flak away from the minister. The involvement of parliamentary secretaries in the decision-making process is usually very modest.

In terms of authority in and direction over a government department, the second in command to the cabinet minister is the *deputy minister*. As administrative head of a department, the deputy minister is responsible for the overall direction and day-to-day operation of the bureaucracy. A deputy minister is not an MP, but is, in effect, the top civil servant assigned to each department. Even though deputy ministers are appointed by the prime minister and are removable by the PM, as career public servants, such a change costs them power, but not job security. Deputy ministers are more directly involved in the political process than most civil servants and, therefore, occupy a rather distinctive position in the bureaucracy. As the "permanent" department head, the deputy minister fulfills not only an administrative role, but a political one as well. Deputy ministers are usually important participants in the policy-making process. As a result, a shuffle of deputy ministers may be more significant as an indicator of changing government priorities than a shift of cabinet portfolios. Because a shuffle of deputy ministers is usually less frequent than one of cabinet ministers, and given their expertise and knowledge, deputy ministers often control the cabinet ministers who in theory direct the department. Arrayed beneath the deputy ministers are the component units of each government department, a structure that varies from one department to the next.

The important political role of the bureaucracy in the decision-making process means that, despite the civil service's supposed impartiality, all governments seek to control its composition and influence. A government that has been in power for any length of time can fashion the bureaucracy in its own political image. At the top of the bureaucracy (i.e., deputy minister level) the government party has the prerogative to appoint and remove civil servants as it desires, while at the intermediate levels, civil service hiring guidelines are flexible enough to allow the government to shape its structures and hiring procedures. The political nature and importance of the bureaucracy is clearly evident when an opposition party, especially one that has been out of office for a lengthy period, wins an election and forms a government. At least some highly visible public servants lose their jobs, if for no other reason than as a symbol of the changing of the political guard – such an interpretation can account for the departure of Privy Council Clerk Michael Pitfield, Trudeau's longtime friend and confidant, shortly after the Clark government took office. Sometimes the leaving of imbedded allies of the former government can be a messy business, as

FIGURE 4.1   *Canada's Executive Branch of Government*

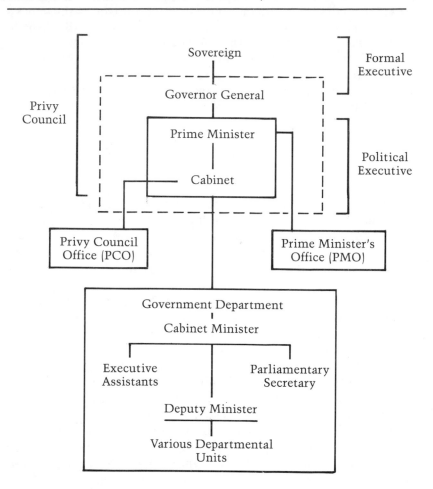

illustrated by the forced departure of Bryce Mackasey as chairman of Air Canada, a federal crown corporation. Mackasey was a veteran cabinet member and Liberal MP whose appointment to head Air Canada before the 1979 election was widely interpreted as a fairly blatant patronage appointment. Because Mackasey refused to leave of his own volition, he was "fired" by Prime Minister Clark. Such problems between a new government and the bureaucracy are common at the provincial level as well, where the bureaucratic turnover after an election is apparently more extensive. For example, upon assuming office in January 1982, NDP Leader Howard

Pawley removed ten top bureaucrats in the Manitoba civil service, replacing most of them with individuals who had ties with the New Democratic Party (i.e., former candidates or party officials). One woman who had been in the civil service, but had temporarily left to run as a Progressive Conservative candidate in the 1981 Manitoba election, was laid off when she sought to return to her job. Once the initial turnover of key positions in the civil service has been accomplished, the government has considerable leeway in establishing and extending its influence throughout the bureaucracy during its stay in office. The concern of all governments to control the structure, operation, and composition of the civil service is a reflection of the political nature of the bureaucracy and its significant role in the policy-making process.

The complex nature of the executive branch of government in Canada reflects, in part, its political role as the core or centre of the political system. The basic features of the executive branch are outlined in *Figure 4.1*. The growth and expansive nature of government in the modern era has been primarily the growth of the executive branch. Through constitutional evolution and political tradition, the formal executive has become a bit player in the drama of Canadian politics, while the political executive, especially the prime minister, has assumed the leading role.

THE BRITISH PARLIAMENTARY EXECUTIVE

In broad outline, the structure and operation of the British executive parallels that of the Canadian. On a number of specific points, however, British and Canadian practices diverge with respect to both the formal and political executives.

The formal executive in Britain – what has been referred to as ''the Rolls Royce of Monarchies'' – is hereditary in terms of succession and constitutional with respect to its role in the polity. Tracing its origins back ten centuries, the slow evolution and public acceptance of the British monarchy has placed it in a far more secure position than its Canadian counterpart. Support and affect for the monarchy and Royal Family are extensive, although some members may be held in less than high regard. The legitimacy of the monarchy is rarely challenged and, when it is, the result is usually an overwhelmingly positive response from the public in defence of the formal executive. The hereditary nature of the office and its public support has effectively allowed the British monarchy to become a unifying symbol of the nation, in sharp contrast to the Canadian experience.

Britain is also an example of a constitutional monarchy, where the chief of state or monarch exercises his/her powers on the advice of the political executive. Historically, monarchs governed as they desired, with few limitations on their roles or powers, a situation sometimes classified as absolute monarchy. However, as Parliament and, much later, the political executive emerged to challenge the monarch, the latter became more and more a figurehead, serving primarily symbolic and ceremonial roles. Thus, the monarch was once dominant over the political executive in Britain. This relationship between the formal and political executives is clearly demonstrated with respect to the Royal Prerogative, that is, the authority that rests with the Crown as the embodiment of executive influence.

> The extent of the Royal Prerogative has not diminished appreciably during the last 200 years. What has happened is that, whereas 200 years ago the reigning monarch performed many or most of these acts at his own discretion, today the monarch performs the acts on the advice of ministers or other persons. The acts are performed in the name of the Crown, but except in a few special cases *the decision is no longer taken by the monarch* (Birch, 1980: 44, emphasis added).

Although the British monarch acts on the advice of the government, a procedure that strongly circumscribes his or her political role, some political functions remain. Given the legitimacy of the monarchy in Britain, the king or queen has more leeway and thus more influence in such matters than the governor general in Canada. On several occasions in the 20th century, the British monarch has been called upon to take an active role in naming a prime minister. For example, in 1957, there was no clear successor within the Conservative caucus to Prime Minister Anthony Eden. Two people were possible successors – Harold Macmillan and R. A. Butler – and after it was clear that the Conservative party could not quickly settle the question among themselves, the Queen asked Macmillan to form a government, thus making him Prime Minister. A more complex situation occurred in 1931 when no party had a majority of seats in the House of Commons. The King took the initiative to bring the various party leaders together for consultation, but, rightly, he did not advocate which of them he preferred as prime minister. What these examples indicate is that the monarch infrequently acts on his or her own initiative and, on those rare occasions, proceeds in an impartial and nonpartisan manner. While in theory the monarch can dismiss ministers, deny a dissolution request from the prime minister, or refuse assent to a piece of legislation, in practice a much more modest constitutional role has evolved for the formal executive in Britain.

The real power of the executive branch is granted to the occupant of Number 10 Downing Street, the British prime minister's official residence. The prime minister in Britain is preeminent with respect to public policy, party, and Parliament to an even greater degree than the Canadian prime minister. Since the political structure is unitary, the prime minister does not share either power or the political limelight with the leaders of an intermediate level of government. Thus, the British prime minister's policy-making role is greater than in Canada, where it is limited by the federalization of responsibility between the national and provincial governments. Moreover, British parties have traditionally been highly centralized in structure and operation, as well as disciplined within Parliament itself. British party leaders, especially Conservative ones, have usually exerted strong control over their party's parliamentary wing. These considerations reveal that a British prime minister is not constrained by some of the typical limitations imposed on any prime minister in Canada.

Cabinet composition is also based on different premises in Britain than in Canada, because the representation principle regarding regional and provincial interests does not apply. Moreover, the major parties have usually received some Commons' seats from all areas within Britain, so regionalism need not be the major factor for cabinet selection or promotion. Instead, ideology plays a significant role in a cabinet's composition, with all major factions included. Party figures with strong support in the party or the electorate are ignored at the leader's peril. Ministers may be appointed from either House of Parliament, although the vast majority are from the Commons. Members from the House of Lords are more frequently used in British cabinets than are senators in Canadian ones, a reflection of the greater status and prestige of the upper House in Britain.

On the surface, the size of the British cabinet is small, averaging about 20 members in recent years. The lack of applying the representation principle in cabinet composition has helped to keep the size of this key decision-making body limited (20 out of 635 members in the British House, compared to 35 out of 282 in Canada). However, the importance of the cabinet can only be appreciated by distinguishing it from the ministry. In Canada, the cabinet and ministry are identical, while in Britain the cabinet is the smaller operative part of the ministry. A British ministry includes all cabinet officers, plus the parliamentary secretaries and parliamentary under secretaries. The ministry may number over 100 members, while only the key portfolios are designated as cabinet ones. The positions included as part of the cabinet are based on tradition and on the desires of the prime minister with respect to how the government should be organized. Thus, the British cabinet is small, while the ministry is large. Appointments to the ministry often provide a means of recruitment and socialization for future cabinet appointees. In Britain, the ministry rarely, if ever, meets, while the cabinet does so on a regular basis. Decisions of the cabinet are based on a consensus approach, with only rare challenges to its authority emanating from the ministry, party caucus, or Parliament.

The power of the prime minister with respect to the cabinet has resulted in the thesis that the prime minister, not the cabinet, is the centre of influence and power in modern British politics. This thesis has been forcefully stated by former professor and Labour party minister Richard Crossman. Because a skillful prime minister can control the party, the Parliament, and the bureaucracy, the concept of cabinet government has become a myth: "the best description of the present system of control is that it is not Cabinet Government any more but Prime Ministerial Government" (Crossman, 1972: 29–30). In effect, then, the concept of collective responsibility has been replaced by prime ministerial responsibility to party and nation, bypassing or at least manipulating Parliament in the process. The facade of power has expanded from the formal executive to elements of the political executive as well: the cabinet reigns, the prime minister governs.

While the thesis of prime ministerial government is becoming a common one in assessments of British politics, it is premature to accept it uncritically. Much depends on the political skills and the political will of the occupant of Number 10 Downing Street. The position of prime minister creates the potential for prime ministerial government, it does not guarantee it. Moreover, the cabinet, if pushed too far, can make life very unpleasant for a prime minister, even to the extent of forcing him or her to resign (e.g., the resignation in 1917 of Prime Minister Asquith). Finally, the prime ministerial thesis ignores the constraints of custom and convention that have limited the prime minister's actual role in cabinet composition, direction, and control (Wilson, 1977). A prime minister must "carry his colleagues" with him (or her) on major policies and programs. To the extent that the prime ministerial thesis emphasizes the key role of the prime minister in modern British politics, it is correct; to the extent that it ignores the collegial nature of that leadership, it is wrong.

The implementation of public policy is carried out by the traditional civil service in the various government departments known as Whitehall. The role of the bureaucracy has been a significant one in the policy-making process, because in Britain, the relationship between the civil service and the government of the day has usually been an intimate one. It appears that the Canadian practice of bypassing the traditional bureaucracy by setting up a counter-bureaucracy around the office of the prime minister has not been a major development in British politics. Instead, a counter-bureaucratic structure has been created, which parallels the structure and political functions of the civil service. These organizations, estimated to number in the range of 30 000, have been labelled as "quangos" (quasi-national governmental-organizations). Since members of the quangos are appointed by the ministers, they are usually patronge-based because normal civil service hiring rules do not apply. Quangos can be used to bypass the traditional influence of Whitehall in the policy-making process. In most cases, however, the quangos accommodate themselves to the existing system: "their basic rationale is representation and advice to governments and the permanent bureaucracy" (Presthus, 1981: 313). The quangos are an interesting and unique example of the expansive nature of government, in general, and of the importance of the bureaucracy, in particular, in the political process of the modern era.

As our discussion shows, the nature of executive power in Britain is divided between an hereditary and constitutional monarch and an elected and temporary political executive. The formal executive retains primarily symbolic and ceremonial tasks, while the prime minister and cabinet have become the engine of the political process. Thus, in broad outline, the tasks of the Canadian and British executives are similar, although they vary in the manner and context of how these functions are carried out. In contrast to these two parliamentary systems, the American presidential executive is based on a single executive office and the separation of powers principle.

THE AMERICAN PRESIDENTIAL EXECUTIVE

The Office of the President of the United States, often described as the most powerful elective office in any democratic system, has become the focal point of the American political process. This central leadership role of the president has clearly emerged in the past 50 years, a development based primarily on political convention rather than any explicit constitutional enhancement of presidential powers. As the national government became the key player in the American federal system, American presidents often seized the opportunity to exert their influence in both domestic and foreign affairs. In the process, the presidency became the symbol of the American nation, embodying high principles of political virtue backed by popular support. American citizens believe "that no matter how the faith may be destroyed elsewhere, at one particular point – the Presidency – justice will be done beyond prejudice, beyond rancor, beyond the possibility of a fix" (White, 1975: 332). This democratization of the presidency allowed for the further growth of presidential power to such an extent that by the early 1970s the office was increasingly referred to as the imperial presidency.

> ... in our own time it has produced a conception of presidential power so spacious and preemptory as to imply a radical transformation of the traditional polity. In the last years presidential primacy, so indispensable to the political order, has turned into presidential supremacy (Schlesinger, 1974: 10).

The public reaction, however, to such misuses of presidential power as Watergate and Vietnam provided for at least a temporary retrenchment of the imperial presidency. The inability of Republican President Gerald Ford (1974–1976) and Democrat Jimmy Carter (1977–1981) to provide successful leadership in either domestic or foreign affairs reflects the decline of presidential power in the 1970s. In contrast, Republican Ronald Reagan's landslide electoral victory in the 1980 presidential contest allowed him to reassert the powers of the presidency upon taking office in January 1981, best illustrated by his initial budget-cutting successes against a Democratically-controlled House of Representatives. This ebb and flow of presidential power illustrates the ambivalent attitude most Americans feel about the presidency itself: they are "excited by its potential for good, yet fearful of the abuse of power" (Pious, 1979: 10).

The creation of the presidency provides for an understanding of such a paradox. The American presidency was designed to be a revised combination of the British formal and political executives of the mid-18th century: as Theodore Roosevelt described it, a position "almost that of a king and a prime minister rolled into one". Thus, the tasks or functions of an American president are extensive, because they include the symbolic and ceremonial duties of a formal executive and the political functions of a prime minister. This fusion of roles is an important basis of presidential power in the American system and illustrates why Duverger (1974: 52) classified the American president as a "democratic transplant of the king of England."

The importance of the presidency in the American political process is clearly revealed in the various roles the president is called upon to play. First, the president is Chief of State, that is, the symbolic and ceremonial leader of the nation. In this capacity, the president carries out the duties of a formal executive in a parliamentary system. A considerable portion of a president's time is spent in greeting foreign leaders, attending social functions such as state dinners, or meeting representatives of various social and economic sectors of society. Under President Richard Nixon, this aspect of the job was so time-consuming and troubling that it was turned over, in part, to Vice-President Spiro Agnew. The attempted delegation of these ceremonial duties to a vice-president was unsuccessful because the vice-president does not hold the same prestige and status as the president. These monarchical tasks have sometimes led presidents to absurd undertakings, as when Richard Nixon dressed up the White House Guard in new uniforms patterned on European lines. The din of the ensuing national laughter was so great that the "tin soldier" look was quickly removed from public view. What President Nixon failed to comprehend was the democratized nature of the monarchical element contained in the American presidency.

An important ingredient of the president's role as Chief of State is the ability to veto legislation, a power similar to the formal executive's granting of assent to a piece of legislation in a parliamentary system. However, unlike the assent procedure, which has become a formality in Canadian and British politics, the veto power is real, effective, and frequently utilized in American politics. A presidential veto usually acts to defeat a bill, although it is possible for Congress to override a presidential veto with a two-thirds vote in both the House of Representatives and the Senate. An important limitation on the veto power results from the fact that the president must accept or reject a bill in total. This procedure means that a president will often compromise and accept a bill because it has at least some favourable provisions. A president can, however, sometimes get the contents of a bill changed prior to its submission for executive approval by threatening to use the veto unless Congress changes some of the bill's provisions, at which point the legislature may compromise. Unlike assent, which is automatic, in American politics presidential approval of a bill need not be: the monarchical element or royal prerogative remains an important weapon in the arsenal of presidential power.

The second major role of the president is that of Chief Executive, that is, the head of the government. This job is equivalent to the prime minister's role in a parliamentary system. As the Chief Executive, the president plays the leading role in the domestic policy-making process and supervises the administration of all federal government departments and personnel (approximately three million civilian employees). The president is a significant actor, as well, in the legislative process, since most major bills are in fact proposed and drafted by presidential advisors. Although the president is not formally involved in passing legislation until the very end of the process (when a bill is either signed or vetoed), political tradition permits the president to take an active role by using the influence of the executive position to persuade the legislature to pass a given bill. Once passed, it is the duty of the Chief Executive to see that the laws are implemented, or, as the Constitution puts it (Article Two, Section Three), "he shall take Care that the laws be faithfully executed." The vast size of the executive structure creates advantages and disadvantages for any president, although typically more of the latter than the former. If a president can exert control over the executive branch, it can become an important resource for and basis of national leadership – if not, the executive structure will frustrate the incumbent's leadership potential.

A third significant job of the American president is the role of Chief Foreign Policy Maker. Subsumed under this heading are the president's tasks of Chief Diplomat and Commander-in-Chief of the Armed Forces. For example, in this diplomatic capacity, the president sends and receives ambassadors, recognizes foreign governments, and negotiates treaties or executive agreements with other countries. Moreover, the direction and content of American foreign policy can be changed solely by the president, as Richard Nixon's rapprochement with Communist China in the early 1970s clearly demonstrates. Backing up the diplomatic role is the constitutionally designated position as commander-in-chief: the president can make war by committing American troops to battle. Once the armed forces have become involved, public opinion will rally round, making it most unlikely that Congress will challenge the presidential authority. For example, no official declaration of war was ever made by the United States during its long involvement in the Vietnam conflict. The significance of the president's role as Chief Foreign Policy Maker has been a major factor in the expansion of presidential power since World War II. The emergence of the United States as a superpower in world affairs automatically thrusts any American president into a leadership position in the international arena, which reinforces the president's domestic preeminence as well.

A final role, and one that is often overlooked, is the president as party leader. Although the president is deemed to be a unifying symbol and national leader, an individual obtains that exalted position as head of a political party. Moreover, if the president wishes to be reelected for a second term, and most do, then party support is likely to be an important ingredient in the campaign. Between elections, the president may find it helpful to be nonpartisan, but the historical record clearly demonstrates that the most successful presidents have been the most party-based presidents. The reason for such a pattern is clear: party support and organization make the president's other roles easier to accomplish, whether it be in terms of passing legislation, having a treaty approved by the Senate, gaining congressional approval or appropriations to be used by the military in foreign affairs, or in asserting control over the vast reaches of the federal bureaucracy.

As the discussion of the role of the president as party leader indicates, the various tasks of the American presidency need not be harmonious. For example, a president often has to choose between foreign policy priorities and domestic ones – usually described as the choice between guns and butter. The success of any American president depends both on an ability to fulfill each role separately and on a political judgment of how to combine the multiple roles when they are in conflict.

While the American presidency combines the typical roles of both the formal and political executives of a parliamentary system, it would be incorrect to conclude that the president of the United States is more powerful than a prime minister in Canada or Britain. Much of a president's power stems from the superpower position of the United States in the international arena. An American president may be the most powerful elected official with respect to world affairs, but in domestic affairs this is not the case, given the separation of powers principle. Since the executive does not control the legislature, no American president can guarantee the passage of a legislative program. In contrast, prime ministers, especially in majority government situations, usually have a success ratio of nearly 100 percent in passing their major policies. For this reason we can conclude that a Canadian or British prime minister considerably more power in domestic affairs than any Ame president. Prime ministers have even more power to control the foreign policy of their countries than do American presidents. For example, a prime minister can conclude a treaty with a foreign country and, unlike an American treaty, it does not need the approval of the legislature before it becomes binding. What makes the American presidency such an important political office is the role of the United States in world affairs, not the president's constitutionally-prescribed duties in the domestic political process.

In addition to the presidency, several other components of the executive branch are worthy of mention. First, surrounding the American leader is the Executive Office of the President, which includes a retinue of personal aides, policy advisors, bodies such as the Council of Economic Advisors, and technical support staff. Simply in the White House, this array of help for the president costs the American taxpayers over $100 million a year and employs over 500 people. The president's staff has assumed a major policy-making role in the political arena in the last 50 years. In American politics, an important political resource is proximity to the president, a fact that gives advisors an often critical role in the decision-making process. In Canada, the growth of the staff of the PMO and PCO parallels this American development and is one reason for the argument that the Canadian polity became "presidentialized" under Pierre Trudeau.

Unlike the various members of the White House Staff, the American cabinet has almost no influence or even an accepted group role in policy making. Since there is no collective responsibility in a system based on the separation of powers principle and because its use and functions depend on the desires of the incumbent president, the American cabinet usually meets infrequently, carries little weight as a group in the policy-making process, and performs primarily administrative tasks. Individual members of the cabinet may have considerable influence, but, if they do, it is because of their relationship with the president and not because of their cabinet title. For example, Henry Kissinger's role as probably the most significant member of Richard Nixon's administration stemmed from his personal relationship with the president, not from his cabinet portfolio as Secretary of State. In the American context, elevation to the cabinet is not usually a political promotion or a stepping-stone to higher office (i.e., the presidency itself).

A final element of the American executive is the position of vice-president of the United States. Elected in conjunction with the president, the vice-president has two main constitutionally-defined roles. First, the vice-president, in the event of the death or disability of a president, becomes the new president. Moreover, holding the office gives a vice-president a head start over party rivals when seeking the presidency at a later date. Since World War II, former Presidents Truman, Johnson, Nixon, and Ford had all served as vice-presidents before assuming the mantle of the American presidency. The second designated task of the vice-president is to serve as President of the Senate, the upper House of the legislature. This position is one of very little influence or power and is primarily ceremonial in nature. Outside of these two tasks, the daily functions of the vice-president are determined by the president. Historically, once in office most vice-presidents have been ignored, although recent presidents have attempted to upgrade the vice-presidential role by allocating to it an effective part in the decision-making process. However, while the vice-president is only a heartbeat away from the presidency, this individual's day-to-day involvement in the direction of the executive branch remains minimal. The key player in American politics is the president, assisted by the White House staff. The cabinet and vice-president rarely grab either the political limelight or much influence in the American political process.

COMPARING EXECUTIVES

Of the various institutions of government, the executive branch was the first created, it remains the most complex, and has re-emerged as the core of modern government. The political process is executive-centred and controlled, even though the specific structures and contexts of the executive branch differ from one polity to the next.

The executive branch is the centre of modern government because it both makes and implements policy with the help of the civil service. Executives have the potential for leadership and typically the will and resources to turn that potential into action and decisions on major matters of public policy: "the nature of our political institutions in both the broad and narrow sense places them at the centre of political consciousness" (Young, 1978: 282). If executives do not lead, then it is most unlikely that any other branch or institution of government will do so – the polity will drift without a rudder. Of course, this should not be taken to mean that a political system will not drift, even with executive direction.

In seeking to provide leadership, the executive branch in democratic systems is typically structured along either parliamentary or presidential lines, with different functions for their component parts. A parliamentary executive is a dual one, with the formal executive performing primarily symbolic and ceremonial duties, while the political executive (prime minister, cabinet, and bureaucracy) governs. The fusion of powers in a parliamentary system guarantees the success of the government's program, at least in a majority situation. In contrast, the separation of powers principle of the American presidential system tends to limit the power of the executive branch, although it remains the centre of the political process in the United States.

In comparing executives, therefore, we must identify the location of executive power, on whose initiative or prerogative that power is exercised, and in what contexts. Such considerations would lead us to the following conclusions in comparing the parliamentary executives of Canada and Britain with each other and with the American presidential executive. While similar in broad powers, the formal executive in Britain has more influence and plays a somewhat more active political role than its Canadian counterpart. Moreover, because the British political executive is not constrained by the factors of federalism or the representation principle of cabinet composition, prime ministerial government is a more correct description of British than of Canadian politics. In both systems, the cabinet is a crucial mechanism of executive power, second only to that of the prime minister.

By contrast to these two parliamentary systems, the American presidency finds itself constrained, particularly with respect to the legislature, given the separation of powers principle. Moreover, other factors such as a two-term limit, the need to gain legislative approval for treaties, and the public reaction to such fiascoes as Vietnam have further limited presidential prerogatives in recent decades. In both domestic and foreign affairs – especially in the former – no American president ever approaches the power of a Canadian or British prime minister. In addition, the American cabinet is a weak and ineffectual body, with most decision-making power residing with the White House staff. Thus, the power of the American president stems, in large measure, from the role of the United States in world affairs, rather than from presidential power over the other branches of government.

Given this comparison, it should be obvious that the idea of "presidentializing" the Canadian parliamentary system would mean a considerable decrease in prime ministerial power. From a comparative perspective one would have to ask why any prime minister would want to be a president and thereby give up this grip on the polity. The expansion of the PMO and PCO has not caused prime ministerial preeminence, for the prime minister has always dominated Canadian politics. What the recent trends in the executive branch have done is to strengthen the prime minister's already firm grasp on and leading role in the Canadian polity, thereby helping to transform cabinet government into prime ministerial government.

SUMMARY

1. The executive branch is the engine of the modern political process, performing the tasks of leadership, policy making, and policy implementation. A parliamentary executive is dual, dividing the executive functions between a formal and a political executive. Founded on the fusion of powers concept, a parliamentary executive operates under the principles of both collective and ministerial responsibility. In contrast, a presidential executive is based on the separation of powers principle, with neither collective nor ministerial responsibility.

2. The formal executive (governor general) in Canada is an appointed, nonhereditary position of limited duration that performs primarily symbolic and ceremonial tasks for the polity. The most significant political function retained by the formal executive is to see that there is always a government in office. In practice, however, the governor general's choice of the prime minister is greatly limited by political traditions. Most of the formal executive's remaining powers are exercised on the initiative of the political executive. The formal executive represents the facade rather than the substance of power.

3. The political executive dominates the Canadian political scene, a role based on custom rather than on the Constitution. The prime minister is preeminent within the political executive, this leading position an outgrowth of the PM's relationship with the public, formal executive, party, and cabinet. In spite of extensive powers over the structure, composition, and function of the cabinet, the prime minister is constrained by the workings of the representation principle. Public policy is under the direction of the prime minister and cabinet, although aided by the bureaucracy.

4. The formal executive in Britain is hereditary, a prime symbol of national unity, constitutional with respect to its powers, and, at times, an important participant in the political process. The centre of executive power is the British prime minister and the cabinet. In contrast to the Canadian political executive, the

British prime minister is not circumscribed by the application of the representation principle, but political tradition does limit the full development of prime ministerial government.

5. The American president performs the combined duties associated with the dual executive in Canada and Britain. The president of the United States is Chief of State, Chief Executive, Chief Foreign Policy Maker, and Party Leader. The ability to fulfill these various roles, and the conflicts between them, largely determine a president's success. Along with the White House staff, the president plays a leading role in the initiation, development, and implementation of public policy. While individual cabinet members may play a significant political role, as a group, the cabinet is of minor importance in the American political process. Vice-presidents have frequently been elevated to the presidency by death, assassination, resignation, or election, but the vice-presidency remains an office of little power in the normal workings of the polity.

RECOMMENDED READINGS

Executive Power: General

DUVERGER, MAURICE (1974) *Modern Democracies: Economic Power versus Political Power*. Hinsdale, Ill.: The Dryden Press.

ROSE, RICHARD and EZRA N. SULEIMAN, eds. (1981) *Presidents and Prime Ministers*. Washington, D.C.: American Enterprise Institute for Public Policy Research.

SMITH, GORDON (1980) *Politics in Western Europe: A Comparative Analysis*, London: Heinemann Educational Books, 3rd ed. See esp. Chapter 8, "Executive Power," pp. 176–205.

The Canadian Parliamentary Executive

CAMPBELL, COLIN and GEORGE J. SZABLOWSKI (1979) *The Superbureaucrats: Structure and Behaviour in Central Agencies*. Toronto: Macmillan of Canada.

GWYN, RICHARD (1980) *The Northern Magus: Pierre Trudeau and Canadians*. Toronto: McClelland and Stewart.

HOCKIN, THOMAS A., ed. (1977) *Apex of Power: The Prime Minister and Political Leadership in Canada*. Scarborough, Ont.: Prentice-Hall Canada Inc., 2nd ed.

MACKINNON, FRANK (1976) *The Crown in Canada*. Calgary, Alta.: McClelland and Stewart West, Glenbow-Alberta Institute.

MATHESON, W.A. (1976) *The Prime Minister and the Cabinet*. Toronto: Methuen.

NEWMAN, PETER C. (1978) *The Distemper of Our Times*, 2nd ed. Toronto: McClelland and Stewart.

_____ (1973) *Renegade in Power: The Diefenbaker Years*. Toronto: McClelland and Stewart.

PUNNETT, R.M. (1977) *The Prime Minister in Canadian Government and Politics*. Toronto: Macmillan of Canada.

RADWANSKI, GEORGE (1978) *Trudeau*. Scarborough, Ont.: Macmillan-NAL.

SIMPSON, JEFFREY (1980) *Discipline of Power: The Conservative Interlude and the Liberal Restoration*. Toronto: Personal Library.

The British Parliamentary Executive

CROSSMAN, RICHARD H. (1972) *The Myths of Cabinet Government*. Cambridge, Mass.: Harvard University Press.

HAMILTON, WILLIE (1975) *My Queen and I*. Don Mills, Ont. Paperjacks, General Publishing Co.

KING, ANTHONY, ed. (1969) *The British Prime Ministers: A Reader*. London: Macmillan.

WILSON, HAROLD (1979) *The Governance of Britain*. London: Sphere Books.

The American Presidential Executive

CEASER, JAMES W. (1979) *Presidential Selection: Theory and Development*. Princeton, N.J.: Princeton University Press.

NEUSTADT, RICHARD E. (1980) *Presidential Power: The Politics of Leadership from FDR to Carter*. New York: John Wiley and Sons.

PAGE, BENJAMIN I. (1978) *Choices and Echoes in Presidential Elections: Rational Man and Electoral Democracy*. Chicago: University of Chicago Press.

PIOUS, RICHARD M. (1979) *The American Presidency*. New York: Basic Books.

SCHLESINGER, ARTHUR M., JR. (1974) *The Imperial Presidency*. Toronto: Popular Library.

5 THE LEGISLATIVE BRANCH OF GOVERNMENT: REPRESENTATION AND LEGITIMATION

It was like looking at Westminster through the wrong end of the telescope. The Governor delivered the Speech from the Throne. The military band outside struck up God Save The Queen with great vigour; the people shouted; the Ins rubbed their hands; the Outs shook their heads; the Government party said there never was such a good speech; the Opposition declared there never was such a bad one; and in short everything went on and promised to go on just as it does at home (Charles Dickens on observing the opening of the Nova Scotia Legislature in 1842).

In most nations, legislators do not legislate. Executives legislate. True, many legislators have a formal role in lawmaking and many continue to debate, review, delay, and legitimize policies. But when it comes to initiating and enacting policies that regulate public behavior and allocate scarce resources, few legislators have much independent authority (Obler, 1981: 127).

TO THE ORDINARY CITIZEN, the legislative branch of government is mysterious and confusing, a little-understood institution, a jumble of rules and procedures with passing relevance to one's daily concerns. Outside of the pageantry of an opening of Parliament, a particularly rancorous Question Period, or the controversy usually accompanying an increase in members' salaries, few citizens pay much attention to their legislators. As a member of the French National Assembly put it, one reason for the public's indifference, perhaps, is that the legislature is a "theatre of illusions" (Servan-Schreiber, quoted in Smith, 1980: 152).

The most basic of these illusions, which we are taught from childhood, is that the legislature is sovereign, that it makes the laws. Historically, however, legislative dominance has been restricted to the last decades of the 19th century and the early decades of the 20th: the golden age of legislatures was one of limited duration. Declining decision-making power of legislative institutions has led some observers to question their continuing relevance. The decline of the lawmaking function, however, has not meant the imminent demise of the legislative branch of government: "while parliament may never have been the sovereign, basic entity described by theoreticians, while it is no longer the majestic law-giver of liberal-democracy, it is still irreplaceable and important" (Duverger, 1974: 150). The continuing legislative functions of legitimating executive actions and representing the public in the governing process remain important duties. While the notion of parliamentary sovereignty may indeed be a myth, so also is the view of legislative nonimportance.

THE DEVELOPMENT OF LEGISLATURES

The significance of legislatures is reflected in the fact that they were the first political institutions designed to give the public a role in the political process, even though initially that public was only a tiny fragment of the total population. Legislatures were developed as representative institutions in the struggle with the king. As the mass public became incorporated into the body politic, the legislature became the symbol of liberal-democracy. Reflective, perhaps, of the public's power through the legislature is the prominence given to it in the American Constitution: Article One deals with the legislature and is twice as long as Article Two, which delineates executive power and structure.

The public's role in the political process through the legislature, however, is once removed: representative government is an example of *indirect democracy*. The people do not rule directly on a day-to-day basis; instead, the people select representatives to govern. In an attempt to guarantee the public's role through the legislature, democratic systems constitutionally require a yearly meeting of the legislature. The origin of legislative institutions suggests, therefore, two key questions for evaluating their current status: first, what is the nature of the legislative-executive relationship and second, what is their role as representative agencies in the political process?

The importance of the legislature as the public's representative is embodied in the principle of *parliamentary supremacy or parliamentary sovereignty*, which asserts the fundamental right of the legislature to make any law whatsoever. As British political leader Disraeli once phrased it, "we are governed not by logic but by Parliament." Those who defy parliamentary authority discover their mistake in short order: for example, Jean-Claude Parrot, head of the Canadian Union of Postal Workers, spent time in jail for his failure to heed Parliament's back-to-work legislation to end a postal strike in the late 1970s. As developed in Britain, parliamentary supremacy includes four essential features: "There is no higher legislative authority; no court can declare Acts of Parliament to be invalid; there is no limit to Parliament's sphere of legislation; and no Parliament can legally bind its successor, or be bound by its predecessor" (Punnett, 1980: 173). In the Canadian context, however, parliamentary sovereignty is circumscribed by the political principles of federalism and judicial review.

An important mechanism for maintaining the supremacy of Parliament is *parliamentary privilege*, a series of rights given to the legislature and to nobody else, in order to ensure that Parliament and its members are collectively and individually free of any outside control. Historically, parliamentary privilege was an outgrowth of the early battles between king and Parliament for control of the political system, with the privileges preventing the detention or arrest of any member during a legislative session. The right of members to carry on the public's business was not to be interfered with. In addition, parliamentary privilege gives the legislature the power to discipline its own members and to determine its own procedure. For example, the use of legislative committees, rather than the full legislature, to consider bills is a decision for the legislature alone to take. Similarly, a member may be expelled from a day's sitting or for longer periods of time, with the legislature having the ultimate right to prevent a duly elected candidate from taking his or her place (e.g., a seat may be declared vacant, with a new election called).

In addition to handling its own affairs, parliamentary privilege guarantees the right of free speech to members carrying out the public's business within Parliament itself. For example, an individual member cannot be sued for libel for remarks made in the legislature; however, if those same statements are repeated outside the legislature, libel suits are a possibility. While such rights can be abused, free speech is considered essential for the conduct of the public's business. A final, and often overlooked, example of parliamentary privilege is the right of the legislature to determine its own worth, that is, to set its own salary. There is no legal limit on what the legislators could decide to pay themselves, although there are some real political constraints, in particular, the fear of electoral reprisal. If any outside body determined salary levels, then control of the legislature would be possible, since the legislators might be bribed by extravagant salaries or forced into submission by reducing their pay to minimal levels.

Although legislatures developed as a means of public representation in the political process, the public's influence was not only indirect but further restrained by the original design of legislative institutions. The first legislatures were *bicameral* rather than *unicameral* in structure. A bicameral legislature is composed of two parts, a lower house (e.g., the House of Commons in Canada and Britain, the House of Representatives in the United States) and an upper house (e.g., the Senate in Canada, the House of Lords in Britain and the Senate in the United States). The lower houses are designed to be the closest to the people – hence they are based on popular election with relatively frequent elections (two years in the United States, with a maximum of five years in Canada and Britain). The upper houses are designed to check the power of popular passion as contained in the lower house by allowing for a ''sober, second thought'' on all legislation.

In order to provide the political basis for resisting the lower house, the upper legislative chambers were insulated from mass pressure by having their members appointed for long terms (e.g., Canada) or by using an indirect method of selection (e.g., senators in the United States were initially chosen by the state legislatures). By contrast, in a unicameral system, where there is only one legislative chamber, there is no mechanism within the legislature itself for checking the decisions it has taken. The national legislatures in Canada, Britain, and the United States are bicameral; all of the American state legislatures are bicameral except for Nebraska; and all of the Canadian provincial legislatures are now unicameral in structure.

A federal political structure and a bicameral national legislature work together in an interesting way: the upper house of the national legislature is used to give representation to the constituent units of the federal system. For example, Senate representation is based on the provinces in Canada and on the states in the American system. The diversity that encourages the adoption of federalism also promotes use of the upper legislative chamber as a means of guaranteeing representation in the national government of various regional, religious, cultural, and ethnic groups. Thus, bicameral legislative structures function both as a safeguard against popular passion and as a tool for representing various interests within the national government.

EXERCISING LEGISLATIVE POWER: THE ROLE OF THE CANADIAN HOUSE OF COMMONS

By the time the Canadian Confederation was established in 1867, the role of the legislature had been well-developed, with the basic principles of parliamentary supremacy and parliamentary privilege accepted as fundamental. However, in contrast to the British pattern, the adoption of federalism and the resulting use of the courts to settle jurisdictional disputes between the two levels of government limited the supremacy of the Canadian Parliament. The federal and provincial legislatures were supreme, but only within their own areas of competence. From the beginning, Canadian federalism has made parliamentary sovereignty something of an illusion.

Likewise, the notion of the legislature making the laws has been a mirage. While in the early years of Confederation governments had their legislation rejected in Parliament (Forsey, 1974: 123–138), defeating a piece of legislation is reactive, and not the same thing as producing legislation. Moreover, it is often forgotten that the so-called golden age of legislatures occurred at a time of extremely limited government: governments passed little legislation in few substantive areas in the late 19th century. The expansion of government in the 20th century is the fundamental reason why executives have become the key actors in the political process. Power between institutions, as with individuals, is relative: executives and legislatures have both gained power in the 20th century, but executives have done so at a much faster rate. Canadian legislatures in the 1980s deal with more topics in a greater number of areas in more detail than ever before; in that sense legislators in the modern era have little in common with their 19th-century counterparts. Finally, although the national legislature in Canada is bicameral, the two parts have never been equal. The House of Commons has always been preeminent and has become more so in recent decades: rarely does the Canadian Senate awake from its institutional slumber to take an active, if fleeting, role in the political process.

Structure of the House of Commons

The institutional and physical structure of the House of Commons influences the way it performs its various political functions. After the 1971 census the size of the House of Commons was raised to 282 seats from its previous number of 264, with further increases projected after each decennial census. Seats are allocated among the geographical units (provinces) primarily on population: the largest province, Ontario, has 95 seats, while the smallest province, Prince Edward Island, has 4. However, other criteria (Sections 51 and 51A of the BNA Act) are also included in the seat allocation process: for example, no province can have fewer seats in the House than members in the Senate, which means that the small provinces are overrepresented in the Commons. In order to protect the French-Canadian minority, Quebec is assigned a given number of seats (75 seats in the Representation Act of 1974) and the other provincial seat allocations are then computed from that starting point. Thus, the membership structure of the House is territorially based around the provincial units, with population the main basis in assigning provincial seat totals.

The physical structure of the Commons is divided between government and opposition members, with the speaker of the House presiding over both. The government sits on the speaker's right and the opposition on his or her left, a seating arrangement with perhaps Biblical connotations. Each member is assigned a particular seat, with government and opposition members facing each other across the centre aisle, symbolic of the antagonistic relationship between them. The prime minister and cabinet occupy the first two rows centre on the government side, with the offical opposition leader and his or her shadow cabinet facing them. Those MPs not in the cabinet or shadow cabinet fill in the remaining rows on each side of the aisle; hence, they are called backbenchers. If more than two parties are in opposition, the minor parties sit on the opposition benches farthest removed from the speaker, with any independents on the far side of them.

The most important position in the House of Commons is that of the speaker. The speaker is nominated by the prime minister but elected by the House. As the presiding officer it is the speaker's job to ensure the smooth and fair functioning of the lower House. In so doing, he or she recognizes those members who wish to participate in the debate, attempts to be impartial in the business of the House, and rules on disputed questions of procedure. Decisions of the speaker should be nonpartisan and fair to all participants: if they are not seen as impartial, then the ability of the legislature to carry out its political tasks becomes seriously impaired. The speaker is expected to be bilingual, with an alternation of those chosen between members with English or French as their mother tongue. A deputy speaker is selected as well, whose primary task is to replace the speaker when the speaker is unable to carry out the job. The deputy speaker needs to be bilingual, although his or her mother tongue is usually opposite to that of the speaker.

The importance of the speaker's role can be seen in the kinds of decisions he or she is called upon to make. For example, the speaker decides who is recognized to talk, and if the speaker chooses not "to see" a member, that member is excluded from the debate. The speaker likewise rules on whether a member has exceeded the time limit for discussion, whether a member's parliamentary privileges have been violated, and resolves disputes about parliamentary procedure, ranging from motions of adjournment to those of closure to acceptable amendments. In a majority government situation, the speaker must pay particular attention to ensure that the government does not trample on the rights of the opposition or of Parliament as a whole (Newman, 1973: 88). The speaker is also faced at times with opposing the government of the day, as in the summer of 1981, when Speaker Jeanne Sauvé ruled out of order a series of government spending estimates, forcing the government to pass each item separately before the House could adjourn. The speaker is also called upon to supervise the running of the House of Commons itself, a not insignificant task, given its $100 million yearly budget. For example, in November 1980, former Auditor General J.J. MacDonnell submitted a report to Speaker Jeanne Sauvé that indicated poor management of the Commons' budget. Indicative of that claim was the discovery in December 1979 that an exclusive restaurant for the senior staff had been opened without either the speaker's knowledge or approval. In July 1981, Speaker Sauvé ruled that the restaurant, which served full course dinners for $2.75, be closed.

In carrying out such tasks, the speaker is expected to be nonpartisan, which, in many ways, is another illusion of the legislative system. Since the speaker is nominated by the prime minister, but technically elected by the Commons, the position has always been a partisan one, even though the person chosen need not be a member of the government party. Most often, the speaker is a government party member who has been bypassed for the cabinet, as illustrated by the selection of Jeanne Sauvé in 1980.

In an attempt to undercut the partisan basis of appointment, recent practice has been for the opposition parties to second the nomination of the speaker. Other steps were taken in the late 1960s to make the speaker more nonpartisan: in the 1968 election, Speaker Lucien Lamoureux ran as an independent, won reelection, and was reappointed as speaker. However, the conclusion (Mallory, 1971: 248) that such events demonstrated that the office of the

speaker was "in the process of evolving from a major political office to one ... essentially above politics" has proven premature, given the developments of the 1970s. With a minority government situation in 1972, the Liberals chose Robert McCleave, Conservative MP from Halifax, as deputy speaker, supposedly with an agreement that he would be elevated to speaker when Lucien Lamoureux retired. However, after gaining a majority in the 1974 election, this deal became inoperative: Liberal MP James Jerome from Sudbury, Ontario was selected, with the Conservatives refusing to second his nomination. As a consolation prize, Robert McCleave later received a judicial appointment in his native Nova Scotia.

Even when a government party member is not picked, the speaker may still have been chosen on political grounds. For example, a common practice of both federal and provincial minority administrations has been to appoint an opposition member as speaker, thus reducing the opposition caucus by one vote and redressing slightly the government's chance of defeat in the legislature. Although the speaker votes only in case of a tie, based on convention, it would be most unlikely for him or her to vote against the government. For such political considerations, Joe Clark renominated James Jerome as speaker following the 1979 election, even though the Conservatives had refused to second Jerome's nomination in 1974. With the demise of the Clark government, Jerome did not run as a candidate in the 1980 election, but, interestingly enough, during the campaign he was appointed by Clark as an associate chief justice of the Federal Court of Canada. Thus, in the experience of one individual we see examples of both the partisan nature of the office of speaker of the House and of judicial appointments as well.

A classic example of picking a speaker on political grounds occurred after the 1978 New Brunswick election, which saw a narrow Conservative majority of 30 to 28 over the Liberals. Premier Hatfield nominated Liberal Robert McCready as speaker. The McCready selection created internal problems for the Liberal party caucus, since McCready had contested leader Joe Daigle in the 1978 Liberal leadership race. In anger over his acceptance of the speakership, the Liberals expelled McCready from their party caucus. Although a minority government may choose an opposition member as speaker, the political nature of the position is clearly evident if that minority government gains a majority position. The opposition member speaker is usually dumped in favour of a government backbencher, as illustrated by the selection of John Turner as speaker of the Ontario Legislature following the 1981 Conservative majority victory.

In addition to the political considerations evident in the selection process, the speaker's role is also political in another sense; that is, the speaker's rulings help to determine the influence of individual members and parties within the House, and, on occasion, in the country as a whole. Rulings on procedural disputes, on matters of privilege, on Question Period, influence individual and party standings in the eyes of the electorate, as illustrated in the famous Pipeline Debate in 1956 (Newman, 1973: 37–43). Thus, although the speaker is usually selected on partisan grounds and even though the speaker's rulings have the potential to greatly affect individual and party influence both inside and outside of the legislature, one of the sustaining myths of parliamentary government is the speaker's impartiality. But as Walter Stewart (1971: 147) explains:

> Myths are the grease that make the machine work, for if the MPs are allowed to call each other cheats and liars, Parliament will break down; if there is no chairman who can rule impartially over the savage debates that shake the chamber, democratic government, with its open, sometimes brutal questioning of the ruling powers, will become impossible.

The work of the House is facilitated by the political party organizations. Each party selects a House leader and party whips, who help to ensure an orderly flow of business. The party's House leader is usually different from the national party leader, so that the party leader is able to be absent from the Commons without disrupting the public's business. The House leader is chosen by the party leader, usually in consultation with the major figures in the party caucus. The government House leader is a cabinet level position, with the person so selected being named in recent years as president of the Privy Council. Party whips help to "whip," at least symbolically, the party members into cohesive groups in the legislature. The job of the party whips is to make sure their caucus members know the party's stand on a given issue, know when the vote is taken, and have their members on the floor of the House to support the party's leadership. An extreme example of a party whip's job was apparent in the events leading to the Constitutional Crisis of 1968: as the division bells were kept ringing for over an hour, the Liberal whips searched the bars of Ottawa, bringing several members back to the party fold, but not enough to prevent defeat (Stewart, 1971: 196–198). The usual business of the party whips is more mundane, since most members are more than willing to follow the decisions of the party leadership.

The importance of the political parties in organizing the work of the legislature is probably best demonstrated in the *principle of party discipline*; that is, the parties work as cohesive groups rather than as an array of disparate individuals. Party discipline is so pervasive and accepted that it is rarely challenged; most party members never vote against their party during the course of their entire political life. Those members who do openly challenge party unity may find their party careers to be of short duration. Most members accept "the whip" or party discipline because they want to, because they know that future party and governmental promotions are dependent on it. Party discipline is strongest in the governing party, where a break in party ranks might cost the party control of office. Opposition parties are somewhat more lenient in demanding party unity, because it makes little difference in their current position. For example, when former Conservative party leader John Diefenbaker voted against his party and successor Robert Stanfield, the party was in opposition and thus a breakdown in party discipline could be tolerated. Retribution for such behaviour when the party is in power is more severe, with the possibility of being refused the party's nomination in your own riding in the next election. For example, Conservative MP Edmond Morris, who abstained on two want-of-confidence motions against the Diefenbaker government, was denied his party's nomination in the 1963 election (March, 1974: 87). Party discipline, which has been firmly established throughout the 20th century, is a key to understanding both party control and executive dominance of the legislative branch of government.

In addition to party organization in the House, the Commons is also structured into a series of small committees, where much of the intensive work of the legislative branch takes place. The use of legislative committees, however, is a recent development in Canada, with the standing committee structure blossoming in the 1965 and 1968 parliamentary reforms. The late adoption of small legislative committees is a reflection of the principle of parliamentary supremacy; Parliament as a whole was very reluctant to give up any of its functions and powers. The reforms were finally adopted in the mid-1960s as a result of the pressures of time; Parliament was becoming so bogged down in the details of bills that little government legislation was being passed.

There are numerous kinds of legislative committees. The two

most important types are the striking or selection committee and the standing committees. The function of the *Striking Committee* is to decide on the membership of all the other committees in the legislature. It meets in the first few days of a session and is composed of the party whips. In practice, the Striking Committee accepts the committee assignments decided on by the parties themselves, rather than getting into the contentious practice of assigning individual members to specific committees. Each party caucus, in consultation with its party and House leaders, decides which of its members will sit on which committees. The party whips then take these committee assignments to the Striking Committee, which approves them. Such a process avoids the possibility that the government party could use its majority to assign the least able opposition members to the most important committees, thereby undercutting the effectiveness of the opposition in the legislature.

The second and most important committee type is the *Standing Committee*, which gives clause-by-clause consideration to each piece of legislation between its second and third readings. It is at the Standing Committee stage where much of the real work of the legislature occurs, in that detailed consideration, sometimes including witnesses both for and against the legislation, is given. The structure of the Standing Committees is roughly parallel to that of the executive departments, with each committee considering the legislation related to one or more departments. For example, while the executive has a Department of External Affairs and a Department of National Defence, the Commons has a single standing committee called External Affairs and National Defence, which oversees the legislation for both departments. Membership on each standing committee is normally 20; cabinet members are not assigned to them but a cabinet minister's parliamentary secretary may be; and they have the legal power to call witnesses, with testimony given under oath. Each committee selects a chair and vice-chair to preside over its meetings.

The composition of the standing committees, as well as all other types, is party-based. The basic principle is that a party's strength in the full House is reflected within each committee. For example, if a party has 60 percent of the seats in the Commons, it will gain approximately 60 percent of the positions on each committee. Since the committees select their own chair and vice-chair, these positions are allocated to the governing party as well. Based on custom only, the Public Accounts Committee, which oversees government expenditures, is chaired by an opposition member. Not even that small token of influence has been granted the opposition in some provinces: in Nova Scotia, for example, during the 1970s, the Minister of Finance was also chair of the Public Accounts Committee, which produced a fairly blatant conflict of interest between his executive and legislative roles.

In a majority situation, the standing committees, given this party base, are not in a position to change government legislation. Even if they do revise a bill, such alterations can be reversed when the bill reappears at third reading before the full House. If a committee does object to a government bill, recalcitrant government committee members can always be removed. In 1976, Liberal MP Simma Holt complained that she had been prevented from attending a meeting of the Broadcasting Committee, which was considering legislation on ending tax concessions to both *Time* and *Reader's Digest*, by then Secretary of State Hugh Faulkner, the minister responsible for the legislation (*Globe and Mail*, February 5, 1976). Four Liberal MPs had already been removed from that committee in December 1975, so as to ensure that the government's bill would emerge in the form desired (Campbell, 1977: 127).

In a minority government, the influence of the committees is temporarily enhanced if the opposition parties can overcome their differences and work together to amend the government's legislation. For example, in 1973, the Conservative and New Democratic parties combined at the committee stage to amend the minority Liberal government's wiretap legislation. The opposition parties inserted a notice provision in the bill, which required the government to inform people that they had been under surveillance, if after 90 days no wrongdoing had been discovered. When the bill came back to the full House the government tried to have the notice amendment deleted, but was unsuccessful. However, even in a minority government situation, the opposition parties usually do not cooperate, since the normal opposition parties at the federal level are either more opposed to each other than to the Liberals or because the NDP, as between 1972 and 1974, supports the Liberals' legislation. Minority governments create the potential for standing committee influence in the legislative process, but they certainly do not guarantee it.

The Passage of Legislation

Having considered the institutional structure and context of the House, we can now proceed to a discussion of how legislation is passed. The rites of passage that turn a bill into a law are extremely complex: it may take a neophyte MP several sessions before even the basic intricacies are mastered. The fundamentals, however, centre around three topics: first, the different types of bills; second, the stages of legislation; and third, legislative procedures such as closure and Question Period.

Any Member of Parliament can introduce legislation, but the kind of legislation proposed and its chance of passage varies depending on whether it is a government bill or a private member's bill. A *government bill* is part of the ruling party's legislative program, is introduced by a minister, and backed by the full weight of the government party caucus. Government bills are given priority and are usually passed, especially under majority governments. *Private member's bills* are those bills introduced by an MP that do not have government support. They are most often introduced by opposition members, but may be introduced by a government backbencher as well. Private member's bills cannot result in the raising and spending of money which is a government prerogative; hence, they are often phrased as suggestions for future government policy. Private member's bills are given little time for consideration in the Commons, are dealt with in the order in which they are introduced (which means that many are not even debated), and are almost never passed. The most common use of private member's bills is to influence public opinion, with the intent of changing future government policy. Reform proposals have usually appeared first as a private member's bill, only to be coopted as a government bill in a later Parliament, as public support and acceptance of the idea becomes apparent.

Although specific details may vary from one type of bill to the next, all legislation goes through six stages: first reading, second reading, committee stage, third reading, consideration by the other House, and royal assent. Even this six-stage process greatly simplifies the actual passage of a bill by Parliament. In most cases, first reading, third reading, and royal assent have become mere formalities; the crucial steps are the second reading and committee stages. At first reading, the bill is introduced into the legislature, by indicating the title of the bill and perhaps giving a very brief statement about the bill's subject matter. The legislation at this point is not open to amendment or debate, although in extremely rare cases it may be rejected. For example, in an almost unprecedented move, the Conservatives in the Ontario legislature denied a member the right to introduce a bill at first reading in May 1981.

The initial debate on a bill takes place at second reading, which is known as ''approval in principle.'' The bill cannot be amended, but must be accepted or rejected in total. Second reading usually involves the major debate on a bill, for once it has been ''approved in principle'' it becomes difficult, although not impossible, to defeat it at a later stage. In contrast to steps one and two, the committee stage does not involve the full House, but only a part of it. In most instances, a bill is sent to one of the standing committees for detailed, clause-by-clause review. It is at this step that the bill can be amended for the first time, in addition to being debated. Witnesses, both pro and con, may be called to testify, and the process may take a number of weeks. Once the committee is finished with a bill, it is sent back to the full House for third reading. It is possible for the committee to make changes in the legislation, but the full House has the right to accept or reject such revisions when it receives the bill back from the Committee. Having given approval in principle to a bill at second reading, plus a detailed look at its contents during the committee stage, means there is little work to be accomplished at third reading. Usually, by this time, it is a foregone conclusion that the bill will pass, although the opposition parties may debate a controversial bill at some length at third reading. Government defeats can happen at this stage, as with the defeat of a tax bill that provoked the Constitutional Crisis of 1968.

Once passed by one of the Houses of the legislature, the same basic steps are repeated by the other House in Canada's bicameral legislature. Although either House may initially consider any bill – except for money bills, which have to originate in the Commons – usual practice is for government legislation to be presented first to the Commons and then to the Senate. Although the Senate may make minor changes in a piece of legislation, for all intents and purposes its approval has become perfunctory. However, in a bicameral legislature, the bill as passed by both Houses must be identical, so that if the Senate amends legislation coming from the Commons, the revisions must be sent back to the lower House for its approval. Rarely is there any dispute between the two Houses over the content of a piece of legislation; if there is conflict, the lower House usually asserts its power and carries the day. The sixth and final stage concerns approval by the formal executive through the royal assent procedure, which takes place in the Senate chamber. Royal assent has never been refused a federal piece of legislation, and the bill usually becomes the law of the land as soon as royal assent has been granted. In some instances, a section or the entire bill itself may not become operative until it is proclaimed. For example, the Canada Act received royal assent in Britain on March 29, 1982, but it did not become effective until it was proclaimed on April 17, 1982.

Given this procedure for the passage of legislation, it should not be surprising to discover that legislative approval is often a long drawn-out process consuming many weeks, months, or even years. If the opposition parties make full use of their rights to talk and debate, as well as to propose amendments, then the government may be delayed, but not defeated, in obtaining legislative enactment of its policy proposals. Each step of the legislative process normally occurs on a different day, with several days required between some steps, as between the committee stage and third reading. If the opposition desires it, the legislative process can become very time-consuming. However, if the parties in the House are in agreement, a piece of legislation can literally breeze through: in July 1981, the bill to increase legislative salaries passed all of the stages in the Commons in five hours. There is nothing like self-interest to make short work of the legislative obstacle course.

Such consensus in the legislature is rare, however; typically the parties confront each other over almost every piece of legislation. If the government has a majority mandate, there is usually no way that the opposition parties can stop the ruling party's legislative program from becoming law. For example, in March 1982, the opposition Conservatives walked out of the Commons, leaving the division bells ringing for two weeks, in order to force the Liberals to compromise on the structure of the energy security bill. The compromise that was finally reached broke the large omnibus bill into eight separate bills, with the Conservatives promising that all eight would be allowed passage by the end of June. This procedural dispute forced a delay in the government getting its legislation approved, but it did not change the content of the legislation. If the opposition parties utilize their delaying tactics and if the government is adamant about the need for a particular measure, then the government can always force it through the legislature by invoking closure. Closure is the cutting off of debate by the government, and it is a powerful tool for ensuring the passage of government legislation. However, it is only occasionally used in the Canadian House. The threat of closure is often sufficient to bring the opposition into line, unless the opposition is attempting to force the government to use closure, so it can then claim that the government is "abusing Parliament." Closure, combined with party discipline, ensures the passage of the government's legislation, especially in a majority context. Using closure, it would take approximately ten sitting days of Parliament for any bill to become law. If a majority government is not successful in enacting a bill, it is for the quite simple reason that it does not really want it passed (e.g., the failure of freedom of information legislation throughout the late 1970s and early 1980s).

With this process of legislative approval, it is apparent that much of the work of the legislature involves disputes about procedure rather than about content or subject matter. The reason for a procedural emphasis is quite clear: with a government that has a majority mandate, the substance of legislation cannot be altered without that government's concurrence. Hence, if the opposition wants to delay a bill, it will try and tie it up in a series of procedural disputes and points of privilege. While such tactics may not defeat a government, they may embarrass it, as in December 1974, when the NDP pointed out to the speaker that a quorum of MPs was not present to vote themselves a 47 percent increase in their own salary. In minority government situations, the opposition may be more successful, for the government may agree to substantive changes rather than risk defeat in the House. However, minority governments have rarely feared legislative rejection: recent examples, such as Trudeau's defeat in 1974 or Clark's defeat in December 1979, probably indicate that the executive wanted to be brought down in each case so as to force an election. It would be hard to demonstrate in either situation that the legislature was exercising effective control over the executive.

Although the government is rarely defeated in the legislature, it is, nonetheless, kept from doing everything it wants. Probably the best check against government pigheadedness, incompetence, or downright malfeasance is the *oral question period* in the Commons. For 40 minutes a day when the House is in session, the opposition members, or once in a while a brave government backbencher, can challenge the government over its past, present, or projected behaviour. Since the government ministers do not know what the questions will be, the opposition attempts to embarrass them over policy, patronage, or corruption. While the opposition cannot force ministers to answer, their failure to do so, or their seeming unwillingness to do so, influences their own and their party's image among the electors. It is quickly apparent whether a minister has control over or an understanding of his or her department. Yet ministers with political savvy can answer a question without really being specific, thereby frustrating the opposition. Another possibility is to take the particular question "on notice," that is, to say that one does not have the answer on hand, but will, of course, search diligently for it and report back. On highly controversial matters, a court case is started or a royal commission appointed to look into the matter. In these situations, the minister refuses to answer the question on the grounds that he or she does not want to prejudice the court case now underway or refuses to respond since a royal commission is investigating the problem. In the late 1970s, anyone appointed solicitor general had to learn two things: first the oath of office and second, a statement indicating an inability to answer any questions about RCMP activities and wrongdoings (because the McDonald Royal Commission was currently investigating the matter).

Such techniques of avoidance have done much to undercut the effectiveness of the question period, but it remains one of the few ways the legislature, and particularly the opposition, can bring the government to task. The fact that the question period is significant in its impact is demonstrated by the lengths governments sometimes go to try to undercut it. For example, the Liberal minority government in January 1974 attacked the opposition's use of question period on the grounds that it was delaying the House from considering important legislation and that it had cost the taxpayer $9 million in 1973 to answer all of the inquiries (Halifax, *Mail-Star*, January 19, 1974). Another undermining of the question period is evident in the practice of not allowing past ministers to answer questions, even if they are still members of the House. A new minister can feign ignorance of past events, and the former minister, sitting only a few feet away, is not forced to respond. Finally, the most serious attack on question period occurred between 1968 and 1972, after Trudeau's first election victory. Arguing that it was inefficient to have all ministers present every single day (an outside observer might assume that it was part of their job), Trudeau introduced the infamous *roster system*, whereby only a given number of ministers would be present (say one-half) on any specific day. Amazingly, a number of ministers who would be absent from question period would appear on the floor once the routine business of the House began. The roster system was rightly attacked by the press and opposition parties as a blatant attempt to muzzle question period. After the Liberals won only a minority government in 1972, the roster system was dropped at the insistence of the opposition members. Although it has not been formally reintroduced, many governments unofficially follow it: a common complaint of federal and provincial opposition members is the poor turnout of government ministers during question period.

Functions of the House of Commons

It should be clear from our discussion of both the structure and procedure in the House of Commons that its role is heavily influenced by the nature of the executive-legislative relationship. In the Canadian parliamentary system, the fusion of executive and legislative power, based on party cohesion and cabinet direction, has meant that the notion of parliamentary supremacy is a myth. Parliament does not write the legislation, revise it to any great extent, or defeat the government's program. Control of the legislature by the executive has, however, produced a system wherein the government of the day has the capacity, if not always the will, to act decisively. Given such a pattern, these questions might rightfully be asked: why is the concept of parliamentary supremacy maintained, and if Parliament does not in any real sense make the laws, what functions does the legislature perform?

The principle of parliamentary sovereignty is retained because it is useful for the legislature in carrying out its two most important remaining and interdependent political functions of legitimation and representation. In approving executive decisions, the legislature legitimates the exercise of influence and power by the prime minister and cabinet; that is, it makes the government's actions acceptable to the public. Because it is a representative institution, the House of Commons can continue to serve as a repository of public authority, even if that authority is effectively exercised by the political executive. People may not like increases in their taxes, but if Parliament has approved, then they will most likely accept them. In many respects, Parliament is based on both traditional and legal-rational bases of authority. If the traditional basis is not sufficient, then the fact that the proper procedure has been followed can be used to justify obedience.

A good example of the legitimation function of the legislature can be seen with respect to a government's budget. Probably no piece of legislation is more fundamental than a budget, for it sets the priorities of the polity. The typical procedure in a budget's preparation, which is done in secret, is for the Minister of Finance, in consultation with the prime minister and perhaps several other cabinet ministers, to set the broad outlines of policy, which are then specified in detail by the bureaucracy. The budget is written and printed before the full cabinet sees it or before the government party caucus is informed of its content. It is then presented by the Minister of Finance in the Commons and becomes the subject of a special debate. However, the budget debate rarely changes the content of the document, but gives the opposition a chance to air public grievances about the decisions already taken. Such a procedure allows the legislature to legitimate decisions that have already been taken by the political executive. If any further evidence of this point is required, then the implementation of wage-and-price controls in the mid-1970s would provide it. Although Pierre Trudeau went on national television in early October 1975 to announce the immediate imposition of wage-and-price controls, the bill authorizing such a move was not passed by Parliament until several months later. The extent to which Parliament can effectively legitimate such actions is based in part on the public's perception of it as a representative institution.

The House of Commons is representative in the obvious sense that the people, through the election process, select its members. However, the representative function usually includes more than simply the process of selection, comprising in most cases the implication that once the members are chosen they will make known the concerns of their constituents and reflect the socioeconomic attributes of the electorate. With respect to the latter point, it is clear that Canadian legislators have never been a mirror image of the general public. Lawyers dominate the membership in the House (usually about 30 percent of MPs are lawyers), with business and the professions running a close second. However, legislators attempt to represent their constituencies by their activities in the House, including the debates, committee hearings, and question period. Through such mechanisms, individual MPs, particularly opposition members, make their constituents' views known and publicize government wrongdoing or incompetence in handling the affairs of the nation. In that sense, then, the "essential day-to-day business of the Canadian House of Commons is not decision-making but representation" (Hockin, 1973: 361).

Although the current legislative functions of representation and legitimation are not as grand as the principle of parliamentary sovereignty, they are important tasks. The House of Commons has adapted to changing circumstances and thereby has maintained a significant place for itself in the political system. In the process, some of the initial patterns of Canadian politics have been altered, such as the lack of party unity in the Commons. Moreover, parliamentary privilege, which emerged historically in the battles between the king and Parliament, is now used to buttress the representational tasks of the legislators, guaranteeing their right to question the government, as well as to raise issues of concern to their constituents. The 20th century has also witnessed changes in the structure of the House (e.g., number of members and number of provinces) and in its procedures (e.g., closure, standing committees). Such changes reflect the evolution of the House of Commons from a lawmaking institution (if it every truly was) to one concerned with the remaining functions of representation and legitimation.

THE DECLINE OF LEGISLATIVE POWER: THE ROLE OF THE CANADIAN SENATE

Unfortunately for Senate admirers (one assumes there are a few, at least, outside of current, former, or prospective aspirants), the upper House of Canada's legislature has neither performed as expected nor adapted to the changing circumstances of the 20th century. As a result, the Senate, although never the equal of the House of Commons, has witnessed a steady erosion of its legislative role. For example, a recent book on the Canadian Parliament uses the "terms parliament and House of Commons interchangeably", because of the minimal legislative power retained by the Senate (Kornberg and Mishler, 1976: 17–18). Technically, however, Parliament includes the Senate, House of Commons, and the formal executive. While the imminent demise of the Senate is not apparent, neither is its rejuvenation. After a brief look at the structure of the Senate, we will consider its current functions in the political process, particularly its relationship with the House of Commons.

Structure of the Senate
The basic institutional composition of the Senate is outlined in Sections 21–36 of the British North America Act. In contrast to the Commons, which is directly elected, the Senate is an appointed body. Although legally chosen by the governor-in-council, Senate selection, for all practical purposes, has become a prerogative of the prime minister, even though others may be consulted in the process. Legal qualifications are fairly straightforward: an individual must be 30 years of age, a resident of the province for which he or she is appointed, a natural born or naturalized subject of the Queen, and have real property, over and above all debts, of $4000. For Quebec senators, the province is broken down into 24 districts, with the person appointed either a resident of that district or meeting the property qualification therein. Based on custom, Senate appointments are spread throughout a province, with senators being desig-

nated for particular areas. For example, legally all of Ontario's representatives could be appointed from Toronto, but such a pattern would be bad politics and, hence, has never happened. Revealing is the monetary requirement of $4000, which has remained constant. A barrier to most people in 1867, the $4000 figure does not eliminate as many people in the 1980s.

The allocation of Senate seats is based on the provinces and regions, with a current maximum total, if all the positions were filled, of 104 members: Quebec 24, Ontario 24, Maritimes 24 (Nova Scotia 10, New Brunswick 10, Prince Edward Island 4), the West 24 (6 for each province), Newfoundland 6, Yukon 1, Northwest Territories 1. Initially senators held office for life, but any senator appointed from 1965 onward must retire at the age of 75. A senator may be removed from office (BNA Act, Section 31) for failing to attend two consecutive sessions, by ceasing to be a citizen, or by failing to meet the requirements of residency or financial solvency.

The main criterion for Senate appointment is based on custom and convention: the upper House is selected on the basis of patronage or party service. Combined with being an appointed body in a democratic age, patronage has seriously eroded the legitimacy of the Senate and has helped to reduce its legislative powers to minimal levels. To classify a practice as one of *patronage* means that the controlling factor in appointment is past party work and loyalty, although that does not necessarily mean that people of talent will not be chosen. The Senate has become a base for national party organization: the work is not too taxing or time consuming and the pay is good and from public, not party funds. Those who raise the party finances and those who organize election campaigns are often made senators. Senator Keith Davey, often dubbed "the rainmaker," because of his influence in the Liberal party organization, is one example.

The patronage base of appointment has also meant a severe party imbalance in the upper House, since one party (the Liberals) has controlled national office for most of the last half century. The Liberals have generally held a four to one ratio over the Conservatives in the upper chamber, with minor parties or independents usually excluded from service. The imbalance was becoming so acute in the late 1970s that Pierre Trudeau adopted policy of appointing Conservatives to fill vacancies caused by Conservative deaths or retirements.

While the final selection is a prime ministerial prerogative, considerable jockeying and infighting occurs within the party organization over who should be called to the Senate. The interests of the provincial and national party organizations must be reconciled, as well as other competing interests (ethnic, religious, and racial). It is not unknown for an individual to campaign extensively behind the scenes for a Senate appointment, as Sam Bronfman did in seeking to become the first Jewish member in the Red Chamber (Newman, 1979: 47–60). A number of vacancies are usually kept open until shortly before an election, in order to exact as much work or money as possible out of Senate aspirants. A good indicator of a forthcoming election, therefore, is a series of Senate appointments, as the governing party tries to use up all of its patronage powers before calling an election that might result in the loss of office. Few parties are willing to gamble that they will win. In contrast, the Liberals were so confident of victory in 1957 (they had, after all, been the government since 1935) that 16 positions were not utilized, which allowed the Conservatives a chance to appoint a large number of new senators after winning power.

Given the party basis of the appointment process, there are many political uses to which the Senate can be put. Before the adoption of a pension plan and the large salary increases of recent years for members of the House of Commons, the Senate was often utilized as a retirement pension for loyal MPs. Senate appointments have also been used to ease members out of the cabinet gracefully, without forcing a long-time minister to return to the backbenches (e.g., Paul Martin's appointment to the Senate). The prime minister may also manipulate the Senate selection process to open up a safe seat in the House. What seems destined to become a classic example of this practice occurred in July 1981, when 45-year-old Peter Stollery, MP for the Spadina riding in Metropolitan Toronto, was appointed to the Senate to make room for Jim Coutts, who had been principal secretary to the prime minister for many years. The Spadina constituency, which was heavily populated with ethnic members who had strong ties to the Liberal party, was touted to be the "safest" Liberal seat outside of Quebec. Stollery, who had spent a decade as a Liberal backbencher, had never been selected for the cabinet and had no immediate prospects for such a development. With the salary increase of 1981, Stollery's Senate appointment, given his mandatory retirement at age 75, was worth over $1 million. Unfortunately for Jim Coutts' electoral career pattern, which was rumoured to include a cabinet position as well as a try for the Liberal party leadership upon Trudeau's departure, the voters of Spadina rejected him in the August 17, 1981 by-election.

Senate appointments also have an impact on general election results. Knowing that defeat was possible, in preparing for the 1979 election, Trudeau appointed Bob Muir, long-time Conservative MP from Cape Breton, to the Senate in the hopes of winning that riding in the forthcoming contest, which the Liberals did. Senate appointments can also help to sow dissension within an opposition party. In the early 1960s Hazen Argue, House leader and briefly national leader of the CCF, was defeated by Tommy Douglas for the leadership of the just-formed New Democratic Party. Argue subsequently became a Liberal, but upon losing his seat was appointed to the Senate in 1966 (Young, 1969: 235–238). An even more blatant attempt to produce internal disunity within an opposition party was revealed in Trudeau's appointment of Claude Wagner to the Senate, again as a prelude to the 1979 contest. Wagner had been Joe Clark's primary rival for the party leadership in 1976, losing by only a handful of votes on the fourth ballot. Moreover, Wagner was one of a few Conservative MPs from Quebec, around whom the party had hoped to rebuild. Although they had tried strenuously to beat him in the previous elections, the Liberals selected Wagner for the Senate because it would hurt the Tory rebuilding effort in Quebec, as well as producing disunity within the Conservative party caucus. Such continuing machinations regarding Senate appointments is a major reason why senators have "on the whole ... turned in what must be considered an undistinguished performance" (Dawson, 1970: 283). Moreover, the patronage and party organization uses to which the Senate has been put have undercut its legislative role and its relationship with the House of Commons.

Functions of the Senate
The initial design of Canada's upper House reflected two main purposes: first, to serve as a check on the lower House and second, to represent the provinces and regions within the national government. Neither function remains viable in the 1980s.

The Senate has never been equal to the House. For example, all money bills must be introduced in the Commons first, and the government is responsible for retaining legislative support there. While the senate can theoretically defeat a bill, such a defeat would not bring the government down. Thus, the power of the Senate in the bicameral federal legislature was designed to be inferior to that of the Commons in 1867 and has become more so since then.

Considerable debate surrounds the extent of the Senate's legislative powers in the 1980s. In theory, the Senate retains the right to reject legislation coming from the Commons; in practice, it almost never happens or, for that matter, the issue of rejection is scarcely even contemplated. An important distinction must be made between vetoing legislation in total or making significant amendments to it, and the more limited approach of revising the work of the Commons. The Senate can make major changes, but only if the Commons does not see them as a challenge to its own dominance in the legislative process. If the House perceives the Senate's actions as a challenge, then a major confrontation between the two Houses occurs, and the House of Commons carries the day.

An example of this took place in late 1973 and early 1974 over the government's wiretap legislation. As discussed earlier, the NDP and Conservative parties had combined forces at both the committee stage and in the House to insert a notice provision to persons under surveillance for 90 days. When the bill reached the upper House, the Liberal-dominated Senate removed the notice provision and sent the bill back to the Commons for approval. Justice Minister Otto Lang recommended to the Commons that the Senate revisions be accepted. In the House, the opposition Conservative and New Democratic parties were outraged, rightly perceiving that the Liberal minority in the House was attempting to use the Liberal majority in the Senate to circumvent the power of the Commons. Press and public reaction were scornful of the Senate, pointing to its patronage and nonelected base – in other words, questioning the legitimacy of its actions. John Diefenbaker, who had once gone so far as not to include any senators in his cabinet, declared that if the Senate wanted "a free-for-all, let's let them have it." Blunt talk of Senate abolition began to be heard. The Commons proceeded to reinsert the notice provision into the wiretap legislation and sent it back to the Senate, daring them, in effect, to have the guts to reject it or to revise it again. The second time the Senate acquiesced, and the legislation was passed in the form preferred by the Commons.

The fact that these confrontations are rare in recent decades is indicative of the dominance of the Commons over the Senate. Such battles are more likely, however, when the Commons and Senate are controlled by different parties, thus giving the Senate-House confrontations a partisan basis (Newman, 1973: 295-321). While it rarely challenges the lower House directly, the Senate not only influences the Commons, but sometimes has been able to convince the lower House to accept revisions to its legislation. While most changes are minor, a recent study has argued that many of the so-called technical changes made by the Senate are in fact significant because they provide a means for business and corporate influence in the legislative process (Campbell, 1978: 10–19). It is in this role of a minor revising chamber that the Senate retains a modicum of influence in the Canadian legislative process in the 1980s.

The second intended function of the Senate in 1867 was to serve as an institution that would provide regional and provincial representation within the national government. The regional allocation of Senate seats prescribed in the BNA Act was designed to guarantee such a result; thus, in a technical sense the Senate continues to be based on regional and provincial interests. However, as a regional voice within the national government, particularly as an effective one, the role of the Senate has been disappointing. From the time of Macdonald's first cabinet, in which he allocated portfolios on a provincial and regional basis, the lower House, through the cabinet, has usurped the Senate's role as the defender of provincial interests. Moreover, the inability of the Senate to defend provincial and regional interests is directly linked to its declining role in the legislative process: minimal legislative influence exacerbates the Senate's failure to be the defender of the provinces, even when it tries to undertake such a task. The patronage base of Senate selection has also meant that many members are not particularly concerned either with checking the work of the Commons or of being effective regional defenders. Few party warhorses at career's end are likely to be political activists, no matter what the intent of the body to which they have been appointed.

If the Canadian Senate does not serve as a restraint on the Commons or as an effective voice of regional and provincial concerns within the national government, what are its current functions? First and foremost, the upper House is a tool for party organization and development: declining legislative functions have been replaced by party tasks, especially for the governing party. Second, the Senate plays a minor revising role in the legislative process. Third, the Senate provides at least symbolic representation for the regions in the affairs of the national government, although the provinces seem less than satisfied with such a continuing role for the Senate in the 1980s. Fourth, occasionally the Senate contributes to the political process over and above its minimal legislative tasks. Several senators have been active in investigating areas of social concern – Senator David Croll's committee's look at poverty in Canada is an example. Such useful tasks, however, seem more dependent on the interests and concerns of an individual senator than a necessary outgrowth of the Senate's overall political role.

Additionally, the Senate-sponsored hearings on Senate reform proposals in the late 1970s led to an advisory opinion from the Supreme Court of Canada in December 1979, that the federal government did not have the power to alter the composition of the Senate without the Senate's consent. Fifth, relatively infrequently, the Senate is called upon to provide regional representatives for the cabinet. Such a use is a result, however, of inadequate provincial representation within the governing party in the House of Commons itself. For example, both Joe Clark in 1979 (for Quebec) and Pierre Trudeau in 1980 (for three Western provinces) made use of the Senate to bolster provincial representation in their cabinets. However, once a party has gained seats in the House from a province, it would be contrary to custom to select senators rather than members of the House for ministerial positions. Given these reflections, the Senate's present role could be summarized as follows: an upper House with minor revising powers in the legislative process and a base for party organization and development, which rarely emerges as a significant actor in the political process.

Reforming the Senate

Numerous reform proposals regarding the appointment and structure of the Canadian Senate have been advanced in recent years. One incentive for reform, in addition to the problems of patronage and minimal legislative duties is simply cost. With the pay increase of July 1981, the price tag of the Senate, for salaries alone, is at least $5 million yearly. Other costs include the parliamentary restaurant and library, printing, upkeep, and a host of ancillary services, which would likely bring the direct Senate burden to many more millions a year. Rather than attempting to reduce its direct costs, the reform proposals have sought to change the Senate's patronage base or to enhance its role in the legislative process.

Reforms dealing with the age and patronage factors are generally modest in their contemplated changes to the Senate, while a greater legislative role would bring into question the current imbalance of power between the Commons and the Senate. Although the reform of 1965 requires any senator appointed since that date to retire at the age of 75, which has led to a 20-year reduction in the average age of senators, nevertheless an age problem remains. It is not so much a problem of mandatory retirement deadlines, as it is of the trend toward appointing senators who are in middle age. While youth may help to rejuvenate the Red Chamber, a person appointed at age 45 has a possible 30 years of service, with no performance review.

Particularly if the appointment of younger persons is the trend, then Senate appointments should be for a fixed term (e.g., five years or ten years), with the possibility of one reappointment. Such a tenure might encourage senators to be active and would not create the problem of a member being a possible nonparticipant for several decades. A second often-suggested reform is to make Senate selections from a wider range of people, especially to include individuals for other than patronage considerations. While such appointments would create a Senate of greater diversity in its social and economic makeup, it is not apparent that such a change is in the self-interest of the parties, particularly the governing party. A third proposed change is to alter the dominance of the federal level in the selection process by giving the provinces control of half of the Senate seats. Such a change would alter the party balance in the Senate, since in the early 1980s not a single provincial government was controlled by the Liberals. Although this reform would alter the party balance, it would not change the patronage base of selection: half of its appointees would be provincial patronage appointments instead of federal ones.

A final set of reforms aim at altering the Senate's role in the legislative process. For example, the Senate may be renamed the House of the Provinces or the House of Confederation, a change that would coincide with the initial intent that the Senate represent regional and provincial interests within the national government. However, to be effective, such a change would necessitate an increase in the Senate's current legislative powers. If the Senate cannot alter legislation, it cannot protect provincial concerns. If Senators are rarely included in the cabinet, how can Senators be effective defenders of provincial interests? We hence come to the pivotal question of Senate reform: what role or functions do we want it to perform in the political process? Unfortunately, this question is not always asked by those making reform proposals.

Changes in the selection process, the age of those chosen, or the tenure of the appointment will do little to alter the current overall position of the Senate: it will remain a minor revising body, patronage-based. Only such changes, in combination with additional powers, will do much to alter the Senate's political role in the current system. To grant the Senate more power would mean a reduction in the current status of the House and, by implication, the cabinet. Senate reform has been inhibited by the self-interest of other political institutions: the major stumbling block to a rejuvenation of the Senate is the House of Commons. For example, one proposal by Trudeau in 1978 would have given the Senate a "suspensive veto" power for six months. *A suspensive veto* is the ability to delay legislation for a given period of time rather than rejecting it outright. In other words, the theoretical total veto would have been replaced by an actual veto of half a year. Many critics wrongly perceived this as a further reduction of the Senate's power. In fact, in our view, a six-month suspensive veto would mean an increase in the power of the Senate, and as such would be unacceptable to the Commons. Another example of a change that would not be tolerated by the lower House would be the consistent use of Senators in ministerial positions. However, such a reform would be necessary to make the Senate an effective defender of regional concerns, since the cabinet is the key decision-making body in the Canadian polity.

These examples indicate that the likelihood of Senate reform is related to the prospects such a change would make in the overall balance of power between the two parts of Canada's bicameral legislature. The greater the proposed change in the Senate's role or powers, the greater will be the opposition to it coming from the Commons. The Senate, thus, finds itself in a Catch-22 situation: even if it wanted to, which it probably does not, it could do little to reform itself. It is not in the political self-interest of the institutions that control its fate – the House of Commons and cabinet – to see a revived and effectively functioning Senate. Any reform is likely to be illusory, leaving the basic role of the Senate intact, with its legitimacy further eroded in the years ahead.

THE LEGISLATURE IN GREAT BRITAIN

While the "mother of Parliaments" is a venerated institution, and while the years have not been totally unkind to her, they have, nevertheless, taken their toll: the British "Parliament does not and cannot" govern (Bradshaw and Pring, 1972: 9). The basic trends regarding the role of legislatures in the political process, or the balance of power between the constituent parts of bicameral institutions, have not bypassed "this sceptered Isle." In the nation of its birth, the principle of parliamentary supremacy has become a myth (Crossman, 1972). The House of Commons dominates the legislature, with the House of Lords continuing to recede in political significance. While in broad outline, the British Parliament resembles its Canadian counterpart, both in structure and function, it differs on a number of important specific points.

The House of Commons

The predominant lower House is composed of 635 members elected in single-member plurality districts. Since the 1971 redistribution, England has a total of 516 seats, with Scotland receiving 71, Wales 36, and Northern Ireland 12. Unlike the Canadian House, the physical structure of the British Commons is composed of benches that provide seats for only about 65 percent of its members. The result of such seating arrangements is an intimacy in the British House of Commons that is lacking in the individual desks or seats of both the Canadian and American legislatures. Interestingly, when the Commons was destroyed by fire during World War II, no increase in the physical size of the legislature was approved.

Internally, the Commons is under the direction of the speaker of the House, who is expected to be nonpartisan. British speakers are more independent than their Canadian counterparts in terms of both selection and tenure. For example, upon selection, the speaker ends previous political connections and ceases to be a member of any political party. Upon retirement, custom prevents a former speaker from taking up the partisan battle again. Once selected, the speaker may run in the next general election as an independent and if returned to the House, is usually reelected to the speaker's post. These conventions have made a British speaker more independent, with greater status, than the more partisan-based Canadian office.

The committee structure in the British Commons is not as well-developed as in Canada. The mother of Parliaments has been less than enthusiastic in delegating some of its authority to its constituent parts. The result has been the rather late and limited development of a standing committee system. The basic function of the standing committees is the detailed consideration of legislation between second and third readings, although their structure and membership limit their power in this task. Usually about ten standing committees are appointed during a session, with a membership of 16 MPs each. Thus, a minority of House members are involved in committee work in Britain. Moreover, membership on these committees is not stable – the composition of the standing committees is altered for each bill that it considers. The rationale for this approach is to have as much expertise as possible on the standing committee for each item it reviews. Typically, those members who have shown an interest in a bill during the second reading debate are appointed to the committee that will consider the legislation. Membership is allocated according to party strength in the full House by the committee of selection. British standing committees are not broken down along departmental lines as in Canada; however, recommendations for parliamentary reform may move Britain along more Canadian lines in the years ahead.

As in Canada, the organization of the British House revolves around the political parties, in particular the principle of party discipline. The cohesive behaviour of the political parties within the legislature has long been cited as one of the distinguishing hallmarks of the British party system. For example, in eight sessions since World War II, governments have successfully passed 100 percent of their legislative program, with the average success rate since 1945 standing at 97 percent (Rose, 1980: 75). Such results indicate that most members of Parliament willingly accept "the whip" and thus support their leader and party, both inside and outside the legislature. Interestingly the whip received its name in typical British fashion from "the hunt": the concept "derives from the whippers-in of the hunting field who keep the hounds working as a pack and prevent them wandering" (Bradshaw and Pring, 1972: 30).

The strength of party discipline is distinguished between one-line, two-line, and three-line whips, which refers to the number of times an upcoming vote is underlined on the outline of the week's expected activities prepared for party members by the party whips. The greater the number of underlings, the greater is the expected loyalty of party members: rarely will a member vote against the party if a three-line whip has been called. Because the national parties play an extensive and direct role in the recruitment of candidates for office, party leaders may deny a straying member renomination in the next election. The 1970s and early 1980s provided examples of members increasingly defying their party whip, but the principle of party discipline remains as a basic operating rule of the British House. The example of a number of Conservatives voting against their government's budget in June 1981 is exceptional behaviour in the House of Commons. More typical is the view of a member of Parliament as "a G.I. in a political army, whose rifle is his vote" (Crossman, 1972: 100).

The passage of legislation follows the usual pattern of three readings, with the committee stage occurring between the second and third readings. While the House of Lords repeats the process, for all practical purposes, the legislative function resides with the House of Commons, which in turn is controlled by the political executive. The government determines the priorities to be dealt with by the Commons and can ensure the passage of its legislation through use of closure. In contrast to the Canadian system, closure is frequently used. For example, between 1950 and 1970, closure was invoked 525 times in the British House (Bradshaw and Pring, 1972: 152), while in Canada closure was only used seven times between 1913 and 1957 (Newman, 1973: 39).

While the British House of Commons does not share legislative power with provincial or state governments and while its laws cannot be overturned by the judiciary, since judical review is not part of the political process, it is nonetheless true that the notion of parliamentary supremacy is illusory. More so than in Canada, given the absence of federalism and judicial review, the British political executive is not constrained by the legislature: the political process is executive-centred and executive-dominated. However, the Commons is still involved in an important way in the representation and legitimation functions. The Commons is representative not only in terms of its geographical constituencies, but also as a mechanism for registering individual and group concerns with the government of the day. Moreover, in its consideration of legislation, in its review and debate of a government's program, the House of Commons helps to legitimate executive actions: "Laws are described as Acts of Parliament, but it would be more accurate if they were stamped: Made in Whitehall" (Rose, 1980: 84–85). In other words, the task of the British House of Commons is "not that of initiating legislation but of authorizing and approving proposals for law formulated outside the legislature proper, most often by the executive" (Loewenberg and Patterson, 1979: 197). In this regard, the British and Canadian Houses of Commons reflect a distinct familial resemblance.

The House of Lords
The upper House of the British Parliament plays a very minor legislative role. The dominance of the House of Commons has long been established in British politics, beginning with the Reform Act of 1832 and consolidated by the Parliament Acts of 1911 and 1949. In many respects, the House of Lords is a monarchical, rather than a legislative institution, given its membership and overall role in the political process (Punnett, 1980: 279–291; Birch, 1980: 51–60).

The composition of the House of Lords is based on appointment, most of which is hereditary in nature. The total number is over 1200 members, although most of these never actively participate in the legislative process: only between 200 and 300 members make an effort at regular participation in the business of the Lords. Approximately three-quarters of the Lords are hereditary members; that is, they either inherited their titles or they were given a peerage themselves as a reward for public service. The remaining members are what are known as life peers, those whose appointment to the upper House ends with their own death. Selection to the Lords is a prime ministerial prerogative, although technically the appointments are made by the sovereign. The result is that the composition of the Lords reflects, in part, partisan control of the Commons: since the Conservative party has dominated British politics over the past century, the Lords is heavily weighted in favour of that party. Moreover, the preponderance of Conservative peers in the Lords reflects their traditional and appointive tie to the nobility. One reason for allowing life peers, beginning in 1958, was to correct this imbalance by giving the government greater flexibility in the appointment process. Most new peers in recent decades have been life peers and these members, as a group, are more active in the Lords than their hereditary counterparts. Since the prime minister has the right to create new peers, he or she can do so to break a deadlock between the Commons and the Lords: usually the threat of such action is enough to bring the upper House into line. The major confrontations between the Commons and the Lords have occurred when the lower House is controlled by a party other than the Conservatives.

The hereditary and appointed composition of the House of Lords has led some critics to refer to it as "a political geriatric unit" with few remaining significant functions in the political process: "a harmless political eunuch, possessing no power and little influence" (Hamilton, 1975: 9, 136). While such an assessment is perhaps extreme, most observers of the Lords would agree that in terms of legislation its major powers "have been reduced almost to nil" (Beer, 1973: 239). The Lords does retain, however, a role as a revising and debating chamber, in addition to its ability to deal with the private member's bills and to consider certain kinds of legislation ahead of the Commons. In these respects, the House of Lords relieves the Commons of some of its heavy workload. Perhaps the most revealing indicator of the remaining power of the House of Lords concerns its ability to veto legislation passed by the Commons, in particular the adoption and use of the suspensive veto.

As in most bicameral legislatures, either House traditionally shared the right to reject or veto legislation passed by the other chamber. The ability to veto measures passed by the Commons was first lost in 1911, when the Lords' total veto was replaced by a suspensive veto of two years' duration. For example, if the Lords rejected a bill and the Commons still wanted it, then the Commons could pass the legislation in three successive sessions (i.e., a minimum period of two years) and it would become law whether the Lords liked it or not. The suspensive veto was further reduced from two years to 12 months in 1949. As might be suspected, the change to a suspensive veto and its decline to a period of one year were both opposed by the House of Lords. However, the Parliament Act of 1911 was passed after two general elections had been held on the issue and after the sovereign threatened, at the request of the Government, to appoint enough new peers to the Lords to ensure the bill's passage. Rather than see their beloved chamber inundated by new and non-Conservative members, the Lords finally acquiesced and accepted the suspensive veto. The change in 1949 to reduce the suspensive veto to one year was passed after the Lords had delayed it for two years. More than anything else, the suspensive veto symbolizes the current role of the House of Lords in British politics: "If we cannot speak of the decline of Parliament, we surely can speak of the decline of the House of Lords" (Beer, 1973: 240).

The legislature in Great Britain can thus be described as bicameral in structure, with the elected House of Commons dominating the appointed and largely hereditary House of Lords. Increasingly peripheral to the political process, the upper House has steadily lost power to the Commons in the present century. While the Commons performs important representation and legitimation functions, it does not govern. Parliamentary sovereignty is illusory, with the Commons itself controlled by the political executive working through the party system.

THE AMERICAN LEGISLATURE

If any legislature in the world could be cited as an example that would belie the "decline of Parliament" thesis, it would be the American Congress. As a result of the separation of powers principle, which provides the potential for an assertive legislative branch, the continuing role of Congress in the lawmaking process runs counter to the trend in most countries. Moreover, the American experience also differs with respect to the relationship between the two legislative chambers: the House of Representatives and the Senate were designed to be coequal in theory and, for the most part, have remained so. In contrast to the Canadian Senate or the British

House of Lords, the American upper House has successfully adapted to the demands of the democratic era. In so doing, the American Senate has preserved a vital role for itself in the political process. Since the House and Senate are coequal partners, we will consider them together with respect to three areas: legislative organization, procedures, and functions.

Legislative Organization

The physical structure of the Capital places the House of Representatives and Senate at opposite ends, symbolizing, perhaps, their distinct role, as well as their often adversary relationship. However, unlike the seating arrangements in most British parliamentary systems, the parties in the American House and Senate do not face each other, but are instead arrayed in a semicircle around their presiding officers. This seating arrangement helps to mitigate antagonism between the parties within each House. Moreover, the concepts of government and opposition found in a parliamentary system would be hard to achieve in a polity based on the separation of powers, because the government, the party in control of the presidency and White House, is not necessarily the majority party within either legislative chamber.

Membership in both the House of Representatives and the Senate is based on direct, popular election, although the constitutional requirements for service and length of tenure varies in each. For the House of Representatives an individual must be 25 years old, a citizen for seven years, and a resident of the state in which his or her legislative district is based. The term of office is two years, with the number of congressional districts allocated to each state based on population. For example, the House of Representatives has a total of 435 members, with the largest state, California, assigned 45 districts and the smallest states, such as Vermont and Wyoming, receiving only one. For the Senate a member must be 30 years old, a citizen for nine years, and a resident of the state that he or she represents in the upper House. The allocation of Senate seats is on a geographical or territorial basis: each state, no matter its size, receives two Senate seats. Thus, with 50 states, the Senate is composed of 100 members. Initially, senators were selected by their respective state legislatures: for example, the New York state legislature would select that state's representatives to the upper House of the national legislature in Washington. However, since the adoption in 1913 of the Seventeenth Amendment to the American Constitution, senators are popularly elected. This reform is a major reason why the Senate has remained an important element in the American governmental system. Senators serve a six-year term, with one-third of the membership elected every two years. For example, one-third of the Senate will be elected in 1984, one-third in 1986, and one-third in 1988; they will all serve a six-year tenure before facing reelection in 1990, 1992, and 1994, respectively.

Both the House and Senate generally organize themselves internally along similar lines. The House of Representatives is presided over by the speaker of the House, who is chosen by the majority party. The person selected has usually been a senior member who has built up a power base within the legislature itself: the job of the speaker of the House is not usually a stepping stone to higher office in the American political system. In addition, each party elects a floor leader, whose function is similar to the Canadian House leader, as well as several party whips. The speaker, majority and minority floor leaders, and party whips are responsible for organizing the day-to-day business and operation of the House of Representatives. The Senate's structure varies slightly from this pattern: its presiding office is the President of the Senate, who is the vice-president of the United States. As Senate president, the vice-president is not an integral part of the legislature: the position is largely routine, with the incumbent casting a vote only in the case of a tie. Often the vice-president does not preside, at which point the presiding officer of the Senate is the president *pro tempore*, a member of the majority party. Effective power lies not with the office of the President of the Senate, but with the majority and minority leaders selected by each party. These positions are often ones of national prominence and can sometimes be used as springboards to national office. For example, Lyndon Johnson's mastery of the Senate as majority leader during the 1950s was one reason John F. Kennedy selected him as his running mate in the 1960 presidential election. Although in 1980, Senate minority leader Howard Baker made an ill-fated try to gain the Republican presidential nomination, the success of the Republicans in the election made him majority leader of the Senate in 1981, a position that may well serve as a launching pad for another try at the presidency.

While the presiding officers and party leaders are influential positions within the legislature, their power is constrained by the nature of party discipline and the committee system. Although the leadership usually gets its way, it may be forced to compromise or even be defeated outright on a particular vote. The reason for this is that, while the political parties work as groups within the legislature, their degree of cohesion and unity is considerably lower than in a British parliamentary system. The legislative parties are neither controlled nor directed by the executive, a reflection of the separation of powers doctrine. Moreover, the use of the primaries for political recruitment and the local power base of both House and Senate members has meant that the party leadership has few resources or sanctions with which to ensure strong party cohesion. As a result, party discipline in the American legislative chambers rarely approaches 100 percent: "Almost every vote in both houses shows a minority of each party voting against the majority of their party" (Hilsman, 1979: 116–117). Although party discipline is weaker than in Canada and Britain, it is still the most important factor in determining how individual members of Congress will cast their ballots.

The second constraint on the party leadership is the committee system in each House. Unlike the committees in a parliamentary system, which are tightly controlled by the government, American committees have an independent power base, which results in considerable clout in the legislative process. While these committees have as their main function the detailed clause-by-clause analysis of a piece of legislation, there is little else about them similar to their Canadian counterparts. Significantly, American committees have the effective power to delay, to amend, or to defeat a bill outright. As such they are a further example of the decentralization and fragmentation of power so typical of the American political process. Moreover, it is in the committees or "little legislatures" that most of the real work of Congress is accomplished.

Each chamber is divided into a series of standing committees: 15 in the Senate and 21 in the House, organized around substantive concerns such as agriculture, justice, and foreign affairs. Individual senators and members of Congress serve on several committees, move from one committee to another on a voluntary basis, and typically remain for many years on the same committees, thus building up considerable expertise in several policy areas. Party strength on the committees reflects the party's overall standing in each chamber, with the parties determining which of its members serve on the specific committees. Each committee is directed by a 'chair', individuals who have traditionally been extremely powerful in the legislative process. Until the reforms of the mid-1970s, an individual committee chair could quite literally tie up the entire legislative process: today they remain key actors in the House and the Senate. For example, Wilbur Mills, from a rural congressional district in Arkansas for many years chaired the House Ways and Means Committee, one of the most important committees in the House of Representatives. During those years, the Democratic members on his committee served as that party's committee of selection, thus choosing all other committee assignments for the Democratic party. As a result, Wilbur Mills was the most influential and powerful member in the legislature. When he briefly entered the presidential race in 1971, one of his colleagues asked him, "Wilbur, why do you want to run for president and give up your grip on the country?" (Green et al., 1972: 71). A few years later, Wilbur Mills was involved in a Washington sex scandal and lost his party and House positions.

These positions as chairs of the standing committees are usually determined by the *seniority principle*, or as critics have called it, the senility system. Based on custom, the chairs are given to the senior member of the majority party on each committee with the longest continuous service. The result of this practice is to reward members from safe districts, since it is necessary to win continuous reelection for many years in order to qualify for one of the key committee chairs. Moreover, many of these districts have traditionally been rural in nature and based in the South. These powerful positions have been filled, therefore, by elderly men from rural and mainly Southern constituencies, at a time when the American population was becoming young, urban, and based in the big city-states of the North. The South may have lost the Civil War, but for a hundred years it controlled Congress and was able to prevent effective civil rights legislation from being passed until the mid-1960s. However, scandals such as those involving Wilbur Mills, as well as the autocratic power of many chairs, led to a revolt in the 1970s against this longstanding custom. For example, in 1975, the Democrats in the House of Representatives ousted three committee chairs. Reforms adopted in the mid-1970s have both given members of the party caucuses more say in the choice of committee chairs and have curtailed some of the more blatant misuses of power. However, the seniority principle remains as the most important factor in selecting committee chairs, whose power is still considerable.

Legislative Procedures
A number of points should be kept in mind when trying to understand the passage of legislation in the American system. First, the

already discussed rites of passage of a parliamentary system scarcely apply to the approval of a bill in a presidential-style process. Second, the American system was designed to make the enactment of legislation exceedingly difficult and it has succeeded admirably. Third, legislative politics are extremely complex because of both the coequal status of the House and Senate and the general fragmentation of power within each legislative chamber. Fourth, this decentralization of power has produced a series of multiple veto points in the legislative process, so that a single member or a small group of legislators can stop the passage of a particular bil. As a result, it is much easier to defeat a bill than it is to pass it. Simple majority support (more than 50 percent) in the full legislature is not enough to win: against determined opposition one must have overwhelming support (two-thirds of those present and voting). In such a system, reform legislation is not necessarily prevented from gaining approval, but the process for such legislation is difficult without strong public and Congressional support.

The passage of legislation can be broken down into four major stages: first, introduction of the bill in both Houses; second, committee action; third, consideration by the full House and Senate, sometimes called floor action; and finally, enactment into law upon presidential approval (Oleszek, 1978: 15). Each stage involves a number of steps, with defeat of the bill possible at any single one. Except for money bills, legislation may be introduced in either House, although it is usually introduced simultaneously in both chambers. A bill must be passed by both Houses in an identical format before being sent on for presidential action.

Submission of a bill is normally routine, with only members having the right to introduce a piece of legislation. For example, the president cannot formally introduce a bill, but can and does get supporters to do so in both the House and Senate. Once introduced, a bill is sent to one of the standing committees. It is at the committee stage that close scrutiny is given to a bill, the so-called clause-by-clause review. A committee may hold public hearings, ask for expert testimony, or have the committee's staff prepare reports on the expected consequences of the bill. Committees may allocate this responsibility to subcommittees, which then hold hearings and consider the bill as well. Once the full committee has reviewed the legislation, it votes either to send it on to the next stage or not. A committee can also "sit" on a piece of legislation; that is, it does not consider the bill and therefore it cannot proceed any further. This is a fate that awaits most bills.

From committee it moves on to stage three, discussion and debate by the full House and Senate. In most cases, there remains the right to amend the legislation at this juncture. However, except on highly controversial bills, legislators usually accept the recommendation of the committee that has considered the bill in detail. To this point, then, the House and Senate have each considered the bill in committee and have each granted approval to it by their total membership. Floor action is not complete, however, until the versions of the bill passed by the two chambers are identical. As the bill has proceeded through each chamber separately, it is quite likely that it has been revised and amended differently. If the versions passed by the full House and Senate are not identical, the bill is sent to the Joint Conference Committee to work out the differences. The Joint Conference Committee is composed of members from both the House and Senate committees that considered the bill at the initial committee stage. If a compromise is reached, the bill goes back to the full House and Senate for final approval, after which it is sent to the White House for presidential approval.

In the fourth stage, the president has several options: to sign the bill; to let it sit for ten days, after which it becomes law in any case; or veto it and send it back to Congress. If both Houses pass the bill a second time with a two-thirds majority – what is called *overriding* a presidential veto – the bill becomes law without the president's signature. When the vetoed bill is returned to Congress, it goes back to the full House and Senate and does not have to go through the committee stage again. If Congress overrides a presidential veto, the bill is not sent back to the president for approval: the president cannot veto the bill the second time around. As this simplified outline should demonstrate, the passage of legislation is extremely complex and difficult in the American system. Moreover, at each juncture a bill can be defeated, while approval only comes after all the possible veto points have been successfully passed.

Although legislative procedures in the House and Senate are very similar, there are several important differences, which not only distinguish each chamber, but demonstrate the extreme decentralization of power in the American Congress. For example, between the committee stage and floor action, the House of Representatives uses a special committee known as the House Rules Committee, through which most legislation must pass before reaching the full membership. This committee determines when a piece of legislation will be considered, how much debate will be allowed, and whether or not amendments to a bill can be made by the full House.

If the Rules Committee refuses to pass "a rule" on a bill, then it has effectively defeated the legislation, because the bill cannot move forward without it.

Distinctive to the Senate is the *filibuster*, the right of individual senators to talk for as long as they want on a piece of legislation. This practice of unlimited debate can be used by an individual or small group of senators to bring the work of the upper House to a halt, thereby either preventing the passage of a bill or forcing the proponents of the legislation to compromise on specific points. Often the threat of a filibuster is sufficient to bring about such changes by the backers of a bill. One of the most successful uses of the filibuster was by former Senator Wayne Morse of Oregon, who used to pin a fresh rose to his lapel and threaten to talk until it wilted. A filibuster can be limited by the use of *cloture*, which cuts off debate and allows a vote on the bill. However, a cloture vote is rarely won in the Senate, because most senators do not want to set a precedent for the device to be used against themselves at some future date. Moreover, until 1975, a cloture vote required a two-thirds majority of those present for passage; since then, a three-fifths vote of the elected membership is needed.

Legislative Functions

While similar to other democractic legislatures in terms of its representation and legitimation functions, the American Congress is unique in terms of its lawmaking tasks: "the constitutional separation of powers has preserved for Congress an independent role that distinguishes it from legislative bodies in most western democracies" (Oleszek, 1978: 215). Moreover, in carrying out its lawmaking function, Congress is further distinctive because of the coequal status of its chambers, which means that the House of Representatives and the Senate each have the power to oppose the wishes of the other. As a result, the American legislature is a major participant in the political process, perhaps best symbolized by its independent power of the purse.

The basis of legislative significance is the principle of separation of powers, which creates the possibility of legislative independence from executive control. Although at times the American Congress has been seen as an ineffective body controlled by a strong presidency (e.g., in the 1960s and early 1970s, there was the notion of an "imperial presidency"), the legislature has reasserted its power in the last decade. More often than not, the American legislature can prevent executive action by vetoing, revising, or delaying a measure, although it is much less likely to take major policy initiatives on its own. The separation of powers doctrine forces a mutual dependence on both the executive and legislative branches: the ability to withdraw its cooperation is often the key to legislative power in the American political process. Moreover, if the executive does not cooperate with the legislature's priorities, then Congress may override a presidential veto to force particular policy upon a reluctant executive. The basis for such a legislative role lies, of course, in the broad power allocated to Congress by Article One of the Constitution. While some of the specified tasks given to the Congress (e.g., the power to declare war) have been modified by events and custom, they remain the foundation for an assertive legislative branch. The result is that "contrary to some popular opinion, Congress plays a major role in national policy-making – both in foreign and domestic spheres" (Hinckley, 1979: 138).

COMPARING LEGISLATURES

While the structures, functions, and procedures of legislatures may vary widely among different types of political systems and historical periods, the view of these institutions as lawmakers is as widespread as it is illusory. Even in democratic systems, where there is the best chance for legislative importance, parliamentary supremacy is clearly a myth in the last decades of the 20th century. Only regarding the American system can one make a strong argument for legislative significance in the policy-making process. This conclusion reflects the basic difference between legislatures in parliamentary and presidential systems.

Key to an understanding of the role of the legislature in a parliamentary or presidential system is the nature of the relationship between the executive and legislative branches of government. The fusion of powers in a British parliamentary-style system between the executive and legislative institutions has reduced the legislature's role from one of policy-making to one of representation and legitimation. Parliament remains a symbol of authority, but effective decision-making power lies in the executive. By contrast, in the American presidential system, the separation of powers principle divorces executive and legislative institutions, thereby creating the potential for an assertive legislature. This potential, when combined with competent legislators and public support, can be translated into an effective policy-making role by the American Congress. Separate institutions sharing the power to pass bills give

Congress a major bargaining chip in order to force compromises and concessions from the executive branch. Thus the variation in executive-legislative relationships between parliamentary and presidential systems creates a somewhat different role for the legislature in each: in the American presidential system there is a policy-making function, in addition to the functions of representation and legitimation.

Presidential-parliamentary differences are also apparent with respect to the passage of legislation. In a parliamentary system, the government (especially a majority one) clearly controls the ebb and flow of legislation, determining when it will be considered, whether it will be labeled a government bill or not, and whether closure or other techniques will be used. As long as party discipline holds, the legislative proposals of the government are assured of passage. By contrast, in the American presidential system, committees and committee chairs are independent bases of influence and power. An individual member of Congress can effectively bring the entire legislative process to a halt. Moreover, there is a series of multiple veto points, which makes it easy to defeat a bill. A good example of the differences between parliamentary and presidential systems can be seen in the techniques of closure in the Canadian House of Commons and cloture in the American Senate. Closure is imposed by a majority vote and is applied against the opposition parties, while cloture requires a three-fifths vote and is applied against groups and individuals, not parties. In Canada, the use of closure is controlled by the government, while in the United States the imposition of cloture is not, thus symbolizing the difference between the fusion of powers and separation of powers doctrines.

In addition to the executive-legislative nexus, an important concern in analyzing bicameral legislatures is the relationship between the upper and lower chambers. The general pattern of the 20th century has been for a decline in the power and importance of the second chambers, again with the exception of the American Senate. What is often overlooked in assessing such a pattern is the fact that in most parliamentary systems, the executive is responsible only to the lower House, which is one reason why upper chambers have receded in significance. Control of the legislature by the executive, or more precisely, by the political executive, is based on executive-dominance in the lower House. As a result, the second chambers have become increasingly superfluous in the legislative process. By contrast, the American Senate remains an integral part of the polity, a result due in no small measure to its coequal relationship with the House of Representatives within the legislature. And, unlike the Canadian Senate or the British House of Lords, the American Senate has adapted, or been forced to adapt, to the demands of a democratic age. While the upper Houses do not necessarily have to be popularly elected to survive, what they do need is a method of selection or appointment that is seen as legitimate by the public. Until such changes are accomplished, the Canadian Senate and British House of Lords will never have the potential for regaining a significant role in the legislative process.

The initial legislative institutions were designed to give the public a voice in government and, although they rarely make the laws in fact, that first function remains a viable one for democratic legislatures in the decades ahead.

> The function of the legislature is to provide a means of ensuring that there are channels of communication between the people and the executive, as a result of which it is possible for demands to be injected into the decision-making machinery whenever they exist and for the executive decisions to be checked if they raise difficulties, problems, and injustices (Blondel, 1973: 135).

SUMMARY

1. While the concept of parliamentary sovereignty may be a myth, so is the view of legislative irrelevance. Legislatures in democratic systems serve both representation and legitimation functions, while in the United States a policy-making role has also been retained. Structurally, legislatures may have either one (unicameral) or two (bicameral) chambers, with federal systems usually adopting a bicameral legislature so as to guarantee regional or cultural representation in the upper House. Typically, bicameral legislatures are now controlled by the lower House, which is selected by direct popular election. Upper Houses based on heredity or appointment have seen a major decline in their legislative role.

2. Canada's bicameral national legislature is dominated by the House of Commons, while the Senate's legislative power is severely constrained. Based on representation by population and selected by direct popular election, the Commons is organized on the basis of party discipline and protected by the principle of parliamentary privilege. While designed as a means for ensuring

regional and provincial representation, the appointive nature of the Senate has instead resulted in its use as a patronage-related institution, undercutting its legitimacy and power in the political process. In the Canadian context, the notion of parliamentary sovereignty is constrained not only by executive-dominance, but by the principles of federalism and judicial review.

3. In Britain's bicameral legislature, the upper chamber or House of Lords is composed of appointed members who hold office either as hereditary or life peers. The power of the House of Lords has been greatly diminished, but it does retain a suspensive veto over the lower House. The Commons contains 635 members selected by direct popular election, is organized along party lines, and is the preeminent legislative chamber. However, even in the nation of its birth, parliamentary supremacy has become a myth.

4. Unlike its Canadian or British counterparts, the American legislature has retained for itself a significant role in the policy-making process, a result of the separation of powers principle. Again in contrast to the Canadian and British pattern, the American bicameral legislature was designed to be composed of two equal chambers and has, for the most part, remained so in practice. The House of Representatives and Senate are both chosen by direct popular election, with the House seats based on population and the Senate seats based on geography. Passage of legislation in the American system is not only extremely complex, but difficult, given the multiplicity of veto points in the process. Influence and power is decentralized within each chamber, symbolized by the filibuster in the Senate and the traditional role of committee chairs in both Houses.

5. In understanding the role of legislatures, a key concern must be the nature of the executive-legislative nexus. In bicameral systems, an additional focus must be the kind of relationship between the two chambers: does one chamber dominate, or are the two houses roughly equivalent in power? While they are rarely lawmaking institutions, legislatures remain an important mechanism of communication between the governed and their governors.

RECOMMENDED READINGS

Comparing Legislatures

BLONDEL, J. (1973) *Comparative Legislatures*. Englewood Cliffs, N.J.: Prentice-Hall.

BRADSHAW, KENNETH and DAVID PRING (1972) *Parliament and Congress*. London: Quartet Books.

LOEWENBERG, GERHARD and SAMUEL C. PATTERSON (1979) *Comparing Legislatures*. Boston: Little, Brown and Co.

OLSON, DAVID M. (1980) *The Legislative Process: A Comparative Approach*. New York: Harper and Row.

The Canadian Legislature

CAMPBELL, COLIN (1978) *The Canadian Senate: A Lobby From Within*. Toronto: Macmillan of Canada.

CLARKE, HAROLD D., COLIN CAMPBELL, F. Q. QUO, and ARTHUR GODDARD eds. (1980) *Parliament, Policy and Representation*. Toronto: Methuen.

JACKSON, ROBERT J. and MICHAEL M. ATKINSON (1980) *The Canadian Legislative System*. Toronto: Macmillan of Canada, 2nd, rev. ed.

KORNBERG, ALLAN and WILLIAM MISHLER (1976) *Influence in Parliament: Canada*. Durham, N.C.: Duke University Press.

STEWART, JOHN B. (1977) *The Canadian House of Commons: Procedure and Reform*. Montreal: McGill-Queen's University Press.

The British Legislature

BUTT, R. (1967) *The Power of Parliament*. London: Constable and Co.

CRICK, BERNARD (1964) *The Reform of Parliament*. London: Weidenfield and Nicholson.

CROSSMAN, RICHARD H.S. (1972) *The Myths of Cabinet Government*. Cambridge, Mass.: Harvard University Press.

The American Legislature

HINCKLEY, BARBARA (1978) *Stability and Change in Congress*. New York: Harper and Row.

OLESZEK, WALTER J. (1978) *Congressional Procedures and the Policy Process*. Washington, D.C.: Congressional Quarterly Press.

SCHWARTZ, JOHN E. and L. EARL SHAW (1976) *The United States Congress in Comparative Perspective*. Hinsdale, Ill.: The Dryden Press.

6

THE JUDICIAL BRANCH OF GOVERNMENT: THE RELUCTANT EXERCISE OF POWER

The problem of the guardianship of a constitution is the touchstone of its efficacy as the basic law of the land. While in a sense all authorities are called upon to protect the constitution, as expressed in their oaths of office, there needs to be an individual or body which has the "last word." Constitutional experience points to the judiciary, and more specifically, its apex, as the least objectionable choice for such guardianship (Freidrich, 1968: 265).

I have long been fascinated with the phenomenon of judicial power in different societies, but especially in our own. It is (or has been) such quiet power, so unacclaimed, so often denied! It is precisely the subtle, ironic strength which our judiciary derives from its hidden nature that so fascinates me (Russell, 1975: 75).

IN DEMOCRATIC SYSTEMS the political process, and the public's perception of it, is dominated by the elected politicians of the executive and legislative branches of government. In most of these polities the third branch of government, the judiciary, rarely comes into public focus and, when it does so, its actions are little understood by the ordinary citizen. Such a lack of attention once led Chief Justice Bora Laskin to call a news conference at which he complained of the media's minimal coverage of the Canadian Supreme Court. Characteristically, the news conference was sparsely attended and its contents only briefly reported. This pattern of low political visibility is a reflection of the judiciary's typical guardianship role in the polity: its legitimacy depends, in large measure, on the public's perception of its neutrality and nonpartisanship. To stay above mere politics necessitates that the court system abstain from active and direct involvement in the daily workings of the political process. However, low visibility does not necessarily translate into little political power and influence, for, despite the public perception of their nonpolitical status, the courts are political institutions that render political judgments with at least occasionally, far-reaching political consequences.

THE NATURE OF JUDICIAL POWER

As with many aspects of the political process, the often significant political role of the judiciary emerged from practice rather than from theory. Of the three branches of government, least attention is typically paid to the judiciary in most constitutions. Moreover, in the American system, the principle of full judicial review was asserted by the judiciary itself, rather than being prescribed in the Constitution. Although the court system was often viewed initially as a kind of disinterested referee of the political process (e.g., in federal systems deciding which level of government could constitutionally exercise which powers), it was also conceived as a potential means for counteracting the effects of popular sentiment on the executive and legislature. In contrast to its conservative intent, the expansion of judicial power has coincided with the democratization of the political process. Paradoxically, an appointed branch of government in a democratic age has had the potential for increasing and protecting human rights against encroachments by the elected political institutions.

The court system's ability to counteract executive and legislative abuses of power reflects the *principle of judicial independence*. In broad terms, judicial independence means the lack of political direction and control over the courts by any outside body, including the executive and legislative branches of government. The fusion of powers between the executive and legislature in a parliamentary system does not extend to the judiciary, while the separation of powers principle in a presidential polity is a major reinforcement of judicial independence. Judicial independence is designed to prevent any person or institution from dictating to the courts the content of their rulings, a reflection of the view that the courts should be nonpolitical.

The independence of the judiciary in democratic systems is protected by giving the judges legal immunity from the consequences of their decisions. If judges in carrying out their official duties, make an incorrect ruling, they cannot be sued as individuals. A redress of grievances can be sought, however, by suing the government. Thus, the courts are protected by a legal immunity, as well as a political immunity, from outside intervention in their affairs. Judicial independence is further enhanced by the nature of judicial tenure. Judges are either appointed for long terms of office or for life, although some systems have imposed a mandatory retirement age. Once appointed, a judge can be removed only for ''cause,'' that is, some sort of improper behaviour (e.g., a criminal conviction). Removal for cause does not mean that people simply disagree with a judge's rulings. Such an action is often made difficult, so as to reduce any chance of government manipulation of judicial personnel. Moreover, salaries of judges cannot be individually tampered with, either up or down, thus preventing political pressure from being applied monetarily.

The principle of judicial independence has often been misinterpreted to mean that somehow the courts are above or outside of the political arena. Nothing could be further from the truth. The myth of judicial impartiality is an important basis for legitimating the political effects of court decisions, even as it provides an incorrect description of the role of the judiciary in the political process.

Courts are inherently political by reason of their composition, the content of their rulings, and the consequences of their decisions. For example, patronage has often been the leading criterion of court appointments in democratic systems, especially at the lower levels of the judicial structure. Even when explicit partisanship is not the prevailing basis of selection, the appointment of court members, so as to reflect particular ideological views or to represent various interests of society (racial, regional, ethnic, linguistic), is often done for political considerations. The contents of judicial decisions are political because they involve the allocation of power and influence within the polity. For example, in a federal structure, court rulings have been a means of settling questions of jurisdiction between the levels of government. Finally, the consequences of judicial decisions are political, for they may alter the existing distribution of power and influence or raise new issues, which must be handled by the other branches of government. For example, court decisions have had the political consequence of helping to alter the initial allocation of powers in both the Canadian and American federal systems. Thus, the principle of judicial independence does not exclude the court system from the political arena, but, instead, creates the potential for its political involvement by keeping the judiciary free from executive or legislative tutelage.

An important means of judicial participation in the political process is what is known as judicial review. Two basic types exist, what we have labeled as *full judicial review* (interpretations of constitutionality) and *limited judicial review* (decisions regarding

the allocation of powers in a federal polity). The political consequences of full judicial review are potentially of far greater significance than those of limited judicial review. For example, a basic
reason for the extensive political impact of the American judiciary
stems from its application of full judicial review, while the more
modest Canadian judicial result is congruent with a limited judicial
review process. In Britain, judicial review does not exist, since its
application would be in direct opposition to the principle of parliamentary sovereignty. The greater the extent of judicial review, the
greater the likelihood of the court system's involvement in politics,
because court cases based on full judicial review often thrust the
judiciary into a policy-making role.

Judicial review has been criticized as undemocratic, since it
allows a small group of appointed officials to overturn the actions or
legislation of elected ones. However, full judicial review has, at
times, expanded civil and political liberties against the conservative
interests that controlled the other two branches of government. A
good illustration of this point is the civil rights rulings that began in
the mid-1950s in the American system. However, the impact of full
judicial review on the polity will depend, to a considerable extent,
on the composition of the courts. Judicial review supplies the legal
basis for the assertion of judicial power. If such a pattern results, it
depends, in large measure, on the individuals appointed to the
judiciary.

Whether the judiciary operates under either full or limited judicial review, the interpretation of a constitution and its application
in specific contexts is often a tricky business. Two broad approaches
to constitutional interpretation can be identified: judicial activism
and judicial restraint. In a pattern of *judicial restraint*, the courts
take a very narrow view of their own powers of interpretation. In
fact, the judges seek to divine the literal and intended meaning of
the initial constitution. This approach implies that it is not the role
of the courts to adapt the law to changing circumstances, but to
apply the law as it was written. If changes in the law are needed,
then it is up to the executive and legislature to respond accordingly.
In contrast, the second pattern, that of *judicial activism*, reflects a
willingness on the part of the judges to use their powers vigorously,
to take a broad view of any powers delineated in the constitution,
and, if necessary, to adapt the law to changing circumstances,
especially if the other two branches are reluctant to do so.

While patterns of judicial restraint or judicial activism depend, in
part, on the individuals appointed to the courts, there is an impor-

tant relationship between trends of judicial interpretation and the two basic kinds of judicial review. Full judicial review creates the potential for an activist judiciary, while limited judicial review makes more likely a pattern of judicial restraint. A pattern of judicial activism or restraint reflects a country's political culture and the prevailing attitudes about the proper role of the judiciary. Moreover, no judicial system is able to decide cases on its own initiative. Conflicts must be brought to the courts before the judicial branch can get involved. Like a car that only starts on a cold winter morning with the help of booster cables, the court system, must be continually jump-started before it can render any decision.

The actual operation of the judiciary in democratic systems embodies several key features. First, an individual is presumed innocent in criminal proceedings until otherwise proven guilty during the course of a judicial hearing. This assumption is a direct result of the principle of judicial independence: the judicial system, not the executive or legislature, decides the question of guilt or innocence. In contrast, totalitarian systems reverse this view, assuming that a person charged by the state is guilty until the individual proves otherwise. In such a system, the judicial structure is not independent, but is seen as a political extension of the state. The role of the courts is to enforce the political decisions of the party, with accusation of wrongdoing being tantamount to conviction.

The second tenet of a democratic judiciary concerns the process for arriving at decisions of guilt or innocence, that is, the adversary or fight system of justice. Both the prosecution, those trying to show that the individual is guilty, and the defence, those attempting to prove the individual's innocence, are given the opportunity to bring the facts of the case, as they see them, before the court. Then, the judge or jury acts as an impartial arbitrator, deciding guilt or innocence on the basis of the testimony presented. Assumptions of innocence and an adversary system of court procedure help to produce what is known as the "due process of law" in democratic polities.

A final significant aspect of court procedure is the principle of *stare decisis* or the rule of precedent. Once a court has ruled on a particular question or type of case, that ruling stands as a guide or precedent for similar cases in the future. Thus, the principle of *stare decisis* provides for some continuity of judicial interpretation, as well as limits the number of cases the court system must handle. However, precedents may not be definitive, since they are often multiple, as well as contradictory. One can always argue that the facts of a particular case are different enough from previous similar cases as to require a further elaboration of the law. In addition, precedents change. Judicial rulings can be applied in new contexts or simply reversed, thereby creating a new precedent for further court decisions.

Once a court has issued a decision, the question of its implementation comes to the forefront. In democratic systems, the executive branch of government, either by constitutional prescription or custom, is usually required to enforce the decisions of the judiciary. Thus, a possible conflict of interest might arise when a judicial decision goes against the executive, for the executive is supposed to enforce such a decision against itself. These cases, however, are infrequent because of the prevalent belief in democratic systems that judicial decisions should be obeyed. Force is rarely needed to gain acquiescence with judicial intent. The legitimacy of the judiciary, based on the belief of its impartiality, is usually sufficient so that court orders are self-enforcing. If they are not, a court can take several actions, in addition to notifying the executive of any nonobservance. For example, an injunction may be issued by the judiciary, which may either command that some action be taken or order that certain actions be stopped. Failure to comply with judicial decisions may also result in an individual or group being held in contempt of court, an offence that carries penalties meted out by the judiciary itself. Thus, the court system is not only lacking a self-starting mechanism, but it is given no direct means for implementing the decisions it has taken. As a result, the judiciary in most democratic systems has often been a reluctant participant in the political process.

THE CANADIAN JUDICIAL SYSTEM

In analyzing the nature of judicial power in any specific polity, four broad areas must be considered: the structure, composition, operation, and consequences of the court system. Comparing judiciaries on the basis of these criteria reveals more variation among Canada, Britain, and the United States than with respect to the other two branches of government.

The structure of the Canadian judiciary is complex, with responsibilities and functions shared between the federal and provincial governments. Moreover, each province has the power to determine the organization of its own court system, thus producing considerable variation of detail. Overall, the Canadian court system is hierarchically structured and composed of three court levels: federal courts (Supreme Court and Federal Court of Canada), provincial courts (a provincial Supreme Court and superior, county, and district courts), and lesser provincial courts (such as family courts).

Responsibilities for the courts is federalized, with the national government controlling the federal courts, the provinces in charge of the minor courts, and federal and provincial governments sharing jurisdiction over the intermediate level. For example, while the provinces determine the number and structure of the major provincial courts, the federal government was given the power of appointment, tenure, and salary of these same courts. Thus, as an area of shared control, the intermediate court level can only function effectively on the basis of federal-provincial cooperation. Defining the law's content was also federalized, with the national government granted the right to define the criminal code and procedure and the provinces allocated powers over civil procedure. Thus, an area such as the decriminalization of marijuana is a federal responsibility, while matters of marriage and divorce are provincially determined.

The federalization of jurisdiction in defining criminal and civil law and of control over the intermediate court level has been incorporated, nevertheless, into an overall hierarchical court structure, now presided over by the Supreme Court of Canada. Although it was first created in 1875 under the authority granted the national government in Section 101 of the BNA Act to provide a "General Court of Appeal" for the Canadian system, the Supreme Court only became the highest court of appeal with passage of the BNA Act (No. 2) of 1949. Prior to this change, the ultimate court of appeal for Canadian cases resided in Britain with the Judicial Committee of the Privy Council (JCPC). Moreover, even after its creation in 1875, many cases were never considered by the Supreme Court, since "it was possible for appeals to go directly from a court of appeal within a province to the Judicial Committee" (Cheffins and Tucker, 1976: 95). The result of such a judicial structure was not only to make explicit the nature of Canada's colonial position, but to give the JCPC the role of being "the major interpreter of the Canadian constitution and the major expander of explicit views on the nature of Canadian federalism" (Stevenson, 1979: 55). Thus, Canada faced the anomaly of having judges trained in British law and its role in a unitary state trying to comprehend and interpret the nature of Canadian conditions and the evolving pattern of Canadian federalism.

While considerable controversy surrounds the overall impact of the JCPC on the Canadian polity, there is little question that its decisions at the end of the 19th century were an important contributing factor to the initial decentralizing trend within the federal system. Since any case that was before the courts at the time of the passage of the BNA Act (No. 2) of 1949 retained the right to appeal to the JCPC, a number of years passed before the Supreme Court of Canada became, in fact, the final court of appeal. Canada was thus in a colonial judicial relationship with Britain until the mid-20th century. With its elevation to the position of the highest court of appeal, the composition, operation, and consequences of the Supreme Court became crucial for understanding the nature of judicial power in the Canadian context.

There is a strong reason to suspect that the composition of the Canadian judiciary is patronage-based, particularly at the lower levels of the court system. From this view it makes little difference which level of government has the appointment power: the party in office at either level rewards its own members more often than not. While patronage is pervasive, it rarely becomes a matter of public attention, as it did in Nova Scotia in the Summer of 1981, when several lawyers openly questioned their ability to have their clients receive a fair hearing. Moreover, although opposition parties traditionally criticize such practices, they are usually quick to adopt them when they gain power. Any listing of patronage-inspired judicial appointments would be lengthy, so a few examples should be sufficient. The appointment in 1979 of former Conservative candidate for the Commons, Julien Chouinard, to the Quebec Superior Court by the Joe Clark government and of Joe Daigle, former provincial Liberal leader in New Brunswick, to the bench in early 1982 by the federal Liberal government, are both illustrative. Several members of a group of young lawyers known as the Silver Seven, associated with former Liberal Justice Minister Otto Lang, have received judicial appointments in Saskatchewan.

While political uses are infrequently associated with the Supreme Court of Canada itself, the selection of its members is still political in the sense of the ideological views the appointees bring to the Court. The selection of Bora Laskin as Chief Justice of the Supreme Court by Prime Minister Trudeau was political because of Laskin's publicity expressed views on the Canadian judiciary. In a similar vein, Prime Minister John Diefenbaker had earlier refrained from appointing Laskin to the Supreme Court because of a critical assessment by then Professor Laskin (1959) of Diefenbaker's proposed Bill of Rights (MacKay, 1981).

In addition to the patronage factor, other considerations influence court appointments. Since judges are appointed from among members of the legal profession, the court members are typically unrepresentative of the total population in terms of such basic sociopolitical factors as race, ethnicity, education, and social class. For example, while the two charter groups of Canadian society are well-represented, those of neither British nor French origin have received few judicial appointments to date. To help ensure French-Canadian representation on the national courts, Quebec is guaranteed three positions on the Supreme Court and four on the Federal Court, although no such guarantees exist for other groups. The main reason for Quebec's representation is to ensure that judges familiar with the civil law tradition of Quebec sit on cases that deal with such matters. Although some effort is made to distribute judicial appointments among the various socioeconomic interests of society, the composition of the judiciary is more immune to the democratic ethos than either the executive or legislature.

The tenure of judges in Canada is indeterminate, extending from their appointment to their mandatory retirement, usually at age 75. Within this period judges are typically not subjected to any formal review or reappointment process. However, judges can be removed for "cause." For example, Section 98 of the BNA Act empowers the federal government to remove any judge of the superior courts after an address by the governor general to both Houses of Parliament. The exercise of this legal power is rare, for a judge in trouble because of personal problems or alleged wrongdoing will usually resign before being removed from office.

The Supreme Court of Canada is composed of nine justices, one of whom is named the chief justice and presides over and directs the work of the court. The position of Canadian Chief Justice is one of influence rather than one of power, for there is nothing that guarantees support from the other justices. On several significant occasions in the 1970s, Chief Justice Bora Laskin found himself in the minority, exemplified by his dissent in 1975 on the power of parole boards to change the conditions of a person's parole without any apparent reasonable justification. The Supreme Court must contain three members from Quebec, with a quorum consisting of five of the nine justices (on any appeal from Quebec, two members of the quorum must be from that province). Those appointed must have considerable legal experience (i.e., ten years of practice as a barrister) or be members of a provincial superior court. These requirements have usually prevented blatant patronage appointments to the highest court.

In addition to the structure and composition of the judiciary, a third important attribute of the court system is its method of operation. The broad functioning of the judicial system in Canada could be described by the concepts of judicial independence, limited judicial review, and judicial restraint. Although the principle of judicial independence has sometimes been violated, its acceptance has never been open to serious attack. The judiciary is designed to be free of executive or legislative control and when violations of such a principle become known, the political consequences can be severe. For example, in Ontario in the late 1970s, one minister resigned because of his alleged intercession with a judge on behalf of a constituent with respect to a pending court case. Similarly, in the famous Judges Affair in 1977, two federal cabinet ministers resigned or lost their portfolios because of reported interventions with a judge with respect to a contempt of court citation against one of their fellow cabinet officers.

Sometimes judicial independence is challenged by the reverse of this process, that is, when a judge intervenes openly into current partisan controversy. Such a case occurred when Justice Thomas Berger of the British Columbia Supreme Court wrote a lengthy critique about the dropping of native rights from the patriation accord, a critique that was published in the *Globe and Mail* on December 10, 1981. Prime Minister Pierre Trudeau, who had appointed Mr. Berger to the judiciary, reacted bitterly to the critique, openly attacking Justice Berger for his views. In April 1982, a complaint against Justice Berger's intervention into the partriation controversy was brought before the Canadian Judicial Council. Justice Berger responded by saying that he would continue to speak out on minority rights in the future. Although such incidents concerning the principle of judicial independence occur, they are relatively infrequent in Canada.

The second operating principle of the Canadian judiciary is that of limited judicial review. This practice of delineating the respective powers of the federal and provincial governments is not directly contradictory to the principle of parliamentary sovereignty, since the judiciary determines only which level of government is supreme with respect to which powers. As already mentioned, such rulings, can, however, have considerable impact on the balance of power between the two levels of government in a federal polity. An example of the exercise of limited judicial review is the Supreme Court ruling on the wage-and-price control legislation of the mid-1970s. The anti-inflation program was held to be within the federal government's powers because of the residual power clause of the BNA Act. Such decisions are classified as examples of limited judicial review because they deal with the kinds of powers and functions that the federal and provincial governments may exercise.

The third operating principle of the Canadian courts is the practice of judicial restraint, that is, the limited exercise of the limited powers given to them. In part, the pattern of restraint reflects the attitudes of the judges themselves (what could be called, perhaps, judicial self-restraint), as well as the overall constitutional position of the judiciary in Canada. Quite frankly, the other two branches of government, usually under some version or variation of the parliamentary supremacy doctrine, have sought to limit any expansion of judicial power. As a result, the umpire of the federal system is called upon to make very few close calls at home plate. Given the workings of limited judicial review and a pattern of judicial restraint, the political consequences of the Canadian judiciary might be expected to be modest. In fact, however, the Canadian courts have played a fairly significant political role, particularly considering the context within which they must operate. Such a conclusion is supported by a political analysis of the Supreme Court of Canada, a body that has not been immune to political controversies.

Since the Supreme Court is the final body to hear matters of federal-provincial conflict and because its members are appointed by the federal government, the provinces have always harboured the suspicion that the Supreme Court is biased in favour of the national government. This view is reinforced by the legal requirement that Supreme Court justices, after their appointments, must live within five miles of Ottawa, thus supposedly helping to overcome any regional or provincial bias they may have had. Premier Peter Lougheed of Alberta put it bluntly in 1978 when he said that it didn't matter where the Supreme Court justices were born, because after 20 years in Ottawa, they all thought alike anyway. In a similar vein, in its constitutional reform proposals of 1978, the province of British Columbia questioned the impartiality of the Supreme Court, because of Ottawa's supposed control over the Court's jurisdiction and composition. However, a perusal of Supreme Court decisions from 1949 onward reveals a mixed pattern, with the court sometimes ruling in favour of the provinces and sometimes in favour of the federal government. The decisions of the Laskin Court of the 1970s have often upheld federal government powers, as in the wage-and-price control decision, but it has also ruled in favour of the provinces (e.g., the December 1979 decision regarding Senate reform). Contrary to provincial perceptions, it would be difficult to make a strong case for inherent Ottawa bias in the decisions of the Supreme Court of Canada or to argue that judges are appointed because they appear to be centralist or nationalist in their judicial outlook.

Instead of an explicit bias in favour of Ottawa, what seems more realistic as the cause of provincial concerns is the following pattern. The typical narrow or legalistic interpretation of the BNA Act by judges operating under a pattern of judicial restraint and limited judicial review has been seen to support the national government because the BNA Act itself remains, in theory, a highly centralized Constitution, unreflective of the decentralized pattern of modern Canadian federalism. Perhaps revealing is a study of the Supreme Court undertaken by the Quebec government following the PQ victory in 1976. Released in 1978, the report claimed that there was no specific bias on part of the Supreme Court simply because it was appointed by Ottawa. Any bias resulted instead from the Supreme Court's literal interpretation of a near-unitary document (*Globe and Mail*, October 18, 1978).

Provincial suspicions remain, however, and help to determine some aspects of federal-provincial relations. For example, the provinces are reluctant to settle federal-provincial disputes in the courts if negotiations can possibly resolve the matter. Fear of federal bias has restricted the judicial alternative, as in the case of the Atlantic provinces' refusal to take questions of jurisdiction over offshore oil and natural gas to the Supreme Court for resolution. In the Fall of 1981, federal Energy Minister Marc Lalonde openly dared Nova Scotia and Newfoundland to seek a court ruling, which they declined to do. Thus, one reason for modest judicial involvement in political disputes has been a provincial fear of a federalist bias on the part of the Supreme Court of Canada.

In addition to the perceived centralist bias of the Supreme Court, a second important political element of judicial operation concerns the use of advisory or reference decisions. Unlike some court systems where only actual cases are heard, the Supreme Court of Canada can be asked to rule on matters or legislation before they are implemented. At the request of the governor-in-council (for all practical purposes, the prime minister and cabinet), the Supreme Court will issue an advisory opinion as to the constitutionality of a proposed course of action. Some of the most significant Supreme Court decisions of recent years fall into this category, including the rulings on Senate reform in 1979, the patriation proposal in 1981, and offshore jurisdiction in 1967. Although actual cases might lead to a challenge of an advisory opinion at a later date, the court is unlikely to change its opinion in the near future. An advisory opinion in its favour is an important political resource for either level of government. However, since the provinces cannot ask for advisory opinions from the Supreme Court, but must work their cases up through the hierarchical court system to the final court of appeal, the federal government has a decided advantage in this regard. Moreover, the federal government is unlikely to ask for such Supreme Court advice unless it feels that the court is likely to rule in its favour. If a negative advisory opinion results, the proposed legislation or government action can be modified to take account of the court's objections. If a positive decision is forthcoming for either level of government, then future court action is unlikely, since the side which has lost will seek a negotiated settlement with the other level of government rather than risking an anticipated loss before the Supreme Court.

A third political effect of judicial decisions has been to make the court system one element among many in Canadian political conflicts: "The court's declarations are often viewed as a factor in political bargaining, rather than as decisive statements" (Mc-Menemy, 1980: 146). The determination to take a conflict or dispute into the court system is a political, rather than primarily a legal decision: "One of the most obvious consequences of judicial review is that political questions often come to the courts clothed as legal, constitutional questions" (Fletcher, 1977: 100). A good example of this political use of the judiciary can be seen with respect to Quebec's Keable Commission's powers. Under the direction of Commissioner Jean Keable, the province of Quebec sought to investigate alleged RCMP wrongdoing in the province. In order to do so, the Keable Commission subpoenaed extensive information from the RCMP's secret files. As a federal body, the RCMP resisted, with the full backing of the Liberal government in Ottawa. The federal government proceeded to take the issue to the judiciary, arguing that no province had the right to investigate police matters, which clearly fell under federal jurisdiction. Moreover, since criminal law was a federal responsibility, if the police had broken any such laws, it was a matter for federal prosecution and, thus, not of concern to the provinces. The province of Quebec, with the support of four other provinces, argued that, since the administration of justice was a provincial concern, the province had a constitutional right to

investigate even a federal police agency. The eventual outcome of
this dispute was a court ruling that backed the federal position and
effectively shut down the Keable Commission.

While it was shrouded in legal principles, what was really taking
place was a political battle between the PQ government in Quebec
and the federal Liberals in Ottawa, with each side seeking political
support within the province. The clear intent of the provincial
Keable Commission was to embarrass the federal government and
to thus increase backing for the independence option, while the
purpose of the federal government was to prevent such an investigation so as to protect its own political flank. However, not all judicial
decisions are as definitive as the one on the Keable Commission, so
that a court ruling may not settle the conflict at all. The ruling of
the Supreme Court on the Canada Act in September 1981 is a case in
point: both the federal and provincial governments claimed victory,
with the battle continuing until a politically negotiated resolution
finally settled the matter.

A further aspect concerning the political consequences of court
actions can be seen with respect to judicial protection of the broad
areas of civil and political liberties. As with a constitution, so also
with a bill of rights: the effectiveness of each depends more on their
implementation than on their wording. Key to the maintenance of
human freedoms is the willingness of the court system to use
judicial power to make them effective in practice. A bill of rights or
charter of rights depends, to a considerable extent, on the willingness of citizens to challenge arbitrary governmental actions and on
the political will of the judiciary to prevent political abuses when
they are given the opportunity to do so.

Unfortunately, the record of the Canadian courts in this area is
not encouraging. For example, the judiciary has typically backed the
powers of the state and has resisted any effort to make themselves
the agents of social change (McNaught, 1976: 160). Moreover, in the
past few years, the Supreme Court has made the following kinds of
decisions. The judiciary has ruled that illegally obtained evidence is
admissible in court, with the only recourse left to the citizen a suit
against the individual police officer involved in the alleged wrongdoing. Of course, a person could be in jail a long time before such a suit
was resolved. In a similar vein, the Supreme Court has upheld the
need to have a public permit for demonstrations in the city of
Montreal, under the suspect view that such an assembly of citizens
might lead to a breakdown of public order and safety. As a result,
any group wishing to protest against local politicians such as Mayor

Jean Drapeau has to gain a permit from the city to do so. Needless to say, such permits are often difficult to obtain. Given these kinds of decisions, it seems that the Supreme Court's desire to protect civil and political liberties may have reached a minimum level.

The potential for judicial protection of civil and political liberties has only been modestly enhanced by the Constitution Act of 1982 (see Chapter 12). The major advantage of the Constitution Act is that it applies to both levels of government, rather than to just the federal one. Thus, the basis for judicial activism has been laid, but willingness to use it probably remains untouched. We must remember that it took nearly a decade before the Supreme Court used the previous Bill of Rights to invalidate a federal piece of legislation. Moreover, the Constitution Act contains several mechanisms, such as the override provision in Section 33, by which basic liberties can be circumvented. Those who seek an activist Canadian Supreme Court will find little solace in the 1982 Constitution Act. The traditional reluctant exercise of judicial power will likely remain an element of the Canadian political process.

THE COURT SYSTEM IN BRITAIN

The most important fact about the British judiciary is its lack of direct involvement in the political process. The practice of judicial review is unknown in the current British polity: "no court of law can override the British Parliament, which is supreme" (Verney, 1976: 35). Parliamentary supremacy has rendered unacceptable any exercise of full judicial review concerning the constitutionality of government actions. As long as the government is exercising the powers granted to it, no court will intervene. If a person or group does not like the law, then the opportunity exists to change the law or to replace the lawmakers with new ones through the electoral mechanism.

In addition to the impact of parliamentary supremacy, the unitary structure of the political system has also eliminated the need for the exercise of a pattern of limited judicial review as used in Canada. Since there is no division of powers between levels of government, there is obviously no logical or practical basis for delineating their respective powers. Instead of settling questions of constitutionality, British courts are involved in interpreting executive or legislative actions in light of their statutory or legal basis. If the executive or legislature has overstepped the authority granted to it (i.e., its statutory power), the judiciary may order a halt to such behaviour. In a similar vein, if proper procedures have not been followed, the courts may nullify government actions. However, as long as government behaviour has a statutory basis, the courts will not become involved. Even if executive or legislative actions are overturned, the government may simply pass retroactive legislation, giving itself authority for its previous behaviour and thus bypassing the court ruling. The consequence of a pattern of neither limited nor full judicial review has kept the political role of Britain's third branch of government modest indeed.

The judicial structure is complex in Britain, divided down into both civil and criminal courts. Included in the civil court wing are the county courts and family courts, while at the bottom of the criminal court structure are the justices of the peace and the juvenile courts. Although there is no supreme court in Britain, appeals from the top civil and criminal courts may be sent to the House of Lords, if they involve a matter of general public importance. Technically the appeal is to Parliament, but the House of Lords has been given the specific judicial function of interpreting the laws of Parliament. However, the Lords in general do not hear such appeals; they are heard by only the Lord Chancellor and the ten Law Lords (technically, the Lords of Appeal in Ordinary). The Lord Chancellor is a member of the government and thus changes when there is a government turnover. The Lord Chancellor and prime minister together share the responsibility for selecting members from the legal profession for judicial posts. The British court system operates under the principle of judicial independence, the judges are selected by the executive, and they may be removed for cause.

Given the pattern of no judicial review of government actions and neither a written constitution nor a specific charter of rights, the British polity utilizes a very different mechanism than either Canada or the United States to protect basic civil and political liberties. Instead of delineating citizens' rights in a bill of rights or a charter of rights, individuals in Britain are given all rights not denied to them by law. Fundamental freedoms "rest simply on the age-old assumption by British courts that a citizen is free to do as he likes provided he does not commit any specific breach of the law" (Birch, 1980: 236). Thus, British citizens enjoy such basic rights as freedom of speech and assembly, even though they are unspecified in law.

THE AMERICAN JUDICIARY

In no other political system does the judicial branch of government play as significant or controversial a role as it does in the American. The basic reason for such a pattern is the exercise of full judicial review by the American court system: "Judicial review is the power of the judges, ultimately those of the Supreme Court, to interpret the Constitution and to refuse to enforce those measures that in their opinion are in conflict with the Constitution" (Peltason, 1979: 27). This tremendous power of full judicial review was not contained in Article Three of the American Constitution, but developed from the initial assertion of judicial power by Chief Justice John Marshall in the famous case of *Marbury* v. *Madison* in 1803. While the details of the case are complex, the result was the acceptance of the view that the courts were the official interpreters of constitutional matters in the American system. The political consequences of this development have been extremely significant, for they have made the court system in the United States more politically oriented and more powerful than the judiciary in any other democratic polity.

The structure of the American court system is federalized in the extreme. Unlike the Canadian court system, which creates a hierarchical and unified structure of federal and provincial courts, the American court system has a complete set of both federal and state courts. Moreover, the large municipalities may have their own court system, thus further decentralizing the judicial structure. The jurisdiction of these court systems stems from the powers granted each level of government by the Constitution: federal courts hear cases involving the powers of the national government, while state courts generally consider all other matters. Some areas of jurisdiction may be shared, thus allowing the accused to be tried in either the state or federal courts, but not in both for the same wrongdoing. At the apex of the judiciary stands the American Supreme Court, which under Article Three (Section 2) hears cases involving the national government or matters of dispute between citizens and governments in two or more states. Cases tried in the state courts can only be appealed from the state supreme courts to the national Supreme Court if they involve important matters of constitutional law under federal jurisdiction.

Composition of both the American federal and state court systems is patronage-based and politically motivated to an even greater extent than in Canada. For example, the creation of federal judgeships is a legislative prerogative, although the president nominates, with the advice and consent of the Senate, the individuals to fill the federal judicial positions. If Congress and the presidency are controlled by different parties, then a stalemate over new positions is likely. Moreover, if a presidential election is on the horizon, the party in control of Congress may wait to see if it is also able to win control of the executive branch, thus enhancing its patronage powers. For example, the Democratically-controlled Congress refused to authorize any new judgeships for Republican Gerald Ford, but was willing to create 152 new federal judicial posts for his successor, Democrat Jimmy Carter.

Once the judgeships have been established, the composition of the courts are further politically influenced because of the party basis of judicial selection. The overwhelming percentage of federal judicial appointments are from the same party as the president, with the rate of partisan selection around 90 percent. Moreover, since federal judicial appointments are held for life, judges often retire early or stay on the job, despite ill-health, in an attempt to get a successor to their position modelled on their own image: that is, a Democratic judge will seek to retire when a Democratic president is in office or will hold on to the judgeship in the hopes that the next president is a Democrat. Finally, federal judicial appointments are highly political because of the practice of *senatorial courtesy*. Based on custom rather than on law, senatorial courtesy gives the senator from the state where the judge will serve a "veto" power over who is selected. This customary veto power is especially strong when the senator has the same political affiliation as the president. Moreover, senatorial courtesy is a good example of the political interdependence created by the separation of powers principle: the executive recommends the nominee that the Senate accepts or rejects to fill a vacancy in the judicial structure. The practice of senatorial courtesy can be used to deny a judicial posting not just on partisan grounds, but on ideological and sociopolitical factors as well. Those of liberal or conservative persuasions tend to have an abiding affinity for their own kind: in patronage-inspired appointments, opposites repel.

While federal judges are appointed, many judicial posts are filled by election at the state and local levels. The most significant aspect of electing judges relates to its impact on the principle of judicial independence. Most court systems assume that an appointed judiciary will be insulated from political pressure. However, the various reform movements in American politics, such as Jacksonian democracy, viewed an appointed judiciary as a bastion of elite influence that had to be brought under public control. Electing judges would free the courts from elite manipulation and possible corruption, increasing their independence from big business interests. Judicial election was designed to enhance judicial independence from the special interest groups in society; at the same time, the judiciary was to be made more responsible to the people. In practice, judicial election has rarely interfered with the principle of judicial independence.

For those judges who are appointed, removal from office can occur through two processes: death or impeachment. In the latter and, some would say, more difficult method, the legislature may remove a judge (or any other civil officer of the United States) for improper conduct. Impeachment, however, is not used to make the judiciary politically accountable for its decisions. Technically, impeachment means bringing charges of wrongdoing against an official before the House of Representatives. If the impeachment resolution passes, then the Senate sits as a court to hear evidence and to possibly convict the accused. If convicted by the Senate, individuals are removed from office, at which point they may be prosecuted as any other citizens would be. Only four federal judges have ever been impeached and convicted.

The structure and composition of the American Supreme Court can be described with respect to its size and method of appointment. The size of the Supreme Court is currently nine, a number determined by the legislature. There have been politically motivated attempts to change this number, the most famous being Franklin Roosevelt's court-packing plan of the late 1930s. In responding to the exigencies of the Great Depression, the federal government sought to lead in the revitalization of the American economy. However, a number of laws giving the national government the power to act were held to be unconstitutional by the Supreme Court. By enlarging the size of the Supreme Court, President Roosevelt felt that he could tip the balance of judicial opinion in his favour. The court-packing plan failed to gain approval, but shortly thereafter, the Supreme Court started upholding the constitutionality of Roosevelt's key economic programs. The Supreme Court usually follows the election returns, even if somewhat belatedly.

Appointments to the Supreme Court are less blatantly partisan than those to the federal courts in general, although political considerations are not entirely removed. Rather than partisanship, ideology is a leading criterion in nominees to the highest court, as well as ethnic, racial, and other sociopolitical attributes. These factors are not legally required, but based on custom and convention. For example, the major religious groups often receive appointments, with an attempt made to select at least one Catholic and one Jewish justice. Justice Thurgood Marshall was the first black elevated to the Supreme Court, and President Reagan placed the first woman, Sandra Day O'Connor, on the Supreme Court in 1981. Although presidential nominees to the Supreme Court must receive Senate approval, the custom of senatorial courtesy does not apply. The Senate will typically approve the presidential recommendation, as long as the individual is deemed qualified. President Nixon had two nominees rejected by the Senate, not because they were conservative and the Senate was liberal, but because they were deemed not to be among the best qualified conservatives available. Once appointed, Supreme Court justices may be removed by impeachment and conviction, but no justice has ever been so treated and removed from office (one justice was impeached, but not convicted).

The operation of the American court system is based on the principles of judicial independence and *stare decisis*, with the Supreme Court standing as the highest court of appeal. Judicial independence is sometimes challenged, particularly when individuals or groups disagree with the content of court rulings. A movement may be undertaken to remove a particular judge, such as the attempt to impeach Chief Justice Earl Warren in the 1960s, or to overturn a court decision by passing new legislation to make a judicial interpretation inapplicable. The most blatant attempts in recent memory to threaten judicial independence were evident in the Watergate episode, particularly the suggestion by the Nixon White House that they might ignore adverse court rulings, even those coming from the Supreme Court itself. The second operating principle, that of *stare decisis*, helps to provide a degree of continuity in a judicial system with over 10 000 federal and state judges.

Several unique aspects of judicial operation are characteristic of the American court system. First, before a case can be taken to court the individual or group must be recognized as having "standing to sue," that is, the right to utilize the judicial alternative. In the American legal system only those who are directly affected by a law or government action have the right to challenge it in court. Trumped up cases or those designed simply to allow judicial involvement do not have "standing to sue" and are rejected by the courts. A second unique aspect relates to the nature of the cases presented: a law or government action can only be challenged after it has been implemented. The American judiciary does not give advisory or reference opinions on hypothetical cases. If the executive or legislature is unsure of the constitutionality of a proposed bill, the only thing they can do is to pass it into law and be preprared for possible judicial intervention at a later date. Third, the Supreme Court itself decides which cases it will hear from the thousands presented to it annually for possible consideration. Usually, only several hundred are selected and these are the cases the justices feel have broad public and constitutional significance.

The crucial element in the operation of the American judiciary is the previously explained principle of full judicial review, the basic reason for the often extensive political impact of court decisions. The pattern of full judicial review has given to the Supreme Court an inherent policy-making role, so that major areas of political conflict become matters for judicial, rather than executive or legislative, resolution.

> In recent years the federal courts have taken the lead in eliminating segregation in public life, ensuring the separation of church and state, defining relationships between individuals and law enforcers, guaranteeing individual voters an equal voice in government, and establishing the right of women to obtain abortions (Dye, 1977: 186).

The exercise of full judicial review is particularly crucial in defence of the civil and political liberties established by the American Bill of Rights. Initially, the Bill of Rights applied only to the national government – no protection was given the citizen from the state and local levels of government. This pattern began to change in the 1920s, when the Supreme Court, in an exercise of judicial power perhaps only surpassed by the *Marbury* v. *Madison* decision of 1803, asserted the applicability of fundamental freedoms to all levels of government. This use of the power of judicial review had the effect of nationalizing the American Bill of Rights, thus providing the political basis for an even more activist Supreme Court in American politics in later decades.

The American judiciary, backed by the various checks and balances, operating under the principle of full judicial review, composed of judges often willing to exercise their potential for power, and repeatedly jump-started into action by a litigious citizenry, has played a significant and, at times, a crucial role in the political process. This combination of factors has given the American Supreme Court a powerful and "often decisive role" in the polity, while at the same time making it the most "unique judicial body in the world" (Oddo, 1979: v).

COMPARING JUDICIARIES: POLITICS, PATRONAGE, AND POLICY

In considering the nature of the judicial branch of government in the democratic polities of Canada, Britain, and the United States, four factors have been analyzed as the basis of comparison: the structure, composition, operation, and consequences of the court systems. Such comparisons stress the role of the judiciary in the political process with respect to three areas: politics, patronage, and policy. Contrary to the legitimating myth of their noninvolvement in the political arena, the judiciaries in democratic polities are intimately involved in political conflicts and the struggle for power and influence. The principle of judicial independence has *not* transformed the third branch of government into a political eunuch, impotent in its relationship with the executive and legislature.

The political nature of the judiciary is clearly evident with respect to the process of judicial selection: in most cases, the court system remains a bastion of political patronage in a democratic era. Judges are often created from among those individuals with past or present partisan ties. Such a criterion does not automatically produce either good or bad judges, for partisan affiliation is not necessarily a causal factor of judicial competence. Probably the most debilitating effect of a patronage-based selection process for judicial appointments is its impact on the legitimacy of judicial power in the eyes of the public. Since the effectiveness of a court ruling is heavily dependent on the public's acceptance of the judicial decision, any factor that undercuts the legitimacy of the judiciary should be a prime area for political reform.

Judges and their actions are also political because of the ideological views brought by them to the bench, which serve as an important factor in the process and content of judicial interpretation. Since judges typically serve long terms of office, these views may continue to have a political impact long after the politicians who appointed the judges have disappeared from the political landscape. Moreover, individual judicial temperament is also an ingredient in producing a pattern of judicial activism or judicial restraint. Some judges are willing to exercise their constitutional powers to the fullest, at times even expanding them, while other judges are content to take a narrow view of their own political role. Finally, judges are political with respect to their constitutionally-defined roles, which can range from no judicial review to limited judicial review to full judicial review. The particular type of judicial review helps to create a specific style of judicial activism or judicial restraint: the greater the powers of judicial review, the greater is the potential for an activist judiciary. Whatever the type of judicial review, the court system is a political player that is sometimes given a bit part and on other occasions a leading role in the polity.

SUMMARY

1. The judicial branch of government is a significant political actor, especially in democratic polities. Basic operating principles of a democratic judiciary include the concept of judicial independence and the interpretive guideline of *stare decisis*. Configurations of judicial review range from its absence in Britain to a limited judicial review process in Canada to full judicial review in the United States. The type of constitutionally-prescribed judicial review is an important ingredient in creating a pattern of either judicial activism or judicial restaint.

2. The Canadian court system is patronage-based and hierarchically organized, even though responsibility for it is shared by the federal and provincial governments. Since 1949, the Supreme Court of Canada has become the highest appeals court, replacing the Judicial Committee of the Privy Council in Britain. Appointed by the federal government, the Supreme Court is viewed with suspicion by the provinces who are reluctant to take federal-provincial disputes into the court system. Operating under the principles of limited judicial review and judicial self-restraint, the judicial branch has nevertheless had significant political consequences for the Canadian polity. Judicial interpretations, for example, have historically been an important ingredient in the evolving pattern of federal-provincial power. However, with respect to judicial protection of civil and political liberties, the Canadian pattern leaves much to be desired. If past performance is any guide to the future, then the Constitution Act of 1982, which increases the potential for an activist judiciary, will have little immediate impact on the traditionally reluctant exercise of power by the Canadian courts.

3. Given the principle of parliamentary sovereignty, judicial review is unknown in the British context. While courts will rule on whether executive or legislative actions are within the statutory powers of these two branches of government, a redress of grievances in Britain must be politically, rather than judicially obtained.

4. The most powerful judiciary in any democratic system is the American, which is also the one most widely selected on the basis of patronage. The custom of senatorial courtesy gives the national legislature control of most federal court appointments, while at the state and local levels a majority of states now elect their judges. The structure of the American court system is federalized, with a complete set of both state and federal courts. The highest court of appeal is the United States Supreme Court, which has often played a significant political role, given the principle of full judicial review. As a consequence, the American judiciary is activist in outlook and intimately involved in the political process, often taking the lead in new areas of public concern, especially when the executive or legislature is reluctant to do so.

RECOMMENDED READINGS

The Nature of Judicial Power

CARDOZO, BENJAMIN (1921) *The Nature of the Judicial Process.* New Haven, Conn.: Yale University Press.

ELY, JOHN HART (1980) *Democracy and Distrust: A Theory of Judicial Review.* Cambridge, Mass.: Harvard University Press.

The Canadian Judicial System

BERGER, THOMAS R. (1981) *Fragile Freedoms: Human Rights and Dissent in Canada.* Toronto: Clarke, Irwin and Co.

FRIEDENBERG, EDGAR Z. (1980) *Deference to Authority: The Case of Canada.* White Plains, N.Y.: M. E. Sharpe, Inc.

LEDERMAN, W.R. (1981) *Continuing Canadian Constitutional Dilemmas.* Toronto: Butterworths. See especially Part III, "The Canadian Judicial System," pp. 107–225.

McNAUGHT, KENNETH (1975) "Political Trials and the Canadian Political Tradition," in Martin L. Friedland, ed., *Courts and Trials.* Toronto: University of Toronto Press, pp. 137–161.

RUSSELL, PETER (1977) "The Anti-Inflation Case: The Anatomy of a Constitutional Decision," *Canadian Public Administration,* Vol. 20. Part 4 (Winter), pp. 632–665.

———— (1975) "Judicial Power in Canada's Political Culture," in Martin L. Friedland, ed., *Courts and Trials.* Toronto: University of Toronto Press, pp. 75–88.

WEILER, PAUL (1974) *In the Last Resort: A Critical Study of the Supreme Court of Canada.* Toronto: Carswell/Methuen.

The Court System in Britain

BIRCH, ANTHONY H. (1980) *The British System of Government.* London: George Allen and Unwin, 4th ed., Ch. 15, "The Rights of the Citizen," pp. 235–253.
VERNEY, DOUGLAS V. (1976) *British Government and Politics.* New York: Harper and Row, 3rd ed., pp. 95–100.

The American Judiciary

COX, ARCHIBALD (1976) *The Role of the Supreme Court in American Government.* New York: Oxford University Press.
ODDO, GILBERT L. (1979) *Freedom and Equality: Civil Liberties and the Supreme Court.* Santa Monica, Calif.: Goodyear Publishing Co.
WOODWARD, BOB and SCOTT ARMSTRONG (1979) *The Brethren: Inside the Supreme Court.* New York: Simon and Schuster.

PART THREE

Political Processes and Political Behaviour

7 POLITICAL CULTURE: THE BELIEFS AND VALUES OF THE POLITY

It is not on political forms, it is on political forces that I dwell.... To really understand the character of social action, its modes of procedure must be studied in light of the character of those who apply them, and of the social and political conditions in which their wills are formed and manifested (Ostrogorski, 1902).

I am convinced that the most advantageous situation and the best possible laws cannot maintain a constitution in spite of the customs of a country; while the latter may turn to some advantage the most unfavorable positions and the worst laws (de Tocqueville, 1835).

Institutions are living things, and they do not easily yield their secrets to the printed word. Predominantly, that is not because they are in themselves mysterious. It is rather because they change with changes in the environment within which they operate, and partly because they differ, from one moment to the other, in terms of the men who operate them (Laski, 1940:1).

THE FOCUS OF OSTROGORSKI on political forces rather than political forms, of de Tocqueville on customs rather than on laws, and of Laski on people and their environment rather than on institutions all stress the importance of political values and beliefs in comprehending and analyzing the political process. Each polity attaches a particular combination of meanings to its political structures and political practices. An understanding of this subjective aspect of political action is necessary, for it provides the context within which the political system operates: "politics makes sense only when we know the political culture, the pattern of thinking and meaning, that participants share" (Bell and Tepperman, 1979: 1).

POLITICAL CULTURE: DEFINITION AND TYPES

As a concept that stresses the meaning of politics for the individual participant, as well as for the wider political community, *political culture* can be defined as the attitudes and beliefs people have about the political system: it is a "shorthand expression to denote the emotional and attitudinal environment within which the political system operates" (Kavanagh, 1972: 10). A political culture defines the nature and scope of legitimate political activity, the attitudes towards various political institutions and processes, and the individual's role in the polity. From the individual's perspective his or her political self or political identity is a specific combination of the major themes of a country's political culture, while from the viewpoint of the political system, the political culture of a country is the total combination or mixture of political attitudes held by its members. A country's political culture reflects its history and shapes its future, while it influences the present operation of the polity.

Types of Political Culture
Numerous ways of classifying political cultures have been developed. For our purposes, the most useful typologies are those that relate political culture to the role of the individual in the political process, focus on the degree of consensus in political values, or link political cultures to their ideological composition.

The role of the individual in the polity can be used as the basis for classifying political cultures as parochial, subject, or participant (Almond and Verba, 1965: 11–26). A *parochial political culture* is one in which a specific political system has not developed and hence no particular role has been assumed for the individual. In a sense, then, these systems are prepolitical. While no pure parochial cultures remain in the modern era, pockets of parochialism may exist within other systems. For example, a so-called national government in a capital city, headed by an autocrat, may have no relevance to isolated rural groups, which remain apolitical or parochial in outlook. In a *subject political culture*, the individual is aware of the specialized political structure, is affected by its decisions, such as paying taxes or serving in the army, and may accept the legitimacy of the system. The role of the individual is a passive one, however, confined to obeying the decisions of the state. A *participant political culture* is one in which the person is given an explicit political role, with various opportunities provided for participation.

All political cultures represent a mixture of parochial, subject, and participant orientations. For example, at the individual level, each person reflects a unique combination of political values as part of his or her political self, values that likely include subject ones (e.g., a willingness to obey laws) as well as participant ones (e.g., a desire to vote or to influence political leaders). At the system level, each political culture is mixed in the sense that different regions, classes, and ethnic groups may have varying conceptions of politics. Thus, one region might be classified as more participant or more subject in outlook than other regions in the same system. Generally speaking, democratic systems have participant political cultures, autocratic systems usually have a combination of subject and parochial values, while totalitarian systems stress subject orientations with participant values grafted on.

A second way of classifying political cultures is dependent on their degree of unity with respect to fundamental political values. On this basis, two types of political culture can be identified, with many possible variations between these extremes. A *fragmented political culture* is "one whose population lacks broad agreement upon the way in which political life should be conducted," while an *integrated political culture* has developed a consensus about a core set of political beliefs (Rosenbaum, 1975: 37-57).

In a fragmented political culture, many people identify with governmental units other than the national government; patriotism and national identity are weak; distrust between the major sociopolitical groups is evident and often widespread; and the legitimacy of the existing political regime may be in question, as various sectors of the polity demand major changes in the social, economic, and political structure. Fragmentation may be based on factors of race, religion, class, ethnicity, region, or language. When these various bases of fragmentation coalesce, conflict and violence may erupt, which further decreases the level of unity in the polity. Highly fragmented political cultures may spawn movements or parties that demand separation or independence from the larger political system.

In contrast, an integrated political culture is characterized by identification with the national government; strong patriotic sentiments; a moderate to high level of social trust; acceptance of the existing social, political, and economic arrangements; and rare occurrences of open conflict and secessionist threats. Fragmented political cultures are often associated with unstable political systems, for the bases of such fragmentation may be unresolvable through normal political processes. For example, questions of language, culture, and religion are often so intense that the political system may be torn asunder. Integrated political cultures have either dealt successfully with such issues in the past or they have managed to keep such issues from becoming focal points of contention. For example, the doctrine of the separation of church and state in Western society is one way of keeping religious issues from becoming politicized. The fragmented or integrated nature of a country's political culture influences the way in which the political institutions are structured initially, as well as how they continue to function.

Our third way of analyzing political cultures focuses on their attitudinal and ideological composition: what are the specific beliefs that comprise their core elements? For example, such values as nationalism and social trust have often been seen as key elements of political culture. From a somewhat broader perspective, we might focus on a political culture's ideological mixture in terms of the major political ideas of the modern era: conservatism, liberalism, and socialism. The ideological approach to political culture emphasizes the content of beliefs, while the fragmented-integrated distinction focuses on the degree of consensus evident with respect to these fundamental political values.

Each of the three approaches to political culture suggests that a specific political culture will not only be complex, but also mixed, comprising a variety of values and beliefs not necessarily consistent with each other. What often happens is that certain segments of the polity acquire a set of beliefs that distinguishes them from the dominant pattern. We refer to such a pattern as a *political subculture*. These subcultures may be based on any of the major socioeconomic cleavages such as class, religion, race, and ethnicity, as well as around a particular ideology. When such factors not only distinguish a group from the dominant pattern, but also place the group in a specific geographical location, then we refer to the subculture as a *regional political culture* (Landes, 1979). Some political cultures lack any subcultures, while others have many. Generally, we would expect, for example, that integrated political cultures based on one dominant ideology would be unlikely to produce subcultures, while fragmented political cultures with a mixture of ideological beliefs might contain several distinctive subcultures.

THE CANADIAN POLITICAL CULTURE

The pattern of core political beliefs in Canada can be summarized with respect to four major themes: elitism, regionalism, dualism, and continentalism. Each one has had a significant impact on the structure and operation of the political system. After analyzing these themes, we will discuss their interaction by taking a look at the nature of consociational politics in Canada.

Our first major theme is that of *elitism*, which can be defined as a pattern of decision-making in which "small groups of people ... exercise considerable power" (McMenemy, 1980: 95). While it is difficult to put an exact figure on the size of the elite, it is quite likely a very small group, based on any kind of percentage figure in comparison with the total population. A figure of one percent, for example, would produce an elite of 240 000 members, given the 1981 census figure of 24 000 000 Canadians. Some, including this author, would argue that such an estimate is much too large. But for our purposes, an elite is a small group with both control over the crucial political resources and a willingness and ability to use such resources to determine the outcome of the decision-making process. Moreover, the elite is not a unified grouping, but, as our definition indicates, is composed of a series of subgroupings. For example, democratic polities are usually seen as having a plurality of elites, which would, at least, include political, economic and bureaucratic components. The exact nature of the Canadian elites – with respect to their structure, composition, and influence – is a controversial topic. However, observers agree on one conclusion: the various elites are seen as exercising considerable clout in the Canadian context (Panitch, 1981; Forcese, 1978; Presthus, 1973).

Evidence of elitism is pervasive in the Canadian system. For example, the Official Secrets Act prohibits disclosure of government information, even if that information has nothing to do with national security, although it might have something to do with the governing party's political security. Moreover, the federal government can, on its own initiative and authority, impose the War

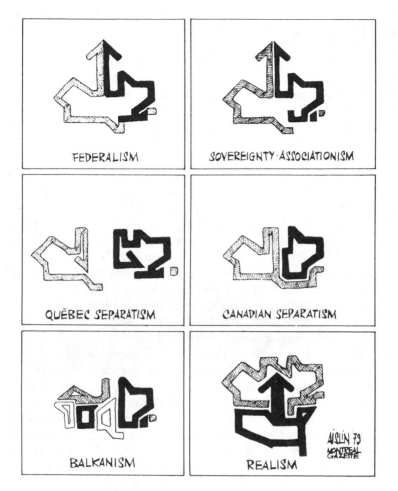

FEDERALISM

SOVEREIGNTY-ASSOCIATIONISM

QUÉBEC SEPARATISM

CANADIAN SEPARATISM

BALKANISM

REALISM

AISLIN 79
MONTREAL GAZETTE

Measures Act, which in effect places the entire polity under martial law. Canada has been governed by such means during the October Crisis of 1970 and throughout both world wars. The longest imposition of the War Measures Act occurred between 1939 and 1954, although the period from 1945 to 1954 was less restrictive than a full imposition of governmental control would have allowed. During this 15-year period Canada was governed by what can be described as a constitutional dictatorship – a not so inaccurate description of politics in Canada even when the War Measures Act is not in place.

The elitist pattern of Canadian politics is also evident in numerous actions by which governments can exempt themselves from the existing rules of the game. For example, cutbacks in Via Rail service during the Summer of 1981 were done on the authority of an order-in-council (i.e., a cabinet decision) rather than by legislation, wherein the government exempted itself from the authority of the Canadian Transport Commission to rule on such matters. An order-in-council was also used to implement the "gag law" with respect to Canada's alleged participation in an international uranium cartel. When accusations of wrongdoing began to be heard in the mid-1970s, primarily as a result of the release of information and the findings of several investigations in the United States, the Canadian cabinet issued a regulation in 1976 that prohibited the release or disclosure of any documents relating to "production, import, export, transportation, refining, possession, ownership, use or sale of uranium or its derivatives or compounds" between 1972 and 1975. Even the 1960 Bill of Rights could have been bypassed if the government so wished, simply by the government declaring that a specific law was exempted from its protection (Bill of Rights, Part 1, Section 2). The ability of the government to override certain protections in the new Charter of Rights and to circumvent existing laws or to pass new regulations to protect its own possible wrongdoing can only occur in a political system in which influence is centralized and accepted as legitimate by most people – in other words, in a polity characterized by elitism.

Consistent with an elitist pattern of control are deferential attitudes towards authority, limited means for citizen participation, and political structures that embody such values. Deferential views of authority can be seen in Canada's continuing ties to the monarchy and traditional forms of authority: after all, monarchical institutions are historically based on the assumption that a small group has a right to rule. It must also be remembered that the Fathers of Confederation were not fervent believers in democracy: Confederation itself was more of an attempt to stop democratic ideas from crossing the Canadian border than it was a means for the extension of the democratic ideal. The political system constructed in 1867 was federal, but it was a highly centralized structure in which few citizens participated. Indicative perhaps of what lay ahead were the methods used to create the new system: the "procedures restricted effective participation to a very small number of persons, and even symbolic participation by the voters was virtually excluded" (Stevenson, 1979: 45).

Although the polity has become democratized during the past century, reflected best by the extension of the suffrage, few direct avenues for political participation are provided. Other than voting in federal, provincial, or local contests, most citizens rarely seek to

influence their leaders between elections – an attitude and behaviour pattern encouraged by the political elite itself. Typical of the
elite view of the public's participatory task is that expressed many
times by Pierre Trudeau: "he says that the role of the government is
to govern, and the role of the public is to judge him on the quality of
his performance when he chooses to call an election" (Stewart,
1971: 103). Such a pattern of limited mass participation has been
classified as "quasi-participative politics" (Presthus, 1973: 38). A
good example of quasi-participative politics can be seen in the rare
use of the referendum: the public is only asked to decide on an issue
when the elite chooses, but even when a referendum is held, the
results do not bind a government to any specific policy. The last
time a referendum was held in national politics was in 1942 over the
conscription issue during World War Two. The vote (80 percent in
favour in the English-speaking provinces and 72 percent against in
Quebec) served to release Mackenzie King from his no-conscription
promise.

A number of historical developments have contributed to the
strength of elitist values in Canada. In addition to the monarchical
ties, Canada has not experienced a revolution, but has evolved
slowly towards nationhood. The political culture of an evolutionary
pattern of development is more conservative and traditional than a
revolutionary society, perhaps best symbolized by the phrase in the
BNA Act that describes its purpose as "Peace, Order, and Good
Government." Confederation was an act of counterrevolution,
which sought to preserve the power of the elite. Moreover, such
factors as the hierarchical class system, (e.g., the Family Com-
pacts); the non-egalitarian school system, dominated by the private
schools such as Upper Canada College; religious groups, such as the
Anglicans and Roman Catholics, which are hierarchically organized; and a weak sense of national identity have all helped to
produce and to preserve elitist values in the Canadian context
(Lipset, 1970). In particular, the governmental structure embodies
and perpetuates the significance of elitism.

> What insulates the elites in the British Commonwealth countries is the
> political system. The cabinet-parliamentary system with its disciplined
> legislative parties, which fuse executive and legislative powers in the
> cabinet, makes for a governmental system strong enough to withstand
> very great public pressure.... The effect of the British parliamentary
> system is to damp down the waves of public agitation (Truman, 1971:
> 511-512).

The second major theme of the political culture is that of *regional-ism*, a reflection of the fact that "nature and history have conspired to make geography central to the Canadian existence (Schwartz, 1974: 1). Regionalism is both a cause and consequence of the regional political cultures, producing different patterns of politics across the country. As an old saying about Canadian politics puts it, in the Atlantic area politics is patronage, in Quebec a religion, in Ontario a business, in the Prairies a protest, and in British Colum-bia entertainment. Regionalism is so pervasive that it is rarely overlooked, although once in the late 1970s the Canada Day celebra-tions in Ottawa forgot to include New Brunswick as one of the participants. Similarly, in 1977, an individual from Newfoundland who applied for a job in a Toronto hospital was told that foreigners were not hired and that before his request could be seriously considered he would have to seek landed immigrant status (*Globe and Mail*, September 16, 1977). In a more serious vein, regionalism is a continuing political issue with respect to constitutional reform, as well as in relation to everyday political decisions. For example, in 1978, the British Columbia government asserted that in any revised constitution the province must receive official recognition as a distinct region, rather than being grouped as simply a part of Western Canada. With respect to policy making, almost every major decision, whether it concerns unemployment insurance benefits or Via Rail cutbacks, has differing consequences for the various regions of Canada.

Regionalism reflects diversity of geographic factors and economic concerns that are politically important and are perceived as such by members of the political system. However, it is difficult to specify precisely the nature of the regional units in the Canadian system. With few exceptions, most writers have assumed that the prov-inces, or some combination thereof, adequately delineate regional boundaries. The first technique is to equate provincial boundaries with regional units. For example, in a significant article, John Wilson (1974: 440) argues that there "must be at least one political culture for every independent political system." Since the provinces are such independent units, they each have a separate political culture. The second way of defining regions is to group various provinces together to form larger political units. The most typical way is to combine the eastern provinces together as either the Maritime or Atlantic provinces and the Western provinces together as either the Prairies and British Columbia or as simply the West. The usual rationale for such groupings is that the various provinces within each region are seen as relatively homogeneous in nature.

The grouping of several provinces together to form a single region, however, has been questioned in recent investigations of the Canadian political culture. For example, the Maritime/Atlantic region is dismissed by those most familiar with the area as a reflection of the "annoying tendency of Canadians west of New Brunswick to assume the existence of an integrated Atlantic region" (Cameron, 1971: 25). The further one is removed from the area, the greater is the commonality perceived. Such a conclusion is demonstrated, perhaps, by British Columbia's constitutional reform proposals of 1978, which called for the formal union of the Atlantic provinces into a single political entity. Within the Eastern provinces the notion of a Maritime Union has no appeal, while outside of the area it is still seen, at times, as a viable option. In analyzing the supposed commonality among the Eastern provinces, Professor Murray Beck (1977: 16) came to the conclusion that "the familiar entity, the Maritime Provinces ... has no existence." In the following analysis, we will assume that regional boundaries, more often than not, coalesce around the provincial units.

While such considerations should caution us against grouping various provinces together to form larger regions, we should also be aware that equating provinces and region may lead us to neglect the extent of diversity within each provincial unit. The provinces themselves are not necessarily homogeneous in either socioeconomic structure or in political attitudes. For example, considerable differences in quality of life and political values are evident between northern and southern Ontario, between northwestern and southeastern New Brunswick, between Cape Breton Island and mainland Nova Scotia, and between northeastern British Columbia and the crowded southern mainland. Such internal differences are true of every province, although they are minimal in the smallest province of Prince Edward Island.

Having discussed the nature of regionalism and the ways in which regional units have typically been classified, we can now deal specifically with the content of the regional political cultures in Canada. The regional political cultures are, in effect, a series of political subcultures based around the territorially defined provincial units. These political subcultures reflect differences in the economic base of each region, their access to and abundance of natural resources, their rate of economic development and modernization, and the varying effects of urbanization and industrialization. The result of such factors has been to produce a series of regional economies. As one study by the Economic Council of Canada (1977: 212) put it, "no amount of juggling with statistics can lead any reasonable person to deny that economic well-being is sharply affected by the region in which one happens to be born or brought up. In short, disparities are real." In addition to economic indicators, the various regions of Canada differ with respect to their cultural, linguistic, and ethnic composition. English-French differences are important in Quebec, Ontario, and New Brunswick, but less so in the remaining provinces. The idea of bilingualism in these regions may be popular and refer to the English and French languages, while in Cape Breton, English and Gaelic and in Saskatchewan, English and Ukrainian would be the two most useful languages to know. The various regions also differ with respect to their religious composition and class structures.

The consequences of the regional economies and of the varying social and cultural make-up of each province have been the production of differences in political values and behaviour, that is, the creation of a series of regional political cultures. These regional cultures are distinctive in terms of their core beliefs, reflected in individual attitudes toward and active participation in the political process (Schwartz, 1974). For example, a study by Simeon and Elkins (1974) found significant variations among the regional political cultures in terms of political efficacy and political trust. Based on answers to a series of questions from national political surveys, the Simeon and Elkins' analysis discovered that individuals in the Atlantic provinces ranked low on the efficacy indicators, while persons in Ontario and British Columbia reflected high efficacy ratings. With respect to political trust, individuals in Ontario, British Columbia, Manitoba, and Saskatchewan rated high, while those persons in the Eastern provinces, especially in New Brunswick, ranked low. Overall, they concluded that "there are strong differences among the citizens of Canadian provinces ... in some basic orientations to politics" (Simeon and Elkins, 1974: 432).

In addition to variations in efficacy and trust, the regional political cultures are distinctive with respect to attitudes towards specific aspects of the political process. For example, although patronage occurs in all of the provinces, it is seen as a legitimate activity in some (the Atlantic provinces and until the mid-1970s in Quebec), an unsavoury practice in others (Saskatchewan), and a tolerated activity, as long as it remains limited and out of public view, in provinces like Ontario. Moreover, the regional political cultures often exhibit different types of parties and party systems (Wilson, 1974). In British Columbia, the two main provincial competitors are the Social Credit and New Democratic parties, although in other provinces, like Nova Scotia, neither party has had much success. Parties in Quebec are nationalist in orientation, a rare concern for parties in the other provinces. Such differences in parties and party systems, attitudes toward patronage and the political process, and feelings of efficacy and trust are some of the core values that distinguish the regional political cultures in the Canadian system.

Paralleling the variations in basic political orientations, the regional political cultures are also seen as composed of individuals with regional loyalties and identities. Regionalism implies a perceived commonality, that is, a regional consciousness among the individuals within each of the political units. On a general level people do recognize regional divisions and they do express an identity along regional lines (Clarke et al., 1979: 41-66). However, these regional identities are both very general and unsophisticated among many individuals. Given the significance of regionalism in the Canadian polity, the level of regional consciousness among the mass public is lower than might be expected. We would suggest that regional consciousness may be strongly felt by the political elites in a country, while it is only weakly or modestly perceived by the mass public. This elite-mass distinction could account for a pattern whereby relatively low regional consciousness exists among the Canadian public, while at the same time regionalism remains a vital element affecting the operation of the polity.

Such an interpretation reveals that regionalism, in addition to being a major characteristic of the Canadian political culture, is also a valuable political resource, which the federal and provincial political elites seek to manipulate in order to enhance their own influence and power. For example, federal political leaders can argue that a strong central government in Ottawa is needed so that they can preserve national unity by overcoming the deleterious effects of regionalism. In contrast, provincial political leaders demand greater powers from the federal government so that they can fulfill the regional aspirations of their constituents. Conveniently, such a demand also helps to insulate the provincial political elites from their own people. As long as a province is fighting with Ottawa or the other provinces over regional interests, then political support at home is increased, since it is difficult to attack a government that is seen as the defender of provincial interests in the larger political system. As a result, those parties in control of a provincial government prefer to run against Ottawa in a provincial election campaign than against the provincial opposition parties. These ideas suggest that, once the pattern of regionalism became established in Canada, it has been maintained more as a result of elite perceptions and behaviour than because of the attitudes held by the mass public (Gibbins, 1982: 188).

The presence of regionalism and the regional political cultures has significantly affected the structure, operation, and customs of the Canadian political system. For example, with respect to the political structure, Canada was made a federal system in order to preserve the various regions in existence at the time of Confederation. Explicit recognition of Canada's regional nature is reflected in the structure of the Senate and the House of Commons, as well as in relation to many other institutions of government. Moreover, the decision-making process, both federal or provincial, must continuously deal with the regional implications and possible consequences of any issue, whether it is one of constitutional reform, economic development, or social policy. Finally, the customs and conventions of the Canadian polity are rife with regional practices, perhaps best exemplified by the representation of the provinces within the federal cabinet.

The third major theme of political culture is *dualism*, that is, the impact of and relationship between Canada's major cultural groups. While Canada has become a multicultural society, especially since World War II, the political system has been slow to accommodate such changes. Instead, the political structure reflects and the major concern of domestic politics focuses on the continuing problems between the two "charter groups." In addition, the pattern of dualism has combined with regionalism to produce Canada's most distinctive political subculture in Quebec.

As the largest minority group in the political system, which has continually feared its fate at the hands of the English-speaking majority, French Canada has developed several unique political values. First and foremost French Canada, which in recent decades has become increasingly concentrated within the province of Quebec, has used the political process as a means of cultural defence. The key concern of French Canada has always been a preservation of its language and culture. As a result, the relationship between Quebec and the other provinces and Ottawa, as well as the nature of politics within Quebec itself, has focused on the values of nationalism. It is not by chance that the provincial legislature in Quebec is named the National Assembly. Moreover, all parties in Quebec, whether at the federal or provincial levels, are nationalist in orientation. It is ironic, perhaps, that within the provincial party system there has not been a serious "federalist" party competing for at least several decades, while the party that represents Quebec in the national legislature in Ottawa is the one perceived to be the best defender of French-Canadian interests in the federal system.

The necessity for cultural defence, combined with an agrarian society and hierarchical church structure, helped to produce an adherence to the values of centralized authority and elitism within the traditional political culture in Quebec (McRoberts and Posgate, 1980). As a result, the political orientations in French Canada have usually been classified as parochial and subject in nature, at least in comparison to the more participant values of English Canada. A reflection of such beliefs, perhaps, was the late extension of the suffrage to women in Quebec, an enfranchisement that was about two decades later than in other provinces. The lack of participant values was typified by French Canada's attitude toward democracy: "French Canadians have not really believed in democracy for themselves ..." (Trudeau, 1968: 103). Parliamentary democracy was foreign in origin and design, and instead of being used as a mechanism for the democratization of Quebec society, it became a means for the defence of French-Canadian interests in the larger federal system.

A third attribute of traditional political values is revealed in attitudes toward the proper role of the state in the Quebec polity. Historically, the role of the state has been limited in Quebec, with the scope of governmental activity and purpose narrowly conceived. This core value of "anti-statism" is illustrated by the pattern of economic development under Maurice Duplessis: "it was assumed that economic processes should remain in the hands of private interests; the economic responsibility of the provincial government was to facilitate the pursuit by private interests of their own objectives" (McRoberts and Posgate, 1980: 61). What was true of the economy was applicable to other sectors as well, including the areas of both social and political reform. Quebec was a late entrant into the era of the expansive welfare state.

The characteristics of the traditional political culture in Quebec thus included a defence of the French language and culture and a resulting emphasis on nationalist values, acceptance of a centralized authority and a pattern of elite decision-making, and a negative view of the role of the state in the political process. Such attributes were dominant through the 1950s, but beginning with the Quiet Revolution in the 1960s, several of these core values were fundamentally altered. While the defence of the French-Canadian community remained fundamental, the method of survival was changed. Rather than defending the status quo, Quebec began demanding greater powers from the federal government so that the provincial unit could more adequately preserve French Canada's language and culture. Paralleling these new powers was a change in attitude towards the role of the state. Government acquired positive functions, with a corresponding increase in the scope and extent of state activity. Two prime examples are the creation of Hydro-Quebec in the early 1960s and the James Bay project in the 1970s. Greater powers for defence led inexorably to an increased role for government in matters of social, economic, and political reform. Moreover, such changes modified the participatory elements of the political culture, moving Quebec into the forefront of democratic sentiments. For example, the use of the referendum in May 1980 is revealing in that the public was seen as a necessary source of legitimacy for any move towards the independence option, a view uncharacteristic of the previous elitist pattern of decision-making. Legislation regarding the public funding of election campaigns and the control of political party finance has helped to make Quebec a leader in democratic reforms in recent years. Thus, several of Quebec's traditional core political values have been modified, but constant throughout has been a concern for defending the language and culture of French Canada.

Much of the continuing conflict between English and French Canada is reflected in concerns over language, perhaps best summarized in Richard Joy's (1972) *bilingual belt thesis*, which argues that a bilingual zone around Quebec increasingly isolates an English unilingual population from a French one. This buffer zone extends roughly from Sault Ste. Marie, Ontario, to Moncton, New Brunswick. While the Canada of the 19th century was a linguistic checkerboard of various languages, in the 20th century, English and French have become dominant. Moreover, these two preeminent languages have been increasingly separated on both a geographical and a practical basis. Within the territorial boundaries of the bilingual belt live over 90 percent of those claiming French as their mother tongue. In terms of language use, bilingualism is most often found among those with French as their initial language, although a very small percentage of the total population is bilingual. The result of such a configuration is that, while Canada may be officially a bilingual country, it is overwhelmingly composed of unilingual citizens (Joy, 1972: 3-15).

A number of historical factors help to explain the development of such a pattern. Within the bilingual belt, the French language has been preserved because it is used in daily discourse, while outside it is dying the slow death of assimilation from nonuse and from the preference for English in terms of the economic system. Moreover, those pockets of French culture in English Canada have lost more than the battle of language use: in recent decades, additional French-speaking immigration into those areas has dwindled to negligible levels, while young people who want to live in a French milieu are increasingly returning to Quebec. Inside Quebec, the birth rate has changed from the highest in Canada to the lowest, while the large waves of non-English and non-French immigration into Quebec have overwhelmingly chosen English as their new language. Moreover, French-Canadian emigration from Quebec has historically gone to the United States rather than to other areas of the Canadian system. On the basis of these historical trends, Joy (1972: 135) concludes that "two languages of unequal strength cannot co-exist in intimate contact and that the weaker must, inevitably, disappear."

In an attempt to prevent such a development, both the federal government in Ottawa and the provincial governments in Quebec have passed legislation designed to protect the French language. At the federal level, the 1969 Official Languages Act declared both French and English to be the official languages of Canada, set up bilingual districts – where numbers warranted – so that citizens could deal with their federal government in the language of their choice, and sought to make the status of French equal to that of English throughout the country. The reaction of Quebec – one that was largely correct – was that the Official Languages Act was too little and too late, since, as the bilingual belt thesis argues, the French language outside of Quebec had already been lost. Instead, the Quebec provincial governments of the past two decades, whether they have been formed by Liberal, Union Nationale, or Parti Québécois members, have all sought to use the powers of the provincial government to promote and defend the French language within Quebec itself. In that sense, the genesis of Bill 101 passed in 1977 by the Parti Québécois is the relationship between English and French in the rest of the country: accepting the defeat of French outside of its borders, the PQ is determined to prevent such a pattern within Quebec itself. Generally Bill 101 moves Quebec toward being a unilingual French province (or will do so in the future), thereby seeking to emulate the English dominance in all the other provinces. The reaction to Bill 101 inside Quebec has been enthusiastic from the French-speaking segment, while English-Canadians and recent immigrant groups have been strongly opposed. Those individuals most upset are in fact emigrating from Quebec, a trend which in the long run will help to consolidate the growing unilingual nature of the province.

While the dualism theme is perhaps best symbolized by current disputes over language, its impact is also clearly evident with respect to the structure and operation of the polity. For example, the federal principle was adopted as a means of guaranteeing the existence of both the English and French cultures, with the provinces given control of "those matters where the traditions of the English- and French-speaking communities of the former province of Canada differed significantly" (Smiley, 1980: 20). Moreover, within the federal government itself, English-French duality is indirectly recognized, as in the allocation of provincial seat totals in the House of Commons. The customs and conventions of Canadian politics also reflect the theme, exemplified by the selection of the speaker and deputy speaker of the House of Commons, cabinet representation for Quebec as well as for francophone areas in New Brunswick and northern Ontario, and the regular alternation of French and English leaders within the Liberal party. Thus, through both institutional structures and political customs has the theme of dualism remained a significant influence on the Canadian political process.

In contrast to the themes of regionalism and dualism, which are based on internal realities and problems, our fourth theme of *continentalism* reflects the importance of external factors, namely, the impact of the United States on Canadian politics. American influence runs the gamut from basic principles of government, such as federalism, to political practices, such as the use of national party leadership conventions. In some cases we have imitated American practices, while in others we have resisted their encroachments. However, overall, the impact of the United States on Canadian politics has been extensive.

One of the reasons, of course, for the movement towards Confederation in the 1860s was the fear of American expansionism and the attempt to prevent the absorption of the English colonies into the American orbit. While the results of the War of 1812 prevented a military conquest, Canada remained apprehensive about possible American intervention until the early decades of the 20th century. For example, until the 1920s, Canada maintained a secret contingency plan of how to respond to an American invasion, even though such a threat had not been very likely for some time. The result has been an element of anti-Americanism among basic Canadian political values – as Frank Underhill once described us, Canadians are the "world's oldest and continuing anti-Americans." One consequence of the American impact has been a low sense of national identity, which in itself is defined in negative terms: we know what we are not (i.e., American), but we do not know what we are (i.e., the essential attributes of being a Canadian).

The desire to contain and possibly to reduce American influence in Canada led to a growing movement of nationalism, particularly economic nationalism, during the past few decades. For example, the preferential tax position for *Time* and *Reader's Digest* has been removed, Canadian content regulations have been established and implemented for the mass media, and most recently – with the National Energy Program of 1980 – the energy sector is becoming "Canadianized." In response to the impact of multinational corporations in Canada, a Foreign Investment Review Agency (FIRA) was established to screen all takeover bids; however, the subsequent success of takeover applications has been high, usually in the neighbourhood of 80 percent. In foreign affairs, Trudeau's policy review and his later actions during the 1970s were based on an attempt to reduce Canadian dependence on the American superpower and to give Canada a more independent position in the international arena.

Policies aimed at limiting the extent of American influence in Canada are a reflection of the kind of control exercised by the United States, particularly in relation to the economic sector. During the 19th and early 20th centuries, when Britain was the dominant foreign power in Canada, a pattern of *indirect investment* allowed control to remain in Canadian hands. In contrast, American investment has been *direct*, with control shifting to the multinational corporations. The distinction between the two types of investment is significant because "indirect investment is basically a financial transaction that can be paid off, while direct investment involves at least partial ownership and control" (Redekop, 1978: 38). Because of the pattern of direct investment, economic decision-making power has shifted to the American system. For example, during the 1970s, several instances occurred of the application of American law on Canadian territory. The Canadian branch plants of the American multinationals were prevented from dealing with a country such as Cuba, even though Canadian law did not prevent such business transactions. What is true of the economic sector is also found in other areas such as culture, defence, and politics. Continentalism seems destined to remain a significant factor in Canadian politics in the decades ahead, though at the same time further attempts to check American influence may be made in the 1980s.

Having discussed the four major themes of elitism, regionalism, dualism, and continentalism, we can now classify the Canadian pattern of core political beliefs in terms of the basic types of political culture. Overall, Canada has a fragmented political culture composed of a series of regional political orientations. The most distinctive political subculture is that of French Canada, which is increasingly centred in the province of Quebec. By comparison to most countries, Canada's political culture is participant, but the strength of elitism indicates pockets of subject and parochial values that limit extensive participation in the political process. Moreover, the elements of regionalism, dualism, and continentalism have all contributed to a lack of national identity and unity, that is, to a pattern of attenuated nationalism. From an ideological perspective, liberalism has been dominant, although it must compete with both conservatism and socialism to retain such a position (Horowitz, 1968: 3-57). Canadian conservatism is unique in its collectivist emphasis and willingness to use the power of government for national objectives (e.g., John A. Macdonald's National Policy). Similarly, Canadian socialism is characterized by its British heritage and its belief in democratic socialism rather than Marxian socialism. This particular mixture of ideologies has helped to solidify the unique characteristics of the Canadian political culture.

Given the ideological, regional, and cultural fragmentation of basic political values, the next concern might be with trying to explain how the overall system manages to stay together. The answer that has often been given is that Canada exemplifies a political system that can be classified as a consociational democracy or as a pattern of elite accommodation (Presthus, 1973; McRae, 1974). Based on the experience of how the smaller European democracies have been able to function successfully despite linguistic, cultural, and ethnic differences, the theory of consociational democracy indicates that a system's survival is heavily dependent on the intention and ability of the political elite to make it work. Effective decision-making power is given to the elite so that it can successfully accommodate and mediate among the various social, economic, and political interests. In addition, there is often the fear of an external threat, which reinforces the need of the elite to control the system. The policies adopted by the elite are pragmatic rather than ideological in scope, thus allowing for conciliation between the political subcultures. In such a system the masses must be willing to delegate political authority to the elite, refrain from interference in the conciliation process, and accept the bargains struck by the political leadership. Mass participation is limited and is generally confined to voting in elections.

These characteristics of a typical consociational democracy are consistent with the four major themes of the Canadian political culture. The elitist nature of the British parliamentary structure allows for the exercise of considerable power in the accommodation process, while the deferential attitudes toward authority make such a pattern legitimate. A limited degree of nationalism among the masses, along with a pattern of quasi-participation, restricts their ability to upset the bargains made by the elite. Fear of an external threat is symbolized by the American presence in Canada: that is, continentalism is a major incentive to keep the present system going. The themes of regionalism and dualism reveal two of the fundamental policy areas that must be continually accommodated by the elite. Such conciliation is more effective when the elites themselves are representative of the various political subcultures.

The future of this pattern of elite accommodation has obviously been thrown into question by the election of the Parti Québécois in the Quebec provincial contests of 1976 and 1981. The assumption that the key actors of the political elite want to make the system work is no longer tenable. It is in the long-term interests of a separatist party to show that the existing system does not and cannot be made to work, thereby providing justification for independence. No amount of political reform or constitutional tinkering can accommodate or satisfy the national aspirations of the Parti Québécois. Until the Parti Québécois gives up on its dream of making Quebec a nation-state, the pattern of elite accommodation will become less and less feasible as a means of keeping the current political system together.

THE BRITISH POLITICAL CULTURE

Because Britain lacks a comprehensive written constitution, political custom and convention play a vital role in the political process. These conventions embody the core values of the British political culture, which include the importance of tradition, deferential attitudes toward political authority, and a consensus regarding key political norms and practices. In many respects, especially in its elitist and quasi-participative tendencies, the pattern of British political beliefs resembles the Canadian one.

The first characteristic of British political culture is the significance of *tradition*, a reflection of the evolutionary nature of the polity over the course of many centuries. The weight of history is heavy, as new beliefs and practices merged with existing ones. Two institutional survivors are the monarchy and the House of Lords. For example, while the substance of monarchical power is no longer exercised by the monarch, the institution remains in place: "The

British monarch is a powerful living symbol linking the British of today with a rich past and a royal future" (Roth and Wilson, 1980: 11). The role of tradition is emphasized by the symbols and ceremonies of the polity, what Walter Bagehot called the "theatrical show of society," such as the opening of Parliament or the pageantry of a royal marriage. One major result of the evolution of tradition has been to give a pragmatic thrust to British politics, which in most instances has taken precedence over ideological concerns.

The role of tradition is reinforced by the second characteristic of British political culture, namely, *deferential* attitudes toward political authority. Deference or respect for authority can be seen in the support of traditional political institutions, as well as in the acceptance of a class-based society and an elitist pattern of decision-making. The "dignified" parts of the system – "those which excite and preserve the reverence of the population" (Bagehot, 1867: 61) – are a means of legitimating the power of the political elite to rule between elections. A further indicator of deferential beliefs is the acceptance of the "rule of law" and the notion that violence is not a legitimate means for achieving political goals. This deferential nature of political values parallels the structure of the British polity. A system that is unitary in form, based on the principle of parliamentary supremacy, and without a pattern of judicial review is inherently elitist in style and operation. Such a pattern may be democratic in form, but the overall result is a system "of government of the people, for the people, with, but not by, the people" (Amery, quoted in Beer, 1973: 140).

The third attribute of the British political culture is its *consensual* nature: that is, there is widespread agreement on political fundamentals. The rules of the political game have not been seriously challenged for several centuries: "Since the end of the seventeenth century, the British constitution and the government have been generally accepted" (Finer and Steed, 1978: 35). One reason why a political consensus has long dominated British politics is the ability of the political system to adapt to changing circumstances. No major group has been excluded outright from the political system, although several have "peacefully" forced their entry into the political game. Gradual adaptation rather than a politics of confrontation has successfully coopted the major socioeconomic interests into accepting the legitimacy of the political structure. In addition to its adaptability, a second factor contributing to consensus has been the relatively homogeneous nature of British society. There have been few sharp cleavages, such as language or ethnicity, which might tear the political fabric asunder. Finally, the geographical compactness of Britain has helped to minimize the development of regional differences, which often characterize larger systems like Canada and the United States.

The traditional, deferential, and consensual characteristics of the British political culture all support the view that it is an integrated political culture, with a high sense of national identity and purpose. While generally participant in outlook, the deferential attitudes toward political authority reveal strong subject orientations as well. Few political subcultures can be identified and regionalism is minimal, with the major ideological differences revealed in the class-based structure of the polity.

While this interpretation of the British political culture is a fairly typical one, it can be challenged on several grounds. First, the characteristics apply better to England than to the United Kingdom (England, plus Wales, Scotland, and Northern Ireland). The inclusion of these areas greatly increases the diversity of core political values, reduces the homogeneity of the overall political culture, and recognizes the crucial factor of regionalism. Second, while violence may have been excluded from the normal political process, it most certainly is an important ingredient in the internal politics of Northern Ireland, as well as in the conflict between that area and the British government in London. Third, the pervasive nature of deference as a distinguishing characteristic of British values has been questioned in recent years (Kavanagh, 1980). Fourth, the social homogeneity of Great Britain has also changed, given the large increase in non-white immigration in the past several decades, as well as the resurgence of nationalism in both Scotland and Wales. Finally, class-based tensions have become magnified, symbolized by the Conservative government's confrontation with the coal miners in the early 1970s and the radicalization (i.e., leftward movement) of the Labour party in the early 1980s. While these developments may have begun to limit some of the traditional, deferential, and consensual aspects of the polity, by comparison to most systems, the British political culture remains a highly integrated one.

The impact of the core political values can be seen in many aspects of the political process. For example, with respect to voting behaviour, the Conservative party, which represents the middle and upper classes, receives about one-third of its total vote from members of the working class. A partial explanation for such a pattern is the deferential attitudes toward authority, whereby some groups see others as having a "right to govern." Continued support for the monarchy, with high levels of political affect for that institution, reveal the elitist tendencies of the British polity. The nature of particular institutions and their role in the political process is, more often than not, based on a "tradition of behaviour" rather than statutory requirements. The relationship between institutions (e.g., House of Commons and House of Lords) is a reflection of the historical evolution of the various structures of government. These examples illustrate the integral nature of the core political beliefs in analyzing the structure and operation of the British polity.

In comparison to the fragmented Canadian pattern, the British political culture is an integrated one. The set of Canadian political beliefs reflects a diversity of cultures and regions, two factors of modest historical importance in a more homogeneous Britain. Both systems are elitist, quasi-participative, and deferential in outlook, but because of Britain's unitary and centralized political and parliamentary structure, these attributes are more significant than in Canada.

THE AMERICAN POLITICAL CULTURE

The core values of the American polity differ in certain key areas from the beliefs of both the Canadian and British political cultures. Overall, the American pattern is an integrated one, although for different reasons than in Britain. Born out of a revolution, the United States was forced to define the nature of its core political values from the outset, in contrast to the evolution of political ideas in Canada and Britain. This delineation of goals was embodied in the writings of the English political theorist John Locke, as interpreted by the American founding fathers in such writings as the *The Federalist Papers*.

Essentially the core political values embraced the doctrines of liberalism, which came to be seen as synonymous with the "American way of life." The dominance of liberalism was so pervasive that ideological diversity was discouraged, with the result that a consensus on political fundamentals quickly congealed. Symbolized by the Declaration of Independence and the American Constitution, this consensus has remained in place for 200 years. The manner in which diversity has been handled in the United States has served to reinforce this liberal preeminence. While socially complex and composed of immigrant groups from many lands, the melting pot emphasis of the school system and of society has helped to produce a unity of political outlook and sense of national identity that few other political cultures can match. As a result, the American political culture is a highly integrated one. The most significant regional political culture in American history has been the South, but the last two decades have witnessed its incorporation into the mainstream of American politics.

To define the nature of the American political culture, therefore, is to describe the main tenets of liberalism, as they have been adapted in the American context (Mitchell, 1970: 105-121). First, Americans are inherently suspicious of political power and its uses, seeing it at best as a necessary evil that must be circumscribed in practice. If political power is evil, then the institutional organization of power, that is, government, is likely to be seen in a similar light. One result of such a view is a rather negative perception of politicians. Another consequence has been the desire to limit government's role and effectiveness, summarized in the view that "the government which governs least governs best." To minimize the possible abuse of power, government is structured in such a way as to make difficult its accumulation in any single institution or individual. Such an outlook is the basis for the separation of powers principle and a Bill of Rights as elements of the American Constitution.

Even though government was to be limited in both scope and purpose, the government that was created was to be controlled by the people. Lincoln's phrase that American government was a "government of the people, by the people, and for the people" symbolizes the importance of popular, not parliamentary, sovereignty in the United States. Participation was to be encouraged, with public officials elected rather than appointed and serving relatively short terms of office. State judges, county officials, and special tax districts of one kind or another are electorally based. The ballot is extensive, often containing numerous tax proposals, constitutional amendments, and referendum questions. Thus, the belief in popular sovereignty led to the adoption of a political structure designed to promote public participation in and control over the elected political elite.

A third theme of American liberalism concerns the importance of individualism and its emphasis on the values of liberty and equality. Self-reliance is necessary in a system of limited government where liberty is defined typically as freedom from state intervention. Moreover, self-reliance or individualism parallels the American conception of equality as an "equality of opportunity" rather than an "equality of condition." An equality of opportunity philosophy puts the burden for one's own success, or lack thereof, on the individual. While liberty and equality are goals and are accepted by most Americans as admirable political values, their application in practice often leaves much to be desired, as the battle over civil rights illustrates.

A fourth theme of the American political culture can be called political moralism: "The moralistic fervor of many Americans has long been a source of both amusement and confusion to perceptive foreigners" (Mitchell, 1970: 118). One result of this moralistic outlook is that politicians, because they deal with power that is evil, must try to be better than an ordinary citizen, to set an example of proper or exemplary behaviour. Corruption, dishonesty, or other lapses of morality can cost one political office, as the Watergate Scandal of the early 1970s illustrates with respect to Richard Nixon. An emphasis on political morality has also led, through the course of American history, to alternating periods of political reform and political conservatism. Another outgrowth of political moralism concerns the typical and traditional American view of their own political system as not only unique, but superior to that of all other countries.

These themes of the American political culture, an outgrowth of liberalism, have been challenged in recent decades in terms of both foreign and domestic crises. They are goals of the polity that most people would agree with on a general level, but that become points of political conflict when applied in specific contexts or with regard to particular issues; for example, equality as a goal, but not necessarily busing as a means to achieve equality of educational opportunity. Such conflicts become frequent when the goals of a polity are seen as possibly unattainable by major sectors of the political system. However, the dominance of liberalism remains largely intact; from a comparative perspective, it is a highly integrated and ideologically unified political culture.

COMPARING POLITICAL CULTURES

In describing the major themes of the Canadian, British, and American political cultures, we have focused on three ways of comparing their core political values: the role of the individual in the political process (parochial, subject, participant); the degree of consensus on political fundamentals (integrated or fragmented); and the ideological mix of political ideas (the content of the core political values). While other ways of classifying political cultures could be considered, these three approaches all emphasize the influence of political beliefs on the structure and operation of the polity.

With respect to the political structure, the core political values translate statutory requirements into working institutions of government. For example, while the BNA Act details many of the considerations that must be taken into account in making Senate appointments, that most important factor, that of patronage, is based on beliefs and customs rather than law. In the American system, constitutional duties set the parameters of the presidential office, but the dominant place of the president in recent decades stems from public beliefs about the proper presidential role, not from constitutional prescriptions. In all three of the systems considered, support for and protection of civil and political liberties are more heavily dependent on popular and elite beliefs that these rights should be protected, than on their specification in law. Thus do political beliefs transform legal structures into operating institutions of government.

A second manner in which beliefs influence the polity can be seen in the various functions of particular institutions and the way these change over time. When first created, a political structure might be designed with a specific task or function in mind. However, as beliefs change, so do the functions of particular institutions. For example, one of the initial functions of the Canadian Senate was to be the voice of provincial and regional concerns within the national government. However, from the time of Macdonald's first government, the cabinet has performed this task. The initial delineation of Senate functions has not been changed, nor has such a task been assigned to the cabinet in law; however, the practice of Canadian politics has been so modified. Likewise, the evolution of the relationship between the formal and political executives in Canada represents primarily changing public expectations about the proper role of each structure in the political system, rather than legally defined modifications. Thus, beliefs can alter the functions of various political institutions, while the political structures themselves remain in place.

If the core political values help to transform political structures into working institutions and if they help to modify the functions of these institutions over time, then political beliefs are an important mechanism for adapting the polity to changing circumstances. Beliefs are more readily transformed than are political structures. By modifying both the structures and functions of government, the core political values are an important mechanism of political change. Generally speaking, the beliefs and structures of the political system should reinforce each other. When they do not, then demands for political reform begin to be heard, with the aim being a reintegration of structures, functions, and beliefs.

SUMMARY

1. The political culture of a system refers to the attitudes and beliefs people hold about the polity and their role in it. Some political cultures have developed a consensus around key political values and hence are integrated, while others are internally divided along the lines of the basic sociopolitical cleavages and therefore are fragmented. Each political culture is a particular mix of ideological elements, illustrated by their various political values. Political cultures also vary with respect to the role of the individual in the political process (parochial, subject, or participant).

2. The Canadian political culture is characterized by the themes of elitism, regionalism, dualism, and continentalism. As a result, Canada has a fragmented political culture composed of an important series of political subcultures. The most distinctive of these regional political cultures is now centred in Quebec, whose main political preoccupation is a defence of the French language and culture. Despite its fragmented nature, the Canadian system has managed to survive by operating a consociational style of political management.

3. The British political culture centres around the political values of tradition, deference, and consensus. The lack of a comprehensive written constitution enhances the importance of political beliefs and customs in the British context. Although increasingly challenged in recent decades, the integrated nature of the British political culture is high in comparison to most political systems.

4. The overwhelming dominance of liberalism in the United States means that the American political culture is, for all practical purposes, defined in terms of its characteristics. Attributes of American liberalism include a negative view of political power and government, an emphasis on popular sovereignty, a stress on individualism, and a strong strain of political moralism. The political culture is an integrated one, although the application of the tenets of liberalism in specific contexts may lead to political conflict.

5. Political beliefs are an important factor in comparing political systems, because they shape both the structures and functions of government. Moreover, the influence of beliefs on both the structures and functions of the political system is a significant mechanism for adapting the polity to changed circumstances.

RECOMMENDED READINGS

Political Culture: General

ALMOND, GABRIEL A. and SIDNEY VERBA (1965) *The Civic Culture: Political Attitudes and Democracy in Five Nations.* Boston: Little, Brown and Co.

GIBBINS, ROGER (1982) *Regionalism: Territorial Politics in Canada and the United States.* Toronto: Butterworths.

KAVANAGH, DENNIS (1972) *Political Culture.* London: Macmillan.

ROSENBAUM, WALTER A. (1975) *Political Culture.* New York: Praeger Publishers.

Canadian Political Culture

BELL, DAVID and LORNE TEPPERMAN (1979) *The Roots of Disunity: A Look at the Canadian Political Culture.* Toronto: McClelland and Stewart.

GIBBINS, ROGER (1980) *Prairie Politics and Society: Regionalism in Decline.* Toronto: Butterworths.

HOROWITZ, GAD (1968) *Canadian Labour in Politics.* Toronto: University of Toronto Press. See Ch. 1 "Conservatism, Liberalism, and Socialism in Canada," pp. 3-57.

MCRAE, KENNETH, ed. (1974) *Consociational Democracy: Political Accommodation in Segmented Societies.* Toronto: McClelland and Stewart.

SCHWARTZ, MILDRED A. (1974) *Politics and Territory: The Sociology of Regional Persistence in Canada.* Montreal: McGill-Queen's University Press.

British Political Culture

BAGEHOT, WALTER (1867, 1963) *The English Constitution.* London: Collins, The Fontana Library.

KAVANAGH, DENNIS (1980) "Political Culture in Great Britain: The Decline of the Civic Culture," in Gabriel A. Almond and Sidney Verba, eds., *The Civic Culture Revisited.* Boston: Little, Brown and Co., pp. 124-176.

American Political Culture

BOORSTIN, DANIEL (1959) *The Genius of American Politics.* Chicago: University of Chicago Press.

HARTZ, LOUIS (1955) *The Liberal Tradition in America.* New York: Harcourt, Brace, Jovanovich.

MITCHELL, WILLIAM C. (1980) *The American Polity: A Social and Cultural Interpretation.* New York: The Free Press.

8 POLITICAL PARTIES: THE ACQUISITION AND RETENTION OF POLITICAL POWER

Parties were created out of a blend of public and private interests. They are agencies for the acquisition of power, not selfless political versions of the Red Cross, to whom citizens may go crying in time of need (Lawson, 1980: 23).

The rise of political parties is indubitably one of the principal distinguishing marks of modern government. The parties, in fact, have played a major role as makers of governments, more especially, they have been makers of democratic government (Schattschneider, 1942: 1).

As they tussle for votes in the current election campaign, loyal Grits and loyal Tories are damning each other's politics with the gutsy passion of a Sicilian vendetta. Yet the jaundiced elector trying to summarize the real difference between them may end up with only one item on his list: the Liberals are in power; the Conservatives want to be (Newman, 1972: 96).

WHILE IT WOULD BE DIFFICULT to imagine how the Canadian political system could operate without political parties, it is also true that most political systems have only recently discovered their usefulness in organizing and operating the political process. On the whole, political parties are predominantly products of the past century, with the first major theoretical analyses of parties written in the early decades of the 20th century. The recognition of their important role in modern politics was undefined in the works of the classical democratic theorists, so much so, that parties have been referred to as "the orphans of political philosophy" (Schattschneider, 1942: 10). Born of circumstance rather than by design, political parties represent an organizational means for governing the political system.

THE NATURE OF POLITICAL PARTIES

Most definitions of political parties exhibit a common theme, namely, that parties are organizations that seek to physically control the government by nominating candidates for office and winning power through the election process. A typical view is that of Sartori (1976: 64), who defines a party as "any group that presents at elections, and is capable of placing through elections, candidates for public office." Thus, parties aim to acquire power and to retain such power once it has been won, organizing both the electorate and the government in the process.

The Origin of Parties
The historical development crucial in the origin of political parties was the acceptance of the idea that the mass of people had to be taken into account in the organization of the polity. Throughout the 18th century and well into the 19th, a very small segment of the population was eligible for political participation. For example, in addition to such items as property qualifications, until the early decades of the 20th century, over 50 percent of the population was prevented from participation by the disenfranchisement of women, a restriction which was not lifted until the 1940s in Quebec, France, and Italy. It is not merely coincidental that the expansion of the suffrage (i.e., the right to vote and to participate in politics) paralleled the development of political parties in countries such as Britain, the United States, and Canada. As the number of potential participants in the political process expanded, a mechanism was needed to organize the mass of people now legally qualified to vote. Such a structure was the political party.

While one can find historical antecedents that trace back many centuries, the origin of the modern political party dates from approximately the mid-19th century. In the United States, the experience of Jacksonian democracy in the 1830s, in Britain, the series of Reform Acts in the 19th century, and in Canada, the achievement of representative and responsible government by the beginning of Confederation, all laid the basis and necessity for party organizations. The historical development of a political party is a reflection, therefore, of the acceptance within a country's political culture of the legitimacy of mass participation: "the emergence of a political party clearly implies that the masses must be taken into account by the political elite" (LaPalombara and Weiner, 1966: 4). However, it is important to realize that being taken account of can mean either mass participation and control over the elite, as in democratic systems, or elite control over the masses, as in totalitarian systems. In either case, the political party serves in an intermediate position between individual and government. In carrying out such a role, political parties connect individual preferences with public policy, linking the governors with the governed in the process.

Party Functions

Although the tasks, jobs, or functions that political parties carry out vary from one political system to the next, two basic functions of parties can be identified: organizing the electorate and organizing the government.

The *electoral function* of parties can be seen in the way in which they recruit candidates to run for political office, dominate the election process, and serve as focal points for individual and group attachments. In a Canadian federal election, literally hundreds of people must be found to compete in the election process. Most of these individuals are recruited to run for office by the political parties – there are few self-starters in Canadian politics. While parties are crucial mechanisms in the recruitment of individuals for electoral competition, it should not be forgotten that parties are also key recruitment agencies for numerous nonelective positions. Electoral success provides the party with the opportunity to place party members within the bureaucracy and the various agencies, boards, and commissions of government. The surest route to a political sinecure is to be a defeated candidate of the winning political party.

Parties also serve an electoral function by organizing campaigns and simplifying the choices presented the individual citizen. With over eleven million people voting in recent Canadian federal elections, some way is needed to sort out, from among all the theoretically possible courses of action, a limited set of alternatives for public judgment. Moreover, the party campaigns help to stimulate public interest in the issues of the day, aid in the registration or enumeration of voters, and promote more widespread participation in the political process. Citizens may also identify with a particular party by developing an emotional tie with it, what is known as a partisan attachment. While not the only factor, such partisan attachments help to influence how the citizen will vote in a specific election campaign.

The second major task of parties can be called a *governing function*. As an electoral organization that seeks to gain control of the government, the winning party serves as an integrating mechanism for getting the various branches and agencies to work together across institutional boundaries. For example, in Canada, a party with a majority mandate gains sole control of both the legislative and executive branches of government and thereby acquires the effective political power to implement its party's platform and policies. However, as electoral organizations, parties are self-interested structures that seek power: "parties formulate policies in order to win elections, rather than win elections in order to formulate policies" (Downs, 1957: 28). Good examples of this assertion include the Liberals' stand against wage-and-price controls in the 1974 campaign, a program they later implemented in the Fall of 1975, or their promise in the 1980 election, later forgotten, not to raise the price of energy by as much as proposed in the Conservative budget. In other words, parties propose policies in order to win votes, thereby linking their electoral and governing functions.

Parties serve a governing function not only by integrating the various institutions of government and providing policy direction, but also by determining the leadership options presented to the voter. The Canadian citizen indirectly chooses the prime minister from among those individuals who lead a recognized political party. Parties put forth the pool of available talent from which the electorate picks its leaders: in 1980, the Canadian voter could have selected either Pierre Trudeau, Joe Clark, Ed Broadbent, or Fabien Roy by casting a ballot for that leader's representative in his or her particular constituency. Thus, the process of national party leadership selection is significant because it sets the outer boundaries of electoral choice. By organizing the electorate and the government, parties provide a linkage mechanism between the citizen and the political structure.

Party Types

While innumerable classifications of party types have been developed, the most useful are those which relate party type to both the party's origin and the manner in which the electoral and governing functions are carried out. Three basic classifications will be considered: first, with respect to a party's origin, the difference between internally and externally created parties; second, in relation to party structure, the variation between cadre and mass parties; and third, in light of ideological concerns, the difference between programmatic and pragmatic parties.

Circumstances of party origin influence both a party's structure and ideology. The parties that emerged from within the legislative branch of government are referred to as *internally created or parliamentary parties*. Developing out of the various factions contending for control of the legislature, internally created parties were the first to appear historically. They have been primarily electorally-oriented organizations intent on winning power rather than on implementing programs of reform. Loosely structured, except during elections, such parties have accepted the legitimacy of existing political arrangements, have rarely been ideologically inclined, and have dominated the party politics in most democratic political systems. Examples of internally created or parliamentary parties include the Liberal and Conservative parties in Canada, the Republican and Democratic parties in the United States, and the Conservative and Liberal parties in Britain.

In contrast, *externally created or extra-parliamentary parties* are of more recent historical vintage, with origins outside of the legislature. These parties have usually challenged key aspects of the existing social, economic, and political structure, have been more intent on implementing programs than on winning power, have usually been better organized and ideologically articulate than their internally created counterparts, but have generally been electorally frustrated (Duverger, 1964: xxiv-xxxvii; LaPalombara and Weiner, 1966: 7-14). Examples of externally created parties include the Communist, Socialist, and States Rights parties in the United States, the Labour party and nationalist parties (Scottish Nationalist Party and Plaid Cymru) in Britain, and the Parti Québécois, Social Credit and New Democratic parties in Canada.

A second classification of party types focuses on variations in party structure and membership. A basic structural distinction is that between cadre and mass parties. In a cadre party, the organization exists primarily for electoral purposes, with little formal activity undertaken between elections. A *cadre party* is a "grouping of notables" whose primary goal is attaining office. Membership is loosely defined, with no formal admission procedures or registration forms. The party's ideology is general rather than specific, if it is defined at all. Party finance is dependent on large individual and corporate donations. The major North American parties, the British Liberal and Conservative parties, and most moderate European parties exemplify this type of party structure. In contrast, the *mass party* is characterized by permanent organization and effort even between election campaigns, by formal membership requirements, and by an emphasis on ideology and platform rather than simply electoral success. Mass parties have based their party finances on individual membership dues, trade union support, and in recent years, the public financing of election campaigns. The closest examples to mass parties in Canada are the Parti Québécois and the New Democrats, while in Britain the Labour party is a prime example.

Our final look at party types centres on the nature of a party's ideology. The parties that have long-term goals and platforms can be called *programmatic parties*, while parties with little ideology and short-term goals (usually meaning winning the next election) can be classified as *pragmatic parties* (Epstein, 1967: 261-272). A programmatic party would rather educate the public on the need for reform than win power, if electoral success means giving up the party's reform ideals. In a pragmatic party, policy is a matter of electoral convenience, a tool for gaining power. In Western democratic systems, pragmatic parties have generally prevailed over programmatic ones.

Although presented separately, these three classifications of party types based on origin, structure, and ideology are interdependent. Parliamentary parties are usually cadre structures with pragmatic policies, while extra-parliamentary parties are typically mass structures with specifically delineated programs. These three typologies have for the most part dealt with the nature of individual parties. However, a party's origin, structure, and ideology also influence how it interacts with other parties, thus leading us to a discussion of the nature of party systems.

Party Systems
A *party system* refers to the competitive relationship between two

or more political parties (Rae, 1971: 47). If only one party exists, then a party system is logically impossible. However, simply because a party exists does not mean that it is a relevant member of the party system. To say that a party is relevant implies that its presence more than marginally affects the behaviour of other parties; that is, it has an impact on the network of competitive relationships (Sartori, 1976: 121-125). For example, in recent Canadian federal elections the Marxist-Leninist Party of Canada has been an officially registered political party. However, because its presence has not visibly affected the campaign strategies of the other parties, because it wins only a minute percentage of the popular vote, and because it wins no legislative representation, the Marxist-Leninist Party of Canada is irrelevant in discussions of the current Canadian party system. On such criteria, the Canadian federal party system has contained four relevant parties in recent decades – the Liberal, Conservative, New Democratic, and Social Credit parties. With the elimination of the Social Credit party after the 1980 federal election, the Canadian federal party system has been reduced to three relevant groups. The United States usually has only two parties that affect the competitive relationship, although once in a while a minor party must be included (e.g., John Anderson's effort in 1980 or George Wallace's group in 1968). The growth of small parties in recent years has greatly increased the number of significant parties in Britain; the relevant groups would now include the Conservative, Liberal, Labour, Scottish Nationalist, Plaid Cymru, and National Front parties, as well as the recently formed Social Democratic party.

If a party system concerns the interaction between two or more parties, then different types of party systems are possible. Two basic patterns are evident: competitive and non-competitive party systems (LaPalombara and Weiner, 1966: 33-41; Sartori, 1976: 131-243). *A competitive party system* exists when the government of the day can be replaced through an election by an opposition party; in other words, the government must compete with and be challenged by another party that is capable of forming a new government. The struggle for power between two or more parties that have a chance of winning an election is the primary condition for calling a party system a competitive one. By such a criterion, the Canadian, British, and American party systems are competitive. A *noncompetitive party system* exists when one party dominates governmental office, is not effectively challenged for power through the electoral process, and, as a result always forms the government of the day. Opposition parties exist, but they pose no real threat to the governing party. A classic example of a non-competitive party system is Mexico, where the PRI (Partido Revolucionario Institucional) has totally dominated the party battle. Many of the party systems in the developing countries are examples of the non-competitive pattern.

Our typology of competitive and non-competitive party systems does not, however, cover all of the possible configurations of party politics, because in some political systems only one political party is allowed to exist. However, we can classify these one-party polities as party-state systems, rather than simply party systems (Sartori, 1976: 42-47). In a *party-state system*, a single party exists, no organized political opposition challenges it for power, and control of the party gives the party leaders control of the state. Party-state systems are usually associated with totalitarian political systems, such as Nazi Germany and the Soviet Union. The essential assumption of a party-state system is the necessary congruence of interests between the sole political party and the governmental apparatus. As described by Yugoslav dissident Milovan Djilas (1957: 70), the party-state system "originates from the fact that one party alone ... is the backbone of the entire political, economic, and ideological activity." Party-state systems are usually based on a comprehensive ideology or revolutionary doctrine, with the single party perceived as the mechanism for transforming society. In Marxism-Leninism the single party is necessary so that the working class can overthrow the existing political arrangements. The single party is seen as the organizational weapon of the working class.

The competitive, non-competitive, and party-state systems reflect the origins, structures, and ideologies of the individual parties. For example, the Communist Party of the Soviet Union, which originated under Czarist autocracy as a means of overthrowing the existing political system, adopted a cohesive structure and an all-encompassing ideology and thus rejected the need for or the possibility of establishing a competitive party framework. The result was a party-state system rather than a party system. Non-competitive party systems that originated in the struggle to throw off colonial rule and to set up new nations have not yet fully accepted the legitimacy of political opposition, arguing instead that nation-building is a higher priority than party competition. In democratic systems, the initial origin of parties within the legislature, the gradual extension of the suffrage, the pragmatic concerns of the major parties, and the acceptance of the legitimacy of political dissent and political opposition have created the conditions for competitive party politics.

THE CANADIAN PARTY SYSTEM

As with any particular aspect of a political system, the political analyst must be concerned not only with general patterns, as exemplified by the above classifications of party types and party functions, but also with how these patterns have developed within specific historical contexts. The interplay between general patterns and the specific Canadian milieu can be seen with respect to both the characteristics of the individual parties and the attributes of the party system.

Characteristics of Canadian Parties

While the emergence of political party organizations can be traced to pre-Confederation Canada, the birth process was an arduous one, consuming nearly half a century in an extended gestation period. As a consequence, modern political parties were not developed until the end of the 19th century (Thorburn, 1979: 2). In the initial decades of Confederation the nascent parties were very loose coalitions of various factions within the legislature, poorly organized, and lacking party discipline. For example, Macdonald's "party" was composed of those interests favouring Confederation and his National Policy, while the opposition factions were, in the beginning, opposed to Confederation and its implications. Several characteristics of the election process helped to produce such a pattern.

Following Confederation, the federal electorate voted in a system of non-simultaneous elections, in which the federal vote was taken on different days in different constituencies. The government would call the election first in those constituencies that supported it, and then work outward to the remaining areas, attempting to build up a bandwagon effect as it went. Such non-simultaneous elections might occur over an extended period, as in the 1867 election, which stretched over six weeks. Combined with the lack of a secret ballot, which meant that the government knew how one voted, non-simultaneous elections produced legislative factions of ministerialists, members whose primary political aim was to be on the winning side in order to reap the rewards of office. As elected Members of Parliament who were uncommitted to any particular coalition, these ministerialists would support the government of the day on the basis of what they or their constituency might receive from that government. Such ministerialists constituted a significant element in "all of the early parliaments: Macdonald called them 'loose fish', George Brown, 'the shaky fellows', and Cartwright, 'waiters on Providence'" (Reid, 1979: 13). While the elimination of non-simultaneous elections and the introduction of the secret ballot for most electoral areas in 1878 gradually helped to solidify party organization and cohesion by the 1896 election, the effect of such initial election practices was to keep the emerging parties poorly organized, while at the same time emphasizing the rewards of a pragmatic style of party politics.

The success of the Liberal and Conservative parties is directly linked to their parliamentary origins and the attributes thus acquired. Born in the struggle for power in the legislature and for control of the new political structure after 1867, the Liberal and Conservative parties have been electorally-focused organizations whose primary goal has been winning power and the spoils of office. With such an aim the major parties have been "practical, flexible, and manipulative" (Winn and McMenemy, 1976: 11). As Pierre Trudeau said of the Liberal party in the 1960s, a statement often true of the Conservatives as well, the party will say anything and do anything to win power. An NDP supporter in 1963, Trudeau viciously attacked Prime Minister Pearson for his decision to accept nuclear weapons on Canadian soil:

> I would have to point out in strongest terms the autocracy of the Liberal structure and the cowardice of its members. I have never seen in all my examinations of politics so degrading a spectacle as that of all those Liberals turning their coats in unison with their Chief, when they saw a chance to take power.... The head of the troupe having shown the way, the rest followed with the elegance of animals heading for the trough (Trudeau, quoted in Stewart, 1971: 11).

However, practical politics resulted in similar behaviour after Pierre Trudeau became leader of the Liberal party in 1968 (e.g., the wage-and-price control reversal in 1974-1975). Such actions would seem to confirm the view that "politicians are hardly notable for their consistency – and the sweet fruits of office can lead men through strange manoeuvrings of conscience and conviction" (Hamilton, 1975: 109).

This pragmatic style of the two dominant parties is clearly illustrated with respect to party platforms, principles, and policy positions. Rarely do either the Liberal or Conservative parties take a stand that clearly differentiates it from the other. Specificity of purpose limits a party's electoral appeal. As a result, party platforms are general in nature, or at least, open to multiple interpretations, especially after the campaign is over. For example, the Liberal party was unwilling or unable in the 1980 contest to explain the meaning of a "blended, made in Canada" price for oil, even though Pierre Trudeau made numerous general statements about the need for such a policy. Perhaps even more revealing was the decision of the Liberal party to keep its total platform secret during the 1980 contest, a decision subsequently maintained even after victory had been achieved. One can assume, perhaps, that this approach to policy had the interest of the voters at heart – there is no point in confusing people with facts, especially in the midst of an electoral contest. The Conservative party's failures in recent years are attributable, at least in part, to its explicit policy positions, such as its budget, which became the central issue in the 1980 contest, its stand in favour of wage-and-price controls in 1974, or its views on conscription in earlier times. In that sense, the Conservatives have not been as pragmatic as their Liberal counterparts, sometimes forgetting that the "fortunate parties are those whose names no longer carry meaning to the electorate" (Mallory, 1954: 168).

The pragmatic nature of the Liberal and Conservative parties is clearly evident in relation to the question of party membership. At the mass level, a person is usually considered to be a party member simply by claiming such an affiliation. Offer your services at election time and you will, in all likelihood, be welcomed with open arms: background checks on previous partisan ties are not a precondition of current partisan loyalty. At the elite level, numerous examples abound concerning the flexible nature of party membership. An outstanding historical example would be that of Joseph Howe: although initially opposed to Confederation, and elected to the House of Commons on that basis in 1867, he joined Macdonald's cabinet only two years later, after renegotiation of Nova Scotia's annual subsidy from the federal government (Winn and McMenemy, 1976: 11). More recently, Paul Hellyer's switch from the Liberal to the Conservatives and back to the Liberals shows the continuing presence of the flexible nature of partisan loyalty.

With respect to party organization, the Liberal and Conservative parties are weak. Since they are electoral organizations, the party structure is only fleshed out prior to and during an electoral engagement – between elections, the party organization remains a paper tiger. Most elements of the party structure, such as the constituency organizations or the provincial parties, hold an annual meeting of little consequence. Even when an election is expected or called, most party units are unprepared for the electoral battle. A considerable portion of the early weeks of the campaign is simply spent in nominating candidates in each of the constituencies. A corresponding aspect of party organization concerns the component units of the federal Liberal and Conservative parties. While they appear to be hierarchically organized, in fact, much of the real power of the federal Liberal and Conservative parties lies in their provincial units: in other words, the party organizations are decentralized. As with constitutions in general, party constitutions are rarely accurate descriptions of the internal power relationships within either of the two old-time parties.

The characteristics of Canada's major parties, the Liberals and Conservatives, therefore, include the following: their parliamentary origin; their pragmatic style of party politics with respect to platform, ideology, and membership; and their weak and essentially decentralized party structures. Electorally-based organizations, the Liberal and Conservative parties are coalitions of individuals, groups, and regions intent on winning for themselves the spoils of office.

In addition to the two dominant parties of parliamentary origin, since the 1920s, Canada has seen the rise and development of a series of minor parties. These newer parties typically illustrate opposite attributes from those identified for the Liberals and Conservatives, for the simple reason that their origins, structures, and functions are different. Parties such as the Progressives, the Cooperative Commonwealth Federation – which later became the New Democratic Party – and Social Credit are extra-parliamentary in origin and ideologically-based. The externally created parties have often been outgrowths from social movements that have sought extensive changes in the economic and political structure of Canada. Since they have a need to justify such proposed changes, these extra-parliamentary parties have usually propounded an ideology that attacks the existing order and suggests the outlines of a new pattern of power relationships. Membership in such an organization entails acceptance of the party's ideology and platform, with enduring organization between election campaigns. These characteristics are exemplified by the only remaining relevant national minor party in Canada in the 1980s, that is, the New Democratic Party.

Although officially formed in 1961, the New Democratic Party's predecessor, the Cooperative Commonwealth Federation (CCF), began in 1933, itself the outgrowth of some remnants of the Progressives of the 1920s. The CCF, as an externally created party, clearly attacked the existing economic and political structures of capitalism. The ideological commitment of the CCF was enunciated in the Regina Manifesto, the party's initial declaration of principles. Membership obligated one to support the party's principles and to help in party finance through annual membership fees.

The CCF was both a social movement and a party, with inevitable strains between these varying conceptions of its role in the political system (Young, 1969: 286-302). The evolution of the CCF from 1933 onward demonstrated this basic conflict between the demands of a political movement and those of a political party. Gradually the CCF became more electorally-focused, with an increasing concern for electoral results, symbolized by the role of David Lewis as national party secretary from 1936 to 1950. The radical thrust of the Regina Manifesto became blunted and was eventually replaced in 1956 by a more moderate statement of party aims known as the Winnipeg Declaration. However, the attempt to refurbish the party's image failed, and combined with the Diefenbaker sweep of 1958, encouraged the CCF moderates to seek the establishment of a new party aimed at implementing social democracy in Canada. The result was the creation of the New Democratic Party in 1961, a party more power-oriented than the CCF, which sought to establish a union of farmer and labour groups within the party, and was predicated on a strategy of appealing more to urban than to rural voters. Thus, the formation of the New Democratic Party is itself a reflection of the pervasive nature of the pragmatic style of Canadian politics.

Many of the initial patterns of party structure, organization, and membership used by the CCF were continued by the NDP after 1961. As well, the inherent tension between reform and electoral victory persisted: "the NDP is both an electoral organization and a political movement, pledged to the eventual transformation of society" (Morton, 1974: 3). Within the NDP, the moderate wing, which focuses more on power than on principle, has carried the organization behind it in terms of leadership selection, party policy, campaign tactics, and parliamentary behaviour. The pragmatic nature of the current NDP is perhaps best exemplified by its support of Pierre Trudeau's Liberal minority government between 1972 and 1974. Although more moderate than the CCF, the NDP still stands apart from the Liberal and Conservative parties with respect to its emphasis on platforms and ideology, internal party democracy, mass party membership, and reform of the social, economic, and political institutions cf Canada.

Canadian parties, therefore, are not created from a uniform mold. The two major and long-dominant parties are parliamentary in origin, pragmatic in style, nonideological in philosophy, and electorally-centred coalitions whose primary goal is winning power. The series of minor parties since the 1920s have been, by contrast, extra-parliamentary in origin, programmatic in style, ideological in appeal, and both political movements and partisan organizations. This combination of cadre and mass parties has helped to produce a unique party system in the Canadian context.

Characteristics of the Party System

The most important attribute of the Canadian party system is the fact that it is a competitive one, although it is not an equally-balanced pattern of interaction. Historically, one party has tended to dominate national politics, with the Conservatives monopolizing that role from Confederation until 1896 and the Liberals bearing the mantle of power for most years since 1921 (approximately 80 percent of the time). This pattern has led one author (Thorburn, 1979: 45) to suggest that the national party system contains the normal government party (the Liberals), the normal opposition party (the Conservatives), and the normal minor party (the New Democratic Party). Such a system rarely produces party turnover in government; instead, "the important alternation is not between different parties in office but between majority and minority Liberal governments" (Meisel, 1979: 128).

The second characteristic of the party system is that it is federal in structure, paralleling the federal organization of government. While our main focus is on the national party system, the federalization of party politics has an important bearing on which party wins power in Ottawa. Federalism has created 11 arenas for the party battle. Moreover, the parties have been differentially successful in these various political contests. For example, while the Liberal party may be the normal governing party in Ottawa, in recent years it has become either the major opposition party in provinces like Quebec and Ontario, or has been, for all practical purposes, eliminated from the partisan battle, as in Alberta and British Columbia. With the defeat of the Trudeau government in 1979, not a single Liberal government existed in Canada. By contrast, the Conservatives, who have been the normal opposition party in Ottawa, have become the most successful party in provincial politics, entering the 1980s in control of Alberta, Manitoba, Ontario, New Brunswick, Nova Scotia, Prince Edward Island, and Newfoundland (some analysts would also include British Columbia, since it was controlled by the Social Credit party, a conservative analogue).

The impact of federalism on the minor parties has been even greater than on the Liberals and Conservatives. Federalism has helped to promote minor parties, while at the same time it has limited their ultimate national success. By creating provincial units that are worth contesting for, given their powers in the Canadian system, federalism has encouraged new parties at the provincial level of government. However, even if a party wins control of a provincial government, it may find it difficult to expand successfully into the national party system. For example, it is difficult to conceive how the Parti Québécois might be extended either to other provinces or into control of the national government in Ottawa. Thus, federalism promotes the emergence of new parties around the provincial units, while at the same time it inhibits their success in national politics. In the 1970s, the New Democratic Party won provincial elections in British Columbia, Saskatchewan, and Manitoba and had become the official opposition in Ontario, yet in national politics in the 1980 federal election it was denied representation in six of ten provinces (Alberta, Quebec, New Brunswick, Nova Scotia, Prince Edward Island, and Newfoundland).

In addition to having an important effect on the success of the political parties in the various political arenas, federalism also influences a party's structure and ideology. The national parties are themselves federal organizations: for example, "it is an important part of Liberal mythology that the party, like the country itself, is a federation" (Wearing, 1981: 81). As federal structures, the party organizations have ended up granting considerable power to their provincial components. The result has been that Canada's national parties are decentralized around the provincial organizations and that unity of effort, ideology, and personnel is rarely achieved.

A policy that is in the interest of the national party may be detrimental to provincial party success. For example, the emphasis of the federal Liberal party on the themes of national unity and bilingualism may be good politics during a national election, but are not very successful in provincial elections, as the provincial Liberal parties in Western Canada have discovered over the last decade. In a similar vein, the federal Conservatives' attempt in 1979 to placate Alberta by moving to the world price for oil produced an unofficial split between the national party organization and its Ontario wing under Premier Bill Davis. Such inconsistencies have sometimes led to the setting up of completely distinct party organizations for the national and provincial arenas. For example, the provincial Ontario wing of the Liberal party established its own structure in 1976, as had the Quebec component in the 1960s.

Even without a formal split between the national and provincial wings, federalism has an important bearing on party policy and platforms. There is no necessary agreement on policy or ideology between the party units that operate at each level of government. A

Liberal provincial government or a Conservative one cannot assume ideological congruence from their federal counterparts, or vice versa. While in the early 1980s Pierre Trudeau (national leader of the Liberal party) and Claude Ryan (leader of the provincial Liberal party in Quebec) were both Liberals, their positions on constitutional reform were diametrically opposed. Such disagreements are typical and widespread within all the party organizations.

One result is that, regardless of party label, provincial parties often campaign against Ottawa during provincial elections, rather than against the opposition provincial parties. For example, existing provincial governments, in announcing an election, ask their electorates for a strong mandate so as to increase their bargaining power with Ottawa – a tactic as true of the Nova Scotia Liberals as it is of the Alberta Conservatives or the Saskatchewan New Democrats. The result of such a system is a pattern of "federal-provincial schizophrenia" within the Canadian party organizations (Black, 1979: 90). In some instances it may turn into paranoia, where the party at one level of government may actually campaign against the party at the other level, as when "in the early part of the Second World War, Liberal Premier Hepburn of Ontario openly cooperated with the Conservatives in an attempt to oust the Liberal government of Prime Minister Mackenzie King" (Smiley, 1980: 146). And the federal Liberal party, despite public protestations to the contrary, did not seem overly embittered by the defeat of the Quebec provincial Liberals by the Parti Québécois in the Spring 1981 provincial election. Such examples show that important aspects of internal and external party relations in Canada are affected by the federal nature of the political system – a factor that is "so obvious as to be almost taken for granted, and yet so important that it can scarcely be overestimated" (Whitaker, 1977: 402).

The third characteristic of the Canadian national party system is its regional and sectional basis. Each of the national parties has regional strongholds and wastelands. For that reason it has often been suggested that "in reality, a Canadian national election is a series of regional contests, with the party competitors in each region varying in strength from coast to coast" (Landes, 1981: 105). The 1980 election results presented in Table 8.1 illustrate such a pattern.

In the Atlantic region, the party battle is dominated by the Liberals and Conservatives, although the NDP does have pockets of strength, such as industrialized Cape Breton in Nova Scotia. Historically, the NDP has only won a single seat in Newfoundland, has never obtained a seat in either New Brunswick or Prince Edward

TABLE 8.1   *1980 Federal Election Results*

| | SEATS WON FOR EACH PARTY | | | |
Province	Conser-vative	Liberal	NDP	SC
Newfoundland	2	5	0	0
Nova Scotia	6	5	0	0
New Brunswick	3	7	0	0
Prince Edward Island	2	2	0	0
Atlantic Total	13	19	0	0
Quebec	1	74	0	0
Ontario	38	52	5	0
Manitoba	5	2	7	0
Saskatchewan	7	0	7	0
Alberta	21	0	0	0
British Columbia	16	0	12	0
Western Total	49	2	26	0
Northwest Territories/Yukon	2	0	1	0
TOTAL SEATS (282)	103	147	32	0

Island, and is only competitive in a few of the Nova Scotia constituencies. Thus, in the overwhelming number of Atlantic seats, the election is a Conservative-Liberal confrontation.

Since the 1960s, the Quebec ridings in federal elections have been primarily contests between Liberal and Social Credit candidates. The NDP has never won a seat in Quebec and in recent elections the Conservatives are lucky to win several – in 1980, they survived in only a single constituency. Particularly since Mackenzie King's sweep of all the federal seats in 1921, Quebec has been the bastion of Liberal dominance. In 1980, Trudeau won 74 of 75 constituencies, wiping out the Social Credit party in the process. With the demise of its main challenger, the Liberal party thus seems assured of continuing and massive support in Quebec in future federal elections. The prospects of either a Conservative revival or a New Democratic Party breakthrough seem unlikely.

In Ontario, the three parties are more evenly matched than in any other region, especially in the metropolitan and industrialized sections of the province. However, because of the workings of the electoral system, out of a possible 95 seats the NDP won only 6 seats in 1979 and 5 seats in 1980. Ontario is a crucial region in federal elections not simply because of its large number of seats, but, more importantly because many of these constituencies are swing ridings. A *swing riding* is one in which party strength is evenly matched, so that a small change in the popular vote totals can swing the victory from one party to the other. Thus, the distribution of seats in Ontario usually determines whether the Liberals or Conservatives will win the election. For example, in 1979, the Conservatives obtained 57 seats to 32 for the Liberals and formed a minority government, while in 1980, the Liberals gained 52 seats to 38 for the Conservatives in winning a majority government. Given their continuing lack of support in Quebec, these swing ridings in Ontario are particularly crucial for the Conservatives.

The final regional battle takes place in Western Canada. Since John Diefenbaker's electoral sweep in 1958, the Conservative party has become strongly based in the Prairie provinces, and in the 1970s in British Columbia as well. In the 1980 contest, the Conservatives picked up 49 seats in the four Western provinces, compared to 26 seats for the NDP and only 2 for the Liberals, who were blanked out in Saskatchewan, Alberta, and British Columbia. Western Canada is thus, in most constituencies, a two-way contest between the dominant Conservatives and their main challenger, the NDP.

More dramatic than the 1980 election results themselves is the impact of regionalism on the ensuing composition of the various party caucuses. The Liberal party has increasingly become the party of Central Canada (i.e., Quebec and Ontario). Half of the Liberal party caucus is elected from Quebec (74 of 147 seats), with 85 percent from Ontario and Quebec (126 of 147). The Conservatives are regionally imbalanced as well, with 50 percent of its caucus based in Western Canada (if we include the North, a total of 51 out of 103 seats in 1980) and less than 1 percent of its caucus in the House from Quebec. The greatest regional imbalance is evident for the NDP – it is locked out of representation in 6 of 10 provinces, with 80 percent of its caucus from three Western provinces (26 of its 32 seats). Such regional influences on the party system, in terms of representation and caucus composition, carry important implications for the ability of our political parties to successfully perform their electoral and governing functions.

The fourth characteristic of the national party system concerns the typical pattern of interaction among the parties. The party system is centre-based, with the Liberal party monopolizing the midpoint of the political spectrum (Alford, 1963; Horowitz, 1968). As a general ideological classification of the federal parties, the following placement would seem to be an appropriate summary of party positions over the past several decades: as a social democratic party, the New Democratic Party is on the left; the Liberals are in the centre, usually on the left of centre but flexible enough to move to the right of centre if political conditions require it; the Progressive Conservatives are a centre-right party; and Social Credit is on the right of the political continuum. With the demise of Social Credit in the 1980 election, we are left with a party system composed of a large centre party challenged from both the left and the right.

Since the majority of voters are in the centre of the political spectrum, the major parties both seek to occupy that position. However, once a party has gained control of the centre, it is difficult to dislodge, which is a key reason why a single party has dominated the federal government since the 1920s. In appealing to the centre, the winning party must find a theme that rallies people to its cause, while at the same time making it difficult for the opposition parties to disagree with it. The current Liberal party discovered such a theme in its emphasis on national unity, just as Macdonald's National Policy worked for the Conservatives in the 19th century. When the electorate does not feel that it is the key issue, as in 1979, the Liberal party fares badly. When the national unity theme is paramount, as in 1968, the Liberals win a majority victory. The opposition parties are put in the unenviable position either of arguing against a theme such as national unity, and thus appearing unpatriotic, or of trying to distinguish their policy from that of the Liberals in the minds of the electorate, a difficult undertaking.

Having established a key theme such as national unity as the basis of their political dominance, the centre-based party then utilizes several tactics: first, it ignores new policy options or issues, hoping that they will disappear so that no action is required; second, if a new issue is gaining public acceptance, the centre party seeks to undercut it by reemphasizing their key theme; and third, if the first two tactics fail, the dominant party takes over or co-opts the issue, remaking it in its own image. As a result, if the challenge to the centre party is from the left, the party moves left; if the challenge is from the right, the party moves right. The centre party thus establishes a moving equilibrium: its position on the left-right spectrum may change, but its placement between the other parties does not. This technique is currently exemplified by the Liberal shuffle: three moves left, five right, three left, and one right produces a lot of action, but the party ends up in the same place as it started. Movement becomes mistaken for leadership, with the retention of power the ultimate party goal.

This pattern was first developed for the Liberals under Mackenzie King and has served as the party's most significant operating principle ever since. For example, in addressing the national Liberal meeting in the Spring of 1978, Pierre Trudeau was asked by a reporter whether the party was moving to the right in preparation for the next federal election. Trudeau responded that the Liberal party was the party of the "radical centre" and would remain so. Thus, after years of extensive federal government expansion, by the mid-1970s Trudeau had announced government cutbacks, promised a tightening up of welfare and unemployment benefits, increased military expenditures with the purchase of new tanks and planes, and even curtailed the federal government's bilingualism programs. In effect, the Liberal party in the 1979 campaign ran against its first ten years in office in an attempt to move to the right of the political spectrum to undercut growing Conservative strength. By contrast, in the 1972–1974 period the Liberal party moved left, passing such legislation as the 1974 Federal Elections Expenses Act and establishing Petro-Canada, in order to acquire NDP support in Parliament and to undercut NDP strength in the electorate. While the move to the right was not immediately successful in the 1979 election, it did lay the foundation for the Liberals' return to power within a year. The move to the left in the early 1970s had an even more immediate impact – NDP strength in the 1974 election was cut in half from its 1972 seat total. Such tactics have allowed the Liberal party to dominate national politics since the 1920s, occupying the "triumphant centre" of the Canadian political spectrum (Horowitz, 1968: 29–44). As Mackenzie King (quoted in Morton, 1950: 22) said in 1921, the "Liberal party with its traditions and aspirations offers a means of escape from both extremes, neither of which is in the national interest."

The Canadian party system is, therefore, best described by four key characteristics: it is competitive, federal, regional, and centre-based. However, underlying each of these attributes is the social, economic, and political diversity of the country. For example, federalism was adopted as a principle of government to help ensure the preservation of the two main cultural groups at the time of Confederation. Not surprising, then, is the finding that such diversity continues to exist and is channeled through the party system, exemplified by the regional basis of party support. Diversity also helps to explain the importance of the centre-oriented strategy of party politics, with a dominant party regularly challenged from both ends of the political spectrum. Finally, diversity makes it impossible for one party to represent all of the social, economic, and political interests of the nation, thereby promoting the development and maintenance of a competitive party system.

The Selection of National Party Leaders

The characteristics of the individual parties and the party system have had a significant impact on both the type of leader chosen and the process of selection. Electorally-oriented parties in a competitive party system, for the most part, prefer leaders who promise the chance of electoral success. Moreover, the significance of our national party leaders is enhanced because Canadian politics has always been leader-oriented (Perlin, 1980: 13–27). The history of Canadian politics is a history of its political leaders, such as John A. Macdonald, Sir Wilfrid Laurier, Mackenzie King, and Pierre Trudeau.

The success of any political party in winning votes and elections is directly linked to the appeal of its leader, his or her personality, and the policies for which he or she stands. One reason Pierre Trudeau dominated national politics for a decade and a half was that his personal appeal, his intellect, and his style far outshone other party leaders, such as Joe Clark and Robert Stanfield. Moreover, political parties often make the question of leadership the focus of their election strategy, as the federal Liberals did with Trudeau on several occasions (e.g., the 1979 theme that "a leader must be a leader") and as the Ontario Progressive Conservative party did with Bill Davis in the 1981 provincial campaign. If Canadian politics is indeed leader-oriented, then it is important to know how those leaders are selected.

National party leadership selection is also significant because, in a democratic political system, we expect our party leaders to be chosen according to certain political principles. For example, the selection process is representative (several thousand delegates are selected to attend from the various local, provincial, and national party organizations), open (public in nature and covered by the press and media), competitive (several candidates seek the leadership, thereby giving the delegates a choice between leaders), based on the majority principle (the first candidate to receive a majority of votes is declared the new leader of the party), with votes cast using the individual secret ballot (a way of guaranteeing the political equality of each delegate). While the general public may not be directly involved in the selection of party leaders, the national party leadership selection process is used as a way of giving party members a direct voice in the choice of their particular leader.

All major parties in Canada now select their leaders through a *national party leadership convention*, which is a gathering of party members from across the country who meet to choose the individual who will become their new leader. In this way, the current practice of leadership conventions varies from the older Canadian tradition of having the party members in Parliament select the leader, a pattern that was used until 1919 in the Liberal party and until 1927 by the Conservatives.

Certain general rules of the selection process are typically employed by the various political parties, although specific details vary between parties or from one leadership convention to the next. The first thing a party must do is the obvious one of deciding to have a leadership convention. In some cases, the decision is straightforward, as when a leader resigns or announces the intention to do so as soon as a successor has been picked (e.g., Lester Pearson's decision to resign as Liberal party leader in December 1967). However, a party leader who wants to retain the position may be forced to call a leadership convention against his or her will (e.g., John Diefenbaker's position in the mid-1960s). Those not satisfied with their party leader may make use of the *leadership review process*. The major party constitutions allow delegates to the national meetings to propose and vote on a resolution that asks for a leadership review. If such a resolution passes with a majority vote, the party then calls a leadership convention. Thus, the party members who select their leader may have the final say over how long he or she remains at the head of the party. Even if a leadership review resolution does not pass, a strong minority vote in favour of it is a clear indication to the party leader that the rank-and-file members are unhappy with the leadership. In 1981, for example, 33 percent of the delegates to the national Progressive Conservative meeting and 31 percent of the delegates to the New Brunswick provincial Liberal party meeting voted in favour of a leadership review. While such votes were not large enough to force an immediate review, they clearly put Joe Clark and Joe Daigle on notice that large sections of their parties were unhappy with their leadership. Moreover, within a few months, Joe Daigle had resigned as party leader, left elective politics, and had become a judge in New Brunswick.

Once a decision to call a leadership convention has been made, the next order of business is to determine how the delegates to the national party leadership convention will be selected. The rules for delegate selection are important; if they are biased towards a particular candidate or region, for example, they may end up predetermining who has the best chance of winning. A party usually sends several delegates from each local or constituency organization (there are 282 constituencies, one for each seat in the House of Commons), a number of representatives from the provincial party organizations, and a group of delegates from the national party organization. Delegates are included from the party's youth and women's organizations, the elected members of the party in both the provincial and national legislatures, and senators and privy councillors. On occasion defeated candidates from the past election, as well as delegates-at-large appointed by the party leadership, have been given the right to participate. The delegate selection process produces a gathering of several thousand party members, who then choose the party's new leader.

The next stage is the nomination of candidates. In most cases, individuals seeking the position of party leader have announced their candidacy long before the convention begins, in order to have time to win the backing of delegates to the convention. Party leadership contests now last for several months before the convention, they are widely covered by the news media, and they can cost a candidate several hundred thousand dollars in expenses. To be officially nominated, a party usually requires the candidate to be a known party member and to have his or her nomination papers signed by a given number of party members (about 50 delegates attending the convention). Few restrictions are placed on who can run for the party leadership, although "frivolous" candidates (those with no party support or those unknown to the party) may be denied the right to enter the contest. These few restrictions have not prevented a large number of people from being nominated in recent leadership conventions: 9 candidates on the first ballot in the 1968 Liberal meeting and 12 candidates in the 1976 Progressive Conservative leadership convention.

Once the candidates have been nominated, they are given the opportunity to address the delegates. Following the speeches by the candidates, the voting procedure begins, according to the following rules. First, the voting is done by secret, individual ballots. Since no one else knows how they have voted, delegates are free from political intimidation by a leadership candidate. The secret ballot has also produced an effect known as the Flora Syndrome, named after Flora MacDonald's leadership bid in 1976. The Flora Syndrome refers to a delegate publicly declaring support for one candidate, and then voting differently in the privacy of the voting booth. This pattern was also evident in the 1981 Conservative party's annual meeting, where few people publicly were willing to call for a leadership review, but when the time came, 33 percent voted for such a review process.

The secret ballot thus increases the importance of the individual delegate, since a vote from Newfoundland counts as much as a vote from an Ontario delegate. As well, since no candidate can win simply as a regional spokesman or "favorite son," each leadership hopeful must appeal to the delegates on a national or countrywide basis. For example, a candidate from the largest province, Ontario, cannot win solely as a favorite son candidate, even if all of the delegates from Ontario vote for him or her, because the Ontario delegation comprises only about one-third of the total number of participants.

A second operating rule is that each successive ballot (first ballot, second ballot, third ballot, etc.) is held almost immediately. As soon as the first ballot is finished, the second ballot begins, with only a short interval between. Ballots are held until one nominee receives a majority of votes cast. The quick succession of ballots means that candidates have very little time to decide whether they will remain in the contest or to make deals with the other candidates.

A third rule allows for the elimination of minor candidates after each ballot (e.g., those candidates not receiving a minimum number of votes, such as 50), and for the elimination of the least-placed candidate (e.g., the candidate with the fewest votes, once all minor candidates are no longer in the contest). This third operating rule helps to ensure a relatively quick decision by the convention. For example, in the 1968 Liberal convention, the original nine candidates from the first ballot were reduced to three by the fourth ballot, while in the 1976 Progressive Conservative meeting, 12 first-ballot nominees were cut to two by the fourth ballot.

The victory of Joe Clark in the 1976 contest illustrates that the eventual winner need not be the most popular on the first ballot. Clark won because most of the candidates who were eliminated between ballots threw their support to him. For example, between the first and second ballots, Gillies, Stevens, Grafftey, and Fraser withdrew and supported Clark, while Hellyer withdrew and gave his support to Wagner. Between the second and third ballots, MacDonald withdrew and supported Clark, while Horner and Nowlan aligned themselves with Wagner. However, more important than how many leadership candidates withdraw and give their support to a remaining candidate, is the loyalty of their delegates. Since delegates use the secret ballot, leadership candidates cannot guarantee how their supporters will vote after they have withdrawn or been eliminated from the contest. Because of the quick succession of ballots, all a leadership candidate can do is to ask supporters to cast their future ballots for a specific candidate, or to make some sort of symbolic gesture, such as sitting with a remaining candidate. However, many delegates simply ignore such a request, and vote for their own choice anyway. For example, even though Jack Horner moved to the camp of Claude Wagner, it is doubtful that many of his delegates from rural Alberta voted for Wagner on subsequent ballots. The result of such voting rules is to make it possible for a relatively unknown candidate to win the leadership of a major Canadian political party.

Leadership selection in the New Democratic Party is based on a different philosophy than that of the two parliamentary parties. As an extra-parliamentary party that seeks to control its leader, the NDP requires that the party leader be selected on a regular basis. The NDP leader chosen ''is to be held accountable for his term as leader by the members of his party meeting in convention, and he is expected to ensure that the party convention policy decisions are implemented once he and his colleagues have gained power" (Courtney, 1973: 174). As a result of this view, the party leader must automatically seek reelection at the NDP's biennial convention, thus eliminating the need to push for a leadership review process, as in the Liberal and Conservative parties. However, in fact, no serious challenge to the party leader has ever developed within the NDP, thus resulting in a secure tenure of office. For example, in the July 1981 NDP meeting, while 37 percent of the delegates voted against their leader's stand on the constitutional issue, discontent over policy did not result in a challenge to Ed Broadbent's continuing leadership of the party.

Although all federal parties use the national party leadership convention to select their leaders, the type of leader chosen by the parties has differed between the Liberals and Conservatives (Smiley, 1968; Courtney, 1973; Perlin, 1980). In the Liberal party, candidates from Ontario and Quebec dominate, with every leader thus far selected coming from Central Canada. Conservatives are more likely to select nominees from either Western Canada or the Maritimes. Thus, the regional nature of the party system and party support is reflected within the parties, as well as between them in election campaigns. Conservatives have relied on those who were veterans of elective office, especially on people who have served as provincial premiers. Liberals, in contrast, have rarely chosen a leader who has ever contested a provincial election and have been receptive to candidates who have had little political experience. In this sense, the Liberals have been more pragmatic than the Conservatives in the selection of their leaders, even accepting a candidate such as Trudeau, who had vehemently attacked the Liberal party shortly before joining it. Such pragmatism is also evident in the Liberal party's alternation between French and English leaders (King, St. Laurent, Pearson, Trudeau): the party of Ontario and Quebec rarely forgets where its power base lies. By contrast, Conservatives have failed to appeal to Quebec in terms of their leadership selection, as exemplified by Claude Wagner's defeat in their 1976 convention.

The type of leader selected varies not only between parties, but with other forms of leadership selection as well. For example, since the adoption of the national party leadership convention, the role of the party caucus has greatly diminished, thereby increasing the opportunity for the selection of outsiders. It is highly doubtful that either Joe Clark or Pierre Trudeau would have been chosen to lead their parties if the party caucus method had been used in either 1976 or 1968. Moreover, being selected by a national party convention has enhanced the power of the leader over his or her party caucus, since leaders now argue that they can be removed only by such a convention. However, if a leader is removed, as Diefenbaker was in the 1967 Conservative convention, then the caucus is likely to become split between the supporters of the old and new leaders, as Robert Stanfield discovered. After his ouster, Diefenbaker remained a member of the party caucus, "emitting all the baleful radiance of a whore at a family wedding" (Young, 1978: 290). Finally, if the major parties are electoral coalitions, then the basic factor in leadership selection is whether the new leader can enhance the party's electoral prospects. As a result, the leaders so picked have been pragmatic politicians, nonideological in outlook, with the primary goal of electoral victory. Those leaders who cannot produce such results immediately come under attack, with internal party conflict over leadership replacement usually occurring after an electoral defeat. Since Canadian politics is leader-oriented and because the easiest way to change a party's image is to select a new leader, the Conservative party, as the usual losing party in federal elections, has had a history of internal party conflict over questions of leadership, dubbed in one recent analysis as the Tory Syndrome. However, enduring battles over leadership undercut the viability of the opposition party in the public's mind, thereby further contributing to that party's electoral decline (Perlin, 1980: 200).

Party Finance
If parties are primarily electoral organizations, then it is not surprising to find that the major expenses facing the parties are campaign expenditures. As a fundraiser who worked for both the Conservatives and Liberals, Israel Tarte's statement (quoted in Dawson, 1970: 478) that "elections are not won by prayers alone" points to the importance of financial considerations in the success of a political party. Changes in campaign techniques in recent decades, in particular the emphasis on costly mass media advertising, have greatly increased the necessity for party funds. Parties also need money to carry the organization through the inter-election period, an especially vulnerable situation for opposition parties.

The pattern of party finance differs between the cadre and mass party types. Traditionally, the cadre parties (Liberal and Conservative) have relied on contributions from the corporate sector, with large donations from relatively few sponsors. In contrast, mass parties have taken a grass-roots funding approach, depending on small donations from numerous individuals or on union support.

In the initial years of Confederation, party leaders had to concern themselves directly with matters of party finance. The inevitable soon occurred: a party leader, John A. Macdonald, was involved in questions of party funding and corruption. The Pacific Scandal of 1872 brought the downfall of the Conservative government and almost wrecked Macdonald's career. Consequently, party leaders have since sought to isolate themselves from matters of party finance by having specific party organizers for fundraising activities. These "bagmen," who are often appointed to patronage positions such as the Senate, operate outside of the party leader's sight, so that when the political scandal eventually hits, the party leader is able to disassociate him or herself from any involvement in political wrongdoing. Seeing no evil allows the party leader to profess innocence, while the party's bagman may be charged with criminal wrongdoing by the government controlled by his party and left to defend himself, as Senator Louis Giguère discovered in the Sky Shops Affair.

This pattern of fundraising by the Liberals and Conservatives, based on large corporate donations, has endured, in slightly modified form, to the present. The financial backing thus received helped to reinforce the dominance of the two major parties, since new parties were often hard-pressed for cash. Moreover, because the extra-parliamentary parties represented a challenge to the existing social and economic interests of Central Canada, they neither wanted, nor were they typically offered, corporate largesse. As a result, they sought a new means of party finance, attempting to use the mass-funding techniques of the European social democratic parties. This grass-roots approach centred on two sources of potential party income: annual dues from individual members and contributions from trade unions and interest groups. The initial attempts at mass funding through individual contributions were not particularly successful, usually leaving the party perpetually short of funds, as the experience of the CCF demonstrates. However, dues paying members combined with labour union contributions have helped to give the NDP a more solid financial base then its predecessor. In the 1960s, trade union financial support for the NDP amounted to approximately 40 percent of party funds, allowing the party to challenge the financial dominance of the Liberals and Conservatives (Paltiel, 1970: 56–61). The most successful mass-funding party in Canadian history is the Parti Québécois, which not only sent back corporate donations in the 1973 and 1976 provincial election campaigns, but proceeded to make such contributions to parties illegal after they became the government in 1976.

The traditional pattern of party finance for the Liberals and Conservatives utilized several basic techniques, although these practices were regularly denied by the party bagmen. The essential first step in fundraising was to select bagmen who had access to the financial and corporate elite: as Mackenzie King (quoted in Wearing, 1981: 63) put it, ''you need millionaires to get money from millionaires.'' These fundraisers would then visit wealthy individuals and corporate executives for their annual contributions. A longtime practice was for the donations to be split 60 percent for the government party and 40 percent for the opposition. Such contributions thus ensured that no matter which party won the next election, the individual or corporation, having donated to the party coffers, could count on access to the political leaders.

If such donations were not readily given, the governing party could institute the practices of toll-gating and kickbacks (Wearing, 1981: 58–64). In toll-gating, government contracts or business would be allocated to those firms that had given to the party coffers, while a kickback scheme meant that once a firm had received government work, a certain percentage would be returned to the ruling party, usually by way of campaign contributions. Finally, the party in power could also use patronage appointments to bolster party finances. Those receiving such appointments are often expected to contribute a portion of their salaries to the party that appointed them. These practices clearly favour the party in power, with electoral defeat often creating a crisis of party finance.

The major change in this traditional pattern of party finance came with the passage of the 1974 Election Expenses Act, which attempts both to regulate party fundraising activities and to provide public subsidies for election expenses. The adoption of such a measure has an interesting political lineage: the Liberal minority government between 1972 and 1974 needed the backing of the NDP caucus to stay in power and election finance reform was one payoff for their continuing support. Not surprisingly, the 1974 reforms have greatly benefited the NDP, putting the party on a more equal financial footing with the major parties. We would also suggest a further reason for the 1974 Election Expenses Act: campaign expenditures were increasing so rapidly that all of the parties feared their inability to raise adequate funds in future elections. As a result, the parties collectively turned to public funding and proceeded to raid the public treasury without greatly changing the existing practices of party finance.

One requirement of the Election Expenses Act is that the parties have to file an annual financial report with the Chief Electoral

Officer. The first reports, which covered the 1974–1975 fiscal year, indicated that it costs about $2 million to operate a national party in a non-election year (*Globe and Mail*, February 10, 1976 and February 11, 1976). By the 1980s, that annual figure for party spending had reached $4 million to $5 million. Moreover, the corporate sector, with few exceptions, gave exactly the same contribution to both major parties. The difference between cadre and mass party funding approaches was also evident: while 6400 individuals contributed to the Conservatives and 9900 to the Liberals, 28 000 persons made a donation to the NDP. While approximately 30 percent of Conservative funds and 50 percent of Liberal funds come from individuals, 85 percent of NDP donations originate from party members.

In addition to requiring an annual report, the Election Expenses Act seeks to limit the amount of money that parties and candidates can spend, provides for the disclosure of the sources of party and candidate incomes, grants subsidies for candidate expenses and party media advertising, and establishes a tax credit for people contributing to party funds (Paltiel, 1975). Although in effect as of August 1, 1974, the first election to which these provisions applied was the 1979 contest. The July 1974 election was conducted under the traditional pattern of party finance – an example of "once more for old-times sake" before the reform legislation became applicable.

The impact of the Election Expenses Act can be seen in the extent of public subsidies to parties and candidates in the 1979 and 1980 election campaigns (Seidle and Paltiel, 1981: 275–276). Subsidies to the parties came to $4½ million and to $17 million for the various candidates. Since its adoption in 1974, public support for election expenses has totalled close to $50 million.

While the 1974 Election Expenses Act represents a considerable improvement over past practices, its effectiveness is open to challenge. For example, the limits on party and candidate expenditures were set relatively high, so that if the Act had applied to the 1974 election, no party would have exceeded them. Moreover, before the Act was applied the first time, these limits were raised in 1977 and the base year for indexing the spending ceilings was changed from 1974 to 1976, which added a possible $23 million to potential party and candidate costs. In other words, limits which are set so high that no party approximates them in no way curtail party spending in campaigns. In fact, since the public now subsidizes these expenses, the costs of the campaigns have soared to unprecedented levels. A second defect concerns the amount of individual contributions: any donation over $100 must be disclosed, but no limit is put on how much can be given. Thus, the financial dependence on small groups of financial backers has not been greatly undercut. Third, the enforcement provisions for violations of this Act are weak – it is up to the public or the various parties to lay complaints with the Chief Electoral Officer. With the "live and let live" attitudes of the parties, few violations will be investigated. Given these limitations of the 1974 Election Expenses Act, the traditional pattern of party finance remains largely in place, with public funding grafted on. The parties successfully raided the public treasury without giving the public effective control over the area of party finance.

Party Functions

Matters of party finance are significant because they help to determine whether a party will be successful in carrying out its electoral functions: money cannot buy electoral victory, but electoral victory is difficult to achieve without it, given the expensive nature of modern campaigns. Canadian parties are electoral organizations not only in the sense of aiming for victory, but also because they are important actors in organizing the electorate. For example, parties help get the individual voters on the appropriate polling lists, provide the voters with information on the issues of the contest, and help to stimulate voter interest and participation. Parties are also the key structure in recruiting candidates for office, thus providing the electorate with someone to vote for or against, as the case may be. As Dalton Camp (1979: 231) has observed, the "essentials of Canadian politics are few: the system needs enough good men to make it work and enough fools to make it interesting."

Parties also help to structure the electorate by serving as political objects with which people can identify. These partisan attachments are some of the earliest linkages an individual develops with the political system. Although individual partisan attachments may vary, in the aggregate they help to structure the partisan coloration of the electorate. A party's national vote total on a percentage basis rarely changes by more than a few points between election campaigns. One reason for this is the extent of partisan ties among the electors: there is a reservoir of support for the parties, which they receive regardless of the issues or leaders in a particular campaign.

In addition to serving as objects of individual emotional ties, parties help to structure the electorate, because the major socioeconomic cleavages of society differentiate the group bases of partisan support in the Canadian polity. Historically, different regions, religious, ethnic, and linguistic groups have become linked with specific parties. The way these groups align themselves with the parties gives historical continuity to the party system. The most obvious example of this point is the preference of English-Canadians for the Conservative party and French-Canadians for the Liberal party. Such group basis of party support reveals that the Canadian "party system is organized around the usual regional, religious, and social class oppositions to which is added a specific linguistic cleavage" (Laponce, 1972: 284).

The party that wins the election undertakes, in addition to its electoral functions, a number of what can be called governing functions. In the Canadian parliamentary system, the governing party is the key mechanism for achieving the fusion of the executive and legislative branches of government. Walter Bagehot's famous description of the mid-19th century British cabinet as "the hyphen which joins – the buckle which fastens – the executive to the legislative part of the state" is obsolete since the advent of parties. It is the party that lays the foundation for the fusion of executive and legislative powers, and only after the party does so can an institution such as the cabinet implement the fusion of powers on a day-to-day basis. In the modern era, cabinet government is predicated on party government; Walter Bagehot's buckle has a party label. Failure to realize this relationship has often led to a denigration of the significant role parties play in the governing process.

Parties help to organize the government in several ways. It is the electoral success of a party, in terms of it winning more seats than any other party in the legislature, which provides the group basis of government organization. Except in rare circumstances, the leader of the party with the largest block of legislative seats is asked by the formal executive to form a government. Thus, control of the legislature gives the party control of the executive. While it is true that once a government has been formed, the cabinet may dominate the party caucus and the legislature, the legislative base of the cabinet is often lost sight of. In a parliamentary system, the political executive retains office only as long as it has legislative support, and that support is provided by the party organization through the principle of party discipline. Only when a *free vote* is called (i.e., when party discipline is relaxed and the legislative members decide on an individual basis how to vote) does the group basis of legislative power momentarily recede.

An additional governing function of the successful party is that it directly provides the personnel to fill the cabinet portfolios. Except for the one experience of coalition government during World War I, all subsequent cabinets have been formed by the individuals from a single party. In this way, the party literally takes over physical control of the government by placing its members in positions of executive authority. Moreover, the cabinet, once formed, controls thousands of further job appointments to the various departments and agencies of government. Through the use of patronage appointments, the governing party oozes its way through the structure of government, linking unto itself the disparate realms of power and influence. Patronage is the interstitial glue of politics, fusing together the otherwise inchoate elements of government. A good example of this process was evident when the Conservatives won power in 1979. After securing office, the party set up, under one of its defeated candidates Jean Pigott, a screening process for all government appointments. A list of all jobs over which the government had appointment power was prepared, so that when vacancies occurred these positions would be filled by people with Conservative party ties. Moreover, a longstanding practice in Canadian politics has been to appoint a political minister for each province, who oversees and directs the filling of vacant federal governmental positions within his or her province. By such mechanisms, parties seek to organize the disparate structures of government into a working, if not necessarily a cohesive, organization.

A final governing function of parties is to contribute to policy direction and leadership for the political system. In most cases, the parties play only a small role in this process. Once a government is formed, the policy process is dominated by the cabinet and bureaucracy, with the party organizations relegated to a minor role. However, parties are an essential basis for the implementation of policy, because they provide the necessary support in the legislature for its passage. In addition, parties may play a policy-making role by providing the party platforms for election campaigns. Overall, however, the party organizations have a limited role in the policy process, serving instead as supporters of policy decided elsewhere.

While all parties have various electoral functions, it is only the winning party that directly participates in the several governing functions. However, the opposition parties are indirectly involved through their participation in the legislature, which can be used to attack or to suggest changes in government policy. Although no minor party has ever formed a government in Ottawa, they have often acquired limited governing functions because of the frequent occurrence of minority governments. As a result, minor parties have sometimes had a direct impact on government policy, which has enhanced their role as innovators in the Canadian party system.

COMPARING PARTIES AND PARTY SYSTEMS

Britain and the United States are two examples of competitive party systems. In these polities, current practices reflect the origin and development of the individual parties.

British Political Parties

Historically, parties first emerged in the European context, with Britain leading in the development of these new political mechanisms. By the middle of the 17th century, factions, the forerunners of the modern party organizations, were present within the legislature. However, the importance of these new groups was not immediately appreciated, as evidenced by the labels Tories and Whigs, nicknames "given in a spirit of derision," since "Tories were bandits on the highways of Ireland" and the "Whigs a band of Scottish insurgents in 1648" (Duverger, 1972: 78). By the middle of the 19th century, the factions had developed into the parties of the modern era. With the Reform Act of 1832, these parties expanded from their legislative birthplace to seek greater support among the electorate, in the process establishing party structures at the local level and cohesive groups within Parliament. Adopting the names Conservatives and Liberals, instead of Tories and Whigs, the two initial parties of parliamentary origin dominated the party system for three-quarters of a century.

However, parties of extra-parliamentary origin have had a major impact on British politics in the 20th century. The most significant event was the formation of the Trade Union Congress in 1900, which aimed at establishing a mass-based, socialist, working-class party. Adopting the name Labour Party in 1906, this group gradually emerged as a challenger to the Liberals and Conservatives. By the 1920s it had become the second largest party in Parliament, replacing the Liberals, and the first Labour government was formed in 1923. Since the 1930s and the ensuing decline of the Liberal party, Britain has had primarily a two-party battle, between the Conservatives and the Labourites.

In addition to the expansion of the Labour party in the early decades of the present century, Britain experienced the growth of a series of nationalist parties based on the regional and cultural concerns of Ireland, Scotland, and Wales. The most significant nationalist party was the Irish, which held 80 seats in the House of Commons from 1910 to 1918 and eventually succeeded in gaining Home Rule or independence for Ireland. More recently, the 1970s saw seats in the Commons obtained by both the Scottish Nationalist Party (SNP) and the Welsh Nationalist Party (Plaid Cymru), with their strength peaking in the October 1974 election and falling off somewhat in the May 1979 contest. In addition to these nationalist parties, other groups such as the Communist Party and the National Front (a neo-fascist group) have competed in recent elections, but have had little electoral success and no great impact on the longstanding parties in British politics.

While the internally created parliamentary parties (Liberal and Conservative) and the externally created parties (especially the Labour party) show the characteristics of the cadre and mass type of parties, respectively, British parties have some unique features as well, which reflect certain attributes of societal and governmental organization. Most important is the fact that Britain is both parliamentary and unitary, with the parties reflecting the resulting centralization of power. For example, while the Liberals and Conservatives may be traditional in organization, they are "rigid elitist parties" in operation (Duverger, 1972: 7). In comparison to Canadian parties, the British parties are more centralized in structure, recruitment, and leadership. British parties are also more ideological than their Canadian counterparts; parties run on explicit platforms or party manifestos that they are expected to implement if they acquire office. Thus, the major parties in Britain in the 1980s (Labour and Conservative) can be classified as ideological in content and programmatic in function. One result of programmatic and centralized parties was the early development of unified groups within Parliament, with strict party discipline being seen historically as one of the hallmarks of British party organization. Although party discipline was increasingly challenged in the late 1970s, the Labour and Conservative parties are still unified and cohesive organizations in Parliament, except on rare occasions.

In addition to their more ideological style and centralized structure, British parties are less regional than their Canadian analogues. Although there is a regional basis of party support even within England itself, the Labour and Conservative parties are more national in composition than either of the two major Canadian parties (Drucker, 1979: 217). Moreover, the centralized nature of the political system has forced nationalist parties to compete for seats in the national legislature. The result has been a greater impact of new parties in British than Canadian politics, although the appearance of such parties in Britain has been less frequent. In Canada, federalism has helped to contain nationalist sentiment, exemplified by the Parti Québécois and its power in provincial politics, while in Britain, nationalist emotion led to the granting of Home Rule for

Ireland. Although the characteristics of the major parties are reflective of the general origin and development of the cadre (Conservative) and mass (Labour) types, their evolution in the British milieu has produced these unique features as well. The British parties remain, however, electorally-oriented parties: "the goal of the British political party is to win elections" (Finer, 1980: 167).

The party system in Britain can be described as competitive in nature, dominated by two major parties, increasingly challenged by both the growth of the nationalist parties and a corresponding decline in public support for themselves (Drucker, 1979). The two major parties have controlled governmental office since 1945, with no other party participation and, unlike Canada, election results have regularly produced majority governments, except for the February 1974 contest. Moreover, the two main parties have alternated in office, although the Conservatives have more often been the government party since 1945. At the end of Margaret Thatcher's first term of office, the Conservatives will have governed for 22 years since 1945, with no party in office for longer than 6 years since the Labour victory in 1964. This turnover pattern makes the British party system more competitive than the Canadian.

In addition to its competitive nature, the two-party battle between the Conservative and Labour parties, and party alternation in office, the British party system is further characterized by the historical dominance of the Conservative party: from 1885 to 1945 the Conservatives "were in government for almost 75 percent of the time" (Gamble, 1979: 26). The normal governing party in British politics is the Conservative party, while in Canada it has been the Liberals. Moreover, the tactics of both parties have been similar, with their appeals to national unity. The cleavage basis of the British party system in the 20th century has been the class division, which replaced the predominant religious cleavage of the 18th and 19th centuries (Butler and Stokes, 1971: 95–134). The transformation of the cleavage basis from religion to class had a significant influence on the party system: it destroyed the basis of Liberal party support and allowed for its replacement by the Labour party. In contrast, the continuing significance of the religious, ethnic, linguistic, and regional cleavages in Canada has been a key factor in the dominance of the Liberal party and has prevented the expansion of the NDP, which appeals to voters on the basis of class considerations.

The British method of picking party leaders is through selection by their respective party caucuses. If the leader of a British party resigns, members of the party caucus meet and vote from among those candidates who have declared themselves for the office. Successive ballots are held until one candidate has achieved a majority. For example, in October 1980, James Callaghan resigned as leader of the Labour party. In November, British Labour MPs selected their new leader, Michael Foot, after two ballots of the party caucus.

There are several advantages to choosing party leaders this way. First, only current members of Parliament have a chance of being selected, thus ensuring that the leader chosen will be well-known, at least to the party. However, selection by the party caucus has a corresponding disadvantage of producing a closed process: it is practically impossible for an outsider or an unknown to win. The second advantage of the British practice is that a decision can be reached on a new leader in a matter of weeks (hours or days, if necessary). In contrast, the Canadian pattern now takes at least several months to complete, and sometimes longer. The third advantage of caucus selection is that the candidate so selected to lead the party in Parliament will have majority support in the caucus. By contrast, in Canada, a leader selected by the convention method may find that he or she lacks the support of a significant section of the parliamentary caucus.

Although the caucus is the key element in the party leadership selection process, there are some interesting differences between the British parties. Prior to 1965, the Conservatives did not take an explicit vote: instead a leader "emerged" from the ranks of the party caucus. While this was a somewhat mysterious process even to party insiders, the system worked well until the 1960s, when no clear-cut leader appeared. As a result, reforms adopted in 1965 provide for an actual vote among Conservative Members of Parliament. This method of leadership selection, especially prior to the reforms of the 1960s, reinforced the leader's control: the "most striking feature of the Conservative party organization is the enormous power which appears to be concentrated in the hands of the Leader" (McKenzie, 1967: 21). Initially the British Conservative leader, once selected, was not required to face reelection by the party organization; however, since 1975, reelection is required at the annual meeting.

The selection and power of the Labour party leader reflects the extra-parliamentary origins of the party. In such a mass-based, ideological party, the party organization seeks to exert control not only over the party caucus, but over the party leader as well. At least in theory, both the leader and caucus are subject to the organization's directives and policy decisions; in fact, in most cases, the parliamentary leader and caucus have managed to retain a considerable measure of autonomy from the extra-parliamentary organization. One way of seeking to ensure control of the leaders has been the traditional practice of making them stand for annual reelection by the party organization, although in practice they are almost never opposed. The result has been to place Labour leaders in a less dominant position within the party hierarchy than their Conservative counterparts, particularly when the Labour party is in opposition. Although subject to outside advice and interference, if not control, by the extra-parliamentary organization, the party leader, prior to the 1980s, has always been chosen by the caucus, using a voting procedure similar to that of the Conservatives.

The longstanding battle between the parliamentary and extra-parliamentary wings of the Labour party finally became so intense in the Fall of 1980 as to provoke a change in the party's leadership selection process. The basic method of leadership selection, beginning in 1981, is based on a widening of the election process to include not only the party caucus but the trade unions and constituency parties as well. An electoral college type of mechanism was adopted in January 1981, which gave the party caucus 30 percent of the vote, the constituency associations 30 percent, and the trade unions 40 percent. This new pattern was designed to give the extra-parliamentary wing of the party, dominated by the trade unions and the more leftist elements, control of the leadership selection process in the Labour party.

The 1981 change in the process of selecting the Labour party leader is the most important political development in the British party system since the formation of the Labour party in 1900, for it has had profound effects on the competitive party battle. First, the British Labour party has split, with a number of key members and former ministers leaving the party to found a new centre-based Social Democratic Party. Polls in the Winter and Spring of 1981 indicated the new party was more popular than either of the major parties. Second, this new party, by aiming at the centre of the political spectrum, is seeking to capitalize on the increasing polarization of the old-line parties, as the Labour party moves left and the Conservative party moves right. Third, the new party is rekindling life into the Liberal party, which has had little influence in the party system for over 50 years. In June 1981, the Liberals and the Social Democrats agreed to a joint strategy for the next general election, in that they will not compete against each other at the constituency level. Such a tactic should maximize both parties' support, to the detriment of the Labour and Conservative parties.

Given these developments, the potential success of the Social Democratic Party may have a profound impact on the British party system, and ultimately on the nature of the larger political system. For example, by the Spring of 1982 the new Social Democratic Party had won several significant by-elections and, together with the Liberals, had over forty members in the House of Commons.

Since the rise of the class alignment in the 20th century, the key factor in the social bases of party support in Britain is the class cleavage, with the middle and upper classes supporting the Conservatives and the working class backing the Labour party. However, both major parties appeal to members of all social classes. If party strength corresponded to rigid class support, then the Conservatives would never win an election. However, with about 30 percent of their support coming from the working class, the Conservatives have done well in their contests for office. Moreover, in recent decades, white-collar workers have given substantial support to the Labour party. The basic class patterns of party support in Britain are not evident, however, with respect to the nationalist parties, which appeal to cultural and regional loyalties instead. Thus, unlike the major Canadian parties, which show little class basis, British party support reflects the class divisions of the 20th century.

Patterns of party finance show predictable characteristics in Britain. The Conservative party is dependent on the cadre type of party finance, with individual and business contributions from relatively few donors. The party has been more than able to finance itself, has opposed public subsidies, has been successful in constituency level finance, and, as a result, clearly outspends the Labour party both between and during election contests (McKenzie, 1967: 653–659; Finer, 1980: 105–110). The Labour party is heavily dependent on trade union financial backing, which now accounts for 80 percent of party funds (Birch, 1980: 109). With individual party membership declining and with the local constituency associations unable to raise adequate revenue, the Labour party favours extension of the public financing of parties and election campaigns. While local campaign costs have been limited since 1948, there is no limit on the amount spent by the national parties (Punnett, 1980: 57). Public subsidies cover such items as free TV party broadcasts, but the parties still need several hundred thousand pounds to support the national party advertising campaign during an election. In a non-election year, total national party costs run between one and two million pounds. In contrast to the Canadian pattern, the major donors to the Labour and Conservative causes do not contribute to both parties, a reflection, perhaps, of the more ideological and class-based party system in Britain.

While British parties have developed certain unique features of structure, style, and interaction, we should not lose sight of the fact that British parties, like their counterparts in other competitive polities, continue to be significant governing mechanisms.

American Political Parties

Reflective of the political culture's suspicion of power and its concentration is the traditional American attitude towards political parties: at best, parties are viewed in an ambivalent manner; at worst, they are perceived as downright detrimental to democracy. In his famous Farewell Address, George Washington sought to alert the American public to "the baneful effects of the Spirit of Party," and even Thomas Jefferson (quoted in Hofstadter, 1972: 2, 123), who was instrumental in the development of the longest lasting political party in history – the Democratic party – remarked that "If I could not go to heaven but with a party, I would not go there at all." However, this aversion to parties was overcome, as in other countries, due to practical considerations, primarily the need to govern in a system of fragmented power.

The initial parties were of legislative origin, created in the early years of the 19th century. However, it was not until the era of Jacksonian democracy in the 1830s that the parties emerged as necessary ingredients of the governing process. The 19th-century origin of the American parties is crucial in understanding their structure, organization, and attributes.

American parties are the preeminent examples of the cadre type of political party: "highly decentralized, status-quo oriented, and win-centered" (Blank, 1980: 55). The goal of electoral victory has produced another attribute of American parties – they are usually nonideological. Ideological specificity repels rather than attracts voters, thereby leading to similar policy views for both the Republican and Democratic parties and to the charge that the two parties are interchangeable in office. When a party becomes ideologically distinct, as the Republicans did with Barry Goldwater in 1964 and the Democrats achieved with George McGovern in 1972, a massive electoral defeat occurs. Although Ronald Reagan may have begun and sustained his political career by his image as a "man of the right," his years as governor of California and his 1980 presidential election victory demonstrate his ability to moderate his views and to move to the centre of the political spectrum in the search for electoral victory. As a result, American parties appeal to a wide social and economic base; they are heterogeneous in makeup, not class-based. Party membership is not clearly defined; membership cards, annual dues, and agreement with a party's policy positions are basically unknown in the American context.

In terms of structure, the parties are extremely decentralized, and power resides at the state and local levels. National party coalitions are created around the presidential contest every four years – between such events, the parties survive on a local base. The decentralization of power is evident in terms of party finance, membership and recruitment. This dispersal of power is a reflection of several of the key principles of the American system of government, namely federalism and the separation of powers. The decentralized pattern has been greatly strengthened in the 20th century by the use of the primary method of candidate selection, which has countered the centralizing or nationalizing trends with respect to some aspects of American politics. If anything, the parties are more decentralized now than they have ever been.

Within the parties, the decentralization of power is reflected in the lack of strong party cohesion both inside and outside of the legislature. While party members share a common label, they rarely share a common purpose. American parties are highly factionalized, with candidates forming their own organizations in their bids for elective office. If successful, candidates thus owe little loyalty to the party organization but considerable loyalty to the group that helped them to win power. Candidate-centred groups have been strengthened by the use of the primary method of nomination for office, where the party can no longer even control who runs under its party label.

The effects of the decentralized pattern are clearly evident in the legislature, where party discipline is weak. Party members, with almost total immunity from retribution from their party leaders, can vote as they wish, for the simple reason that the party leadership has few political resources to turn against them. Party unity is often dependent on the issue being considered. Moreover, each party contains both liberal and conservative factions, which may desert their party leadership on specific matters of public policy. Majorities are often forged across, rather than within, party lines. For example, Republican President Ronald Reagan, despite the fact that the House of Representatives had a solid Democratic majority, was able to win large cuts in government programs in his first few months in office in 1981 by aligning Republicans and conservative Democrats together in a working majority.

The two, long-dominant major American parties, therefore, can be described as cadre parties, election-oriented, nonideological, heterogeneous in social composition, decentralized, with weak party unity. These attributes are reflected in and conditioned by the nature of the party system. The American party network is competitive, dominated by the two major parties, and highly discriminatory against new or minor parties. The electoral battle between Democrats and Republicans, however, has not been, from an historical point of view, an equal battle. One party, as in Britain and Canada, has tended to dominate for long periods: the Republicans from the time of the Civil War to the 1920s, the Democrats from the 1920s to the 1960s, with the last two decades showing a more balanced competitive pattern, at least in presidential elections. The two-party competition focuses on control of the centre of the political spectrum. However, unlike the Canadian system, where the centre is regularly occupied by one party, the centre of the political spectrum in American politics is up for grabs – either party may occupy it, and both try to do so. The battle for the political centre is a key reason why the Democrats and Republicans are nonideological and socially diverse parties.

One of the most often described characteristics of the American party system is that it is a two-party system, dominated by the Republicans and Democrats since the middle of the 19th century. However, it is not true to say that only two parties exist – many parties officially compete, for example, in a presidential election. What is significant is that these other parties rarely affect the pattern of competition between the two major parties, exemplified by the failure of John Anderson's National Unity Ticket in 1980, which received only seven percent of the popular vote and no delegates in the Electoral College. New parties or minor parties are regularly formed, but their success is limited.

Minor parties usually emerge around a specific issue or are based on a particular ideology, thereby limiting their appeal to the majority of the American electorate. If such a party begins to show signs of electoral success, its programs and leaders may be co-opted by one of the major parties, whose nonideological stance allows for considerable flexibility and pragmatism in such matters. Moreover, the decentralized structure and weak cohesion of the major parties often entices new groups to work within one of the major parties, instead of forming a new party (e.g., Goldwater within the Republican party in 1964, McGovern within the Democratic party in 1972). The most successful new groups or movements in American politics have been those that have worked within the existing parties. Finally, the rules of the electoral system are designed to discourage minor parties. New parties, for example, find it difficult to get their names on the ballot: in the 1968 presidential race, "George Wallace had a staff of twenty-five lawyers traveling from state to state researching election laws, filing suits, and getting petition signatures to meet local requirements" (Huckshorn, 1980: 70). Moreover, the plurality electoral formula used in the United States makes it difficult for a minor party to win legislative seats even when it wins a sizable share of the popular vote. For these reasons, minor parties have rarely disturbed the two-party battle between Republicans and Democrats.

Why do minor parties develop in the first place and what accounts for their relative electoral success in a system such as the Canadian and their failure in others like the American? The reason for new parties in both systems is the same – social and economic diversity. The way these new groups operate varies because of the differing institutional contexts in Canada and the United States. It is wrong to assume that Canada has produced more minor parties than the United States – on a numerical basis it has not. However, Canada has produced more minor parties that have affected the pattern of competition in the party system. The basic explanation for Canada is that diversity, combined with federal and parliamentary principles and party discipline, encourages the formation of new parties. In contrast, the decentralized parties and the various election laws, which discriminate against new groups in the American system, make it likely that they will work within one of the existing party organizations. In Canada, a George McGovern or a Barry Goldwater would have formed a new political party; in the United States, they simply seized control of the existing party structures.

Given the characteristics of the major American parties and the party system, the essential aim in selecting party leaders is to win elections. The American parties have been in the forefront of developing new mechanisms of leadership selection, although it is open to question whether these new techniques have improved the quality of the nominees for political office. The current system of leadership selection is an amalgam of historical practice, containing elements of caucus, convention, and primary techniques. The most significant aspect of the change from one method to the next has been the desire to give the public, rather than the party bosses, control of the nomination and leadership selection process. In contrast to the Canadian system of party members meeting in a national party leadership convention, or the British pattern of the parliamentary caucus casting a ballot, current American practice aims at providing an opportunity for involving the mass public in choosing party leaders.

American party leaders are selected through a two-stage process: first, delegates are chosen to attend a national party convention and second, the national party convention selects the party leader. Unfortunately, what seems straightforward at first glance is exceedingly complex, since each of the 50 states set its own rules for delegate selection, procedures which may change from one election to the next.

The first stage of leadership selection uses two basic approaches – the primary and caucus techniques. The most important of the two methods of delegate selection is the presidential primary, which in 1980 picked about 75 percent of the delegates to the national conventions and was used by 37 states and territories. A *presidential primary* is an election among party members to choose their delegates to the national convention, which in turn selects the party's presidential candidate. Those candidates seeking their party's nomination enter a number of that party's presidential primaries. If a candidate wins 30 percent of the vote in a primary, he or she will receive approximately 30 percent of that state's delegates to the national convention. By winning sufficient strength in the primaries, a candidate can win the party's nomination for president. Presidential primaries are held between February and June in an election year. These primaries have become the crucial component in the party leadership contest, since a candidate can win enough delegates to be guaranteed a first ballot nomination victory at the leadership convention. In recent decades, all party leaders have won first ballot convention victories; in other words, the real decision-making power in party leadership is the delegate selection process, with the convention simply ratifying the choice already made.

The second method of delegate selection to the national convention is the caucus technique. The term caucus, as used in the American presidential system of delegate selection, is not the same as a caucus in a parliamentary system. In Britain and Canada, a party caucus means the group of party members in the legislature. In the American delegate selection process, caucus means a meeting of party members from the mass public who decide on their delegates to the national convention. These caucus meetings begin at the local or precinct level and work their way up through district, county, and state-wide conventions. About a dozen states used this procedure in the 1980 presidential race. While it allows for public participation, the caucus method of delegate selection usually involves far fewer rank-and-file party members than does the primary technique.

Several aspects of the American delegate selection process need to be emphasized: first, at the mass level, party members are given the right to participate in the selection of the party leader in both the primary and caucus states and second, at the elite level, anyone has the right to run for the leadership of the party. Both these characteristics emphasize the extent to which the political party, as an organization, has lost control of the nomination process: it controls neither who participates in the delegate selection mechanisms nor who can run for the leadership of the party. Such a pattern of selection might be characterized as "garage-sale politics": one never knows in advance who will show up to offer items for sale or to purchase the goods presented. The only thing that is definite is that few Van Gogh's will ever be found among the dusty artifacts of life, or, as one writer phrase it, "the primary-dominated system of nomination is an unqualified disaster" (McWilliams, 1981: 170).

Following the primaries and caucuses, each party holds its national convention during the summer months of July or August. The conventions previously held centre-stage in the selection of party leaders: the satirist H. L. Mencken once said that there is "nothing quite as entertaining as a hanging or a good convention." In recent decades, there is nothing quite as boring as a national convention, because it has lost the effective power of choice – it merely ratifies the winner determined by the primaries and caucuses. Only if the primaries and caucuses fail to coalesce behind a single candidate would the national convention reacquire effective decision-making power.

The operating rules of an American national convention differ significantly from those utilized in the Canadian national party leadership conventions. First, balloting is open, not secret, and done by states, rather than by individuals. Until the reforms of the 1970s, this rule meant that large blocs of votes could be controlled by party leaders and that deals between leaders and state delegations could be arranged, because a state voted as a group in favour of one or the other candidates, a procedure known as the unit rule. Although the unit rule no longer applies, voting is still done on a state-by-state basis, with delegates openly declaring their support for one of the nominees. Second, such a voting procedure is cumbersome, with the interval between ballots at least several hours, if not longer. Third, there is no rule for the elimination of candidates between ballots, so that a nominee can stay in the race until someone receives a majority vote. The result, historically, has been long conventions, with the 1924 Democratic meeting holding 103 ballots. These rules of procedure make an American convention very different from a Canadian national party convention. Finally, although we have assumed that a party's presidential nominee is the party's leader, in non-presidential election years, especially for the party that loses the presidential race, there is no set way of deciding the question of leadership. For example, after their defeat in the 1980 presidential contest, who was the leader of the Democratic party? Democrats would likely have agreed on only one thing – that Jimmy Carter was no longer their leader. The decentralized structure and fragmented power of the American parties means that the party's legislative leaders in the Senate or House of Representatives, as well as the various leaders in state politics, have as legitimate a claim on that role as the party's defeated presidential nominee.

The dominance of the Republican and Democratic parties has traditionally been reflected in the extent of partisan attachments: electors overwhelmingly identify with the two main parties. A chief characteristic of partisan loyalties in the United States is their public nature – most people are not reluctant to declare which party they support. Moreover, the strength of these partisan ties to the two main parties has often been cited as one important reason why minor parties have had little success at the polls: if people already have an emotional commitment to either the Republicans or Democrats, then it is difficult for a new party to gain adherents. In addition, partisan ties reveal the continued dominance of the Democratic party in American politics, even though the party has been defeated in the presidential elections of 1952, 1956, 1968, 1972, and 1980. For the past 30 years, approximately twice as many voters have identified with the Democrats as with the Republicans, one reason why the Democratic party is classified as the normal majority party in American politics.

The extent of partisan attachments gives each of the major parties a pool to draw on in any particular election. While appealing to the wider electorate, the Republicans and Democrats have traditional groups that support them. Each party seeks to put together a large enough coalition of such groups to win power: the ''supporters of the two American political parties have been distinguished from each other by economic, religious, and national-ethnic differences'' (Nie et al., 1979: 213). The social bases of party support in recent decades can be summarized as follows. First, the higher one's position in the social class hierarchy, the more likely is one to be a Republican. Second, with respect to religion, Jews are more Democratic than Catholics, who in turn are more Democratic than

Protestants. Third, minority groups, particularly racial and the more recent immigrant groups, show a marked proclivity to support the Democratic party. Fourth, regional differences, noticeably the South as a bastion of Democratic strength and Republican dominance in the Middle West and Northeast, has declined in recent years. Thus, the American parties, while socially diverse, do not appeal equally to all major groups in the polity. Although the majority Democratic coalition has been severely weakened during the past two decades, the Republican party has not been able to transform discontent with the Democrats into identification with themselves. Instead, more and more Americans are declaring themselves to be Independents, so that in many surveys more individuals claim such a status than those willing to specify the Republicans or Democrats as the party of their attachment.

The socially diverse support base of the two major parties is not reflected, however, in the area of party finance. As the preeminent cadre parties, the Republicans and Democrats have long depended on corporate backing and large individual contributions. Similar to other systems, the area of party finance has been regularly associated with major political scandals, with Watergate being only the major recent example from among many. Party finance is particularly important in American politics because of the large number of officials selected through the election process. With over 500 000 people chosen for government service in a presidential election year, the amount of money spent by the parties and candidates is approaching the half-billion dollar mark. These expenditures have rapidly escalated, given the heavy emphasis on television advertising in both presidential and congressional elections.

The costs of campaigns, along with the Watergate scandal, produced a climate of reform in the United States in the early 1970s. Although regulation of campaign donations had been on the books since the 1920s, such laws were regularly ignored or violated, given their very weak enforcement provisions. The reforms of the 1970s have put more effective limits on contributions and spending for both individual candidates and parties. In a major departure from past practice, the United States in 1974 adopted provisions for the public financing of presidential election campaigns. A party's presidential nominee who accepts public money is prevented from obtaining private donations for general election expenses. A second major reform concerns the development of political action committees or PACs for short. PACs may be formed by any group to support a particular cause, candidate, or party: by the 1978 congressional elections and the 1980 presidential election, they had become a major source of political funding in the American system.

The characteristics of the American parties and the party system thus reflect certain unique patterns of origin, development, and operation. However, in broad comparisons with other political systems, the American parties show basic similarities with their counterparts in Canada and Britain, the most important attribute being the competitive nature of these three party systems.

POLITICAL OPPOSITION AND PARTY FUTURES

Political parties can perform any number of roles or functions in the political process. In our consideration of parties in Canada, Britain, and the United States, we have focused on two basic tasks of the party organizations, which we designated as their electoral and governing functions. The origin, development, and characteristics of the individual parties and party systems in each country have resulted in different techniques in the performance of these functions. However, a third task of parties in democratic systems is to provide the essential structural means to oppose the government of the day.

Parties and Political Opposition

For those who have grown up in a democratic system, the acceptance of the idea of a political opposition institutionalized through the role of competitive parties appears normal. Historically, however, and even for the vast majority of current political systems, this is not the case. While political opposition functions may be carried out by various political mechanisms, such as an independent judiciary, interest groups, or a free press, the primary organizational agent of political opposition is the political party (Ionescu and de Madariaga, 1972: 52–62). The distinguishing characteristic between competitive party systems (Canada, Britain, and the United States) and a party-state system (the Soviet Union) turns on the role of parties: in the first instance, organized opposition challenges for power, in the second it does not. While opposition exists in all systems, in a party-state pattern it is unorganized and takes place in private within or through the single party organization; in a competitive party system, opposition is organized and occurs in public, primarily through the battle for office. Elections by themselves do not make a system democratic, but elections with organized parties competing for power add immeasurably to such a result. Given the allure of the democratic ideal in the 20th century, party-states nominate candidates for office and hold elections – events which in no way change their classification as totalitarian systems.

Political opposition is not only significant in that it provides for a competitive struggle for power, but also because it is one way of handling the conflict that lies at the basis of politics: "political opposition ... is the most advanced and institutionalized form of political conflict" (Ionescu and de Madariaga, 1972: 16). Allowing people and groups to contest for power through legitimate channels such as the party system increases the likelihood that violence will not be resorted to. Conversely, when the opposition feels that it cannot fairly contest for power through the party system, then violence and coercion may become the reciprocal tools of opposing and governing, as reflected in the events leading to the 1970 FLQ Crisis in Canada. Providing organized political opposition continues to be an important function of the political parties in the democratic systems of Canada, Britain, and the United States.

Political Party Futures

Predicting the future of political institutions such as political parties is very risky. However, the past can at least tell us that some events are more likely in the future than others. And an historical appreciation of the origins and functions of political parties cannot only help us to understand their present status, but it can keep us from denigrating the present because of our ignorance of the past. In recent years, a common criticism of parties in democratic systems is that they are failing to perform adequately. Implicit in most such assessments is the view that previously parties were more effective and more efficient in carrying out their electoral and governing functions. Critics have gone so far as to suggest the possible demise of parties altogether (and they sometimes seem more than pleased by such a prospect).

Such views fail to appreciate either the historical or contemporary contributions of political parties to the political process. Historically, parties, while not the sole creators, contributed strongly to the development of the democratic polity. Currently, the nomination of candidates, the selection of leaders, the organizing of election campaigns, the raising of party funds, and, for the successful party, the burdens and rewards of office are no small feat. In fact, it would be difficult to conceive how other institutions might carry out these functions if the parties were to disappear. The disparagement of parties indicates, perhaps, that we expect too much of them, based on a false analogy that in the past they somehow performed better. Reformers are perpetually upset with the nature of the democratic parties.

Concern with the supposedly declining role of parties in democratic systems is evident in Canada, Britain, and the United States. Concomitant with such negative views are a number of more specific party-related developments, including a decline in the trust and confidence the public has in political institutions in general and parties in particular, and an erosion of partisan attachments for the major parties and a growth in support for either new parties or for being independent from partisan ties. However, such developments need not herald the end of the significant role of political parties in democratic systems. What they do portend are some changes in the way the parties perform their traditional electoral, governing, and opposition functions.

SUMMARY

1. Political parties are a way of giving the mass of people control over their leaders in democratic systems and a means of elite control over the masses in totalitarian systems. Parties may be classified according to their origin (internally versus externally created parties), their structure (cadre versus mass parties), and their ideology (programmatic versus pragmatic parties). Party systems are either competitive or non-competitive, while a one-party situation is classified as a party-state system. All parties serve both electoral and governing functions; parties in democratic systems also provide a political opposition function.
2. The major Canadian parties are electorally-oriented coalitions, pragmatic in style, parliamentary in origin, structurally decentralized around the provincial units, and cohesive in the legislature. The minor parties since the 1920s have been, by contrast, extra-parliamentary in origin, programmatic in style, ideological in appeal, and political movements as well as partisan organizations. The Canadian party system is competitive, federal, regional, and centre-based. Party leaders are chosen by national party leadership conventions, with party finance the key remaining area of political corruption.
3. British political parties are more centralized, ideological, class-based, and programmatic than their Canadian counterparts. The British party system is competitive between two major parties (Conservative and Labour), but increasingly challenged by nationalist parties (Scottish Nationalist Party and the Plaid Cymru)

and by old (Liberal) and new (Social Democratic Party) minor parties. Party leaders are selected by the party caucuses, although the Labour party decided in 1981 to begin using an electoral college type of selection procedure.

4. The major American parties (Republicans and Democrats) are cadre parties, election-oriented, nonideological, heterogeneous in social composition, decentralized, with weak party unity. The American party system is competitive, dominated by the two major parties, and highly discriminatory against new or minor parties. Party leaders are selected at national party conventions, but the key area of choice is the delegate selection process, which is now dominated by the presidential primaries. Unlike Canada or Britain, the mass public may be involved in the selection of party leaders in the United States.

5. Despite some obvious shortcomings, parties, especially the competitive parties in democratic systems, continue to be important political institutions. However, the way in which the existing parties carry out their traditional electoral, governing, and opposition functions may change in the future, as the parties adapt to a changing environment.

RECOMMENDED READINGS

Political Parties: General

DUVERGER, MAURICE (1972) *Party Politics and Pressure Groups: A Comparative Introduction*. New York: Thomas Y. Crowell.

_____ (1964) *Political Parties: Their Organization and Activity in the Modern State*. London: Methuen and Co.

EPSTEIN, LEON D. (1967) *Political Parties in Western Democracies*. New York: Praeger Publishers.

MICHELS, ROBERT (1962) *Political Parties: A Sociological Study of the Oligarchical Tendencies of Modern Democracy*. New York: Collier Books.

SARTORI, GIOVANNI (1976) *Parties and Party Systems: A Framework for Analysis*. London: Cambridge University Press.

Canadian Parties

COURTNEY, JOHN C. (1973) *The Selection of National Party Leaders in Canada*. Toronto: Macmillan of Canada.

ENGELMANN, F. C. and M. A. SCHWARTZ (1975) *Canadian Political Parties: Origin, Character, Impact.* Scarborough, Ont.: Prentice-Hall Canada Inc.

PERLIN, GEORGE C. (1980) *The Tory Syndrome: Leadership Politics in the Progressive Conservative Party.* Montreal: McGill-Queen's University Press.

THORBURN, HUGH G., ed. (1979) *Party Politics in Canada.* Scarborough, Ont.: Prentice-Hall Canada Inc., 4th ed.

WINN, C. and J. MCMENEMY, eds. (1976) *Political Parties in Canada.* Toronto: McGraw-Hill Ryerson.

British Parties

DRUCKER, H. M., ed. (1979) *Multi-Party Britain.* London: Macmillan Press.

FINER, S. E. (1980) *The Changing British Party System, 1945–1979.* Washington, D.C.: American Enterprise Institute for Public Policy Research.

MCKENZIE, ROBERT (1967) *British Political Parties: The Distribution of Power Within the Conservative and Labour Parties.* London: Heinemann Educational Books, 2nd rev. ed.

American Parties

BLANK, ROBERT H. (1980) *Political Parties: An Introduction.* Englewood Cliffs, N.J.: Prentice-Hall.

GOLDWIN, ROBERT A. (1980) *Political Parties in the Eighties.* Washington, D.C.: American Enterprise Institute for Public Policy Research.

KEY, V.O., JR. (1964) *Politics, Parties, and Pressure Groups.* New York: Thomas Y. Crowell, 5th ed.

LADD, EVERETT CARLL, JR. (1978) *Where Have All the Voters Gone? The Fracturing of America's Political Parties.* New York: W. W. Norton.

Political Opposition

DAHL, ROBERT A., ed. (1966) *Political Oppositions in Western Democracies.* New Haven: Yale University Press.

_____ ed. (1973) *Regimes and Oppositions.* New Haven: Yale University Press.

IONESCU, GHITA and ISABEL DE MADARIAGA (1972) *Opposition: Past and Present of a Political Institution.* London: Penguin Books.

9 THE ELECTORAL PROCESS: POLITICAL RECRUITMENT AND ELECTIONS

... one needs the disposition of a test pilot and the arse of a cowboy to endure modern life on the campaign trail (Camp, 1979: 215).

The disproportionate advantage of male, educated, high-status elite recruits increases as we move up the political stratification system. The "law of increasing disproportion" seems to apply to nearly every political system; no matter how we measure political and social status, the higher the level of political authority, the greater the representation for high-status social groups (Putnam, 1976: 33).

... in a modern mass democracy the ultimate political decisions concern not what the rulers shall do but who the rulers shall be. Determining who shall rule through periodic elections of public officials remains the sovereign people's weapon-of-last-resort for influencing what government does (Ranney, 1965: vii).

THE ORCHESTRATED cacophony of an election campaign is at once both the most visible and most vital ingredient of the public's role in the political process of democratic systems. Unfortunately, few voters understand either the mechanics or the consequences of the electoral process, both of which have a profound impact on the distribution of influence and power in the polity.

THE NATURE OF ELECTIONS AND POLITICAL RECRUITMENT

Elections have become an important characteristic of all forms of government in the 20th century. However, there is considerable variation in the structure and functions of the electoral process in different types of political systems. In democratic systems, elections are competitive: that is, several candidates openly contest for power, with the winning party acquiring control of government through a peaceful and public transfer of power. In totalitarian systems, elections are non-competitive: only one party runs a single candidate for each office. The real political battle is carried on in private among the political elites, with elections serving to ratify or legitimate the selection already made by the single party. In autocratic systems, elections may include several candidates or parties, but the result is never in doubt. The dominant party is assured of winning either through intimidation or electoral manipulation, exemplified by the success of the Islamic Republican Party in controlling the electoral process in Iran in the early 1980s.

In democratic polities, the basic function of elections is to select those individuals who will govern and direct the political process until the next campaign. By choosing the governors and forcing them to return to the people at regular intervals for a renewed mandate, the mass public indirectly influences the content and direction of public policy. The public's role in the electoral process is often misunderstood because the connection between the governors and governed is assumed to be immediate and direct – most often it is not. Elections are a blunt instrument of popular control, because they are infrequent and party-based. Between elections, the selected elite has a relatively free hand in governing, although they must always keep their eye on levels of public support if they wish to retain office in the future. Governments are most responsive before an election campaign, usually providing new programs or promises of future improvements in public policy. After an election, governments may undertake unpopular measures (e.g., raising their own salaries, wage-and-price controls), in the hope that their effects on the public will be forgotten or forgiven by the time a new mandate is sought. Given this pattern, it is not unreasonable to suggest that governments should face the wrath of the electorate on a yearly basis. One reason why minority governments in Canada have typically been more responsive than many majority ones, can be attributed, at least in part, to this electoral connection.

In the modern era, elections are party contests for power, not simply a series of individual battles in the various constituencies. Moreover, each party usually takes a stand on a series of issues, so that the electorate may have difficulty in determining which party to select. For example, if you think Party A is on the correct side of two issues, and Party B reflects your sentiments on two others, for which do you cast your ballot? Many people – quite likely a majority of voters – determine their party choice on factors other than policy, including items such as religion, family ties, social class, personality, looks, and charisma. No wonder then that it is often an indirect impact that elections make on public policy. The electorate chooses their leaders, who in turn decide the content of the political agenda. Thus voters rarely grant a specific mandate to any party with respect to the content of public policy, even though winning parties usually act as if their program has, in fact, received the public's benediction.

While the broad purposes and structures of electoral politics are similar in parliamentary and presidential systems, they differ on several important characteristics. In a parliamentary context, election time periods are variable within a maximum tenure of office, typically five years. Election writs are issued after the formal executive grants a dissolution of Parliament, but only on the initiative of the political executive. Individuals are eligible to vote if they meet minimum standards of age and citizenship and have their name included on the voters' list as a result of an enumeration process. Candidates for public office must qualify as a voter and also be nominated by a number of their fellow citizens, with most nominees running under a party label. The selection of candidates is carried out by the parties at the local or constituency level, usually without direct intervention from national party headquarters. Election campaigns are of short duration, in most cases.

In a presidential system, elections are constant (e.g., every four years for the American presidency, every two years for the House of Representatives) and constitutionally prescribed: there is no leeway in the election call, since it is mandated by law. While historically, the parties have exercised power over candidate selection, in the United States, the introduction of the primary technique has undercut the role of parties in the nomination process. Moreover, citizens must take the initiative to have their names included on the list of eligible voters due to a registration, rather than an enumeration, procedure. Election campaigns may be very long: even though the formal American campaign extends from Labor Day to the first Tuesday in November in presidential elections, the informal campaign starts in January, and, in some cases, up to a year or more before that (i.e., nearly two years in total). The different election procedures utilized in presidential and parliamentary systems help to determine the types of parties that will compete and the kind of candidates nominated for public office.

Through the election campaign, the public decides which set of party leaders will govern, while a second important election ingredient, and one prior to the election itself, is the nomination and selection of party candidates. Even though an individual may contest office as an independent, the nomination process is overwhelmingly a party matter, and will be so treated in the ensuing analysis. Parties are the prime agents in the *political recruitment process*, a concept that refers to those "processes that select from among the several million socially favored and politically motivated citizens comprising the political stratum those several thousand who reach positions of significant national influence" (Putnam, 1976: 46). The political recruitment process is significant because, by determining who stands for office, it ultimately selects the makers of public policy. Moreover, it should not be overlooked that in many democratic polities nomination is tantamount to election, given the existence of safe seats for each party. A *safe seat* for a party is a constituency in which that party has consistently won with large vote pluralities over the other parties. Under normal circumstances, the party's candidate will win, no matter who that candidate happens to be. In these situations, the real electoral choice is made by the party at the constituency nomination meeting, not in the general election. At the federal level in Canada, probably 50 to 60 percent of the seats in the House of Commons could be so classified, with an even higher figure applicable in Britain.

While theoretically it is possible for a considerable portion of the public to become involved in the process of political recruitment, either by becoming a candidate or by helping to nominate one, no known instance of such involvement has ever been observed. Instead, from among the many, few directly participate in the candidate selection process, with fewer still ever chosen to become official candidates. The recruitment process can be symbolized, perhaps, as a funnel, with the mouth of the funnel representing the electorate and the narrow end, those nominated and elected to public office. The further into the funnel one moves, the fewer are the number of people involved, but the greater is their power in the political recruitment process. Those individuals who are directly involved in the choice of candidates are often referred to as the *selectorate*, typically a small group in most democratic polities. The selectorate at the constituency level in parliamentary systems may range from several hundred to over a thousand delegates in those ridings in which there is a battle for the nomination. Since the nomination of candidates is an internal party matter with limited mass participation, the recruitment of candidates in a parliamentary system can be classified as *closed*. In contrast, the American presidential system has an *open* recruitment process. The use of primaries to nominate party candidates allows for extensive public participation in the selection process. Moreover, the primaries permit almost anyone a try at gaining the nomination, although in many cases it is the party-backed individual who wins.

The nature and operation of the recruitment process, therefore, reveal much about the political stratification of the polity, for the ability of the selectorate to control who leads ultimately determines the content of public policy. Moreover, those who recruit and are recruited are never a mirror-image of society, but represent, instead, the political elite. A paradox is thus created: representative government is often composed of individuals unrepresentative of some of the major sectors of the sociopolitical milieu. If this discrepancy becomes too great, then the legitimacy of the polity itself might be called into question.

POLITICAL RECRUITMENT IN CANADA

Although parties have traditionally controlled both the recruitment and nomination of candidates for public office in Canada, the fiction was long maintained that those candidates were simply individuals rather than party representatives. For example, it was not until the 1972 federal election that a candidate's party affiliation was included on the ballot. As private organizations, the parties determine their own recruitment and selection procedures. The result, historically, has been for a pattern of elite control of the political recruitment process.

The legal qualifications to be a candidate are minimal. Generally speaking, any person qualified to vote – that is, any elector – has the right to stand for nomination and election to public office. However, certain classes of people, such as those who have violated provisions of the Canada Elections Act in the previous campaign, or government contractors, are excluded. A separation between the federal and provincial political arenas is maintained in the recruitment process at this point, since members of one level of government cannot be officially nominated or contest the election of the other level without resigning from their current office. For example, before former Premier Gerald Regan entered federal politics as an official Liberal candidate in the 1980 election, he resigned his seat in the Nova Scotia House of Assembly. Since the eligible electorate in the 1979 and 1980 federal elections was approximately 16 million, the potential number of candidates is very large indeed.

A second set of legal requirements, in addition to being qualified as an elector, must be met before an individual is officially nominated. Nomination papers, properly executed, must be filed before the date set for nominations to end. Although some minor differences exist between federal and provincial requirements, the general pattern is that candidates must have their nomination papers signed by a number of qualified electors (25 in federal contests) in their electoral district. When the nomination papers are filed, a fee or deposit (federally it is $200) must be paid. This filing fee is returned after the election if the candidate wins or if he or she has received 50 percent of the votes cast for the winning candidate. This practice was designed to prevent frivolous candidates from running for office, but in practice it does not appear to be a serious impediment to those with electoral ambitions: in recent federal elections, over 1400 individuals have been officially nominated. Given that 282 seats are being contested for in the House of Commons, this number averages out to approximately five candidates for each constituency. Finally, the nomination papers must contain a witnessed declaration by the candidate that he or she is willing to stand for election to public office.

To choose from a potential 16 million candidates slightly under 1500 who will actually contest for office in a federal election campaign reveals that the political recruitment funnel in Canada narrows quickly and precipitously. Between the potential and actual candidates stands the selectorate, the party activists who involve themselves in the nomination process. Although there are no exact figures on the size of the Canadian selectorate, a rough approximation can be calculated as follows. If we assume that in future federal elections all three parties (Liberal, Conservative, NDP) nominate candidates in all 282 constituencies and that each party also holds a constituency nomination meeting attended by about 300 people, then the size of the Canadian selectorate is a quarter of a million electors (282 constituencies × 3 parties = 846 meetings × 300 average attendance = 253 800 individuals).

We would suggest that this figure greatly exaggerates the number of electors who are effectively involved in the recruitment process. Most recruitment decisions are taken by the party elite before the nomination meetings are held, so that in many constituency contests only one individual is presented for consideration. While party rules allow for more than one name to be presented, so that the process appears to be competitive and democratic, a contested nomination is usually a sign that the political elite has either refused to coalesce around a single candidate or that, even when it has, some individual or group in the party fails to recognize the legitimacy of such backroom decisions. Thus, the vast majority of individuals who attend their party's constituency nomination meeting are not really given an effective voice in the political recruitment process: their task, instead, is to legitimate the choice of the party elite. The effective Canadian selectorate, therefore, might range all the way from one (e.g., the party leader) to several hundred or more, depending on the historical period, the competitiveness of the electoral district, and the extent of the political elite's control over the party organization.

The traditional pattern of political recruitment has been for the party leader and a few key party organizers in each constituency to control the process. Perhaps the longest-lasting example of a party leader's control over the recruitment and nomination process at both the provincial and federal levels occurred in Newfoundland under Liberal Premier Joey Smallwood (1975: 186):

> For a hundred years in Newfoundland, the leader of a political party exercised an authority that disappeared in mainland Canada long ago. It was the leader of the party who personally selected and appointed every individual candidate of the party in each election.

Although the number of federal candidates that must be nominated tends to preclude a leader's control over all of them, party leaders may still play a significant role, either directly or indirectly through their key aides. The following description of the role of Jim Coutts, then principal secretary to Prime Minister Trudeau, in the recruitment of some highly visible Liberal candidates in the 1970s illustrates this point.

> Above all, Coutts is indispensable because his own greatest strength is Trudeau's greatest weakness: the management and the manipulation of people. Coutts, particularly in recent years, has become Trudeau's talent

scout and fixer, doing for him what Trudeau cannot or will not do for himself. He recruited Jack Horner, the Conservative frontbencher, a transient success that turned into stupendous failure because Horner, simply by leaving, transformed the Tory caucus into a united team. He tried to recruit Ed Schreyer to the cabinet, and almost succeeded. He recruited John Evans, the former president of the University of Toronto, a much-heralded political comet, until he was brought down in the 1978 Rosedale by-election. He recruited as a Liberal candidate Maurice Strong, former chairman of Petro-Canada, until Strong, recognizing his ineptitude for politics, withdrew. He lured three Conservative M.P.s – Claude Wagner, Jack Marshall, and Bob Muir into the Senate, thus opening up by-elections in promising constituencies (Gwyn, 1980: 173).

Control by the current leader and other members of the party elite has often been highly visible in the recruitment of a new party leader, a statement that is particularly applicable to the federal Liberal party. For example, Mackenzie King chose Louis St. Laurent (Whitaker, 1977: 171–178) who in turn selected Lester Pearson (1973: 299–303). While not as open about his preference for a successor as previous Liberal leaders, the record seems clear that Prime Minister Pearson favoured Pierre Trudeau as his replacement (Radwanski, 1978: 79–87). One of the paradoxes of Trudeau's leadership of the Liberal party was his inability to find a successor: those who wanted it he shunted aside, such as John Turner, while those he seemed to favour, such as Maurice Strong, John Evans, Donald Macdonald, and Jim Coutts, were either unwilling or unable to gain both party and electoral support.

While the role of the party leader may be strong, the trend in recent decades is for increasing decentralization, with much of the control over political recruitment residing with the executive of the party's local constituency association. Although control is most often localized, a party leader may take the rare decision to disassociate himself and his party from a particular candidate, as Robert Stanfield, leader of the Progressive Conservative party, did in 1974 when he refused Leonard Jones of Moncton, New Brunswick the right to run as a party candidate. A similar situation occurred in March 1979, when Prime Minister Trudeau refused to accept two Manitoba Liberal candidates who had been openly critical of their leader. Moreover, a leader may help to parachute a candidate into a local riding, but most such cases have been unsuccessful in Canadian politics. In *parachuting*, a local association may have no obvious candidate or they may desire one with more national stature, so that the party leader may bring in an outsider to receive the nomination. Because there is no legal residency requirement at the constituency level (i.e., a qualified elector may seek the nomination in any of the 282 ridings), such practices are possible. However, political tradition works strongly in favour of a local candidate, so that most candidates either live in the constituency they represent or close by.

The local executive of a party's constituency organization attempts to maintain control of the recruitment process by several different methods. First, and most effectively, the local party elite must keep tabs on the sentiment within the constituency organization, so that they know about and are able to defuse possible challenges to their control of the recruitment process. Second, the party elite must work out behind the scenes the candidate to be nominated and then ensure his or her success by coalition-building among the disaffected elements of the party organization. Third, if a contested nomination meeting is expected, then the rules of the game are often changed to limit last-minute memberships, to put an age requirement on those able to vote (e.g., 18), and to restrict access of the challengers to party membership lists. A wise constituency executive never assumes that the obvious will happen – to do so may mean political failure. If the above caveats are not followed, then a constituency nomination meeting will become uncontrollable, as many outside, underaged, and recently-arrived party members vote for the party's candidate. For example, in the Trudeaumania of 1968, the Liberal association in the Davenport riding found that its membership "rose from 150 to 5,445 in a few weeks," with the outcome "determined by non-residents and ten-year-olds who, under the rules, could not be debarred from voting" (Beck, 1968: 401).

A sudden surge in party membership at the constituency level prior to a nomination meeting indicates that the political elite's control is being challenged and that the nomination process will likely be a competitive one. For example, in the Liberal constituency association of Rosedale in the Spring of 1978, membership swelled from 100 to 2000 as Ann Cools and Dr. John Evans vied for the nomination. The candidate of the party elite, Dr. John Evans, was a touted successor to Pierre Trudeau and won the nomination for the 1978 by-election. The fact that he had to contest vigorously for it shows the power of the local constituency association in the political recruitment process. Dr. Evans was defeated in the by-election and decided not to stand for the later contests, which resulted in the nomination going to Ann Cools.

Although the executive of the local constituency association has considerable leeway, and thus potential influence in the recruitment process, a national party leader may, through influence, challenge the local results. In what seems destined to become a classic case of the Canadian political recruitment process, Conservative leader Joe Clark, while suffering an initial setback, succeeded in 1977 in taking a nomination away from Stan Schumacher and thus forcing him to leave the Conservative caucus.

The unusual scenario began in 1976 with Joe Clark's selection as national party leader. As a moderate in the party, Clark was seen as suspect by the right-wing members of the Tory caucus. Moreover, the fact that Clark had defeated Jack Horner, a fellow Albertan and close ally of Schumacher, aggravated the Clark-Schumacher relationship. Because of the electoral redistribution, which gave Alberta two additional seats for the 1979 election, the boundaries of many districts were greatly altered. The new leader wanted to run in the Bow River constituency, because it contained his hometown. However, Schumacher also had a legitimate claim on the Bow River riding, since it included part of his old electoral district. One must remember that all of the Alberta seats went Tory in 1974 and were expected to do so again in the next election, so Clark and Schumacher were both expected to be returned to the Commons, no matter in which riding they received the nomination.

The Battle of Bow River received national attention from August to October 1976, at which point Joe Clark, realizing the Schumacher forces had control of the local constituency association, withdrew from the race. However, the Battle of Bow River was not over, for a year later, when the official nomination meeting was held, Stan Schumacher lost, not to Joe Clark, but to Gordon Taylor, a former Social Credit member of the Alberta legislature. The constituency meeting was packed by new members – Schumacher charged that they were from outside the riding as well, meaning loyal to the national leader. There then ensued more bickering, as the local constituency executive (i.e., Schumacher forces) ruled that the first meeting had been improperly held, and ordered a new one. That decision was itself overturned by the party's provincial executive loyal to Clark and later upheld by the national party executive. If the new leader was unsuccessful in getting the Bow River nomination, he was able, nonetheless, to prevent his opponent from getting it. This case is very revealing in that Joe Clark could more easily win the national leadership of the Conservative party than he could his party's constituency nomination in his hometown!

The recruitment and nomination process, as well as the nature of the selectorate, demonstrate the "law of increasing disproportion." Nominees and elected representatives are not a mirror-image of Canadian society, but are individuals from the better-off segments of society in terms of education, occupation, social class, and most other basic socioeconomic attributes. As one recent study concluded, "Canadian MP's, in comparison to a cross section of the population, have always had elite social and political backgrounds" (Kornberg et al., 1980: 5). Moreover, the largest contingent of public officials have been lawyers – usually about one-third of the total. The most glaring deficiency of the political recruitment process is the virtual exclusion of women: "... Canadian women remain conspicuously absent from Canadian legislatures" (Brodie and Vickers, 1981: 324). In fact, while women make up 50 percent of the population, in the 20th century less than one percent of elected representatives at both the federal and provincial levels have been women. Many reasons can be advanced for the causes of this pattern, the most obvious of which is simply discrimination against females: "Male dominance in politics generally and in elite political institutions in particular is an established fact" (Kornberg et al., 1979: 186). The unrepresentative nature of the candidates nominated and elected and the relatively closed procedures utilized are the bases for the conclusion that "candidate selection seems to be one area of Canadian party politics which departs widely from the democratic ideal" (Qualter, 1970: 76).

THE ELECTION PROCESS IN CANADA

If the recruitment and nomination of political candidates departs from the democratic ideal, how can an election between candidates so selected be seen as contributing to the democratic nature of the larger political system? The key is in the choice between candidates and their respective parties. The overall system is democratic because it gives people a choice between competing candidates and not because those candidates have been selected in a democratic manner. The electoral battle in democratic polities allows the public to choose their governors at regular intervals – it rarely allocates to the ordinary citizen a role in selecting who those competitors will be. Between election campaigns, the individual is given few opportunities to influence the course of events. As Prime Minister Pierre Trudeau said on several occasions during his long tenure in office, if the people don't like government policy, then they kick out that government at the election. Such a view implies, of course, that attempts by the public to control their governors between campaigns may not be seen as a particularly legitimate activity by the political elite.

In Canada, the life of any Parliament is limited to a maximum term of five years. Based on political tradition, majority governments usually return to the people after four years. Governments seek a new mandate when they perceive that the time is auspicious for success, which usually means, in the modern era, that the public opinion polls are in their favour. Minority governments may be forced into an election after only a short term in office if they suffer defeat in the legislature (e.g., the federal Conservatives in December 1979). However, most minority governments hold an election when they feel they can gain a majority (e.g., the federal Liberals in 1968 and 1974). Since World War II, minority governments have been of limited duration, not usually because of their lack of support in the legislature, but as a result of their desire to fashion a majority in a new election or of their belief that, if an election were to be forced by the opposition, they would be reelected.

The five-year maximum life of Parliament may be extended under special circumstances, if the decision for such an action is not opposed by more than one-third of the members of the House of Commons. Only once (during World War I) was this extension provision utilized, so that over six years intervened between the federal elections of 1911 and 1917. Because to extend the life of Parliament requires, in effect, a two-thirds vote in its favour and because the official opposition party normally has at least one-third of the seats in the Commons, it is politically improbable that a government could take such action simply to avoid an anticipated defeat at the polls.

The mechanics of the election process are relatively straightforward. Having requested and received a dissolution of Parliament from the formal executive, the prime minister and cabinet instruct the chief electoral officer to issue the election writs for each constituency. The election procedure in each riding is under the direction of the returning officer, whose job it is to prepare the voters' list, to make ready the necessary ballots, and to receive the nomination papers from those individuals who seek to be recognized as official candidates in the election. The tasks of the returning officer also include designating the various polling stations in each constituency, which may range from several dozen to upwards of 500, supervising the vote on election day, counting the ballots, and then declaring a particular candidate elected. Thus, the returning officer in each riding is responsible for the administration of the election in a fair and nonpartisan manner.

Of major significance for the citizen is the preparation of the voters' list. At the federal level, and for most provinces, the list is prepared by an *enumeration* process, that is, a door-to-door registration of urban voters after the election writs have been issued. In rural areas, voters' lists are open, in that exclusion from them does not prevent a person from voting. Enumerators are patronage positions, with two required in urban ridings (one from each of the two leading parties in that constituency in the last election) and one in rural settings. Given the number of individuals and households that must be contacted in short order, there is considerable pressure on the enumerators to proceed as quickly as possible. The result is some inaccuracy in the voters' lists, since enumerators rarely inquire as to the citizenship, age, or residency of the individuals who happen to be at home when they knock on the door. Contrary to correct procedure, enumerators often add to the list the names of individual family members who are not at home. It is thus possible to get one's name on the voters' list without meeting all of the legal requirements for voting.

Although the current practice of having enumerators from both major parties in the urban ridings prevents most corrupt practices, in the past, control of the enumeration process has been used for partisan purposes. For example, what was known as the *graveyard vote* could be used to swing the results in closely contested ridings. If the government controlled the choice of enumerators, they could then list dead people on the voters' list and have a party worker show up on election day to cast the ballot. More than anything else, what probably prevents such practices in recent decades is simply the size of the constituencies: so many names would have to be manipulated that it would be obvious to the parties contesting the election. A related historical practice was to have the same person register more than once, using slightly different spellings of his or her name. Such techniques were widespread in Western Canada, particularly after the large waves of immigration from Eastern Europe in the 20th century. For example, in Manitoba, the government often traded beer and favours in exchange for votes, a practice made possible because "undecipherable Slavic names made voters' lists elastic and impersonation unchallengeable" (Peterson, 1978: 66). While such practices have largely disappeared and while the voters' lists appear to be reasonably accurate, the major remaining deficiency seems to be the number of individuals whose names appear who do not meet all of the legal qualifications for voting.

The preparation of voters' lists is carried out each time a federal election is called. Thus, Canadian elections are based on what is known as a *temporary voters' list*, because it is only used for a single election before being discarded. A recent exception to this practice occurred in 1980 with the unexpected defeat of the Clark government. The 1979 voters' lists were used in 1980 as well, with the normal enumeration period spent in revising and updating the records. Such a practice, however, seems unlikely to serve as a precedent for the introduction of a *permanent voters' list*, which would be continued from one election to the next.

The use of a temporary voters' list has had one major impact on the nature and organization of election campaigns in Canada, namely, to make them lengthy. Because the enumerators in urban areas must begin their canvass on the forty-ninth day before the election date and because it takes a week or two to get enumerators appointed and trained, the duration of a federal campaign has to be at least two months long. The only practical way to shorten the election period is to utilize a permanent voters' list. Instead of an eight- or nine-week contest, an election campaign might be held in four to six weeks. Shorter campaigns would likely be welcomed by the parties and their candidates, and probably joyously received by the public as well.

A further significant element of the electoral process concerns the way in which citizens cast their ballots and the way votes are counted in determining the winning party. Although other patterns have been experimented with in several provinces, the basic system currently used is the single-member district with a plurality electoral formula. The *single-member district* means that only one candidate is elected from each riding, while the *plurality electoral formula* refers to the fact that the person with the most votes in each riding wins (see Chapter 10).

Based on the 1971 census figures, the number of single-member districts in the House of Commons came to 282, an increase from the 264 seats that was the total used until the 1979 election. After each census, an automatic revision in the number and distribution of seats among the provinces is carried out. However, a time lag always exists, so that the estimated figure of 310 seats in the Commons as a result of the 1981 census will probably not be in effect for federal elections until at least the mid-1980s. The allocation of provincial seat totals was initially outlined by a series of rules specified in the BNA Act (Section 51), with the most recent revision contained in the Representation Act of 1974. Although the rules are complex, seats in the House of Commons are primarily distributed on a population basis, with certain safeguards for Quebec and the smaller provinces. For example, Quebec is assigned a given number of seats, with the other provincial seat allocations determined from that base.

TABLE 9.1 *Provincial Seats in the House of Commons*

	CENSUS		
Province	*1961**	*1971***	*1981****
Ontario	88	95	105
Quebec	74 ·	75	79
British Columbia	23 ⸓	28	33
Alberta	19	21	27
Saskatchewan	13	14	14
Manitoba	13	14	15
Nova Scotia	11	11	12
New Brunswick	10	10	10
Newfoundland	7	7	8
Prince Edward Island	4	4	4
Northwest Territories	1	2	2
Yukon	1	1	1
Total	264	282	310

*Results first applied in the 1968 election.
**Results first applied in the 1979 election.
***Results not likely to be applied before 1975. Based on preliminary results of the 1981 census, as published in *The Globe and Mail*, January 20, 1982.

Table 9.1 presents the seat totals for each province on the basis of the 1961, 1971, and 1981 (estimated) decennial censuses. Several significant patterns are revealed by these data. First, the dominance of Ontario and Quebec is clear, since together they receive, on the basis of the 1971 census, 170 seats out of 282 or 60 percent of the total of all elected representatives to the national legislature. Second, although somewhat delayed in their impact, shifting population growth patterns are also apparent. For example, the four Atlantic provinces, while retaining the same number of seats in 1961 and 1971, are in fact losing representation in the Commons (32 seats out of 264 in 1961 and 32 seats out of 282 as a result of the 1971 figures). In contrast, the four Western provinces, most notably British Columbia and Alberta, are gaining seats. Third, Central Canada, especially Ontario, continues to gain seats as well. Although the West is gaining seats at a slightly faster rate than Central

Canada, it will be many decades before the electoral dominance of Ontario and Quebec is seriously challenged.

When provincial seat allocations are altered due to population changes, then an *electoral redistribution* takes place, that is, a redrawing of the constituency boundaries. Historically, federal redistributions take place after each census, although for the provincial level several decades might pass before such a procedure is undertaken. The consequence of infrequent redistributions was a situation known as *malapportionment*. Because of population shifts, some constituencies ended up with many more voters than others, thus undercutting the supposed equality of each citizen's vote. Until recent decades, malapportionment favoured those parties with a rural base, since urban ridings would usually end up more densely populated. In the past 20 years, the major population trend has been to the suburbs, so that these areas have typically been underrepresented in the legislatures. Since provincial redistributions are usually decided upon by the government of the day, the decision to reallocate constituency boundaries often carries important political consequences. If a party feels that it would benefit, then a redistribution will occur. In contrast, if the party in power perceives that a redistribution will undercut its base of support, then it will be postponed as long as possible.

A closely related technique to that of malapportionment is the practice of *gerrymandering* constituency boundaries, that is, the drawing of the boundaries to maximize the political support of your party and to minimize that of the other parties. The name derives from American history: in 1812, Governor Elbridge Gerry of Massachusetts redistributed electoral boundaries in such a way that the electoral map looked like a salamander, hence the word gerrymander. The way the process works can be illustrated as follows. If the constituencies are not required to be of equal population size (i.e., malapportionment), then put as many of the opposing party's areas of strength in as few ridings as possible. Concurrently, spread your own political support over as many constituencies as possible, but in such a way as to ensure a majority position within each one. Even when the ridings must be of roughly equal size, constituency boundaries can still be drawn in such a way as to help some parties and hinder others. Throughout Canadian history, gerrymandering has been a regular feature of political life. However, at the federal level, since 1964, such practices have been greatly minimized, with nonpartisan boundary commissions now responsible for the redrawing of constituency boundaries during the redistribution process. At the provincial level, a number of provinces have retained the traditional practice of the government controlling when and how redistributions take place. As a result, gerrymandering remains an accepted practice of provincial politics.

A final distinction concerning the Canadian electoral process is the difference between a general election and a by-election. A *general election* results from a dissolution of Parliament, so that all seats in the House of Commons are contested in a nationwide election. A *by-election* is an election in a single constituency to fill a vacancy that has developed between general elections. A vacancy may occur as a result of a member's death or resignation from the legislature. When notified of a vacancy by the Speaker of the House, the prime minister, within six months, can select the date of the by-election. Although the prime minister must act within the six-month limit, the actual date can be anytime in the future, up to the holding of the next general election. Thus, a prime minister can quickly call by-elections in those vacant constituencies the party feels confident of winning, and postpone, at least for a while, those in ridings the party is likely to lose.

The results of a by-election sometimes register the prevailing national political sentiment, sometimes shifts in it, or sometimes serve simply as a means of venting the electorate's anger against the government of the day. As a result, opposition victories in by-elections do not accurately predict the results of the next general election. For example, the provincial Liberal party in Quebec won an impressive series of by-election victories after the general election of 1976, but ended up losing the provincial general election of 1981. The protest aspect of by-elections helps to account, at least in part, for the federal Liberal's extensive losses in the 15 by-elections held in October 1978 and for the win by the separatist candidate in the Alberta provincial by-election in Olds-Didsbury in February 1982. The victorious party in the by-election often interprets the result as an indicator of political trends, while the losing party dismisses it as an aberrant result due to local or other special features not likely to be repeated in a general election. By-elections take on added significance if the government is in a minority position or if it has only a slim majority. In these situations, the loss of several by-elections might cost the government its right to remain in office.

BRITAIN'S ELECTORAL PROCESS

The recruitment and nomination of candidates for the British House of Commons reflects several unique attributes. If the Canadian recruitment process is closed, then the British one is even more so. Candidate selection is a private, internal party matter, a practice which the major parties seem bent on retaining. A consequence of this tightly controlled recruitment process is that the British selectorate, under normal circumstances, is quite small. The selectorate's power, however, is extensive, because up to 75 percent of the seats in the House of Commons are safe ones.

The control of the national and local party elites over the recruitment process is clearly demonstrated by the practice of *short listing*, which works as follows. When a constituency organization for a party is looking for a candidate, those who wish to have the nomination indicate their desire to the executive of the local organization. Other names may be brought forward by the national party office or by members in the local organization. From this pool of possible candidates, which may be anywhere from a few people to several hundred, a short list of the most desirable candidates is prepared. The short list typically contains up to half a dozen names and is prepared by a screening committee of local party officials. This screening committee may contain one to two dozen members and is often described ''as the most critical single stage of the entire selection process'' (Ranney, 1975: 42). The short-listed individuals then appear before a meeting of local party members, usually several hundred, known as the *selection conference*, a group roughly similar to the constituency nomination meeting in Canada. After listening to a presentation by each potential candidate, the selection conference votes for one person, who becomes the party's candidate for public office. A final step involves the approval of the candidate by the national party organization. With rare exception, this procedure puts the control of the recruitment and nomination of candidates effectively in the hands of the party elite.

In addition to the closed nature of the recruitment process, several other characteristics of British practice are worthy of mention. Although similar to Canada in not requiring candidates to be residents of the constituency in which they seek office, the British nonresidency rule has resulted in a considerable movement of possible candidates between constituencies from one election to the next, in contrast to the Canadian convention. In fact, there is a pecking order among constituencies for each party in terms of the likelihood of victory. Before gaining a nomination in a safe seat, positions that are usually reserved for the party leaders and incumbent MPs, individuals will contest an election in a constituency in which they have almost no chance of winning. If a candidate makes a credible showing, he or she may be given the opportunity to run in a more winnable constituency in the next election – and so on, until gaining a seat in the Commons. Except as a result of an electoral redistribution, such movements by candidates between ridings are rare in Canadian politics.

A second distinctive aspect of the recruitment process in Britain is the early selection of candidates prior to an election call. All major parties select a considerable portion of their candidates well in advance of an expected general election, so that they are ready to do battle on short notice. This early selection of candidates is, in part, a reflection of the brief election campaigns in Britain: the parties cannot waste half of the official campaign simply getting their candidates chosen. In contrast, Canadian parties, especially the Liberals and Conservatives, select most of their candidates for office after a dissolution of Parliament has been granted. The initial weeks of a Canadian campaign are an exercise in political recruitment, not a battle focused on the other parties.

A third important attribute of the candidate selection process in Britain concerns the potential role of the national party leader and organization. In comparison to their Canadian counterparts, British parties are not only well-organized, but also highly centralized. At least in theory, this centralization of party organization extends to the candidate selection process. For example, as outlined above, after being named as the party's nominee by the selection conference at the constituency level, the candidate must still be approved by the national party headquarters, a practice true of both the Labour and Conservative parties. Moreover, the national parties maintain lists of possible candidates that the local parties are expected to consult and use, whenever feasible. The national party offices may even recommend to a specific constituency particular candidates they wish to be considered.

The centralization of national party control over the candidate selection process, however, is more apparent than real. Most nominations are decided by the local parties without interference from the national organization. While the national party leadership can step into the process and reject a locally selected candidate, this rarely happens. It would be most accurate to see national party control as a reserve power that is rarely exercised.

These characteristics of the British candidate selection process help to quickly narrow the political recruitment funnel. From a population of 55 million, nearly 40 million individuals are qualified as electors and thus, also, as potential candidates for public office. For the 1979 election, the narrowly-based selectorate reduced this large number of potential candidates to 2576 official candidates, who then competed in the general election.

The closed nature of the candidate selection process, not surprisingly, has resulted in nominees for public office who are unrepresentative of the socioeconomic characteristics of British society. Even more so than in Canada, the British political process is male-dominated, a statement that remains true, despite Margaret Thatcher's success in becoming Prime Minister in 1979. Further, education from one of the elite public schools (comparable to the private schools in Canada) characterizes the candidates of both the Conservative and Labour parties, especially the former. In one study, the "Oxbridge" connection (university education from Oxford or Cambridge) was found to have been true of all prime ministers, 72 percent of all cabinet ministers, 37 percent of all Members of Parliament, but less than 1 percent of the total British population between 1955 and 1974 (Putnam, 1976: 35). Other socioeconomic considerations reveal a similar pattern, so that one researcher concluded that "whatever else MPs may be representative of, it is not the social composition of their constituents, nor even the social composition of their own voting supporters" (Pulzer, 1972: 70). The class-based and deferential aspects of Britain's political culture are clearly revealed in the "law of increasing disproportion," which characterizes the results of the candidate selection process.

The mechanics of a British election resemble those of a Canadian one, with a few significant exceptions. The power to precipitate an election resides with the prime minister, who requests a dissolution of Parliament from the Queen. Because Britain has typically had majority governments since World War II, the prime minister has had considerable leeway in such matters. The only recent exception would be the defeat of the Callaghan government on a non-confidence motion on March 28, 1979. Rather than giving the leader of the opposition party a chance to form a government, a dissolution of Parliament was sought and received by the Labour Prime Minister.

The length of the ensuing election campaign is revealing: only six weeks passed between the defeat of the Labour government in the Commons and the first meeting of the new Parliament under the victorious Conservative leader, Margaret Thatcher (Punnett, 1980: 33–34). The official campaign was even briefer: Parliament was dissolved on April 7, election notices were published on April 11, with the actual vote taking place on May 3, 1979. Thus, the official campaign was only four weeks long, one-half of the duration of a typical Canadian election! The short electoral battle reflects the impact of a permanent voters' list and the tradition in British politics of quickly resolving disputes about which party shall lead the country.

The general election is contested in 635 single-member districts, which utilize a plurality electoral formula. Considerable malapportionment exists: in 1979, the largest constituencies had over 100 000 members, with the smallest one containing under 20 000 electors. Although boundary commissions were first created in 1944, their work is not carried out at regular intervals. Since their recommendations must be put into effect by the government, the implementation of a distribution scheme is a political decision. The last redistribution occurred in 1970, an allocation that is likely to remain in place until the mid-1980s. Historically, blatant gerrymandering was a common political technique, but one that has receded in the modern era of British politics.

The nature of British parties has had an important impact on election campaigns. The ideologically-distinct and class-based parties, which offer the voters a clear choice between their programs, give the British citizen a greater possibility of making a connection between his/her vote and public policy than is true in Canada. Moreover, the shortness of the campaign period means that the parties have little opportunity to change a person's voting intention. Elections in Britain, more often than not, simply register public sentiment as it existed prior to the campaign. As a result, British election campaigns are "quiet in comparison with campaigns in most other democratic countries" (Birch, 1980: 74).

AMERICAN ELECTIONS

A characterization of the electoral process that certainly does not apply to the United States is that it is quiet. In contrast to Britain, election campaigns are noisy, lengthy, expensive, and nearly continuous in the American polity. Moreover, the doctrines of individualism and popular sovereignty have been extended to the internal operations of the political parties themselves, so that a considerable portion of the public has the potential to become involved in the political recruitment process. Candidates for public office are nominated by an election method known as the direct primary – one of the most unique aspects of the American political arena. However, involvement in the process of candidate selection, as well as frequent elections, do not necessarily lead to effective control of public policy. The nonideological nature of the American political parties and the dominance of two competitive parties in the national party system have resulted in election campaigns that choose leaders, not the content of public policy.

In the American presidential system, elections are mandated by law, so that the executive has no control over when they are held. No matter what the state of the economy or world affairs happen to be, the election process continues. For example, the November 4, 1980 presidential election was held, much to the despair of the incumbent Carter administration, on the one-year anniversary of the seizing of the American diplomats by the revolutionary government in Iran, a timing that was less than auspicious for the Democratic party, which was seeking reelection. Elections take place in single-member districts, under a plurality electoral formula. The election of the President is accomplished through the electoral college, which is a special and complex variation of this basic format (see Chapter 10).

The practice of malapportionment has long characterized the American electoral process, although its worst effects have been minimized in the last two decades. Because the constituency boundaries of the congressional districts in the United States House of Representatives are drawn by the respective state legislatures, which means, in fact, that they are drawn by the majority party in that state, manipulation of constituency size used to be a common political practice. However, in 1964, the Supreme Court ruled malapportionment among congressional districts unacceptable and ordered a redrawing of their boundaries on the principle of "one man, one vote." The result has been a virtual elimination of malapportionment in the lower House and an increase in the number of seats from both the urban and suburban areas. However, malapportionment is guaranteed in the Senate, since each state receives two seats: a senator from Maine represents one million constituents, but a senator from California 23 million. An electoral redistribution for the House of Representatives now takes place after each decennial census, with the Midwest and Northeast losing seats and the South and West gaining them. Unlike Canada, which often adds seats to the Commons during a redistribution, the size of the House of Representatives remains constant: if some states are to gain seats, others must lose them.

Although a reduction in malapportionment minimizes, somewhat, the leeway for gerrymandering the constituency boundaries, it has certainly not eliminated this finely-honed practice from American politics. Gerrymandering, once described as "ingenious exercises in political geography" (Key, 1964: 302), has particularly characterized state legislatures, serving as one means, for example, of discrimination against minority groups, especially blacks. An almost sure sign that district boundaries have been gerrymandered is their misshapen outline: often districts were drawn right down to the individual block or house, instead of following more natural dividing lines, such as major streets, county boundaries, or geographical partitions, such as rivers.

Probably the most unusual, as well as the most significant aspect of the American electoral process concerns the potential role of the ordinary citizen in the candidate selection procedures. Most candidates are now nominated through the use of direct primaries – a technique that remains uniquely American. A *direct primary* is an election among party members that selects that party's candidates for the general election. The direct primary was developed as a means of undercutting boss rule and giving to the ordinary citizen control over the nominees for political office. First adopted by the state of Wisconsin in 1903, the direct primary is the basic mechanism of political recruitment, although limited elements of older practices (e.g., conventions, caucuses) still remain. The thrust of the direct primary has been to democratize the candidate selection process, both in terms of the individuals who may seek office and in respect to the size of the selectorate. As a result, the American recruitment process, at least in theory, is the most open in the world. Presidential primaries, which are used in the selection of presidential candidates, are a special version of the direct primary technique.

Election campaigns in the United States are, therefore, a two-step process: first, a series of primary elections to select the party nominees for each office and second, a general election in which the various party candidates, so selected, compete with each other. Primary elections for all elective officers are normally held on the same day, usually several months, at least, before the general election. The typical pattern of primaries is as follows: on primary election day, a voter, who is registered as a Democrat, will be given a ballot containing the names of all those seeking the Democratic nomination for each office. The candidate receiving the most votes in the Democratic primary for each office (i.e., a plurality system) becomes the officially recognized Democratic candidate in the ensuing general election. A similar procedure is followed for Republican voters on primary day. Thus, a primary election is best seen as an internal party election by party activists and supporters of their candidate, who will then compete in the general election against the official candidates of the other parties.

Although the intent of the direct primary was to give the general public or at least party members a role in the candidate selection process, its effect in practice has been far from that ideal. For example, the rate of participation in primaries is usually a small percentage of those eligible, ranging anywhere from 10 percent in some cases upwards to 70 or 80 percent in others. The right to participate does not necessarily lead to actual participation. At the candidate level the law of increasing disproportion still operates: few ordinary citizens are likely to enter the battle for a party's nomination. Again, although the legal right is there, other factors work to limit a citizen from seeking and gaining nomination through the primary route. A major factor in this regard is a financial one: it may cost several hundred thousand dollars or more to run a primary campaign for a major political office. Without public funding for nomination campaigns, few citizens can afford the attempt to gain their party's nomination, let alone pay for the costs of the general election if they happen to be successful at step one.

Even though the direct primary has enlarged the number of citizens who participate in the selectorate, the effectiveness of the public's involvement is open to challenge. The primary mechanism has introduced public competition into the candidate selection process, by giving party members a chance to select which individual from the party's political elite will compete in the general election under the party label. Whether such a result, to an outside observer, is worth the cost and complex method of primary elections is not important, for it seems to be so to the American citizenry: "The American political tradition caps decisions made by popular vote with a resplendent halo of legitimacy" (Key, 1956: 133).

Although the American polity has enshrined the principle of popular sovereignty throughout its election process by electing more public officials in more elections on a more frequent basis than any other democratic polity in the world, neither the rate of political participation in voting nor the effectiveness of popular control over government has been necessarily improved. The potential avenues for active political participation are widespread, but, in reality, the average citizen plays a more modest role. Likewise, as in other countries, elections are primarily a means of choosing government leaders, not a particularly effective technique for controlling the content of public policy: "To choose a government is not to choose governmental policies" (Pomper, 1968: 51).

COMPARING ELECTORAL PROCESSES

The nature, operation, and consequences of a polity's electoral process reflect the party and constitutional context within which it operates. In turn, elections condition and modify both the party and constitutional systems. As a result, the type of electoral process utilized by a particular country is often a good indicator of the nature of the overall political regime. Competitive elections characterize democratic systems, while non-competitive ones are typically associated with the autocratic and totalitarian political systems. Within the democratic variety, presidential and parliamentary systems differ with respect to both the political recruitment process and the mechanics of their election campaigns.

In making a comparative analysis of the recruitment and nomination of candidates for public office, the nature of the selectorate must be a critical concern. The group that has the effective power and influence to serve in this capacity has the ability to control the kinds of candidates from among which the public will choose their governors. While all systems reflect the law of increasing disproportion, the basis of that inequality may be education in one system, race in another, and religion in a third. The open or closed nature of the recruitment process will determine the size and composition of the selectorate, as well as the type of individual chosen for public service. As a result, a country's political stratification system is clearly revealed by the operation and consequences of the political recruitment process.

Comparing election campaigns in democratic polities focuses on such matters as their timing, length, and electoral formula. Further aspects that often have significant political consequences include the problems of malapportionment and gerrymandering, as well as the frequency and partisanship of electoral redistributions. While governments and oppositions typically seek mandates from the public for the content of policy during an election battle, rarely does the public clearly register its policy preferences. Elections are a largely unrefined tool of public control over the content of the political agenda. Instead, elections allow the governed to choose which members of the political elite will govern them.

SUMMARY

1. The most significant difference between elections in democratic and totalitarian systems is the degree and effectiveness of the choice presented to the voter: in the former, the choice is real, in the latter, it is merely apparent.

2. In parliamentary systems, the election call, within a five-year maximum, is at the prerogative of the political executive, except in rare circumstances. Elections are party-based, of relatively short duration, with either a temporary or permanent voters' list prepared by an enumeration of eligible participants. Presidential systems operate elections under fixed time constraints, put the burden of involvement on the citizen to register to vote, and are typically lengthy. A two-stage election process is utilized in the United States, with stage one selecting party candidates and step two allowing the voter in a general election to choose between the party candidates so selected.

3. Political recruitment is the process of finding and nominating candidates for public office. Given the number of safe seats in democratic polities, nomination for office is often tantamount to election. The selectorate in any system is usually small, as the political elite attempts to control the holders of public office by determining which individuals are nominated to contest an election. Whether operating in a closed or open pattern, the political recruitment process produces candidates who are often unrepresentative of some of the major socioeconomic interests of society. Generally, any person who is qualified as an elector is also legally entitled to run for and serve in public office.

4. Canadian elections are competitive, relatively lengthy, and based on single-member districts, which utilize a plurality electoral formula. Voters' lists are temporary, and constituencies are allocated among the provinces primarily on a population basis, with federal electoral redistributions required after each decennial census. In the process of redistributing electoral districts, malapportionment and gerrymandering have been greatly reduced at the federal level. The selectorate in Canada is small, although more decentralized now than in the past. In most cases, effective control resides at the local level, although a national leader can, at times, challenge and overturn the decisions so made. The process of candidate recruitment diverges rather sharply from the democratic ideal.

5. British campaigns are short, based on a permanent voters' list, called at the request of the prime minister, and are quiet, but usually decisive, in that they typically produce majority governments. Candidate selection is a secretive, internal party matter, under the control of the party's elite through the use of such practices as short listing. Centralization of national party control over candidate selection exists in theory, but is rarely exercised in practice: local ridings have considerable autonomy to choose the candidate they desire.

6. American elections are noisy, lengthy, expensive, and nearly continuous. Popular sovereignty is imbedded in the two-stage election process through the use of the direct primary technique to nominate candidates for public office. Extensive avenues for political participation have not resulted, however, in high rates of actual involvement. The American election process, as in Canada and Britain, chooses the governors of the polity, not the priorities of the political agenda.

RECOMMENDED READINGS

The Electoral Process: General

BUTLER, DAVID and AUSTIN RANNEY, eds. (1978) *Referendums: A Comparative Study of Practice and Theory*. Washington, D.C.: American Enterprise Institute for Public Policy Research.

BUTLER, DAVID, HOWARD R. PENNIMAN, and AUSTIN RANNEY, eds. (1981) *Democracy At The Polls: A Comparative Study of Competitive National Elections*. Washington, D.C.: American Enterprise Institute for Public Policy Research.

EULAU, HEINZ and MOSHE M. CZUDNOWSKI, eds. (1976) *Elite Recruitment in Democratic Polities: Comparative Studies Across Nations*. New York: Halsted Press Division, John Wiley and Sons.

PUTNAM, ROBERT D. (1976) *The Comparative Study of Political Elites*. Englewood Cliffs, N.J.: Prentice-Hall.

ROSE, RICHARD and HARVE MOSSAWIR (1969) "Voting and Elections: A Functional Analysis," in Charles F. Cnudde and Deane E. Neubauer, eds., *Empirical Democratic Theory*. Chicago: Markham Publishing, pp. 69–97.

Canada's Electoral Process

BECK, J. M. (1968) *Pendulum of Power: Canada's Federal Elections*. Scarborough, Ont.: Prentice-Hall Canada Inc.

CAMP, DALTON (1979) *Points of Departure*. Ottawa: Deneau and Greenberg.

KORNBERG, ALLAN, JOEL SMITH, and HAROLD D. CLARKE (1979) *Citizen Politicians – Canada: Party Officials in a Democratic Society*. Durham, N.C.: Carolina Academic Press.

LANDES, RONALD G. (1981) "The Canadian General Election of 1980," *Parliamentary Affairs*, Vol. XXXIV, No. 1, pp. 95–109.

PENNIMAN, HOWARD R., ed. (1975) *Canada At The Polls: The General Election of 1974*. Washington, D.C.: American Enterprise Institute for Public Policy Research.

_____ (1981) *Canada At The Polls, 1979 and 1980: A Study of the General Elections*. Washington, D.C.: American Enterprise Institute for Public Policy Research.

QUALTER, TERENCE H. (1970) *The Election Process in Canada*. Toronto: McGraw-Hill of Canada.

Britain's Electoral Process

PENNIMAN, HOWARD R., ed. (1975) *Britain At The Polls: The Parliamentary Elections of 1974*. Washington, D.C.: American Enterprise Institute for Public Policy Research.

_____ (1981) *Britain At The Polls, 1979: A Study of the General Elections*. Washington, D.C.: American Enterprise Institute for Public Policy Research.

PULZER, PETER G. (1972) *Political Representation and Elections in Britain*. London: George Allen and Unwin, 2nd ed.

RANNEY, AUSTIN (1965) *Pathways to Parliament: Candidate Selection in Britain*. Madison, Wisc.: University of Wisconsin Press.

American Elections

KESSEL, JOHN (1980) *Presidential Campaign Politics: Coalition Strategies and Citizen Response*. Homewood, Ill.: The Dorsey Press.

POLSBY, NELSON W. and AARON WILDAVSKY (1980) *Presidential Elections: Strategies of American Electoral Politics*. New York: Charles Scribner's Sons, 5th ed.

POMPER, GERALD M. (1968) *Elections in America: Control and Influence in Democratic Politics*. New York: Dodd, Mead and Co.

10 COMPARING ELECTORAL SYSTEMS

In a really equal democracy, every or any section would be represented, not disproportionately, but proportionately. A majority of the electors would always have a majority of the representatives; but a minority of electors would always have a minority of the representatives (Mill, 1861: 190).

While it is probably the fate of man forever to pursue the better gadget, the power of man as an inventor seems to have found its real focus in the electoral system, where his passion for politics is wed to his passion for gadgetry (Milnor, 1969: 71).

ONE OF THE MOST important consequences of election campaigns and the competitive party struggle in democratic political systems is the actual physical control of the political structure gained by the victorious political party. Control of the political structure provides the winning party numerous political resources that it can use to maintain itself in office. These political resources include such items as the right to dispense patronage and government appointments, the ability to dominate media coverage, the right to determine the course of public policy and to focus the public's attention on certain priority areas, and the acquisition of the role of representative for the country in international affairs. One important power is the ability of the victorious party to modify the "rules of the political game" before the next electoral contest. Possible changes in the rules of the electoral process are rarely neutral or evenhanded in their effects on party competition. Nevertheless, this overt manipulation of the electoral system is often a common feature and tradition in the party battle in democratic political systems.

There are numerous Canadian examples, both historical and contemporary, of the redrawing of electoral boundaries. One of the most blatant historical examples of electoral manipulation is the famous gerrymander of 1882 by the Conservatives under John A. Macdonald (Beck, 1968: 40–41). The redrawing of electoral boundaries can often be utilized most effectively against individual opposition candidates. For example, when in 1945 the riding of Montreal Cartier elected a Communist Member of Parliament, its boundaries were extensively redrawn in 1947, resulting in a Liberal victory in that riding in the 1949 federal election (Winn and McMenemy, 1976: 119). Likewise, in 1978, the provincial Social Credit government in British Columbia proposed, in its suggested redistribution of electoral boundaries, the elimination of the ridings of three of the most energetic members of the opposition New Democratic Party. The New Democratic Party charged that "carefully manipulated alterations of boundaries would, on the basis of the 1975 voting patterns, cost the NDP eight to ten seats" in the next election (Greer, 1978: 46). However, if the party in power is too obvious and blatant in attempting to rid itself of a particular opposition member, it might find the voters returning that member anyway. For example, the federal Liberals tried on several occasions in the late 1940s and early 1950s to rid themselves of John Diefenbaker through the use of a gerrymander, but each time the voters sent Diefenbaker back to the Commons (Newman, 1973: 29–30).

Such manipulation of the electoral process is not unique to the Canadian polity. For example, in the late 1960s, the Labour government in Britain refused to implement the third report of the boundary commissions, which would have changed the electoral outline of 410 ridings. Instead, the Labour government sought to implement changes in a more limited number of constituencies, and when this failed, it laid the report of the boundary commissions before the House of Commons and instructed its own party supporters to vote against it. This tactic was employed to prevent new constituency boundaries from being in place in time for the next general election, because the Labour government feared that the new boundaries would favour the opposition Conservatives.

Electoral manipulation has been more prevalent in France, which has tried several different types of electoral systems since World War II. For example, in the elections for the National Assembly in 1951 and 1956, the Third Force parties, in an attempt to manipulate the electoral system against their chief rivals, the Gaullists and Communists, adopted a system of proportional representation with alliances. This system allowed the Third Force parties in 1951 to win more seats than they otherwise would have been entitled to, although by 1956 the alliance structure had been greatly weakened. General Charles de Gaulle himself was not above electoral chicanery. In designing the Fifth Republic's Constitution, de Gaulle modified the electoral system for National Assembly elections from the Fourth Republic's system of proportional representation and returned France to a system of single-member districts with a two-ballot structure previously utilized in the Third Republic. Later, in 1962, de Gaulle even changed the method of presidential selection in France, from an electoral college system to one of direct popular election. Without that modification of the presidential selection process, it is unlikely that de Gaulle would have been reelected in the 1965 presidential contest.

THE SIGNIFICANCE OF ELECTORAL SYSTEMS

Although such blatant manipulation of the electoral process has declined in recent decades in most democratic political systems, the fact that so much effort has been invested in such exercises leads us to consider the strategic political importance of electoral systems. If the rules of the electoral process had little impact on the political and party systems, then there would be little, if any, incentive to make such changes.

Probably the most significant consequence of electoral systems is their impact on the allocation of political power and influence within the political system. Since they transfer the percentage of popular vote won by the parties in the election into possible governmental control in terms of seats in the legislature, electoral systems help to determine which party actually wins an election campaign. As a result, electoral systems have important long-term effects on political parties' chances of gaining control of the political structure through the electoral mechanism. For example, some systems of electoral law prevent certain kinds of political parties from competing, thereby eliminating any chance for them to gain political power through normal democratic channels. In West Germany, Article 21 of the Basic Law (the Constitution of the Federal Republic of Germany) prohibits political parties that seek "to impair or abolish the free and democratic basic order" of the state (Burkett, 1975: 17). Parties of both the left and right have been banned under this provision: the Communist Party, for example, was outlawed between 1956 and 1969 as a legitimate competitor in the West German party system. Other systems, such as the Canadian, are generous in allowing almost any type of party to compete in the electoral battle. The election of the Parti Québécois in the November 1976 provincial election in Quebec is ample evidence of this point.

However, to compete in Canadian federal elections, political parties must meet certain minimum requirements. These regulations are designed to prevent parties that have no electoral base from either appearing on the ballot or from receiving public monies for their campaign expenditures. The democratic nature of the Canadian electoral process probably does not suffer greatly from the elimination of such fringe groups as the Nude Garden Party as a combatant in federal elections. Thus, by helping to determine which parties are eligible to compete and which parties will be rewarded with seats in the legislature, the first major consequence of electoral systems is their impact on the distribution of political power and influence in the polity.

A second effect of electoral systems is their important interface with the political party systems. The traditional view has been that specific kinds of electoral systems are a major factor in producing certain types of party systems. The most commonly held view is that the plurality electoral system tends to produce a two-party system, while proportional representation helps to generate a multi-party system (Duverger, 1964). While this hypothesis on the relationship between the electoral and party systems has generated considerable controversy, most current interpretations admit that the nature of a country's electoral system does have an important bearing on the type of political party system that emerges (Rae, 1971).

A third consequence of electoral systems is that all types tend to favour large parties over small parties in the allocation of legislative seats. Electoral systems appear to be cognizant of the Biblical injunction: "For whosoever hath, to him shall be given; but whosoever hath not, from him shall be taken away" (quoted in Rae, 1971: 134). As a result, electoral systems tend to favour the status quo parties, since new parties representing new ideas and ideologies are usually small to begin with. However, as a general rule, plurality systems discriminate far more heavily against most small parties than do the proportional representation electoral systems.

A fourth result of electoral systems is a practical one: that is, the problems they present for using national opinion polls to predict the results of forthcoming elections. The percentage of national popular support for a party does not necessarily translate into the percentage of seats that party will win in the election, especially under a plurality electoral system. One reason Prime Minister Trudeau decided not to call an election in the spring and early summer of 1978 was the realization of this important point. Even though the Liberals were leading the Conservatives by a small margin in the national polls, the fact of their overwhelming support in Quebec meant that they might lose the election because of the distribution of sentiment in the rest of the country, particularly in Southern Ontario and British Columbia. In other words, public opinion polls can give an accurate account of national views, but they are a very poor base for predicting election outcomes in terms of legislative seats. The reason for this is clear: it is the distribution of political preferences within the various electoral constituencies, not the national pattern, which will determine the election winner. Only if a poll were carried out within all or perhaps within a representative sample of constituencies could any serious attempt be made to predict the election results in terms of the number of seats that might be won by any political party.

TYPES OF ELECTORAL SYSTEMS

Up to this point in our analysis of electoral systems, we have dealt with their overall importance, without getting into the specifics of the various types. As a starting point, we need to consider a few basic concepts. What do we mean when we talk of "electoral law"? The following definition will serve as our basic guide.

> Electoral laws are those which govern the process by which electoral preferences are articulated as votes and by which these votes are translated into distributions of governmental authority (typically parliamentary seats) among the competing political parties (Rae, 1971:14).

In other words, electoral law is concerned with both the method of voting and the counting of those votes. As such, electoral law has to deal with two basic issues: first, how many candidates are to be elected in each constituency and second, the method for translating the percentage of popular votes into the number of seats won by each party in the legislature. These two issues can be referred to as dealing with the magnitude of the electoral districts and with the selection of an appropriate electoral formula. Using these criteria, we will analyze the two basic types of electoral systems: the single-member district with a plurality electoral formula and multi-member districts with a proportional representation electoral formula.

In relation to our first criterion, the *magnitude of the electoral district*, our concern is with the number of people elected in each constituency, or, in other words, the number of seats to be filled within a given electoral district. In *single-member electoral districts*, only one candidate is elected, no matter how many candidates are running for office in that constituency. In contrast, in *multi-member constituencies*, two or more members are elected, with the number selected depending on the electoral law of the country. Countries that use the single-member district (i.e., a district magnitude of one) include Canada, Britain, and the United States. Political systems using multi-member electoral districts include the Scandinavian countries, France in the Fourth Republic, Italy, Israel, and Austria. The magnitudes of these electoral districts may range from a minimum of two upward to the total number of seats in the legislature. For example, Israel considers the country as one large electoral district and thus ends up with a district magnitude of 120.

Our second criterion of electoral systems concerns the electoral formula for translating the popular vote into seats won in the legislature. There are two basic types of electoral formula: plurality and proportional representation. Under a *plurality electoral formula*, the percentage of popular votes won by a party rarely equals the percentage of legislative seats obtained; in fact, there is often a rather large discrepancy between the two. The reason for this discrepancy is evident if we take a look at the mechanics of the plurality formula. A plurality formula means that the party and/or candidate with the largest number of votes wins the seat or constituency. A plurality winner is not necessarily a majority winner. When only two candidates run for a specific office, the winner will have both a plurality and a majority. For example, let us assume that a constituency has 60 000 voters and that two parties contest the election. If Party A wins 40 000 votes and Party B wins 20 000 votes, then Party A has received both a plurality (more votes than any competitor) and a majority victory (at least 50 percent plus one). However, if three or more parties contest the election, then the winner often ends up with a plurality, but not a majority victory. In our example, let us assume that three parties contest the election, with the following breakdown of the popular vote: Party A receives 25 000 votes, Party B 20 000, and Party C 15 000. Under these conditions Party A still wins the constituency, but the outcome is a plurality, not a majority victory.

When this kind of distortion within a particular riding is multiplied throughout the entire range of constituencies (282 for the House of Commons in Canada), some rather strange results can occur. A party can win on a national basis a respectable share of the popular vote, but end up with a small number of legislative seats. Such a result is especially true of a party whose support is spread rather evenly across the country (what is called a pattern of diffuse or generalized electoral support). In Canadian federal elections, the New Democratic Party feels the impact of this characteristic of the plurality electoral formula. Moreover, because of such distortions, a party can actually lose an election in terms of legislative seats obtained, even though it has received a greater percentage of the popular vote than its opponents. This was the fate of the Liberal party in Quebec in the 1966 provincial election and of the Conservative party in the February 1974 British general election. In the 1979 Canadian federal election, the Liberal party received 40 percent of the popular vote compared to 36 percent for the Conservatives on a national basis, but the Conservatives, who won 136 seats to the Liberals' 114, formed the government. Because the electoral formula can sometimes turn winners into losers and vice versa, it is clear that the electoral system is an important factor in the winning of political power in any political system.

The second major type of electoral formula, that of *proportional representation*, attempts to eliminate the distortion found in plurality systems. Proportional representation electoral formulas seek to have the percentage of popular votes received by a party equal the percentage of seats won by that party in the legislature. The translation of popular support into legislative seats is determined by a specific type of proportional representation electoral formula: the two most common types are the highest average and the greatest remainder formulas. The actual calculations using these formulas can become very complex, so our examples will simply assume that such a system would equalize the percentage of votes and seats won by each party. It is also necessary to remember that proportional representation electoral formulas operate in multi-member constituencies.

Let us assume that a constituency with 100 000 voters selects ten members to the legislature and that the breakdown of the party vote is as follows: Party A receives 60 000 votes, Part B 30 000 votes, and

Party C 10 000 votes. The allocation of legislative seats under proportional representation would thus be distributed among the three parties in the resulting pattern: Party A would win six seats, Party B would obtain three seats, and Party C would elect one legislative member. In this example, each party's share of the popular vote equals its share of legislative seats, although in any real system this perfect equality is never reached.

Having calculated the number of seats won by each party, we must now determine which candidates have been selected. The most common type of candidate selection under proportional representation is the *list system*. In our sample constituency, ten members are to be elected. Each party contesting the election in this constituency would nominate ten candidates before election day and list them on the party's nomination papers in order from one to ten. Once the number of seats won by each party is determined, then the specific members elected are chosen, in descending order, from that party's list of candidates. For example, Party A elected six members, thus, those candidates in positions one through six on Party A's list of candidates would become Party A's elected members from this riding. A similar allocation procedure would occur for Party B and Party C. As this example demonstrates, the basic difference between plurality and proportional representation electoral formulas is in their effects on the allocation of legislative seats: plurality systems often show a great distortion between popular support and legislative representation, while proportional representation seeks to equalize a party's electoral support with the size of its parliamentary contingent.

THE CANADIAN ELECTORAL SYSTEM

In both federal and provincial elections, the Canadian electoral system is an example of the single-member district and plurality electoral formula. The plurality or, as it is sometimes called, the "first-past-the-post" system, is the only type of electoral system ever used in federal elections, although several Western provinces (Manitoba, Alberta, and British Columbia) have experimented with other forms in provincial elections.

Like other political systems that use the single-member district and plurality electoral formula, the Canadian electoral system regularly distorts the relationship between a party's popular support and the size of its parliamentary representation. Such a pattern is evident in the national vote and seat totals for the political parties in the last three federal elections (see Table 10.1). For example, the Liberals in 1974 gained a 10 percent reward from the electoral system, the Conservatives in 1979 received 12 percent, and the Liberals in 1980 gathered 8 percent. In other words, the difference (column 4) between the percentage of a party's popular vote (column 2) and the percentage of a party's seat share (column 3) represents the effect of the electoral system in translating popular support into parliamentary representation.

TABLE 10.1   *Canadian Election Results – 1974, 1979, 1980*

	# of seats	% of vote	% of seats won	electoral system bias %
1974 election				
Liberal	141	43	53	+ 10
PC	95	35	36	+ 1
NDP	16	15	6	– 9
SC	11	5	4	– 1
1979 election				
Liberal	114	40	40	0
PC	136	36	48	+ 12
NDP	26	18	9	– 9
SC	6	5	2	– 3
1980 election				
Liberal	147	44	52	+ 8
PC	103	33	37	+ 4
NDP	32	20	11	– 9
SC	0	2	0	– 2

A few examples of the various parties' fortunes in 1980 should help to clarify the effects of the electoral system in Canada. Even though the Liberal party was advantaged on a national basis by the plurality system, it still was discriminated against in specific provinces. For example, the Liberals received over 20 percent support in the three Western provinces of Alberta, Saskatchewan, and British Columbia (over half a million votes), yet they gained no seats in these electoral contests. Similarly, the Conservatives obtained over 350 000 votes in Quebec, but managed to grasp only one seat out of 75. On a national basis, therefore, the "first-past-the-post" system is usually biased in favour of the major parties, particularly the largest party in terms of votes, at the same time that it may discriminate against the major parties in particular regions of the country.

In contrast, the present electoral system has disadvantages for the New Democratic Party on both a national and regional basis. The NDP's strength, while fairly widespread (20 percent of the vote in the 1980 election), is distributed in a pattern of generalized or diffuse support. In other words, the NDP's support is spread too evenly across too many constituencies for it to gain a fair allocation of seats in the legislature. Minor parties like the NDP with diffuse support are typically discriminated against by a plurality electoral formula. For example, in Ontario the Liberals won 52 seats with 42 percent of the popular vote, but the NDP, with 22 percent support from the Ontario electorate, gained only 5 seats. In the 1980 election the NDP received no seats in 6 provinces, even though it gained as much as 21 percent of the vote in a province like Nova Scotia. Thus, under the present plurality system, the New Democratic Party is heavily disadvantaged on both a national and a regional basis.

The plurality system, however, works to the advantage of minor parties that exhibit strong regional or sectional voting support. The Social Credit party over the last several decades has benefited the most from this pattern. For example, in the 1968 federal election, Social Credit won 4.4 percent of the popular vote and 14 legislative seats, while the NDP obtained 17 percent of the popular vote (4 times that of Social Credit), but only 22 seats (8 more seats than Social Credit). However, in recent elections, Social Credit's popular support has declined to the point where it received no legislative seats in the 1980 contest.

In addition to these national and regional effects on the seat allocations for the political parties, the plurality electoral system in Canada also has a number of other important political consequences (Cairns, 1968). First, in contrast to other political systems, such as Britain, which utilize the plurality formula, in Canada the present electoral system does not produce majority governments on a regular basis. For example, the last six federal elections have witnessed a regular alternation between minority (1965, 1972, 1979) and majority governments (1968, 1974, 1980). In the last quarter century Canada has experienced six minority and four majority administrations. Second, the electoral system contributes to the public's misperception about the nature of the various political parties' status as national political organizations. The public perceives the parties in terms of their parliamentary representation, not in terms of their electoral or voting support. For example, the Liberals are locked out of support in the three most Western provinces in terms of seats, but not in terms of popular voting support, which is over 20 percent. Similarly, the Conservatives' lack of support in Quebec and the NDP's failure to gain representation in six provinces in 1980 is only true in terms of seats, not with respect to voting support. All three federal parties are more national in scope than the plurality electoral system has led us to believe. Third, the plurality electoral system thus reinforces the sectional and regional basis of the Canadian political system, because it tends to reward those parties that have established regional strongholds. The most obvious example is the Liberal party's dominance of Quebec: in 1980, the Liberals won 74 of 75 seats (99 percent of the seats), but in terms of votes they only won 68 percent of popular support. Similarly, the Tories won all 21 seats in Alberta, on the basis of 66 percent support from the electorate.

Finally, the plurality system affects the process of governing. For example, the previously discussed nature of the regional composition of the cabinet is influenced by the workings of the plurality system. By preventing adequate regional Liberal representation from the West and Conservative representation from Quebec in the House of Commons, the plurality electoral system forced the 1979 Clark government and the 1980 Trudeau administration to use the Senate as a temporary base for cabinet selection. Likewise, it is not entirely coincidental that Alberta, which has not elected a Liberal member to the House of Commons since 1968, has been in the forefront of federal-provincial conflict in the past decade. Thus, the present plurality electoral system, in addition to its effect on the translation of popular support into parliamentary representation, has a number of important consequences for the operation of the Canadian political system.

The above effects of the plurality electoral system in the Canadian context have generated numerous proposals for electoral reform. Those reform proposals that have received the greatest attention in the past few years can be broken down into two basic types: limited proportional representation and full proportional representation.

While varying on specifics, *limited proportional representation* proposals suggest adding a given number of seats (ranging from 50 to 100) to the present number of 282 seats in the House of Commons and then distributing these additional seats on a proportional basis among the various political party competitors (Task Force on National Unity, 1979: 104–106; Broadbent, 1980, 1978; Landes, 1980: 2–10; Smiley, 1978: 84–87; Irvine, 1979: 64–67). The allocation of these additional seats would generally correspond to the various parties' popular support and would be calculated under some system of proportional representation, either on a national, regional, or provincial basis. As a result, the Canadian electoral system would become a "mixed" system: 282 constituencies would be selected under the present plurality formula, while the additional seats would be based on proportional representation.

The primary effect of such a reform would be to increase the regional seat representativeness of all three federal parties: no party would be entirely lacking in legislative representation from any region of the country. As an example of a limited proportional representation plan (LPR for short), we present in Table 10.2 the allocation of seats that would have been obtained if the Pépin-Roberts proposal (Task Force on National Unity, 1979) had been in effect for the 1980 election (Irvine, 1980: 22). Such limited proportional representation proposals are a "conservative" way of achieving regional representation without greatly disturbing the overall election results in terms of seats won in the 282 single-member plurality contests.

All of the proposed limited proportional representation schemes, however, leave basically untouched the inequities produced by the plurality electoral formula in the 282 single-member ridings. For those who believe that a party's vote share should equal its share of legislative seats, the obvious answer is to adopt some form of full proportional representation (Irvine, 1979; Quebec Liberal Party, 1980: 46). Under such a plan, a party's legislative representation for each province would approximately equal its share of the popular vote in that province. Table 10.2 includes an allocation of parliamentary seats for 1980 if a full proportional representation formula had been utilized.

The effects of full proportional representation on the parliamentary strength of the political parties would be dramatic. First, the smaller political parties in recent federal elections would be advantaged under any system of full proportional representation. For example, in the 1979 election, Social Credit would have doubled its parliamentary seats (from 6 to 12) and in 1980 would have survived as a political party with 4 seats (compared to 0 under the plurality system). Even more significant would be the results of full proportional representation for the New Democratic Party: it would

TABLE 10.2 *Alternative Electoral Systems 1980**

	LIBERAL			PC			NDP		
	PLUR	*LPR*	*FPR*	*PLUR*	*LPR*	*FPR*	*PLUR*	*LPR*	*FPR*
NFLD.	5	5	3	2	2	3	0	0	0
P.E.I.	2	2	2	2	2	2	0	0	0
N.S.	5	5	5	6	6	4	0	1	2
N.B.	7	7	6	3	3	3	0	0	1
QUE.	74	74	54	1	12	10	0	3	7
ONT.	52	59	40	38	46	35	5	12	20
MAN.	2	4	4	5	5	5	7	7	5
SASK.	0	3	3	7	7	6	7	7	5
ALTA.	0	6	4	21	21	15	0	1	2
B.C.	0	9	6	16	16	12	12	12	10
Y/N.W.T.	0	0	1	2	2	1	1	1	1
TOTAL**	147	174	128	103	122	96	32	44	54

*PLUR means plurality type; LPR means limited proportional representation based on the Pépin–Robarts proposal; FPR indicates full proportional representation based on the highest average formula.
**In addition to the seats indicated in the LPR columns, Social Credit and the Rhinoceros party would each have received one seat in Quebec. Under FPR, Social Credit would have received four seats in Quebec. For the plurality and full proportional representation schemes, the total number of seats is 282, while for limited proportional representation the total seats equal 342.

become overnight a major force in federal politics, with a possible 54 seats (compared to the actual 32 seats) in the 1980 contest. More importantly, not only would the NDP's parliamentary representation approximately double in any election, it would also hold the balance of power within the House of Commons: either the Conservatives or Liberals could govern with the support of the NDP. It is clear that the primary beneficiary of any system of full proportional representation would be the New Democratic Party.

The impact of full proportional representation on the Liberal and Conservative parties, at least from their point of view, would be detrimental: the seat leader under the present plurality system would face major losses. For example, in 1979, the Conservatives would have lost 30 seats, would have found their position as the largest party eliminated, and would not have formed the government (based on the assumption that the largest party in terms of seats would be asked to form a government). In 1980, the Liberals, the leading party under the plurality system, would have lost about 20 seats under any full proportional representation scheme. While remaining the largest parliamentary party, the Liberals would have become a minority, instead of a majority, administration.

A further result of proportional representation would be a dramatic change in the internal regional composition of the three national parties. All three parties would become national parties in the sense of receiving seats throughout the country (with the exception of the NDP in Prince Edward Island). The Liberals would gain strong support in the West and the Conservatives would gain a base of support in Quebec. The major winner in terms of regional representation would be the NDP: it would gain representation in every province except Prince Edward Island. For the Liberals and Conservatives, increased regional representation under proportional representation has the price of the reduction in their total number of parliamentary seats. For the NDP, increased regional representation is combined with an approximate doubling of its legislative caucus. Such consequences would seem to make the adoption of full proportional representation by either a Conservative or Liberal administration very unlikely.

THE BRITISH ELECTORAL SYSTEM

Like Canada, Britain uses the single-member district (635) and plurality electoral formula for elections to the House of Commons. As might be expected, then, many of the consequences of the plurality electoral system are similar in Canada and Britain. For example, in Britain, a party that loses the popular vote can end up winning the largest allocation of parliamentary seats, as the Labour Party did in the February 1974 election (see Table 10.3). Likewise, the plurality system typically works to the advantage of the major parties and discriminates heavily against those parties with generalized or diffuse support (Liberals). For example, the Liberals won 19.3 percent of the popular vote in the February 1974 contest, but gained only 2.2 percent of the legislative seats. In contrast, small parties with strong sectional or regional support (i.e., the Scottish Nationalist Party or the Welsh Nationalist Party) fare much better under the plurality formula than the Liberals. For example, the Ulster Loyalists, with only 1.2 percent of the national vote, won 11 seats in February 1974, while the Liberals, with 19.3 percent public support, gained only 14 seats in the House of Commons. Thus, in both Canada and Britain, the plurality system advantages the major parties (in Canada, the Liberals and the Conservatives; in Britain, the Labour and Conservative parties), discriminates against those

TABLE 10.3 *British Election Results – 1974, 1979*

	# of seats	% of vote	% of seats	Effects of the Electoral System %	# of seats under full PR
February 1974					
Labour	301	37.2	47.4	+ 10.2	236
Conservative	297	38.1	46.8	+ 8.7	242
Liberal	14	19.3	2.2	– 17.1	123
Other	23	5.3	3.6	– 1.7	34
SNP	7	1.9	1.1	– 0.8	12
Plaid Cymru	2	0.5	0.3	– 0.2	3
Ulster Loyalist	11	1.2	1.7	+ 0.5	8
October 1974					
Labour	319	39.3	50.2	+ 10.9	250
Conservative	277	35.8	43.6	+ 7.8	227
Liberal	13	18.3	2.0	– 16.3	116
Other	26	6.5	4.1	– 2.4	41
SNP	11	2.9	1.7	– 1.2	18
Plaid Cymru	3	0.6	0.5	– 0.1	4
Ulster Loyalist	10	1.4	1.6	+ 0.2	9
1979 election					
Labour	268	36.7	42.2	+ 5.5	233
Conservative	339	43.7	53.4	+ 9.7	277
Liberal	11	13.8	1.7	– 12.1	88
Other	17	5.7	2.7	– 3.0	36

parties with generalized or diffuse support (in Canada, the New Democratic Party; in Britain the Liberal party), and either aids parties with strong sectional or regional support or at least does not discriminate against them with the same intensity as it does against those parties with diffuse support (in Canada, the Social Credit party; in Britain, the various nationalist parties: Scottish Nationalist Party, the Plaid Cymru or Welsh Nationalist Party, and the Ulster Loyalists).

The differential effects of the plurality system in the British and Canadian contexts can be seen with respect to two areas: first, the creation of majority governments and second, the regional composition of the major parties. Although similar to Canada in that the winning party rarely has a majority of the vote (the last election where a party won more than 50 percent of the vote took place in

1931), in contrast to Canada, the plurality formula in Britain regularly produces majority governments in terms of parliamentary seat allocations. In the postwar era (1945–1979), 11 elections have been contested, with majority governments resulting in 10 cases. The only exception was the February 1974 election, although the October 1974 Labour majority was so small that it became a minority government within a couple of years through defections, retirements, and deaths. Majority governments have occurred in Britain because, until the 1974 elections and the rise of several nationalist parties, minor parties have received a small number of legislative seats, while in Canada, minor parties have consistently fared much better under the plurality system. In the 1960s and 1970s Canada's four-party system (Liberal, Conservative, New Democratic Party, Social Credit), combined with the effects of the plurality formula, helped to prevent the regular formation of majority governments.

A second difference between the plurality system in Britain and Canada concerns the regional nature of a political party's legislative representation. In the Canadian context, the combination of the plurality system with the regional bases of party support has often resulted in a party receiving no legislative seats from certain regions of the country (i.e., the Liberal party in Alberta obtained no seats in the last four federal elections). In Britain, parties have regional strongholds, but a party is rarely discriminated against to such an extent that it receives no legislative representation (Drucker, 1979: 216–217). For example, even though the Labour party dominates the other parties in the constituencies in Scotland and Wales, the Conservative party continues to receive a block of seats in these regional battles: 16 seats in Scotland and 8 seats in Wales in the October 1974 election (Punnett, 1980: 60–61). Thus, in both countries, the plurality electoral system helps to build and to sustain regional party strongholds, but the extent of this pattern is greater in Canada than in Britain.

Proposals for electoral reform in Britain have centred, as in Canada, on alternatives that would increase the equality between a party's share of the popular vote and its share of legislative seats. The most commonly advocated reform calls for the adoption of a particular type of proportional representation known as the single transferable vote or STV for short (Scammon, 1975: 165–176). While the details of such a plan are beyond the scope of our concern here, the STV System, or any other proportional representation scheme, would greatly alter the electoral fortunes of the various political parties. Since the major parties are as unlikely to commit political "hari kari" in Britain as they are in Canada, prospects for the adoption of any system of proportional representation do not seem likely.

THE AMERICAN ELECTORAL COLLEGE

As in Canada and Britain, the electoral system used in the United States is the single-member district, plurality electoral formula mechanism. For example, in selecting members for the House of Representatives, there are 435 congressional districts, with one member elected in each. For Senate elections, each district corresponds to a state's boundaries, with the person with the most votes (i.e., a plurality) winning a place in the national legislature. In electing a president, a special version of the single-member district, plurality formula is used – the electoral college.

The *electoral college* is only used in selecting the president and vice-president of the United States once every four years, but it is one of the unique aspects of American election practices. It was initially designed to provide an indirect method of electing the American president. The people would elect members of the state legislatures, who in turn would elect the individuals to serve in the electoral college. The members of the electoral college thus chosen would then select the president and vice-president. The ordinary citizen was, therefore, twice removed from direct involvement in the presidential election process. However, as the idea of popular sovereignty became enshrined in the American political culture, the people were granted a somewhat greater say. The people now select the membership of the electoral college when they cast their ballot in the presidential election in November once every four years. Moreover, the electoral college has become a formality, with the real decision made by the people in the presidential election. Although it need not always be the case, the electoral college in the modern era merely ratifies the outcome of the popular vote registered at the polls.

The structure of the electoral college is roughly based on population, since each state receives presidential electors equal to its number of members in the national legislature. For example, California has 2 senators and 43 congressmen, so it has 45 votes in the electoral college. The total number of votes in the electoral college is 538 (a figure equivalent to 100 senators plus 435 representatives plus 3 votes for the District of Columbia). To win, a candidate must receive a majority of votes, that is, a total of 270.

When American citizens cast their ballots in the presidential contest, they are really selecting their state's representatives in the electoral college. Each party or candidate in the presidential race draws up a list of people willing to serve as presidential electors. This slate of delegates is listed after the name of the presidential candidate on the ballot. For example, in 1980 in the state of California, Ronald Reagan, Jimmy Carter, and other presidential candidates listed after their names the names of their nominees to serve as electors in the electoral college. If a candidate wins the race in California, then his or her slate of presidential electors becomes the state's delegation to the electoral college. Moreover, the election in each state is based on the *unit rule*, a special version of the plurality formula. A candidate who wins the popular vote in a state wins all of the state's vote in the electoral college. In other words, in each state, a presidential election is based on a "winner take all" principle. Thus, the presidential vote in November determines the composition of each state's slate of delegates in the electoral college.

The next step is for the presidential electors who have been selected to meet and cast their ballots for the president and vice-president. The electors meet in their respective state capitals in December and cast their secret ballots, which are then sent on to the president of the American Senate (i.e., the current vice-president of the United States). In early January, a joint meeting of the House of Representatives and Senate is held to count the ballots and to officially declare a winner. Thus, the president and vice-president are not technically elected until the votes of the presidential electors are counted by Congress, although for all practical purposes they are elected in November.

A further complicating factor might arise. If two candidates or parties are competing in a presidential election, then the electoral college will produce a majority winner as a result of the workings of the unit rule. However, if more than two candidates compete and if the electoral college vote is splintered among three or more parties, then nobody may receive a majority of votes when Congress counts the ballots in January. If no majority is received, then the House of Representatives selects the president from among the three who received the most electoral college votes, with the Senate choosing the vice-president. This result has never happened in the 20th century, but it is a possibility when more than two parties gain a significant share of the electoral college vote.

The effects of the electoral college on presidential politics are many, though it has largely become a formality in deciding who wins. First, a party can win the presidency by winning the vote in about the 12 largest states. The presidential candidate with the largest national popular vote does not necessarily win a majority of presidential electors in the electoral college. Second, the Democrats and Republicans will most often select as their presidential and vice-presidential candidates individuals from these largest states. This custom is based on the assumption that such candidates will win their home states in the presidential election. For example, in 1960, the Democrats chose John F. Kennedy from Massachusetts and Lyndon B. Johnson from Texas. Third, election campaigns are centred around the largest states, since that is where most of the electoral college votes are determined. Thus, the electoral college not only helps to influence the kind of person nominated for president, but also the nature of American presidential campaigns.

COMPARING ELECTORAL SYSTEMS: THE POLITICAL CONTEXT AND CONSEQUENCES OF ELECTORAL REFORM

In comparing electoral systems, several basic criteria are significant: first, the kind of electoral system used; second, the effects of the electoral system on the party system; and third, how electoral reform is achieved. These three areas are interdependent, since the type of electoral system influences the type of party system created, both of which in turn condition the prospects for electoral reform.

Suggestions for electoral reform are evident in most democratic political systems. Yet most electoral reform proposals have died because of their expected political consequences, real or apprehended. Once a particular electoral system is adopted and used, a pattern of interests develops around its workings and effects; these interests then become opposed to further political change. Those political groups that benefit from the current system will obviously be opposed to and suspicious of political reform efforts, while those political interests disadvantaged by current practices will be the most vociferous champions of political change. In either case, self-interest, not abstract political principles of democracy or equality, determines a group's attitude toward reform proposals. Using Canada as our example, we will analyze the expected political results of adopting either a limited or a full proportional representation electoral formula.

All considerations of alternative electoral systems make one crucial assumption, namely, that voter preferences will remain the same under new election mechanics as they were in previous elections. For example, in Tables 10.2 and 10.3 we based our estimations of the effects of proportional representation in Canada and Britain on the voting patterns of recent campaigns. Such an assumption, of course, is false: as Duverger (1964) noted several decades ago, the first effect of any electoral reform is to modify not only the distribution of seats, but also the distribution of votes. It is probably fair to hypothesize that the greater the difference between the new electoral formula and the present system, the greater the change in the actual distribution of the vote. On this basis, limited proportional representation would produce minimal changes in voter preferences: probably one to two percent of the national vote. The NDP would likely benefit slightly, since the so-called "wasted votes" would at least be rewarded in the allocation of the additional seats in the House of Commons. Under full proportional representation, the NDP would likely, over several elections, increase its base of popular support. It would immediately become a major party under any full proportional representation formula, which might then serve as a foundation for expansion to challenge the dominance of the two old-line parties. A three-party system, similar to that found in Ontario at the provincial level (with the Liberals, however, as the leading party) might result. A change to full proportional representation might lead, over a series of elections, to a realignment of the federal party system along European lines of development (Duverger, 1972: 40-76).

A second possible consequence of electoral reform is a change in the number of parties competing in the federal party system and their relative share of the popular vote and legislative seats. The possible splintering of the national party system under full proportional representation is probably less likely than most observers acknowledge. The Canadian electorate in recent years has shown no predilection for either forming or supporting parties that would be serious challengers to the existing party competitors. In fact, with the demise of Social Credit in the 1980 election, the federal party system has been consolidated, in the sense that the total vote share of the three largest parties is now at a 20-year peak. Moreover, while individual, provincial, and regional voting patterns can shift fairly quickly, the national levels of voting support for the three remaining parties have rarely shifted by more than three to five percentage points between elections. Given the fact that the current partisan alignment and electoral cleavages have remained relatively stable since the 1920s, it is unlikely that a change to even full proportional representation would fracture the federal party system by producing a new party or a series of new partisan coalitions (see, for example, Duverger, 1964: 228–255; Rae, 1971: 148–176; Sartori, 1976).

A further important result of a change in the electoral formula might be in the kind of government (i.e., majority or minority) that results. Systems of limited proportional representation would rarely change the majority-minority decision currently found. In contrast, a proportional representation formula would institutionalize minority governments as the typical Canadian pattern: given the historical voting patterns, it would be rare for any party to end up with a majority of the popular vote and a resulting majority of legislative seats. For example, Pierre Trudeau, while winning three majority governments under the current plurality system, would always have experienced minority governments under any of the full proportional representation schemes. Thus, the proper question seems to be not what kind of government would full proportional representation produce, but what is the stability of the resulting minority situations?

Stability of such minority governments could be assessed on two grounds: first, the frequency of dissolutions of the House and the calling of new elections and second, the frequency of defeats in Parliament and the formation of a new government without resort to new elections. Perhaps paradoxically, full proportional representation would likely lead to more stable governments than the plurality system with respect to the first criterion. Since a party's national vote rarely fluctuates by more than several percentage points between elections, and since proportional representation fairly faithfully reflects in seats a party's share of the popular vote, a return to the people in new elections would rarely change a party's relative standing. Thus, opposition parties or the government might be much less motivated to force new elections than under the current plurality system.

With respect to the second criterion, parliamentary defeats of the governing party might occur on a fairly regular basis. However, in light of the 1968 constitutional precedent concerning the defeat of a minority government, these defeats would not necessarily lead to the resignation of the government. If parliamentary defeats and/or changes in government began to occur on a regular basis, it is possible that some form of coalition government might develop. However, given the previous single federal experience with coalition government, it is unlikely that a coalition government along European lines (i.e., with cabinet portfolios given to the minor party or parties) would be set up. More probable would be agreements to support, for limited time periods, a major party in Parliament by the NDP in return for favourable legislation. Thus, even with respect to the criterion of parliamentary defeats, proportional representation would not necessarily lead to unstable governments in the Canadian context: much would depend on the ability and willingness of the party leaders to make such a system viable.

A change in the electoral system, particularly to full proportional representation, would also greatly alter the internal composition and thus the power of various factions within the political parties. For example, it is not in the political interest of the Quebec Liberal caucus to change to a proportional representation electoral formula: first, about 25 percent of its members would lose their seats and thus, as a second consequence, the Quebec Liberal caucus would play a reduced role within the federal Liberal party. The role of the Quebec Liberal caucus in retaining Pierre Trudeau as the Liberal leader for the 1980 election demonstrates the importance of these internal party considerations. After the 1980 election, the Quebec Liberal caucus had a majority of seats (74/147) in a majority government (147/282): under proportional representation they would have been a minority faction in a minority government. A similar case could be made for the role of the West within the Conservative party. Moreover, even though the New Democratic Party would gain seats under proportional representation, the power basis within the party caucus would shift away from Western towards Eastern Canada. Such reflections indicate likely opposition to full proportional representation from the dominant factions within all of the existing federal parties.

Finally, as long as the Liberal party continues to dominate national politics, it is not in Quebec's interest (at least for federalists) to reform the electoral system. Quebec's relative influence in Confederation would decline: better representation within the major parties only makes sense if these parties regularly alternate in forming the federal government, which of course they do not. The recent proposal by the Quebec Liberal party (1980) to consider full proportional representation at the federal level is a situation that demonstrates that a political party does not always know its own best interest. We would suggest that Quebec's role in and the Liberal party's dominance of the federal level has been crucially dependent on the plurality system, despite the fact that the Liberal party has been ''systematically associated ... with the second province, the second language, and the second religion: an illustration of how to be second in order to be first" (Laponce, 1972: 284). It is also not in the interest of Ontario to see electoral reform proposals come to fruition. The role of Ontario as the key province making or breaking federal governments, due to its large number of "swing" ridings, would be lost in most electoral reforms, especially under full proportional representation. Ontario is now on the winning side with a large bloc of members no matter which major party wins the election: such a situation would be greatly reduced or eliminated under most reform proposals

The above analysis of the political context and consequences of electoral reform in Canada raises a number of significant considerations, which apply to electoral reform efforts in most democratic political systems. First, a change in the electoral system will modify not only the distribution of seats among the parties, but the distribution of votes as well. Second, a change in the electoral formula will have a bearing on the number of political parties that continue to exist or that are likely to develop in the future. In other words, the type of electoral system adopted by a political system has an important bearing on the type of political party system that emerges. Third, electoral systems not only help to determine the minority or majority status of governments, but their resulting stability as well. Finally, the electoral system influences a party's organizational structure and the internal power of the various party factions. Such conclusions support the view that "the electoral system affects the political life of a country mainly through the parties" (Duverger, 1951: 314).

SUMMARY

1. Electoral systems are significant elements of the political process because they help to determine the election winner, influence the number of parties that develop, and affect the internal composition of the political parties.

2. Two basic types of electoral systems can be identified: first, single-member districts with plurality electoral formula and second, multi-member districts with a proportional representation formula. The plurality format usually distorts the relationship between a party's popular vote and its strength in the legislature, while proportional representation seeks to equalize a party's vote and seat share.

3. The Canadian electoral system is an example of the plurality type: it benefits the larger parties and minor parties with regional support, but is a disadvantage to minor parties with diffuse or generalized support. Full proportional representation would greatly help the NDP, but, for that very reason, it is a most unlikely occurrence.
4. Britain's plurality formula has similar effects as its Canadian counterpart, greatly aiding the larger parties and sectional parties, but discriminating against those parties, such as the Liberals, which receive generalized support.
5. The American electoral college is a special variation of a plurality system, which is used to elect the president and vice-president. Although it has typically become a formality in American politics, with the real choice made by the people when they cast their presidential vote, it continues to influence the nomination of presidential candidates and the nature of presidential electoral strategies.
6. Electoral reform often carries with it important political consequences for the existing parties. As a result, electoral reform is often blocked by the current major parties in an attempt to protect their own political dominance in the polity.

RECOMMENDED READINGS

Electoral Systems: General

DUVERGER, MAURICE (1951) "The Influence of the Electoral System on Political Life," *International Social Science Bulletin*, Vol. 3, No. 2 (Summer), pp. 314–365.

MILNOR, A.J. (1969) *Elections and Political Stability*. Boston: Little, Brown and Co.

RAE, DOUGLAS W. (1971) *The Political Consequences of Electoral Laws*. New Haven: Yale University Press, rev. ed.

The Canadian Electoral System

CAIRNS, ALAN C. (1968) "The Electoral System and the Party System in Canada, 1921–1965," *Canadian Journal of Political Science*, Vol. 1, No. 1 (March), pp. 55–80.

COURTNEY, JOHN C. (1980) "Reflections on Reforming the Canadian Electoral System," *Canadian Public Administration*, Vol. 23, No. 3 (Fall), pp. 427–457.

IRVINE, WILLIAM P. (1979) *Does Canada Need a New Electoral System?* Kingston, Ont.: Institute of Intergovernmental Relations, Queen's University.

LANDES, RONALD G. (1980) "Alternative Electoral Systems for Canada." Paper presented to the annual meeting of the Canadian Political Science Association, Montreal, Quebec.

The British Electoral System

FINER, S.E. (1980) *The Changing British Party System, 1945-1979.* Washington, D.C.: American Enterprise Institute for Public Policy Research. See Ch. 2, "Parties at the Electoral Level," pp. 32–71.

SCAMMON, RICHARD (1975) "The Election and the Future of British Electoral Reform," in Howard R. Penniman, ed., *Britain At The Polls: The Parliamentary Elections of 1974.* Washington, D.C.: American Enterprise Institute for Public Policy Research, pp. 163–176.

The American Electoral College

POLSBY, NELSON W. and AARON WILDAVSKY (1980) *Presidential Elections: Strategies of American Electoral Politics.* New York: Charles Scribner's Sons, 5th ed.

WATSON, RICHARD A. (1980) *The Presidential Contest.* New York: John Wiley and Sons.

11 POLITICAL BEHAVIOUR: SOCIALIZATION AND PARTICIPATION

The entire man is, so to speak, to be seen in the cradle of the child (de Tocqueville, 1835).

Indeed, active Canadians appear to approach politics much as they would a hockey game. If the game is good they will come out and cheer. If their team wins they will be happy. If it loses they will be momentarily sad. On election day they may "go to the game" by voting, then watching the returns on television.... If their party wins they will be happy and if it loses they may be temporarily said; but not for long because it really does not matter very much (Van Loon, 1970: 397–398).

IN RECENT CANADIAN federal elections, about eleven and a half million voters dutifully trudged to the polls to cast their ballots for their favourite candidates and parties (a cynic might suggest that they had voted for their least objectionable preference). Unless one makes the probably unwarranted assumption that such behaviour is a reflection of inherited lemming-like traits on the part of the Canadian voter, we are left with the basic question of all social scientific endeavour: why did this pattern occur? At first glance, the answer appears to be deceptively simple: since human behaviour is learned, political behaviour is likewise the result of the learning process.

The attempt to understand adult political beliefs and behaviour has thus led back to an investigation of their origins and development, that is, to a concern with the *political socialization process*. The basic assumption of political socialization research is that the initial learning of political values and ideas in childhood and adolescence influences, to a greater or lesser extent, the later political values and behaviour of adults: "political ideas – like the consumption of cigarettes and hard liquor – do not suddenly begin with one's eighteenth birthday" (Niemi, 1973: 117). Although political learning may begin in childhood, it is also important to remember that it is continuous throughout a person's life. While many orientations and attitudes may be formed in childhood and adolescence, actual experience with and participation in politics as an adult may modify and change previously held ideas. In addition to being continuous and beginning early, the political socialization process, for most people, is also cumulative in nature: that is, the orientations acquired later in life are grafted onto and mixed with those adopted in childhood and adolescence. It is difficult to discard years of learning, political or otherwise, and to start over with a fresh set of beliefs.

Different types of political systems utilize various techniques in attempting to control the learning of political values by the young. In democratic systems, the political socialization process is usually indirect and implicit. Few parents consciously seek to teach their offspring a particular set of political beliefs. Instead, children usually acquire values similar to those of their parents from observing the values parents exhibit in their own behaviour. Even when children are exposed to political content in the educational process, there is usually an attempt to avoid partisan debate. In contrast, both autocratic and totalitarian systems seek explicit control of the political socialization process by directly using state-controlled institutions, such as the school system and mass media, to forge a common set of political values among their citizens. Whether state-directed or not, the various agents of the political socialization process (i.e., family, schools, peer groups, mass media) affect individuals in all political systems. For most individuals, political beliefs reflect a mixture of the influence of socialization agents and personal experiences with the political system.

By the time people reach the age of formal participation in the political process, perhaps best illustrated by the right to vote, their political values, beliefs, and behaviour are generally established. Although a small segment of the public may be politically active in their adolescent years, most are not, a pattern carried over into their adult years. Outside of voting in elections, most citizens participate only intermittently in the political process. The types of political behaviour an individual can use to influence leaders can run the gamut from the unconventional (riots, protest meetings, terrorism) to the conventional (participation in community affairs, campaign activity, running for office) to more passive modes of participation, such as simply voting. Moreover, a segment of any electorate is likely to be apathetic and, thus, does not particpate in either conventional or unconventional political activity (Milbrath and Goel, 1977: 18–19). Although the concept of political behaviour contains a number of kinds of activity, our main focus will be on voting behaviour, because it is the dominant mode by which most citizens seek to influence the operation of their political system.

ACQUIRING POLITICAL BELIEFS: THE POLITICAL SOCIALIZATION PROCESS

While the specific mechanisms utilized in the political socialization process vary from one country to the next, there are many similarities between political systems of each major type. After considering the political socialization process in Canada, we will briefly consider the nature of political learning in Britain and the United States.

Political Socialization in Canada
Politics is not an especially salient focus of concern for the average citizen, which reveals much about the nature of the political socialization process. For most Canadian youth, the learning of political orientations is indirect and implicit and perhaps based on the assumption that "politics, like sex, should be learned in the

streets rather than the classroom" (White et al., 1972: 193). However, the acquisition of political beliefs begins early on a wide variety of topics.

The learning of political information centres initially on political leaders rather than on political institutions (Landes, 1976). By junior high school most children can correctly identify the prime minister, although provincial and local leaders are less well-recognized. Identification of political executives (prime minister, premiers) far exceeds that of the formal executive positions (governor general, lieutenant governors). However, understanding of the more complicated aspects of the political system, such as the job or role of these political leaders, reveals a minimum level of knowledge. For example, the Canadian Student Awareness Survey (Hurtig, 1975) found that 68 percent of high school seniors were unable to name the Governor General, 61 percent were unable to name the BNA Act as Canada's Constitution, and 70 percent had little or no idea what percentage of Canada's population was French-Canadian. Thus, the average Canadian adolescent would appear to have a rather low level of political knowledge. As one researcher phrased these findings, "I feel as though someone out there waged a war on knowledge, and I've been shell-shocked by the 'Ignorants'. Knowledge of Canadian geography is almost nonexistent, political awareness unbelievable, cultural knowledge abysmal" (Hurtig, 1975: 10).

Even though levels of political information are low, children and adolescents still develop an emotional tie to political leaders and the political system. The typical pattern is for the child to personalize the political system (i.e., to perceive politics in terms of leaders) and to develop supportive attitudes and positive feelings toward the polity. For example, a comparative study of English-Canadian and American school children, grades four through eight, found that the Canadian child's affective (i.e., emotional) response to government in terms of benevolence, dependability, and leadership was greater than for his or her American counterparts (Landes, 1977: 68). Although the initial pattern of political affect is usually positive or supportive of the political regime, typically the level of political affect declines during the adolescent years and may even turn into feelings of alienation and cynicism. A particularly important affective tie is the child's early attachment to a specific political party. However, the development of party orientations among young people shows significant regional variations, with the West having the lowest and the Maritimes displaying the highest rate of partisan attachments (Gregg and Whittington, 1976: 78).

In addition to information, affect, and partisan ties, political socialization research has found that the major themes of Canada's political culture are reflected in the political learning process. By the adolescent years, for example, strong patterns of regional loyalties are evident. As Johnstone (1969: 22) concluded, "during the adolescent years Canadian young people become aware of the important sectional, regional, and provincial interests in Canadian life," so that the "adolescent years ... could be characterized as the period of emergent sectionalism." With respect to the dualism theme, a number of studies have discovered that English-Canadian and French-Canadian youth are taught different political values in the political socialization process (Lamy, 1975; Forbes, 1976). For example, an analysis of English- and French-Canadian history textbooks found that almost totally contradictory pictures of individuals and events were presented (Trudel and Jain, 1970). Such findings led one observer to conclude that "political socialization in Canada, then, seems to be for young French and English Canadians a process of socialization into discord...." (Lamy, 1975: 278). Finally, the continentalism theme reveals the American impact on the learning of political values in Canada. For example, the American domination of the mass media has meant that many children are socialized to American rather than Canadian political values. Students often learn little of the Canadian political tradition, but much about American history and politics. As one student in the Canadian Student Awareness Survey concluded, when asked to identify a series of cultural and political leaders, "Never heard of them, so they must be Canadian" (Hurtig, 1975: 13). Combined with the early development of regional loyalties and English-French differences in political outlooks, the American penetration of the political learning process certainly exacerbates the development of a Canadian national identity.

The content of the political socialization process is influenced by the nature of the socialization agents utilized. Although specific political orientations such as partisan attachments may be passed from parents to children, as a general pattern, "most Canadian families, however, are not consciously involved in politically socializing their members" (Kornberg et al., 1979: 228). The family's impact is most apparent in providing the child with certain circumstances of birth (e.g., a social class position, a place of residence in a particular region of the country) which may look nonpolitical to begin with, but which have important consequences for what the child eventually is taught and learns about his or her political environment. In addition, the influence of the family as an agent of political socialization depends in part on the homogeneity of the family unit. If the mother and father have the same political outlooks, then their effect on the child will be greater than if their political beliefs contradict each other. Finally, while the Canadian family in the 1980s remains an important agent in the political socialization process, it is increasingly in competition with the other intermediaries in the learning process.

The significance of schools as agents of socialization is suggested by the frequent battles over attempts to censor school textbooks and reading materials. Censorship disputes are concerned with which community forces will control the content presented by the school as an agent of socialization: "some people fear that insidious professors or evil books may politically subvert the young" (Jaros, 1973: 113). The role of Canadian schools as agents of political socialization can be summarized with respect to the following major points. First, since under the British North America Act (Section 93) education is made an exclusive provincial jurisdiction, "political socialization via the schools is fragmented because of the ten different provincial systems" (Ogmundson, 1976: 181). Second, as a public agent, the schools provide for most Canadians the only "exposure to formal political socialization by an instrument of the state..." (Kornberg et al., 1979: 228). Third, the extent of explicit political exposure through the schools is minimal, confined mainly to history and civics courses. Fourth, what little political content is presented is done so in nonpartisan terms, stressing a consensus version of Canada's political experience. Fifth, the result of the schools' efforts is an uninformed citizenry: "most high school graduates lack basic knowledge of Canadian political studies" (Symons, 1978: 50).

A third significant agent in the political socialization process in recent decades is the mass media, especially television. The potential impact of the mass media rests on two considerations: first, the nearly universal access most people have to newspapers, magazines, and television and second, the ability of the mass media to bypass other intermediaries of socialization and to provide information directly to children and adolescents. Thus, it is not surprising to find that children and adolescents depend on television and the mass media for political news and for help in understanding political events. The mass media have also made available to young children some of the harsher realities of political life, including wars, riots, revolutions, and assassinations. While these events usually occur in other counrties, the fact that they are presented in the Canadian media means that such tragic events are helping to mold the political values and beliefs of our children.

Although other agents, such as peer groups or one's personal contacts with the political regime, may be significant shapers of political values, we will conclude our discussion of the political socialization process in Canada by emphasizing that the content of political learning is heavily influenced by the nature of the socializing agents. For example, the promotion and perpetuation of regional loyalties and French-English differences have been constitutionally facilitated by providing that education is an exclusive jurisdiction of the provincial governments. Likewise, the creation of a common national identity has been hindered not only by provincial control of education, but also by the dominance of American textbooks in the schools and American domination of the mass media. In addition, the indirect nature of political socialization through such agencies as the family and the minimal levels of political content presented to the child through the formal political socialization agent of the schools, has meant the production of an uninformed citizenry, Any reform of this situation must contemplate major changes in both the content and agents of political learning.

The British and American Patterns

Since our general statements about the nature of the political socialization process in Canada apply to most democratic systems, we will focus here on only a few of the distinctive characteristics of political learning in Britain and the United States.

With respect to the content of political socialization in Britain, two areas are significant: deferential attitudes toward political authority and the early acquisition of partisan identifications. As we indicated in the discussion of Britain's political culture, deference and a class-based social structure have long been cited as distinguishing attributes. While all political systems seek to instill respect for authority, the British stands out among democratic ones in this regard, perhaps best reflected in popular support for the monarchy. While such a pattern may be true of England, it is often forgotten that this view does not apply equally well to Great Britain, where sectors of the young may develop anti-English and nationalistic views (e.g., Northern Ireland, Scotland). A second significant aspect of content in the political learning process concerns partisan identifications. While the saying that English children are born as "either a little Liberal or else a little Conservative" would have to be modified since the rise of the Labour party in British politics, it does emphasize the historical importance of learning a partisan attachment in the British context. Partisanship is acquired early and influences a person's attitudes and behaviour in the adult years.

> Partisanship over the individual's lifetime has some of the quality of a photographic reproduction that deteriorates with time: it is a fairly sharp copy of the parents' original at the beginning of political awareness, but over the years it becomes somewhat blurred, although remaining easily recognizable (Butler and Stokes, 1976: 31).

The transmission of partisan attachments from parents to children reveals the continuing importance of the family as an agent of socialization in Britain. Moreover, interest in politics and political activity is often the result of family influence. One fascinating study of British prime ministers has argued, for example, that "the long and meandering road that ends at 10 Downing Street begins its course in an unhappy home," with "the most eminent British political leaders ... distinguished, to an exceptional degree, by childhood bereavement and personal isolation" (Berrington, 1974: 345). Thus, the family in Britain remains an important agent in the political socialization process, particularly with respect to political activity and leadership recruitment. A second distinctive agent of political learning in Britain is the school system, especially the public schools, which are in fact private institutions. The educational system is class-based, with those receiving a university education, especially from the most prestigous schools, dominating the political process (Hall, 1969). Such an educational system helps to reinforce the deferential attitudes and class basis of the British political culture.

The use of two agencies of socialization in the United States has developed rather unique attributes in the American political learning process. First, the school system has traditionally been utilized as a means of developing a homogeneous political culture, as a key agency in achieving the American melting pot. The large waves of immigrants of the 19th and early 20th centuries were to be molded into Americans – social differentiation was discouraged in the search for the common man. The school system was a vital element of this process, teaching people a common language, history, and culture, often through specialized civics courses. Although the school system is probably not as influential today as it once was, it remains an important shaper of values, given the relatively high political content in many American schools. A second significant agent in political learning is the mass media. The early and widespread use of television in the United States, combined with a political process that encourages and demands coverage, has given the mass media an increasingly important role in the learning of political values. Wars, assassinations, elections, and state occasions such as a presidential inauguration receive extensive media exposure. Moreover, even children's programs on television have a high level of political content, as a perusal of Saturday morning shows quickly reveals. For example, one major American network in the late 1970s was less than indirect in its approach, interspersing traditional cartoons with political ones on "how a bill becomes a law" or how the United States became an independent country through a revolution, with the cartoon figures, in Hollywood fashion, doing a song-and-dance act about "no more king, no more king." As a result, the news media are "a significant determinant of children's political attitudes and patterns of political participation" (Conway et al., 1981: 175).

With respect to the content of the political socialization process, the United States is highly nationalistic and patriotic, with an emphasis on the goodness of the American way of life and its values. National loyalty is inculcated early, through symbols such as the flag and through recitation of the Pledge of Allegiance. Extensive sudy of American history is compulsory, with historical figures such as Washington and Lincoln receiving almost saintly status. The uniqueness of the American political experiment is stressed, with an emphasis on the special nature of the land and its people. The typical interpretation of events stresses consensus, downplaying the differences that might separate any group from the mainstream of American political life. A second distinguishing attribute of the political socialization process in the United States is the dominant role of the president in the child's initial perception of politics. This dominance of the presidency is in part a reflection of the consensus image of American politics and the strong sense of nationalism, of which the presidency is a key symbol.

Although each polity may have some unique characteristics with respect to the process of political learning, the goal of political socialization in all sytems is to produce loyal citizens who accept the legitimacy of the existing political institutions. To accomplish such an objective, however, different kinds of systems place varying emphasis on and control over both the content and agencies of the political learning process. In democratic systems, political education is most often implicit and indirect, with little political content taught directly to the child. In totalitarian systems, the process is state-controlled, centralized, explicit, and direct, with a high level of political content contained in the school curriculum. Moreover, such systems place an emphasis on both adult and childhood learning.

The result of the political socialization process for the individual is the learning and acceptance of the main elements of his or her country's political culture. From the perspective of the political system, political socialization processes are significant for their impact on the stability and continued existence of the political regime. All polities seek to influence, if not to control directly, both the agents and content of political education: ''the stakes are simply too high for those in control not to attempt to influence who learns what, especially as that learning affects basic political values'' (Dawson et al., 1977: 170).

CITIZEN PARTICIPATION: VOTING BEHAVIOUR

The impact of the political socialization process is such that by the time people are old enough to vote, their views about and desire to become involved in politics are already well-established. Given the impact of the democratic ideal in the 20th century, people are encouraged to participate in the political process. Although many kinds of political activity are available to the individual, voting is the supreme act of participation for most citizens, especially those in democratic systems.

The rationale for voting can be viewed from the perspective of the overall political system or from that of the individual participant. In the democratic age, voting has become both a symbol of mass participation in the polity and a process for establishing the legitimacy of the political system. Participation through voting is a way of developing and enhancing a person's support for the political system: if one feels that one can influence political decisions by voting, one will be less likely to seek changes in the political structure. The legitimacy of the political system and the individual's corresponding support for it are important consequences of the voting process. From the individual's perspective, voting is also significant because, in democratic systems it is the primary means by which he or she both selects those who govern and seeks to influence their behaviour.

Factors Influencing Participation

Even though a person in a participant political culture may have adopted or learned the need to vote as a result of the political learning process, many other factors influence both the frequency and form of that participation. On a general level, we can identify four major influences on voting participation: legal, social, political, and personal factors.

With respect to legal influences, the 20th century has witnessed a gradual reduction of prohibitions to near minimum levels. While not everyone can vote, restrictions are few and generally limited only by age (usually 18), residency (usually six months to one year), citizenship (usually limited to citizens only), and registration requirements. The latter factor is often overlooked, but the difference between an enumeration process in a parliamentary system such as Canada and an individual registration procedure as in the United States affects the rate of voting turnout. Other legal requirements sometimes influence the extent of voting as well. For example, in most democratic systems, voting is voluntary. Once people have met the requirements of age, residency, citizenship, and registration, they are entitled to vote, but may choose not to do so. However, some democratic systems, such as Australia, have adopted *compulsory voting*, whereby people are legally required to exercise their franchise, otherwise they face a small fine.

Even if one meets all legal requirements, the remaining social, political, and personal factors may circumscribe an individual's political activity. Social characteristics include such things as a person's occupation, education, religion, social class, ethnicity, and region of residence. These factors are often classified as the basic sociopolitical cleavages that divide the political community. Membership in a particular ethnic, class, religious, linguistic, or regional group often has important political consequences. The various sociopolitical groups differentially participate in the political process and as a result wield different degress of influence in the decision-making process. For example, one recent comparative study concluded that the "political advantage of those citizens more advantaged in socio-economic terms is found in all nations..." (Verba et al., 1978: 1). In a similar vein, political advantage accrues to particular ethnic, class, linguistic, and regional groups in all societies.

By political factors we mean the impact of leaders, policies, parties, and events on one's desire to participate. For example, a new leader may galvanize people into participating in the political system. If a particularly salient issue comes to the forefront during a campaign or if people perceive the outcome of the vote to be especially crucial, then participation increases. A political crisis or a referendum on a controversial issue may be the means for taking politics more seriously than in the past. Finally, identifying with a specific political party is often an incentive to increased participation. Such political factors suggest that the political system itself, in terms of its leaders, policies, and parties, has a significant bearing on citizen participation.

Our final factor is the personal characteristics of the individual citizen, which in most cases are psychological. For example, a major incentive to participation are feelings of *political efficacy*, that is, the belief or view that one is capable of influencing the political process. Those persons with high levels of political efficacy participate at a much greater rate than those with low levels. By contrast, those individuals who are cynical, apathetic, or alienated tend to withdraw from active participation in the polity. Such personal characteristics are often developed before the individual becomes old enough to vote and, for the most part, demonstrate the results of the socialization process.

These legal, social, political, and personal factors all influence rates of voting participation, although their specific impact may vary from one individual to another and from one political system to another.

The Canadian Voter

An important point of analysis concerns the problem of how many people participate in Canadian elections in comparison with the number of people who are eligible. Political activity was initially limited to white, adult males. Women were finally granted the suffrage in federal elections in 1918. Property qualifications were eliminated by the early decades of the 20th century. The age requirement for federal elections was reduced from 21 to 18 in 1970, with the age criteria for participation in provincial elections now standing at either 18 or 19. In relation to the citizenship criterion, until 1970 Canadian citizens or British subjects residing in Canada could vote federally, but since 1975, only Canadian citizens are eligible. Landed immigrants cannot vote, which also means that they are excluded from political office, since to qualify as a candidate a person must be qualified as an elector. Residency requirements have traditionally been 12 months, with a person's residence defined as where he/she was living when the election was called.

Legal discrimination has been virtually eliminated from voting criteria, although it was as late as 1950 that Inuit (then called Eskimos) were enfranchised and only in 1960 that discrimination against Indians was removed from the federal franchise. While such legal considerations as age, sex, citizenship, and residence have prevented otherwise eligible adults from voting throughout most of Canadian history, their elimination or reduction to minimal levels during the 20th century means that in the 1980s few individuals are disenfranchised. If an adult Canadian citizen does not vote, it is usually the result of a desire not to participate, rather than a reflection of legal barriers to political activity.

The extent of voter participation is usually measured as the percentage of those individuals on the voters' list who in fact cast a ballot on election day. Over the past several decades in federal elections, the rate of voter turnout has been 75 percent, although in three consecutive elections (1958, 1962, 1963) it reached a high of 79 percent. In provincial elections, voter turnout has exceeded the federal average in some provinces, such as Saskatchewan and Prince Edward Island, while in others, such as Alberta, it has been considerably lower. Although these rates of voter participation are high, when asked whether they have voted in an election, a greater percentage of the electorate claims to have done so than the turnout rates indicate. Such inflated figures appear to be a reflection of the participant theme of Canada's political culture: "Voting is a form of tribal dance around the ballot box in which as many as possible should participate" (Laponce, 1969: 45). Good citizens are supposed to vote, so that when they do not, they are reluctant to admit it. Although voter participation is extensive, it must also be remembered that for "most Canadians political participation is confined to voting in periodic elections" (Clarke et al., 1979: 321).

The high percentage of Canadians who vote means that most of the basic sociopolitical cleavages do not differentiate significant groupings in terms of rates of participation. The variation in voting turnout among these groups has in most cases been small, leading one researcher to conclude that Canadians "lived in a political melting-pot" which produced similar attitudes toward participation (Laponce, 1969: 178). For example, the social factors of ethnicity, religion, gender, and age produce few differences in rates of voter participation (Welch, 1975). Even as pervasive an influence as regionalism seems to have little effect on political participation (Mishler, 1979: 58). In contrast, indicators of social class, such as occupation and education, are related to varying rate of participation: "It appears that Canadians who have a higher level of economic and social resources with which to participate in politics are more likely to do so" (Van Loon, 1970: 390). Although most of the basic sociopolitical cleavages have little impact on the rate of voting, their influence on the total electoral process is significant because of their strong association with partisan attachments, what we labeled as the social bases of party support (see Chapter 8).

A further set of factors that influences participation is political in nature, by which we refer to the impact of parties, policies and leaders. For example, an individual's attachment to a political party is a spur to activity, since parties are so intimately involved in the electoral process. A commitment to a party increases a citizen's interest, knowledge, and activity, while a lack of partisan beliefs is most often found among the inactive segment of the electorate. Moreover, if the parties in a campaign are closely competitive, more voters will be drawn into the electoral process. For example, the battles between Diefenbaker and Pearson in 1962 and 1963 had turnouts of 79 percent, while their repetitive contest in 1965 aroused less interest and a voter participation rate of 75 percent. Similarly, the 1980 election attracted half a million fewer voters than only nine months earlier in May 1979. Part of the reason for the lower turnout seems to have been the expected Liberal victory in 1980, given their 20-point lead in the public opinion polls when the election started. If the citizen views the results of an election as a foregone conclusion, then the incentive to vote is greatly diminished.

With respect to policies, most people do not participate as a direct result of a single important issue. Rarely does an issue appear, which by itself provokes an increase in political participation. A possible exception is the "independence option" in Quebec politics, which seems to have so polarized the political community that high rates of participation resulted. More typically, issues are significant with respect to specific and usually small segments of the electorate, so that their impact on overall voting percentages are small or negligible.

A final example of a political factor that influences participation is the appeal of a particular leader. A new leader may attract people into the political arena by the strength of personality or the policies for which he or she stands. However, a strong personality may also offend many people, so that the overall impact on the extent of political activity is little changed. For example, while it is clear that Trudeau brought many new people into Liberal party ranks during the 1968 campaign, the percentage of those voting in 1968 (76 percent) was only 1 percentage point greater than in 1965 (75 percent).

**The fact he wants to vote
Liberal next time proves
the need for brain surgery.**

Psychological attitudes towards politics, which we have classified as personal factors, have consistently been found to influence political participation. For example, individuals who have an interest in political matters, who have developed an adequate knowledge about their political system, or who have a feeling that a good citizen should be active in politics, have much higher rates of participation than those who do not exhibit such views (Van Loon, 1970: 394–396). Similarly, those citizens who feel that they can influence the political system are most prone to political activism (Mishler, 1979: 76). These findings reflect the importance of perception in the world of politics: if people think they have a meaningful role in it'' they are more likely to participate in the polity.

In examining the four factors that influence political participation (legal, social, political, and personal), we have discovered some items that usually have little impact (e.g., age, sex, legal requirements such as citizenship) and others with more specific political consequences (e.g., education, partisanship, efficacy and interest). Voting participation in Canada is high, but voter turnout tells us about the quantity of participation, not its quality. Recent assessments of the quality of participation have been somewhat pessimistic. However, given the extent of citizen participation in most polities, a comparative view would be mildly encouraging: while "the structure and quality of citizen participation in political life fall far below the democratic ideal, it is also apparent that Canada approaches much closer to this ideal than the great majority of the world's nation-states" (Mishler, 1981: 140).

The British Voter

Throughout the 19th century, the right to participate in electoral politics was severely limited in Britain, although the series of Reform Acts did increase the percentage of adults voting from roughly 5 to 30 percent. Women were granted the right to vote in 1918, although there was a higher age qualification for women (30) than for men (21). Moreover, women were initially entitled to vote only if their husbands met the property qualifications then in existence. The age qualification for women was lowered to 21 in 1928, a legal restriction that stood for both men and women for 40 years until 1969, when adulthood was defined as 18. Although over the last century and a half "the extent of the franchise has been the most important constitutional issue" in Britain (Birch, 1980: 65), it is no longer an area of controversy, since there are now only minimal legal restrictions on the franchise.

An interesting historical aspect of legal qualifications and voting in Britain concerns the use for certain groups of *plural voting*, that is, where one individual was legally entitled to vote more than once. For example, between 1918 and 1948, owners of a business could vote in both the constituency where their business was located and in the constituency where they lived, if separate constituencies were involved. As well, since the 14th century Britain had allowed a limited number of special university seats in the Commons. University graduates were entitled to two ballots: one for the university seats and one in their constituency of residence. Reforms adopted in 1948 abolished both types of plural voting, so that each elector is now entitled to only a single vote.

A further distinctive aspect of the legal qualifications in Britain concerns the electoral register. As in Canada, the government has assumed the responsibility for registering people to vote. However, instead of making up a new list when an election is called, Britain maintains a *permanent voters' list*, which is revised once a year in the fall and which indicates those eligible to vote as of October 10 of that year. This electoral register goes into effect the following February for a one-year period. Most studies have suggested that the electoral register thus produced is quite accurate, with about 95 percent of those eligible to vote contained on the voters' list.

Minimal legal restrictions and a permanent voters' list have helped to produce high levels of voter turnout in British national elections. As a percentage of those included on the electoral register, the 1979 election had a turnout of 76 percent, which is the average turnout in general elections since 1945. The highest level of voting occurred in 1950, with an 84 percent turnout and the lowest rate was seen in 1970 with just 72 percent participating. On a percentage basis, these figures indicate a slightly higher rate of participation in British than in Canadian general elections. However, such differences are very small and can probably be accounted for by the infrequency of British elections and the use of the permanent voters' list.

The impact of the various social, political, and personal factors on voter participation in Britain is comparable to that found in other democratic systems. For example, the higher one's social class, occupation, education and income, the greater is one's political involvement. Similarly, urban rather than rural residents, middle-aged rather than either very young or very old voters, and men rather than women demonstrate greater rates of voter turnout, although such differences may be small. As in Canada, the impact of these sociopolitical cleavages, the most important of which is social class in Britain, is mediated by an individual's party identification. Feelings of political efficacy, as well as having a partisan attachment, also increase the rate of political activity. With respect to political factors, closely competitive or marginal seats have a higher turnout rate than safe seats. The nature of the party system contributes to voter participation as well: programmatic parties, one of which typically forms a majority government in a closely contested election, should enhance the value of the individual's vote.

Since the legal requirements prevent few eligible voters from participating, the reasons for non-voting must be found in a combination of the effects of the social, political, and personal factors. In most British elections, about 25 percent of the eligible voters do not participate. The causes for such a pattern of abstention may reflect a conscious decision by voters that none of the relevant parties or candidates running for office represents their interests. Non-voting may also reflect low feelings of efficacy or the belief that a single vote will not make any difference on the outcome of a general election. Low participation may also illustrate that people are so alienated from the political regime that they do not want to involve themselves in the political process, while for others nonparticipation may exemplify satisfaction with the polity, so that voting is not necessary. While the causes of non-voting at the individual level are complex, from the viewpoint of comparative analysis, the total rate of abstention is revealing for what it demonstrates about the stability of the polity and the general attitudes towards political activity. The rate of non-voting in Britain in this comparative perspective is low: the same conclusion cannot be advanced with respect to political participation in the American system.

The American Voter

The study of political behaviour in the United States has revealed a fundamental paradox: while the opportunities for participation are multiple, the rate of political activity is much lower than in other democratic systems. This paradox is, in large part, the result of a unique combination of legal restrictions, which tend to disenfranchise a significant segment of potential voters.

While the general historical trend has been for a removal of most legal restrictions on the right to vote, so that most adults over 18 are now enfranchised, the extension of the suffrage has produced bitter battles in the political arena. Some of these conflicts have become so salient that they have been resolved through the process of constitutional amendment. If we discount the first 10 amendments, since they constitute the American Bill of Rights, of the remaining 16 amendments, 5 have been concerned with extensions of the suffrage: the Fifteenth Amendment (1870) prohibited discrimination in voting privileges based on race; the Nineteenth Amendment (1920) extended the right to vote to women; the Twenty-Third Amendment (1961) granted residents in the American Capitol the franchise; the Twenty-Fourth Amendment (1964) prohibited the use of the poll tax; and the Twenty-Sixth Amendment (1971) lowered the age of participation to 18 in all elections. These constitutional amendments have been a significant factor in eliminating some of the gross injustices that prohibited significant segments of the population from voting.

Two legal restrictions have remained important factors in non-voting even through the 1960s and 1970s: registration and residency requirements. Unlike the process of enumeration used in most democratic systems, the American voter is responsible for getting his or her name on the voters' list and for keeping it there. The individual must make the effort to register to vote by going to the proper government office, usually several weeks before the actual election. Moreover, states may remove a name from the electoral register if a person fails to vote in several consecutive elections. While the emphasis on the individual's role in registering to vote is a reflection of the individualism theme of the American political culture, its impact on voter participation is significant, since a quarter or more of the population may disenfranchise themselves by failing to register.

Historically, registration procedures have been specifically used as a cover for racial discrimination, especially against blacks in the American South, through poll taxes and literacy tests (Kousser, 1974). A poll tax is a tax, usually only several dollars, which must be paid before a person casts a ballot. Even though the amount was small, it effectively disenfranchised poor blacks and whites. Literacy tests could be rigorously applied against minority groups and not applied at all to majority group members. The result of such practices was that a large segment of the potential electorate in the South could not vote until the end of the 1960s. Elimination of such discrimination began with the outlawing of the poll tax in 1964 and, more significantly, with the passage in 1965 of the Voting Rights Act, which allowed the federal government to send in people to register potential voters in the Southern states. The effects were dramatic: "in Mississippi, for example, the black registration rate jumped from 8.3 percent in 1965 to 67.6 percent in 1970, and the white rate from 57.9 percent to 92.2 percent" (Milbrath and Goel, 1977: 131). Although flagrant abuses of the registration system, such as the discriminatory use of poll taxes and literacy tests, have been abandoned, the need to register before voting remains a major impediment to Americans' political participation in the 1980s.

A second important continuing legal restriction is the residency requirement, which has been quite lengthy in the American system. A residency requirement specifies that a person must have resided within an electoral district for a given period of time before being entitled to vote. The longer the residency requirement, the more people are disenfranchised. In addition, residency qualifications often apply to the state, local, and precinct levels, with a different time period for each level. The state residency qualification has typically been a year. Although there was a trend toward shorter residency requirements in the 1970s, at least for national elections, they continue to be a significant hurdle.

In addition to the legal requirements, several political factors unique to the American system seem to discourage high levels of citizen involvement. For example, both frequent elections and complicated ballots seem to limit participation. Some voters may simply become weary of voting on an almost regular basis and so decide to participate differentially in various kinds of contests. Thus, we find voter turnout highest in presidential election years, lower in congressional election years, and lower still in state and local contests. In addition, American ballots are often long, with the voter being asked to decide on contests for national, state, and local offices, as well as various referendums and tax-related proposals. The ballot in some of the larger states may be several columns wide and several feet long, asking the voter to make numerous separate voting decisions. The result is that as the voter goes through the ballot, more and more of the contests are not judged: faced by voter fatigue or lack of knowledge of the issues, the voter leaves the end of the ballot blank.

Frequent elections, numerous contests, lengthy ballots, registration requirements, and residency qualifications are some of the most distinctive legal and political factors that influence voter participation in the American system. The bearing of the social and personal attributes on voting are similar to those already discussed for the Canadian and British systems. For example, with respect to personal characteristics, those who feel a strong or intense psychological involvement in the political arena are more likely to participate, as well as those with partisan attachments and feelings of political efficacy. In relation to social attributes, those characterized by more education, higher personal incomes, middle age, as well as those who are white, male, non-Southern, and Jewish usually have the highest rates of voting turnout (Hill and Luttberg, 1980: 91). Such findings are consistent with the view that a "major force leading to participation . . . is associated with social status and the civic attitudes that accompany it" (Verba and Nie, 1972: 336).

Given such considerations, it is not surprising that voting turnout is low and, in fact, has been declining in recent decades. For example, turnout in presidential elections in the early 1960s was about 62 percent, while by 1980 it had dropped to 54 percent.

The Role of the Citizen in the Political Process
Our analysis of voting behaviour and the typical factors that influence political activity demonstrates that in the last century all three countries have extended, with few exceptions, the right to

participate to most adult citizens over the age of 18. Bitter political fights often occurred over the successive expansions of the electorate, while the right to vote remained a key domestic political issue well into the 20th century. Although voting rates are typically high in democratic systems, any optimistic conclusion about the impact of individual involvement must be tempered by the realization that for most citizens, most of the time, voting is their only mode of political activity.

If most individuals only participate through voting, what does this say about the role of the citizen in the political process? In democratic systems, voting is usually voluntary and occurs in a free election process characterized by competition between two or more parties fighting for control of governmental office. The individual's vote is thus a means of choosing between leaders or groups of leaders and only rarely indicates a specific choice of policy. It is through their role in selecting the leaders of the polity that most citizens have a say in decision-making. While such a function may be a far cry from the role perceived for the citizen among the writings of the classical democratic theorists (Pateman, 1970), it nevertheless remains a highly significant one, especially when we consider the alternatives.

Given the appeal of the democratic ideal in the modern age, even totalitarian systems seek to nominate candidates and to hold elections. Such elections may even achieve an almost 100 percent turnout of the electorate. However, the key point of comparison is the concept of choice. For example, participation is not voluntary, but expected: nonparticipation is usually interpreted by the state as evidence of dissent, if not downright disloyalty. Moreover, when citizens vote there is no choice presented on the ballot: they are merely ratifying choices already made by the sole party. Elections in such systems are a way of legitimating the regime and its leaders, not a means of citizen influence on or control over the polity: as a consequence "those regimes often appear to be purer than Ivory Soap in voter turnout and approbation" (LaPalombara, 1974: 424). Almost perfect rates of turnout occur when such participation has no bearing on control of the polity: voting in a totalitarian system does not determine who governs. Voting does select who governs in a democratic system, even though such participation is intermittent and rarely controls policy in any direct fashion.

While democratic systems grant most citizens the right or opportunity to participate, individuals from the various social classes, regions, religions, and racial groups differentially involve themselves in the polity. Political activity, such as voting, is seen here as a political resource with which to increase an individual's or group's power and influence in the political process. The sectors of the electorate that vote often select as their leaders those who adopt policies to favour the very groups that elected them to office in the first place. Nonparticipation is not only a consequence, but also a cause, of the nature of political inequality found in democratic systems (Verba et al., 1978). One reason why the suffrage extensions produced such intense political controversies is a reflection of this conclusion: newly enfranchised groups would make use of their vote to ensure more responsive leaders and policies and thereby reduce the existing inequalities in the system. Those groups that benefited from the existing social and political arrangements were thus opposed to the enfranchisement process, while those who desired change argued for universal adult suffrage. The movement to universal adult suffrage has not, however, produced equality in the social, economic, or political spheres. While democratic systems have created the opportunities for extensive citizen participation, a major challenge in the years ahead is to translate more of the potential for involvement into actual participation.

SUMMARY

1. The learning of political beliefs through the political socialization process is one explanation for adult political values and behaviour. In democratic systems, the political learning process is indirect and implicit, while in totalitarian systems it is direct, explicit, and state-controlled.

2. Although political learning begins early in Canada, by high school graduation very few individuals show very much interest in or knowledge about their political system. Initial contact with the political regime is personalized through identification with political leaders and political parties. As the child matures, the major values of Canada's political culture are acquired, especially the attitudes associated with regionalism and dualism. American influence is particularly evident with respect to two agents, the schools and the mass media. The creation of a common national identity has been inhibited by the fragmented and indirect nature of the political learning process.

3. While similar to Canada in their political socialization processes, both Britain and the United States show some unique

traits. With respect to content, Britain stresses deferential attitudes toward political authority and early acquisition of partisan
attachments, while the public schools are an important agent of
political learning and recruitment. In the United States, the
schools and the mass media are significant agents of socialization, with an emphasis on a common national identity and
national loyalty.

4. Citizen participation may take many forms, although the basic
mode in modern systems is by voting in elections. Four major
influences (legal, social, political, and personal) determine rates
of participation in democratic systems. While legal restrictions
are now minimal, the social, political, and personal factors keep
many people from political involvement.

5. Rates of voting are greater in Canada and Britain than in the
United States. In all three polities, participation is greater among
the better-off, among those with partisan attachments, and
among those with feelings of political efficacy. The use of an
enumeration process in parliamentary systems encourages participation, while the registration process in the United States
disenfranchises an important segment of the electorate. Non-
voting can reflect various attitudes, ranging from the cynical and
alienated to the apathetic, to satisfaction with the political
system.

6. Participation in totalitarian systems is nearly 100 percent, but
voting in such a polity is an act of legitimation rather than
control. In democratic systems, voting is a choice between sets
of leaders that determines who will govern, although it rarely
involves a decision on specific policies or issues.

RECOMMENDED READINGS

Political Socialization

BRONFENBRENNER, URIE (1970) *Two Worlds of Childhood: U.S. and U.S.S.R.*
New York: Simon and Schuster.

DAWSON, RICHARD E., KENNETH PREWITT, and KAREN S. DAWSON (1977)
Political Socialization. Boston: Little, Brown and Co., 2nd ed.

LANDES, RONALD G. (1977) "Political Socialization Among Youth: A Comparative Study of English-Canadian and American School Children,"
International Journal of Comparative Sociology, Vol. 18, Nos. 1–2, pp.
63–80.

PAMMETT, JON H. and MICHAEL S. WHITTINGTON, eds. (1976) *Foundations of Political Culture: Political Socialization in Canada*. Toronto: Macmillan.

STACEY, BARRIE (1977) *Political Socialization in Western Society: An Analysis from a Life-Span Perspective*. New York: St. Martin's Press.

ZUREIK, ELIA and ROBERT M. PIKE, eds. (1975) *Socialization and Values in Canadian Society: Volume One – Political Socialization*. Toronto: McClelland and Stewart.

Voting Behaviour

BUTLER, DAVID and DONALD STOKES (1976) *Political Change in Britain*. New York: St. Martin's Press, 2nd college ed.

CLARKE, HAROLD D., JANE JENSON, LAWRENCE LEDUC, and JON H. PAMMETT (1980) *Political Choice in Canada*. Toronto: McGraw-Hill Ryerson, abr. ed.

MILBRATH, LESTER W. and M. L. GOEL (1977) *Political Participation: How and Why Do People Get Involved in Politics?* Chicago: Rand McNally, 2nd ed.

MISHLER, WILLIAM (1979) *Political Participation in Canada: Prospects for Democratic Citizenship*. Toronto: Macmillan of Canada.

NIE, NORMAN H., SIDNEY VERBA, and JOHN R. PETROCIK (1979) *The Changing American Voter*. Cambridge, Mass.: Harvard University Press, enlarged ed.

PATEMAN, CAROL (1970) *Participation and Democratic Theory*. London: Cambridge University Press.

VERBA, SIDNEY, NORMAN H. NIE, and JAE-ON KIM (1978) *Participation and Political Equality: A Seven-Nation Comparison*. London: Cambridge University Press.

PART FOUR

Evaluating the Canadian Political Experiment

12 CANADIAN POLITICS AT WORK: THE 1982 CANADA ACT

Only connect (Forster, 1910).

The dustbin of recent history is littered with discarded constitutions cast aside after brief and withering exposure to reality. Constitutions capable of responding and adapting to the perils of change have sufficient scarcity value to be treated with the deference appropriate to rare achievements. All the more curious, therefore, has been the detached, unappreciative Canadian attitude to one of the most durable and successful constitutions in the world (Cairns, 1970: 483).

The reality of Canadian politics is that it is conducted within narrow limits of probability, so that the power of government is contained well short of adventure and innovation. What remains is the power of governance over the ambitions of others, the small change of preferment and perquisite – old vestments and titles for new men (Camp, 1979: 143).

TO COMPREHEND the interconnections of political life is, at once, both the most necessary and most difficult task of political analysis. The various elements of the body politic represent a pattern, not of random discord, but of discordant harmony. The continuous interdependence of institutions and processes makes the polity complex and, therefore, difficult to understand, but it need not be beyond reason.

One way of bringing together the various ingredients of the political system into a coherent whole is to analyze a significant piece of legislation with respect to both the structures and processes of the polity. While no single political event is typical, the Constitution Act or Canada Act of 1982 provides an excellent example of many of the political relationships and concepts discussed separately in the previous chapters.[1] Moreover, because it provides the Canadian polity with a new constitutional base, an understanding of the Constitution Act is essential for analyzing future developments in the political system. As a leading constitutional writer once put it: "We have a rendezvous with the BNA Act. Its going to come someday" (Scott, quoted in McWhinney, 1979: 137). That someday has now come and gone – whether or not it was a rendezvous with destiny remains to be seen. However, given both the process used and the provisions contained in the Constitution Act, one thing does seem certain: Canadian politics will never be the same again.

1982 CANADA ACT: MAJOR PROVISIONS

Although the immediate gestation period of the Canada Act was approximately two years, its content seems destined to be as well-known by the public as that of its predecessors, such as the BNA Act of 1867 and the 1960 Bill of Rights. To help counter such a situation and to set the basis for our discussion of the passage and implica-

---

[1]Although the terms Canada Act and Constitution Act refer to the same basic document, there is one important difference between them. The Canada Act is the piece of legislation that was passed by the Canadian and British Parliaments, while the Constitution Act is that portion of the Canada Act that was proclaimed on April 17, 1982. The Constitution Act is the Canada Act minus the opening preamble to the Queen. In our analysis, we have used the term Canada Act in discussions of the patriation process, but the term Constitution Act in discussing specific provisions or references to how that statute will affect Canadian politics in the future. Remember, also, that all BNA Acts are now to be renamed as the Constitution Acts.

*"All this talk about constitution.
When I was a boy we ate prunes.
That soon fixed it."*

tions of the Canada Act, it is necessary, therefore, to outline its major provisions. Table 12.1 presents a summary of the Canada Act.

TABLE 12.1   *Basic Provisions of the Canada Act**

SECTION	CONTENT
Preamble	Request to the Queen to submit the Patriation Resolution to the British Parliament for passage.
Constitution Act	
PART ONE: CHARTER OF RIGHTS AND FREEDOMS	
Section 1	*General guarantee of rights and freedoms*
Section 2	*Fundamental Freedoms* (religion, speech, etc.)
Sections 3–5	*Democratic Rights* (voting, yearly sitting of Parliament)
Section 6	*Mobility Rights* (right of citizens to enter and leave country, to move between provinces)
Sections 7–14	*Legal Rights* (protection against unreasonable search and seizure, right to counsel, etc.)
Section 15	*Equality Rights* (protects against discrimination on the basis of race, national or ethnic origin, color, religion, sex, age, or mental or physical disability)

Sections 16–22	*Official Languages* (protection of bilingualism in the federal government and New Brunswick)
Section 23	*Minority Language Educational Rights* (where numbers warrant, education to be provided for from public funds in language first learned by the child)
Section 24	*Enforcement* (right to appeal to the courts if rights in the Charter are violated)
Sections 25–31	*General* (protection of aboriginal rights and equality of males and females, Charter to be interpreted so as to protect the multicultural heritage of Canada)
Sections 32–33	*Application of Charter* (applies to both federal and provincial governments, but an opting out or notwithstanding clause is included)
PART TWO: RIGHTS OF ABORIGINAL PEOPLES	Existing aboriginal and treaty rights of aboriginal peoples recognized and affirmed.
PART THREE: EQUALIZATION AND REGIONAL DISPARITIES	Both levels commit themselves to promote the well-being of Canadians, to further economic development, to provide essential public services, and to maintain equalization payments.
PART FOUR: CONSTITUTIONAL CONFERENCE	Required meeting of all first ministers within one year of the passage of this Act.
PART FIVE: AMENDING PROCEDURE	Details of procedure specified, with several different types of formulas used, depending on which sections of the Constitution are to be amended.
PART SIX: AMENDMENT TO THE BNA ACT OF 1867	Protection of provincial powers over natural resources reaffirmed by adding Section 92A to the BNA Act of 1867.
PART SEVEN: GENERAL	Housekeeping provisions: Constitution of Canada declared to be the supreme law of the land; all BNA Acts are now to be renamed as the Constitution Acts; English and French versions of the Constitution Act are equally authoritative.

---

*Based on the Patriation Resolution as passed by the Canadian Parliament, published as *The Canadian Constitution 1981* (Ottawa: Minister of Supply and Services, 1981). By permission.

Following the preamble, which humbly requests the Queen to act, on our behalf, one last time by laying before the British Parliament the Canada Act of 1982, the Canadian Charter of Rights and Freedoms is specified. The Charter begins with its own mini-preamble, affirming that "Canada is founded upon principles that recognize the supremacy of God and the rule of law," which is followed by a series of political, legal, and language rights in Sections 1 through 34. Approximately one-half of the Canada Act is devoted to these basic civil and political liberties. However, perhaps prophetic in its long-range implications for the Charter is Section 1, which limits these rights and freedoms before they are even recognized: "the rights and freedoms set out in it subject only to such reasonable limits prescribed by law as can be demonstrably justified in a free and democratic society." In other words, the basic rights protected by the Charter can be limited by law, as long as that limitation is demonstrably justified in a free and democratic society. Presumably, the judiciary will be the arbitrator of what the "free and democratic" standard means in specific cases.

Sections 2 through 5 protect some of the basic civil and political liberties, such as the freedoms of speech, assembly, religion, and voting. Section 6 represents a new addition to the traditional list of human freedoms, in that mobility rights are explicitly recognized for the first time in Canada. At the insistence of the federal government, mobility rights were included in an attempt to prevent the "balkanization" of the polity, so that the provinces could not continue to pass legislation designed to hinder interprovincial migration. The necessity of including mobility rights in the Charter reflects the strength of regionalism, as well as an attempt to limit it in the years ahead. However, some restrictions on mobility rights are allowed, if a province's rate of employment is below that of the national average.

The legal rights of Canadian citizens contained in Sections 7 through 14 begin with the "right to life, liberty, and security of person and the right not be deprived thereof except in accordance with the principles of fundamental justice." However, such "principles of fundamental justice" are left undefined, so that the judiciary will be requested, once again, to specify their nature through the decisions they are called upon to make in the course of constitutional litigation. The series of legal rights protected include the right to be free against unreasonable searches or seizures, arbitrary detention and imprisonment, or any cruel and unusual treatment or punishment. One's right to counsel, reasonable bail (not to be denied "without just cause"), and trial ("within a reasonable time") are also specified. Protection against self-incrimination, except in perjury cases, and of being tried a second time for an alleged crime after an initial acquittal are also contained in the section on legal rights. These provisions are basic ones for protecting the individual against the possible abuses of state power.

The equality rights contained in Section 15 guarantee that "every individual is equal before and under the law and has the right to equal protection and equal benefit of the law without discrimination and, in particular, without discrimination based on race, national or ethnic origin, color, religion, sex, age or mental or physical disability." Most of these rights were included in the 1960 Bill of Rights, although the Charter has added protection on the grounds of ethnic origin, age, and mental or physical disability. However, government programs designed to overcome the effects of previous discrimination (i.e., "affirmative action" programs) are allowed. Unlike most provisions of the Canada Act, which became effective as soon as the new constitution was formally proclaimed, the array of equality rights specified in Section 15 of the Charter cannot be applied for three years from the date of the Constitution Act's proclamation (Section 32, Subsection 2). Since many of these rights fell within the areas of traditional provincial jurisdiction, the provinces wanted time to accommodate their existing legislation to those new provisions.

The inclusion of the age clause is of interest and, although primarily aimed at the mandatory retirement deadline of 65, it might also be interpreted to protect the rights of young people. The basic social and economic reason for this age provision is that people are living longer and, as a result, the social protection programs, such as the Canada Pension Plan, will be in financial difficulty in the years ahead unless their funding is improved. One way of achieving that end, of course, is to have people working for more years, that is, past the traditional retirement age of 65. Therefore, from this vantage point, the outlawing of discrimination based on age, rather than acting as an extension of human freedom, might be its exact opposite: the state has laid the constitutional foundation for prolonging individuals' obligations to the state by keeping them working and paying taxes for more years. The expansive nature of government may follow you, quite literally, to your grave.

Protection of Canada's two official languages is contained in Sections 16 through 22, which basically entrench in the Constitution the existing language rights as previously specified in the federal government's Official Languages Act and New Brunswick's version of that Act. Entrenchment enhances the extent of language protection, since constitutional provision for it is less immune to future change than legislative statutes. The official languages are recognized with respect to the procedures of the courts, legislatures, and bureaucracy, although in the latter case only where numbers warrant. Quebec is not included in these provisions, but language protection continues in that province under Section 133 of the BNA Act of 1867 (now the Constitution Act of 1867). However, language protection in Quebec is not extended under this provision to an individual's dealings with the bureaucracy – only language use in the courts and the legislature is specified for Quebec in the 1867 Act. Thus, the combination of the Constitution Acts of 1867 and 1982 guarantees language protection in dealings with the federal government and the provinces of New Brunswick and Quebec. However, given the bilingual belt thesis, the major flaw in this pattern of language protection is the obvious exclusion of the province of Ontario.

Language protection is extended to the educational system by Section 23 of the Charter. Citizens of Canada have the right to education in their mother tongue, where numbers warrant, and to have such instruction paid for out of public funds. The background of this aspect of the Charter is complex, raising the whole issue of minority rights and language use throughout Canadian history. Its inclusion, at the insistence of the federal government, was a reaction to the politicization of the language issue in Quebec during the 1960s and 1970s and the passage in 1977 of Bill 101 by the Quebec government. Section 23 attempts, in effect, to correct, even if somewhat belatedly, an oversight in the original BNA Act.

Contained in Section 93 of the BNA Act of 1867 is protection for the separate school systems desired by the minority religious groups in each province. As Eugene Forsey (1974: 244–245) has pointed out, it was likely assumed by the Fathers of Confederation that a Protestant separate school system in Quebec would in fact be English-speaking, while such a separate school system in English Canada would in fact be Catholic and, thus, by implication French-speaking. However, a literal reading of Section 93 allows a provincial government to determine the language of instruction, as long as the separate school system itself is not attacked. By including Section 23 in the Charter of Rights, the federal government was explicitly challenging the language legislation in Quebec and the attempt by the Parti Québécois to make Quebec a unilingual French-speaking province.

Not surprising, therefore, was the rejection of the Canada Act by the government of Quebec, with Section 23 being a primary reason for its refusal. However, in order to minimize the possible negative reaction to the Canada Act among the French-speaking populace in Quebec, minority language educational rights in Section 23(1)(a) will not apply in that province until they are proclaimed, at some future date, by the queen or governor general (procedure specified in the Charter, Section 59, Subsections 1 and 2). Such a proclamation cannot be issued until it has been authorized by the legislative assembly or government of Quebec. However, once Quebec agrees to Section 23(1)(a), it cannot reverse itself at a later date, because the override clause does not apply to Section 23 of the Charter. Thus, in a future provincial election in Quebec, if the provincial Liberal party won office and committed the province to Section 23(1)(a) of the Charter of Rights, such an action could not be overturned later.

The enforcement of the Charter of Rights is allocated to the judiciary by Section 24. Anyone who feels that their fundamental rights and freedoms have been infringed or denied "may apply to a court of competent jurisdiction to obtain such remedy as the court considers appropriate and just in the circumstances." This explicit recognition of the role of the courts in protecting fundamental rights increases the potential for a more activist judiciary in Canada, if citizens are willing to challenge possible violations of the Charter by bringing them to the attention of the judicial branch.

Sections 25 through 31 of the Charter, labelled General, are a miscellaneous group of provisions not easily accommodated in the previous sections. Section 25 guarantees aboriginal rights, including those that might accrue by means of future land claims settlements. Section 28 specifically recognizes the equality of "male and female persons." These two provisions, at first glance, appear to duplicate the bar against discrimination on the basis of sex and national or ethnic origin contained under Section 15 on equality rights. However, Section 15 does not take effect until three years after the Charter is proclaimed and, more importantly, unlike Section 15, the protections of Sections 25 and 28 cannot be overriden using Section 33 of the Charter. Thus, these two provisions can be applied immediately and cannot be taken away by legislative fiat at some future point. Also contained within the miscellaneous category is an extension of the Charter to the Yukon and Northwest Territories (Section 30), a proviso that the Charter "shall be interpreted in a manner consistent with the preservation and enhancement of the multicultural heritage of Canadians" (Section 26), an assertion that "nothing in this Charter extends the legislative powers of any body or authority" (Section 31), and, in case some rights may have been overlooked, a claim that lack of inclusion of any such rights in the Charter cannot be taken to mean that they do not exist (Section 26).

The final major section of the Charter of Rights concerns its application. Section 32 specifically enforces the Charter on both the federal and provincial levels of government, as well as on the Yukon and Northwest Territories, although the equality rights of Section 15 are delayed for three years. Most significant is Section 33, which allows either the federal or provincial governments to override any rights specified in Section 2 or Sections 7 to 15 of the Charter of Rights. Thus, Section 33 continues the practice of placing the principle of parliamentary supremacy over the application of fundamental freedoms, whether these freedoms are entrenched in the Constitution or not. The use of the override or notwithstanding clause is limited to five years, although it may be reenacted repeatedly in a series of five-year terms. There is no apparent means by which an override action by either the federal or provincial legislatures can be legally challenged by the citizen. The recourse to a misuse of this power must be effected by defeating the government at the next election, rather than through a process of constitutional litigation.

Parts Two through Four of the Canada Act are relatively brief and straightforward. The "existing aboriginal and treaty rights" are "recognized and affirmed" in Part Two, along with a definition of the concept of "aboriginal peoples of Canada" (i.e., Indian, Inuit, and Métis). Part Three reflects the impact on the Canadian polity of regionalism, in that the federal and provincial governments commit themselves, very generally, to the reduction of regional disparities through equalization payments to the provinces. No formula for determining equalization grants or funding levels is included, thereby protecting the flexibility of the governments involved in negotiating these matters. Quite likely, the federal and provincial governments will have different views of what constitutes "sufficient revenues" to the provinces. Part Three was a major concession by the federal government to the poorer provinces in order to try and win their grudging acceptance of the constitutional reform package. Part Four requires that the prime minister convene a conference of first ministers within one year of the proclamation of the Constitution Act. The conference will presumably review the application of the Constitution Act during its first year. Part Four also requires that matters affecting Canada's aboriginal peoples must be considered by this conference, that representatives from these groups must be invited to attend so as to participate in the discussions of these matters, and that elected representatives of the Yukon and North-west Territories will also be in attendance to discuss any matters that directly affect them. For the first time, there is a legal require-ment that someone other than the federal and provincial political executives be involved in the process of constitutional negotiation.

A crucial addition to Canada's constitutional structure is Part Five of the Canada Act, which specifies amending clauses for future constitutional reform efforts. Thus, a major flaw of the BNA Act of 1867 has finally been corrected. However, the amendment of the Constitution Act is complex; in fact, five different procedures are prescribed. For example, within certain limits, the existing right of the provinces to determine their own structure and operation, as well as the power of the federal government to do likewise, is recognized in Sections 45 and 44, respectively. A third variation concerns an amendment that affects at least two provinces, but not all (Section 43). In this situation, a proclamation by the governor general is required, after "resolutions of the Senate and House of Commons and of the legislative assembly of each province to which the amendment applies." The fourth amending procedure (Section 41) differs from the third in that the unanimous consent of all provinces must be obtained with respect to any amendments to the offices of the formal executive (queen, governor general, lieutenant governor), the composition of the Supreme Court, the use of the English or French languages within a province, and the right of a province to have at least the same number of members in the House of Commons as it has senators.

The most general amending procedure, and the fifth possible alternative, is contained in Section 38, which will likely become the heart of the amending process in Canada. Under this technique an amendment is proclaimed by the governor general when author-ized by "resolutions of the Senate and House of Commons" and by "resolutions of the legislative assemblies of at least two-thirds of the provinces that have, in the aggregate, according to the then latest general census, at least 50 percent of the population of all the provinces." However, even if passed under these conditions, the remaining three provinces may opt out of any such amendment. If the amendment opted out of transfers powers in the education or cultural fields to Ottawa, then the provinces are entitled to financial compensation. These amending procedures, particularly Section 38, represent a major change in the nature of constitutional reform in Canada, transforming a process based on convention into one based on constitutional prescription.

An important alteration of the Senate's role in the amending process is contained in Section 47, which gives the upper chamber a suspensive veto of 180 days with respect to all amending procedures except those relating to either the provincial or federal levels changing their own structure and operation. If a resolution authorizing an amendment is passed by the House, but is not passed within 180 sitting days of Parliament by the Senate, then the House can pass the resolution a second time, at which point the amending procedure moves ahead. Because the Senate can be effectively bypassed, if necessary, what Section 47 does is give ultimate control of the basic amending processes to the House of Commons. The Senate can even be gotten around with respect to amendments that change both the powers of and method of selecting members of the upper house. This provision has, therefore, laid the basis for a new round of constitutional reform, which Prime Minister Trudeau contemplated as the passage of the Canada Act neared completion. High on the list of constitutional reform may be changes in the Senate, made easier by inclusion of the suspensive veto in Section 47.

Part Six of the Canada Act amends the existing British North America Act of 1867 by adding a definition of and additional protection for provincial control over natural resources (Section 92A). The newly emerging wealth of Alberta, Saskatchewan, and British Columbia and the hoped for wealth of the Atlantic provinces is based on the natural resource sector, one which these provinces fear the federal government covets. Thus, part of the tradeoff for the Charter of Rights wanted by the federal government was enhancement of provincial control over the natural resources within provincial boundaries.

The final part of the Canada Act (Part Seven, Sections 52 through 60) is another catchall series of provisions: how the Canada Act can be cited, the fact that the English and French versions are considered equally authoritative, and that the Constitution of Canada is the "supreme law of Canada."

Our survey of the major provisions of the Canada Act might lead one to conclude that it is the Rubik's Cube of Canadian politics: what appears simple at first glance is in fact, an extremely complex constitutional document with many significant implications for the future direction of the polity. While it is a consolidation of a number of existing constitutional provisions, the 1982 Canada Act, by itself, is not a comprehensive constitutional document – elements of the 1867 BNA Act, the 1960 Bill of Rights, and the War Measures Act remain as significant ingredients of the total consitutional context in Canada. A considerable portion of the 1982 Canada

Act is simply a repetition of existing constitutional enactments. For example, most of the Charter of Rights was already contained in the 1960 Bill of Rights. However, a number of new elements have been added, including the mobility rights and minority language educational rights in the Charter, the entrenchment of fundamental freedoms in the Constitution, and the Charter's applicability to both levels of government. Outside of the Charter, the Canada Act has also added protection of aboriginal rights, enhanced provincial control over the natural resource sector, and provided a series of constitutionally-designated amending procedures. The major provisions of the Canada Act each represent the result of political accommodations between the federal and provincial governments in the struggle for influence and power in the future Canadian polity. The process used in passing the Canada Act clearly reveals this political nature.

PASSAGE OF THE CANADA ACT: A POLITICAL ANALYSIS

The political bargains struck, the provisions contained in – as well as those left out – and the long-run implications of the Canada Act all demonstrate its significance for the future of Canadian politics. Moreover, the passage of the patriation resolution illustrates many of the conclusions reached in our analysis of the institutions and processes of the Canadian polity. In order to connect our discussion more closely to the actual workings of the political arena, we present in this section a brief political analysis of the passage of the Canada Act. The steps in the passage of the act are outlined in Table 12.2.

TABLE 12.2   *Passage of the Canada Act*

Date	Event
1927–1979	A series of unsuccessful reform efforts, including several by Prime Minister Pierre Trudeau.
May 1979	General election defeat of the Trudeau Government; the Conservatives form their first government since 1963, giving constitutional reform a low priority.
February 1980	Liberals return to power with a majority.
May 20, 1980	*Quebec referendum on sovereignty-association.* The "No" side wins, with Trudeau pledging to keep his promise for significant constitutional changes.

May–August 1980	*A summer of constitutional negotiations* fails to produce an accord, but a final attempt will be made during a Constitutional Conference in September.
September 8–13, 1980	A six-day Constitutional Conference ends in total failure – no agreements on any major reforms are reached.
October 2, 1980	Prime Minister Trudeau addresses the nation, says he will proceed immediately to unilaterally patriate the Constitution, with a Charter of Rights and an amending formula.
October 6, 1980	*Patriation Resolution introduced in Parliament*; debate begins immediately on it. The NDP supports the measure, with Conservatives vowing protracted opposition.
October 24, 1980	Closure imposed by Liberals to end the initial debate of 11 days on the Patriation Resolution.
November 6, 1980	Joint Committee begins hearings on the Resolution. Extension of Committee hearings to February 6, 1981 agreed to on December 2, 1980. Justice Minister Jean Chrétien revises Charter of Rights on January 12, 1981.
February 3, 1981	*Manitoba Court of Appeal* rules 3 to 2 that the Patriation Resolution is legal.
February 12, 1981	Joint Committee reports, with 65 proposed amendments to the Canada Act.
February 17, 1981	*Debate resumes in the Commons*, with Tories stalling for time to allow the judiciary to rule on the constitutionality of the Canada Act. Conservative filibuster begun on March 24, 1981.
March 30, 1981	*Newfoundland Court of Appeal* decides 3 to 0 against unilateral patriation.
April 8, 1981	A deal is struck among the parties in the House to end debate, if the patriation proposals are sent to the Supreme Court for a review of the constitutionality of the Canada Act.
April 15, 1981	*Quebec Court of Appeal* rules 4 to 1 in favour of the federal government's proposals.
April 23, 1981	Final votes in the Commons on the various amendments to the Canada Act. Final approval delayed until the Supreme Court rules.

April 28–May 5, 1981	Supreme Court hears arguments on the appeals stemming from Manitoba, Newfoundland, and Quebec decisions on the constitutionality of the Canada Act.
September 28, 1981	*Supreme Court decision* rules that the Canada Act is legal, but violates the constitutional customs and conventions of the Canadian political system. Both sides claim victory.
October, 1981	Intense bargaining as both sides seek a political settlement. A final Constitutional Conference is decided upon for November.
November 2–5, 1981	*Constitutional Conference*, after several days of stalemate, begins to work out a compromise among the participants. Tentative agreement reached in a late-night session between the federal government and nine provinces.
November 5, 1981	*Constitutional Accord* is announced and is introduced in the Commons. Quebec denounces the agreement. Special protection of women and aboriginal rights not included in the compromise plan.
November 23, 1981	After several weeks of public outcry, the federal government and the nine provinces reach an agreement on including women's and aboriginal rights in the Charter.
December 2, 1981	*Canada Act passes the House of Commons by a vote of 246 to 24.* Quebec moves to challenge the Act in the courts – flags in Quebec lowered to half-mast.
December 8, 1981	*Senate passes Canada Act by a vote of 59 to 23.* Special ceremony held to present the Canada Act to the Governor General at Government House.
December 9, 1981	Patriation Resolution delivered to the Queen by Governor General's Secretary and by Justice Minister Jean Chrétien.
December 1981 to March 1982	*British Parliament approves Canada Act.* The Act is tabled in the Commons on December 21, 1981 and approved at Second Reading on February 18, 1982, by a vote of 334 to 44. House of Lords approves on March 25, with Royal Assent granted on March 29, 1982.
April 17, 1982	*Home At Last, Oh Lord, Home At Last!* Queen proclaims Constitution Act in Ottawa. Quebec stages a series of counter-demonstrations.

One of the major incentives for undertaking constitutional reform, of course, was the perceived inadequacy of the BNA Act of 1867 and other features of constitutional government in Canada (i.e., no entrenched bill of rights). The key provisions of the Canada Act, therefore, are designed to specify and fill in some of the significant gaps in the structure and practice of Canadian constitutionalism. These innovations include a series of amending procedures and an entrenched Charter of Rights, which apply to both the federal and provincial levels of government. Such changes have expanded and helped to codify the nature of constitutional government in Canada.

The impact of federalism was pervasive on both the process and content of the Canada Act. The immediate cause of the constitutional reform effort was the attempt to show Quebec, after the concept of sovereignty-association had been defeated in May 1980, that a renewed federalism could accommodate Quebec's aspirations. However, the rejection of the new Constitution by the Parti Québécois government was inevitable: how could a party and government, whose central purpose was to secede from Canada and form an independent country, agree to any renewal of a federal structure they had so long despised? A renewed federalism would undercut the logic and necessity for independence: politically, René Lévesque could not become a new Father of Confederation.

The importance of federalism was also revealed in the stands taken on the question of patriation by both the federal and provincial governments. Although in his address to the nation on October 2, 1980, Prime Minister Trudeau asserted that his patriation proposal was a "people's package," which would not alter the existing balance of power between the levels of government, the reaction to his plan showed otherwise. The majority of provinces were opposed, not only because they rightly saw that many of the provisions of the Charter of Rights were dealing with matters of property and civil rights over which they wanted to retain control, but also because of their view that, if the Canada Act was to be accepted as initially proposed, the future of the federal system would be weighted in favour of Ottawa. In many ways, the Canada Act illustrates a reassertion of Ottawa's influence and power in the federal system – an outgrowth, no doubt, of Trudeau's view that the political system had become too decentralized in the 1960s and 1970s. By threatening unilateral patriation, the federal government forced the provinces to accommodate, although it ultimately had to do so as well: that threat, however, was a significant political resource that was skillfully utilized by Ottawa. Moreover, there seems little doubt that the Canada Act has altered some of the fundamental rules of the political contest, which will ultimately affect the balance of power in the federal system.

The bitter antagonisms produced during the confrontations over the Canada Act will likely sour federal-provincial relations for many years to come. Most disquieting is the isolation of Quebec, which, if continued for very many years, will do little for the cause of national unity – one of the supposed goals of constitutional reform in the first place. For example, in protest over the Canada Act, the Parti Québécois government adopted a policy of not participating in other than "essential" federal-provincial negotiations. Even before the Canada Act passed the British Parliament, Prime Minister Trudeau had asserted that cooperative federalism was dead (*The Globe and Mail*, February 27, 1982). With such conflicts, the pattern of executive federalism could not long continue unaffected. Distrust of the federal government became pervasive among the provincial premiers, illustrated by the evident hostility during the unsuccessful First Ministers' Conference on the economy held in February 1982.

Only one major addition to the allocation of powers specified in Sections 91 and 92 of the BNA Act was contained in the Canada Act: Part Six amended Section 92 of the BNA Act by strengthening provincial control over the natural resource sector. Notable by their absence were any representatives from the local level of government. The Canada Act was a federal-provincial confrontation in which the local level neither participated nor was recognized: Canada's federal structure remains bipartite.

A further impact of federalism was its influence on the political strategies of both the national and provincial governments. The national government needed some provincial allies to bolster its position, which it found in its tacit alliance with Conservative Premiers Bill Davis of Ontario and Richard Hatfield of New Brunswick. Ontario's backing was crucial, so that both the provinces opposed and the national government sought its support. It should be remembered that Bill Davis played a crucial role in 1979 and 1980 in discrediting the national Conservative administration of Joe Clark. Moreover, during the 1980 campaign, the national Liberal party ran ads in Ontario that quoted Bill Davis and other Ontario cabinet ministers in their opposition to the Clark budget of December 1979. The alliance of Ottawa and Ontario should be seen for what it was – the central heartland seeking to retain its leading role in the Canadian polity. Only a rejuvenated national government could possibly protect the declining dominance of Ontario. The price of Ontario's support was high and undercut the integrity of the national Liberal leader: Ontario would not be included in the bilingual protection contained in Sections 16 through 22 of the Charter of Rights. The province with the largest number of French-speaking citizens outside of Quebec would retain its unilingual posture – a perfect illustration that constitutions are exercises in life, not in logic.

The pattern of executive dominance of the Canadian polity is clearly revealed in the negotiations for the passage of the Canada Act. The constitutional reform process and the political career of Pierre Trudeau became inextricably linked from the mid-1960s onward. For example, Trudeau first rose to national attention as Justice Minister under Prime Minister Lester Pearson. Particularly crucial was the federal-provincial conference on constitutional reform held in February 1968, during which Justice Minister Trudeau, on national television, spurned a special-status solution to Quebec's aspirations. Even before then, his writings on French-Canada and the constitution had brought Trudeau to the attention of the Liberal party hierarchy, resulting in his eventual co-optation into the Liberal fold for the 1965 campaign. Appointment as parliamentary secretary to Prime Minister Pearson and then later elevation to the Justice portfolio put Trudeau in a crucial political role as far as constitutional matters were concerned (Radwanski, 1978: 81–91).

Throughout his many years as Prime Minister, constitutional change was a primary concern for Trudeau, if not always for the nation which he governed. During his initial stay in office, two major attempts at constitutional reform were unsuccessful: the review between 1968 and 1971, which ended with Quebec's rejection of the Victoria Charter (i.e., the tentative agreement on constitutional reform reached at the 1971 Constitutional Conference held in Victoria, B.C.), and the review that began in 1974 and continued on through the presentation of constitutional reform proposals in 1978, entitled "A Time for Action," which also foundered from lack of provincial support. Although Trudeau sought to make constitutional reform and national unity the primary issue in the 1979 federal election, he was unsuccessful. The election of Joe Clark put constitutional reform on a backburner. It was only the surprise defeat of the Conservative budget that provided the opportunity for Trudeau to return to once again undertake his pet project of revising the Canadian constitutional context. According to Trudeau, his brief respite in the role of opposition leader "rejuvenated his spirits" for the long ordeal ahead (*The Globe and Mail*, February 23, 1982).

A fortuitous conjunction of circumstances occurred with the holding of the sovereignty-association referendum in Quebec on May 20, 1980. The intervention of the Prime Minister and the federal Liberal party on the side of the "No" forces was a significant factor in the defeat of the referendum. As a rationale for rejecting sovereignty-association, Trudeau promised major constitutional change in a "renewed federalism," although the specifics of these reforms were left largely undefined. Trudeau then held that his promise was sacred, one that had to be met, thus allowing him to cajole English Canada into accepting the need for a revised Canadian constitution. The fact that Quebec did not want the reforms – they were supported by neither the Parti Québécois nor the provincial Liberals – appeared to be ignored by English Canada: Trudeau had become, once again, the sole defender of Quebec's interests in the federal system.

A final factor prompting constitutional reform was Trudeau's sense of history. Having "promised" that the 1980 campaign would be his last, it was now or never with respect to a new constitution. The push for constitutional revision was instigated, led, and controlled by Trudeau. Despite considerable dissatisfaction from within the Liberal caucus and party organization, the troops rallied behind their leader's third and, presumably, final attempt to achieve constitutional sainthood. Thus, personal motives finally meshed with political circumstances to produce a climate hospitable for constitutional reform. In politics, the timing of political actions is a crucial ingredient of influence and power. It is likely that Trudeau's place in Canadian history will be written largely in terms of his ability to seize the political opportunity, which he himself helped to create, to give the country a patriated and revised constitution.

Not only was the constitutional reform process executive-dominated, it was controlled by the 11 political executives. Federal and provincial political executives were the key actors in the constitutional drama, to the exclusion of almost everyone else. An explicit concern of the political executives was to keep the reform negotiations to themselves; they steadfastly rejected any suggestion, such as a referendum or an election, which might bring the public into the constitutional discussions. Moreover, control over future constitutional revisions by the political executives is clearly maintained in the various amending procedures specified in the Constitution Act. A further illustration that constitutions benefit those who write them can be seen in the refusal by the provincial political executives to recognize local governments as a separate level of government in the Canadian federal state.

Typical of his general position in the polity, the formal executive played a symbolic and ceremonial role in the passage of the Canada Act. For example, the transmission of the Patriation Resolution from Canada to Britain and back was technically carried out by the formal executives or their representatives (e.g., the secretary to the governor general). While Governor General Schreyer likely discussed the progress of the constitutional review process with Prime Minister Trudeau during their weekly meetings, he is unlikely to have altered the intent of the government on the contents of the measure. After the passage of the Canada Act in Canada, in an interview Governor General Schreyer maintained that, if a constitutional agreement had not been reached between the federal government and the nine provinces, he had been prepared to step in and block unilateral patriation by dismissing the government from office, thereby forcing a general election on the issue (*The Globe and Mail*, January 22, 1982).

The ensuing outcry over such a suggestion is instructive. Governor General Schreyer was roundly criticized for publicly making such views known; this action was itself a breach of political propriety. More importantly, expert opinion held that such a move would have been politically unacceptable. For example, Eugene Forsey (*The Globe and Mail*, February 2, 1982) concluded that whether "the situation would have been exceptional enough to warrant dismissing the Government and holding an election is, to say the least, doubtful." Quebec Premier René Lévesque was more blunt in his assessment, saying that "Governor General Schreyer should go back to his normal occupation – sleeping – and stop making noises about the constitution" (*The Globe and Mail*, January 23, 1982). Prime Minister Trudeau then stepped in, asserting that no such threat, or even any discussion of its possibility, had ever been made to him by the formal executive (*The Globe and Mail*, January 27, 1982). The significant point raised by this fracas is the difference between the formal executive's legal powers and his actual role in the political process. While legally entitled to take such a measure, it seems unlikely, from a political perspective, that Governor General Schreyer could have successfully forced an election in this situation.

The Constitution Act seems unlikely, at least in the short run, to change the formal executive's role in the political process. For example, while under the new amending procedures such changes take place on the issuance of a proclamation by the governor general, he only so acts when authorized to do so by the political executive, after the appropriate resolutions have been passed by the various legislatures. However, by severing the remaining linkages with Britain, the Canada Act may allow for an enhancement of the governor general's role in the years ahead. The formal executive's nonpolitical role has been necessary in the past so as to preclude foreign interference in the domestic political battle. By cutting the remaining ties to Britain, the Canada Act might allow the formal executive a somewhat greater political role and more leeway to become involved in the political affairs of the nation (McWhinney, *The Globe and Mail*, February 6, 1982).

The task of the Canadian Parliament in the constitutional reform process was initially designed to be a subservient one, although it didn't turn out that way. Crucial to the patriation plan was the gaining of a majority government by the Liberal party in the 1980 federal election. A majority situation, with strict party discipline imposed on the governing caucus, would ensure the quick and easy passage of the Canada Act through the House of Commons. Even though the government majority was small (147 out of 282 seats), party discipline guaranteed that it was big enough to force unilateral patriation through, if necessary, with only Liberal party support. Thus, the need to compromise with the opposition parties was minimal and closure could always be utilized. If the 1980 election had produced, instead, a minority Liberal government, it seems likely that unilateral patriation would not even have been attempted. Too many compromises would have been needed to gain the support of at least one of the opposition parties in the Commons, with the government possibly facing a defeat over the measure, if no such agreement could have been reached. In addition to its majority in the Commons, the Liberals' huge majority in the Senate appeared to ensure the upper chamber's quick approval of the Patriation Resolution. Given a majority in both Houses, it is no wonder that suggestions for deciding the issue through a free vote, a referendum, or a new federal election were rejected outright by the Liberal government.

The nature and importance of party discipline was clearly revealed in the passage of the Canada Act, although significant breaks in its application occurred within all three parties. For example, at third reading in the House of Commons on December 2, 1981, the vote was 246 in favour of the Canada Act, with 24 opposed. Since the three parties were in support of the Patriation Resolution at this point, all 24 votes against represent breaks in party unity: 5 for the Liberals, 17 for the Conservatives, and 2 for the New Democrats (plus one abstention). In the Senate, the final vote on December 8, 1981, was 59 to 23, with mainly Conservatives opposed, although 5 Liberals ignored party cohesion as well.

Considering the emotional nature of the reaction to the Canada Act, both pro and con, it is difficult to assess the significance of these breaks in party unity. However, it seems unlikely that they will be viewed, in retrospect, as a precursor for any general diminution of the power of party discipline in the normal workings of Parliament. Moreover, the number of individuals willing to break party ranks may have been greater than most people expected, simply because all parties were supporting the final version of the Patriation Resolution. For the Conservatives, lack of party unity would do little to affect their overall political position. Opposition parties are usually less likely to impose strict party discipline than is a governing party. And less than 100 percent party unity neither threatened the Liberal government's hold on office nor the success of the measure itself; thus, some tolerance of dissent was possible. The real test of party discipline in the House would have come if no compromise solution had been reached between the federal government and nine of the provinces at the Constitutional Conference in November, because then any breaks in party cohesion among the Liberals might have cost them office. Rejection of party discipline was more widespread in the Senate than in the House, a result, quite likely, of a senator's more secure tenure, based on appointment rather than election. Moreover, the overwhelming Liberal dominance of the upper house made the vote as close to a sure thing as possible.

Parliamentary procedures and tactics were not as complex and controversial since the great Pipeline Debate 25 years earlier. Several techniques are particularly worthy of mention: the imposition and use of closure, the Conservatives' filibuster, and the role of the speaker in attempting to maintain order and impartiality throughout. Although Prime Minister Trudeau had promised full and extensive debate on his unilateral patriation scheme, the Liberal government also sought to have the measure passed as quickly as possible (the initial date was January 1, 1981). Early in the parliamentary battle, the Liberals were quite willing and able to impose order on the proceedings; by the end of it, however, their control was beginning to dissipate. For example, to move the Patriation Resolution past second reading and forward to the committee stage, closure was imposed in the early morning hours of October 24, 1980. The outcry from the press and at least some elements of the public was so great, that the government was increasingly reluctant, as the patriation battle dragged on, to resort to such measures. One major reason for such reticence concerned the legitimacy of the Canada Act itself: if significant constitutional reform was achieved by brute imposition of the government's majority position in the Commons, would the people and the provinces accept the results of unilateral patriation?

The Liberal party's reluctance to force anything as momentous as the Canada Act through Parliament in a matter of weeks gave the Conservatives a chance to effectively utilize that last bastion of opposition influence in the Commons – namely, time. The goal of the Conservatives was to delay passage of the Canada Act for as long as possible, in the hopes of wringing concessions from the Liberal government. Moreover, a lengthy debate in Parliament was necessary to see whether or not public opinion could be mobilized against the measure, as well as to give the provinces opposed to it a chance to challenge the constitutionality of the Patriation Resolution in the courts and ultimately in the Supreme Court of Canada. By making full use of the opposition's right to debate and discuss each aspect of the resolution, the Conservatives not only delayed its passage for over a year (from October 1980 to December 1981), but, more importantly, forced major revisions in the content of the Canada Act. Most indicative of this pressure was the filibuster during March 1981, which delayed action until the Newfoundland Court of Appeal ruled against the federal plan. This court decision, in conjunction with the Tory filibuster, forced the government to delay final passage of the Patriation Resolution until the Supreme Court could rule on its constitutionality. The opposition's power to delay gave it a limited ability to shape the substance of the process.

Throughout the emotion-charged and lengthy debates, the ability of Speaker Jeanne Sauvé, as well as her impartiality, were put to the test on numerous occasions: given the circumstances, she performed well. The difficult nature of the task of the speaker was clearly revealed when closure was imposed to end debate at second reading. The debate raged on until the early morning hours and when the vote finally came, with the deputy speaker presiding, the tension in the Commons almost spilled over into physical confrontations, as several Conservatives literally charged towards the speaker's chair, and one Liberal member crossed the centre aisle to confront opposition leader Joe Clark. Probably the most significant decision made by Speaker Sauvé was the one not to end the Conservative filibuster in March 1981, a move that asserted her independence from the government of which she had been a former member. Moreover, by allowing the debate to continue, Speaker Sauvé bolstered her support among the opposition parties, in addition to protecting the legitimacy of the Canada Act itself. Without the acquiescence of the speaker, the Tory filibuster could have been quickly ended.

Although Parliament ultimately became involved in altering the content of the Canada Act, it should not be overlooked that throughout much of the process, it was effectively bypassed. Symbolic, perhaps, of Parliament's intended role was the date of the federal-provincial agreement. November 5 is Guy Fawkes Day in Britain, named after the 17th century radical who attempted to blow up Parliament. After a constitutional agreement was reached on November 5, 1981, Prime Minister Trudeau rejected attempts by the federal opposition parties to bring about further changes, on the grounds that any alterations by the national Parliament might lead to a breakdown of the federal-provincial agreement! When native and women's rights were reinserted into the Canada Act in November, it was done by Parliament, but only after the federal and provincial governments had agreed to such modifications. A pattern of executive federalism between levels of government leads to a denigration of the role and powers of the national Parliament.

The nature of the Canadian judicial process greatly influenced the political strategies of the contending parties in the patriation battle. Most revealing was the attempt by both those supporting and those opposed to the Canada Act to keep the judiciary from becoming initially involved: the political executives did not want to relinquish their control over the constitutional reform process to the courts. This strategy on the part of the federal government was clearly outlined in the Kirby memorandum, which was "leaked" to the premiers and the press during the Constitutional Conference in September 1980. Named after its author, Michael Kirby, who was then secretary to the cabinet for federal-provincial relations, the Kirby analysis argued that the federal government should proceed quickly with unilateral patriation before any court challenges could be mounted. Only an assumption that the courts might rule against the patriation resolution could serve as the basis for such a strategy.

Moreover, the Kirby memorandum, which is an excellent example of political analysis, was amazingly prescient in its description of the strengths and weaknesses of the political positions of the provinces opposed to the unilateral patriation move. A suspicious person might even suggest that the Kirby memorandum was purposely leaked by the federal government on the first day of the Constitutional Conference so as to preclude any agreement with the provinces. Failure of the Constitutional Conference in September 1980 provided the necessary rationale for unilateral patriation in October, without the federal government having to make any compromises with the provinces at all.

The reluctance to involve the judiciary was also evident among the eight provinces opposed to the Canada Act. Although they had threatened possible court action throughout the period of negotiations, it was only after the federal government seriously moved on unilateral patriation that the opposing provinces turned to the judicial strategy as their last resort. Court challenges were mounted by the opposing provinces in Manitoba, Newfoundland, and Quebec, in the hope that at least one such challenge would be successful, or alternatively, that they would provide a means for ultimately appealing the case to the Supreme Court of Canada. Throughout the patriation battle, the federal government, meanwhile, sought to prevent a court ruling on the constitutionality of its reforms. Only after the adverse ruling by the Newfoundland Court of Appeal did the federal government finally relent, agreeing not to pass the Patriation Resolution until the Supreme Court could consider it.

The judiciary was being asked to rule on the validity of constitutional reform by the federal government when Ottawa had not first obtained provincial consent for such changes. In other words, the Supreme Court was brought in to arbitrate which levels of government had the right to decide and to be involved in both the process and content of constitutional amendment – one of the classic concerns of a pattern of limited judicial review. Because the Patriation Resolution had not yet passed Parliament and, as it turned out, was not yet in its final form, the Supreme Court did not rule on the validity of the Canada Act as passed on December 8, 1981, but on an earlier version of it. Thus, the fact that the judiciary does not have a self-starting mechanism is clear throughout – the courts could only act on the initiative of others in the political process. Moreover, the Supreme Court did not have to accept the need to issue a ruling on the case at all – it could have decided that the Patriation Resolution was a political problem and have refused to render a decision. In fact, when arguments were first made before the Supreme Court in April 1981, the federal government so argued, in the vain hope that a judicial decision might still be averted. Right to the bitter end the federal government sought to limit the exercise of judicial power.

The slow-moving nature of the court system was quite likely another reason why the federal government sought to prevent the judicial branch from becoming involved in the constitutional reform process. There was a five-month period between hearing arguments on the constitutional issue and issuing a decision by the Supreme Court. Perhaps symbolic of the Supreme Court's role was the way the decision was announced. In order to enhance the visibility of the Supreme Court, public access was provided as the Chief Justice rendered the decision. However, technology refused to cooperate – the microphones were so poor that the content of the decision was not immediately evident, which added to the confusing nature of the decision itself. What the Supreme Court decided, in broad outline, was that the federal government's constitutional reforms were legal, while at the same time they violated some of the important customs and conventions of Canadian constitutional practice. For example, provincial agreement was a custom, not a legal necessity of constitutional reform, but that agreement need not be unanimous ("substantial agreement" by the provinces was left undefined).

The typical reluctant exercise of power by the judiciary is clearly demonstrated: the Supreme Court arbitrated the case in such a way that both sides could claim victory. Appeal to the Supreme Court did not settle the matter; it forced the federal and provincial governments back to the negotiating table in order to achieve a political, rather than a legal, settlement of the controversy. In that sense, the referee of the federal system sent both parties into an overtime, sudden-death period – the Constitutional Conference of November 1981. The consequence of the Supreme Court ruling was to make necessary a politically-determined process of constitutional reform, a conservative result that is consistent with a pattern of limited judicial review and judicial restraint.

In addition to the specific role of the courts in the passage of the Canada Act, a long-term consideration must be whether the Patriation Resolution will alter the role of the judiciary in the political process. While some features of the Constitution Act create the potential for a more activist judiciary (e.g., an entrenched Charter of Rights applying to both levels of government), others seek to limit judicial power (e.g., the override provision). One of the main complaints of the opposing provinces was that the Canada Act, as initially proposed, would expand judicial power and thus, by implication, undercut not only provincial power, but the principle of parliamentary supremacy. The override provision of Section 33 was devised to limit judicial involvement, as is the assertion in Section 1 of the Charter of Rights that rights and freedoms can be prescribed by law, if such limitations can be "demonstrably justified in a free and democratic society." Moreover, the judicial branch only enters the political battle through litigation – cases must be brought before the courts before they can do anything. Judicial personnel will only slowly change, and there is no guarantee that new court appointments will be any more "activist" in orientation than those whom they replace. One highly symbolic exception is the selection of Bertha Wilson on March 3, 1982 to the Supreme Court – the first woman ever so appointed in the Court's 107-year history. This appointment reflects, perhaps, the initial impact of the Canada Act, which protected, in two separate provisions, the equality of men and women. How could an all-male Supreme Court maintain its legitimacy in deciding future cases involving matters of sexual equality? However, one important appointment does not alter the overall composition of the judiciary. While some groundwork has been laid that could serve as the basis of a more activist judiciary, it seems unlikely that such a result will materialize, particularly in the short run.

In the preceding analysis of the Canada Act, we have briefly dealt with the impact that basic political structures (i.e., the constitution and the three branches of government) had on its content and passage. In addition, the political processes of the Canadian polity also significantly shaped the constitutional reform battle.

The overall context, as well as the specific strategies of the contending parties, reflected some of the main themes of the Canadian political culture. Most important was the role of custom and convention and the various participants' use and interpretation of it. The half-century process of constitutional failure reflected a longstanding assumption that unanimity among the participants was preferred in matters of constitutional reform. Thus, a single province such as Quebec could, in 1971, stop the Victoria Charter from going forward. This assumption about the importance of consensus was wrongly interpreted by the provinces to mean that unilateral patriation by the federal government could not be achieved. The provinces clearly thought that the federal government was bluffing, but in a major challenge to political tradition, the Liberal government went ahead after the Constitutional Conference failed in September 1980. This bold move by Ottawa put the opposing provinces on the defensive, and it took them many months to recover their momentum. As Justice Minister Jean Chrétien said on the day of the Supreme Court decision, "conventions change." The flexibility of tradition has been an important means of constitutional adaptation in Canada. Thus, the Canada Act has not only transformed several key aspects of convention into law, but in the process altered its content.

The difficulty of achieving constitutional reform is an obvious reflection of the fragmented nature of Canada's political culture, while the isolation of Quebec, with its distinctive subculture, reveals the continuing strength and problems of both dualism and regionalism. The debate over the amending formulas was another illustration of regionalism, since all provinces initially wanted to retain a veto as a symbolic sign of their equality in the federal system. On this point, at least, there was some accommodation. Elitism was epitomized by the political executives' dominance of the constitutional reform process, while the fear of continentalism was expressed in the desire not to turn the Canadian judiciary into a replica of the activist American judiciary, which is based on the principle of full judicial review. Finally, the notion that Canada can be held together by a process of elite accommodation has been sorely tested. Not only has Quebec been isolated in the federal system, but the attempted unilateral patriation and resulting two-year political battle did little to cement the system together at the leadership level. At probably no time in modern Canadian political history have the political elites been more in conflict than at the present, operating under a pattern that could be called contentious self-righteousness. It would be a magnificent irony indeed, if the search for a new constitution which would promote national unity, turned out, in retrospect, to have produced exactly opposite results.

The constitutional review process created a number of internal problems for each of the political parties. Two such areas of particular importance were questions regarding party leadership and federal-provincial party relations. For the Liberals, successful completion of the constitutional quest generated anew speculation about Pierre Trudeau's anticipated retirement. Once constitutional reform had been achieved, there would be little rationale for his continued stewardship: the question was not "if," but "when" his retirement would come. The dominance of the leader in the Liberal party structure, however, did not make such a result inevitable: the decision to exit would be Pierre Trudeau's, not that of the party organization. In addition, the successful job of Justice Minister Jean Chrétien throughout the patriation battle vaunted him into a leading role as a possible successor to Pierre Trudeau.

For the Conservatives, questions of the continuing leadership of Joe Clark served as a backdrop to the constitutional reform process. Clark's decision to vigorously oppose unilateral patriation and his considerable success in doing so enhanced his stature within the Conservative party and in the country as well. By the time the Canada Act had been sent to Britain, Clark had survived a challenge to his leadership and had emerged, with his party leading the public opinion polls. While the Conservative's public support in the Winter of 1982 had to be attributed, in part, to the neglect of the economy by the Liberals during the two-year review process, some of it undoubtedly reflected their role as a "viable opposition" and possible alternative government during the passage of the Canada Act.

Although the continued leadership of Ed Broadbent was not in question, his actions in committing the New Democratic Party to support of the Liberals' unilateral patriation move caused serious dissent within the party organization. Apparently without consulting his caucus, Broadbent threw his support behind Trudeau. The ensuing outcry was so great, particularly from the party's Saskatchewan members, that party discipline was challenged, and the NDP's constitutional critic, Lorne Nystrom, resigned from his assigned task. By the end of the patriation battle, however, Broadbent was consulting his caucus before committing his party's support to amendments of the Canada Act during the course of parliamentary debate. In this respect, the NDP was similar to the old-line parties: the party leaders, by and large, determined their party's stand on the patriation question.

Matters of federal-provincial party relations were more complex than those of leadership, and possibly had greater long-term effects. Each of the parties suffered serious federal-provincial strains, which revealed that none of them was truly a "national" party. For example, while provincial Liberal leaders in the West rejected Trudeau's patriation plan, more serious was the challenge from Quebec Liberal leader Claude Ryan. Beginning with the October Crisis of 1970, the Trudeau-Ryan relationship had never been overly friendly. The federal Liberal party's move to unilaterally patriate seriously weakened the appeal of the provincial party in Quebec, so much so that, contrary to their impressive string of by-election victories and a several-year lead in public opinion polls, the provincial Liberals were defeated by the Parti Québécois in the Spring 1981 provincial election. Claude Ryan directly attributed his party's loss to the federal Liberals and their constitutional reforms. When the agreement of November 5, 1981, which isolated Quebec, was reached, Claude Ryan condemned it and then helped to write a resolution in the Quebec National Assembly that reasserted the powers and privileges of that province in the federal system. In response, the federal Liberal party in Quebec openly questioned the competence of its provincial counterpart.

Federal-provincial strains in the Conservative party were most apparent with respect to Ontario and to a lesser extent with New Brunswick. Most provinces in the 1980–1982 period were controlled by Conservative governments that were opposed to the unilateral patriation plan. However, the Conservative government in Ontario under Bill Davis supported the national Liberal government of Pierre Trudeau, thereby creating a serious split within the party. This Ontario desertion was particularly significant because the province is not only the largest, but also crucial for any Conservative victory in a national election. The rejection of Clark by Ontario voters in 1980 guaranteed his defeat: Ontario's alliance with the federal Liberals continued this convenient relationship between Bill Davis and Pierre Trudeau. For example, immediately after Ottawa moved to unilaterally patriate the constitution, Ontario Premier Bill Davis held a news conference at which he not only backed the plan, but attacked those who rejected it on "narrow partisan grounds" – a not too subtle reference to the federal Conservatives. Moreover, Premier Davis publicly called on all Members of Parliament and Senators – especially those from Ontario – to support the Patriation Resolution (*The Globe and Mail*, October 4, 1980). These attacks did little for the credibility of either the national Conservative party or its leader. In addition, it seems likely that the alliance between Davis and Trudeau, while it did nothing to hurt Premier Davis's popularity in Ontario – as illustrated by his majority provincial election victory in 1981 – would present major obstacles to any attempt by Davis to become national leader of the Conservative party.

Internal division in the New Democratic Party centred on the split in the party between its Western and Ontario wings. While its leader and a considerable portion of its voting support were from Ontario, its seats were from the Western provinces: 26 of the NDP's 32 seats in the 1980 general election. This east-west division in the

NDP was exacerbated by the federal-provincial split over the Canada Act. NDP Premier of Saskatchewan, Allan Blakeney, disagreed with his federal counterpart, Ed Broadbent, and opposed Trudeau's unilateral patriation scheme. Thus, the only elected NDP government in the country broke with its national party over the Canada Act, as it was initially presented to Parliament.

THE OUTCASTS

The final major aspect of the constitutional reform process that is illustrative of the workings of the Canadian polity is the electoral mechanism and the public's role therein. Although the contending parties often argued that they represented the public, no government had, in fact, a specific electoral mandate from which to proceed. For example, only the most partisan could interpret the Liberal victory in the 1980 election as a mandate for constitutional reform. The public rejected the Clark Conservative government, particularly with respect to its budget – it did not select Trudeau in order to bring about constitutional change. All the governments spoke eloquently of their right to interpret and to defend the public's interest in the reform process, while none of them were elected to office on any such grounds. Only when the patriation battle was well underway in 1981 did the Consevative government of Bill Davis in Ontario and the PQ Government of René Lévesque in Quebec hold provincial elections that might be so interpreted. The perceived mandates of the political executives to negotiate constitutional change were more apprehended than real.

The public was excluded from any direct involvement in the process of constitutional reform. Only indirectly through the mass media and public opinion polls was the ordinary citizen given any attention. Media advertising campaigns, and extensive ones at that, were conducted by both the federal and provincial governments. Private party polls, as well as the Gallup ones, were widely cited. In fairly typical fashion, the same public opinion results were interpreted to support both those in favour and those opposed to unilateral patriation. Perceived public support was a political resource that both sides sought to manipulate to their own advantage. However, by largely excluding the public from the two-year constitutional reform process, it is quite likely that the ordinary citizen will return the favour by ignoring the final product. The Canada Act was primarily the result of a political confrontation between the federal and provincial political elites that was carried out in the name of the public interest.

CONCLUSION

Our discussion of the content of the Canada Act reveals that its major provisions represent a series of political compromises between the federal and provincial governments. While some new features – such as an entrenched Charter of Rights and a series of amending formulas – were added, most of the Canada Act is a refinement of existing arrangements. In fact, the 1982 Constitution Act may be misnamed – it does not provide Canada with a new, comprehensive constitution. What it does do, primarily, is consolidate existing provisions into one act and make a series of amendments to others. Thus, a more accurate title might have been the Constitutional Amendment Act of 1982. Overall, the content of the Constitution Act seems to sustain the view that Canadian politics is contained well short of adventure and innovation.

The passage of the Patriation Resolution seems consistent with our analysis of how the basic political structures and processes of the Canadian polity actually operate. Once proclaimed, the long-term impact of the Constitution Act may be to alter some of the traditional institutional and political relationships (e.g., the political role of the judiciary). At this point, it is still too early to assess whether or not the Constitution Act itself, or the changes it may promote in the future, will make the Canadian polity more capable of responding to evolving political circumstances.

13 THE CANADIAN POLITY: A COMPARATIVE ASSESSMENT

Most Canadians, throughout their history, have been proud of the fact that they do not think reflectively about the profound questions of politics (Christian and Campbell, 1974: 1).

A familiar and rueful Canadian joke holds that, while Canada had hoped to achieve a synthesis of British governance, French culture, and American know-how, it has been left, instead, with the residue of British know-how, French governance, and American culture (Friedenberg, 1980: 107).

A political system is an accident. It is an accumulation of habits, customs, prejudices, and principles that have survived a long process of trial and error and of ceaseless response to changing circumstance (Banfield, 1980: 148).

STUDYING THE POLITICS of one's own country should be an enjoyable experience, and at the same time it is a necessary prerequisite for effective participation in the polity. Knowledge and understanding are fundamental ingredients of a politically-educated citizenry. While no book – and, especially, no textbook – can answer all of the questions about the polity, it can present a basis for students to arrive at their own conclusions about the nature, advantages, and disadvantages of their political system.

COMPARING THE CANADIAN, BRITISH, AND AMERICAN POLITICAL SYSTEMS

A comparative approach to the Canadian polity was adopted as a particularly appropriate task, given the historical and contemporary impact of Britain and the United States on the origin and evolution of the institutions and processes of the political system. Moreover, a comparative perspective facilitates an appreciation of the Canadian polity by delineating the similarities and differences among the political structures and procedures of these three governments. In political analysis, the more specific the basis of comparison, the greater the differences appear to be. Conversely, the broader the comparison, the larger are the perceived similarities. Since most of the analysis contained in Parts Two and Three centred on specific comparisions of Canada with both Britain and the United States, differences rather than similarities were often stressed. As a way of summarizing the discussion, Table 13.1 presents a brief topic-by-topic comparison of the major characteristics of government and politics in the Canadian, British, and American polities.

The conclusions arrived at in any comparison depend, of course, on the unit of analysis, that is, on which particular aspect of the polity is being investigated. A comparative analysis might focus on political institutions, as we did in Part Two, or on political processes, as we did in Part Three. The goals of comparative political analysis are multiple, not the least of which is a better understanding of not just the world, but of ourselves. Comparison is a way of discovering similarities as well as differences, both of which can help to overcome one of the "marked characteristics" of the political community, namely, the "Canadian preference, in spite of the clearness of our physical climate, for living constantly in an atmosphere of mental haze" (Underhill, 1960: 118). While the problems facing the political system are, quite likely, immune to any quick-fix solutions, they will never be successfully dealt with unless we think reflectively about their nature and resolution.

TABLE 13.1   *Governmental and Political Characteristics of the Canadian, British, and American Polities*

Basis of Comparison	Canada	Britain	United States
1. *Constitution*	Constitutional government based on a federal and parliamentary structure. Federalism has become decentralized in recent decades. The 1982 Canada Act has added an entrenched Charter of Rights and amending clauses to the Constitution. Constitutional conventions remain an integral part of the overall pattern of Canadian constitutionalism.	Constitutional government based on a series of documents and on political traditions. Britain is both unitary and parliamentary, which leads to a concentration of political power. In practice, the concentration of power is limited by the conventions of the polity.	Constitutional government based on the view of political power as evil. American constitutionalism seeks to limit and fragment power by such devices as the separation of powers, checks and balances, federalism, and a Bill of Rights. Presidential and federal in structure, with American federalism now highly centralized.
2. *Executives*	A dual executive structure, with the formal executive performing primarily symbolic tasks. The political executive dominates the political process.	A dual executive structure, with an hereditary monarch as the formal executive. Political executive predominates even more than in Canada, although prime ministerial government is constrained by the collegial nature of cabinet government.	A single executive, with the president carrying out both the symbolic and political functions of executive power. The American cabinet is of minor importance in the political process.
3. *Legislatures*	Bicameral structure, with an appointed Senate playing a minor legislative role. The House of Commons dominates and is based on direct election, with the government of the day responsible to it.	Bicameral legislature, with an appointed House of Lords and a directly elected House of Commons. The Lords has been a minor legislative body in the 20th century, with the government responsible to the Commons.	Bicameral structure, with both parts equal in theory as well as in practice. Executive not responsible to the legislature. American legislature has retained an important policy-making role.

4. Judiciaries	Reluctant participants in the political process, the courts operate under the principle of limited judicial review and judicial self-restraint. Canada Act is unlikely to make the judiciary more activist in outlook. On the whole, civil liberties have been weakly protected by the courts in Canada.	Given the principle of parliamentary sovereignty, judicial review is unknown. A redress of grievances is a political, not a judicial, concern. Civil liberties, historically, have been protected by the freedom to do that which is not proscribed by law.	The most powerful judicial branch in any democratic system, the American courts operate on the principle of full judicial review. The judiciary is activist in outlook and intimately involved in the political process. Civil liberties protected in the Bill of Rights, but often ignored, historically, in practice.
5. Political Culture	Characterized by the themes of elitism, regionalism, dualism, and continentalism, the political culture is fragmented.	Political values of deference, consensus, and traditionalism predominate in a relatively homogeneous or integrated political culture.	Liberalism is triumphant, with an emphasis on individualism, popular sovereignty, and political moralism. Political power is seen as inherently evil.
6. Political Parties	Major parties are pragmatic in style, election-centred, parliamentary in origin, structurally decentralized, and cohesive in the legislature. The party system is competitive, federal, regional, and centre-based.	Parties are more centralized, class-based and programmatic than in Canada. The British party system is competitive between the Labour and Conservative parties, but increasingly challenged by the new centre-based coalition, the Social Democrats.	Parties are election-centred, decentralized, non-ideological, with weak party unity. The party system is competitive between the Republicans and Democrats, but highly discriminatory against minor parties.
7. Electoral Process	Elections are competitive, lengthy, and based on temporary voters' lists. Recruitment is primarily a party matter, with the selectorate small in size.	Elections are competitive, short, and based on a permanent voters' list. Candidate selection is a secretive and closed process, under the direction of the party elite.	Elections are competitive, lengthy, nearly continuous, and based on individual voter registration. The direct primary allows members of the mass public to become involved in the nomination of candidates for public office.

CONT'D....

CONT'D.

Basis of Comparison	*Canada*	*Britain*	*United States*
8. *Electoral Systems*	Based on single-member districts, with plurality election, the electoral system rewards the major parties and those minor parties with regional support. Electoral reform is unlikely, since it would benefit the NDP.	Based on single-member districts and the plurality formula, the electoral system discriminates most seriously against the Liberal party. As in Canada, electoral reform is unlikely.	Traditional dominance of Republicans and Democrats depends, in part, on the plurality electoral formula. Selection of the president through the electoral college mechanism is a particular variation of the plurality format.
9. *Political Behaviour*	Political learning begins early, but does not result in a politically-educated citizenry. In terms of voting turnout, participation is high, but between elections political activity is minimal.	Political learning is class-based and deferential in outlook. Participation is extensive during a general election, but weaker between campaigns.	Political learning is more explicit than in Canada and Britain, with an emphasis on national loyalty. Opportunities for participation not matched by actual behaviour.

A basic assumption of our analysis has been that one can only understand the political process by studying it. The goals of comparative analysis include description, explanation, and prediction. While our analysis has focused on descriptions and explanations of the institutions and processes of these three democratic polities, our final concern is to venture forth into the area of political reform. It is in the expected consequences of different patterns of political change that prediction becomes an essential tool of political analysis. However, political reformers must be cognizant of the fact that a political system is a pattern of interconnections that may well be, from an historical perspective, accidental in nature.

The result of such a view is to realize that changes in political institutions and processes may have two consequences: first, immediate or proximal effects and second, long-term or distal effects. The *proximal effect* of political reform alters the nature and operation of a specific institution or process, while the *distal effect* may transform the pattern of relationships between various institutions and processes. A polity is a patterned set of interactions, that is, a system of behaviour. As a result, it is nearly impossible to reform a single structure or mechanism by itself. For example, a change in how party leaders are chosen may alter the chances various individuals or groups have of winning control of that party (a proximal effect). However, such a change by one party is also likely to have an impact on the way other parties select their leaders, on the competitive relationship between the parties, and, ultimately, on the direction of public policy (distal effects). A further example of the proximal and distal effects of political reform would be the representation principle of cabinet composition. Adoption of that operating guide from 1867 onward influenced not only the makeup of the cabinet (a proximal effect), but the political function of the cabinet (a distal effect). Moreover, the representation principle has altered the institutional relationship between the cabinet and the Senate, helping to make the former the key decision-making body and the latter increasingly superfluous to the political process.

Before any specific ideas for political reform can proceed, we must be clear, first of all, in our understanding of what currently exists and second, in our view of the kind of polity we wish to produce through the proposed political reforms. Thus, to discuss political reform is to deal with the normative aspects of the polity, that is, the shape of the polity yet to come. Our basic perspective is that of liberal-democracy, in that we prefer that type of polity to all others; at the same time, we wish to improve the way specific institutions and processes operate. As Winston Churchill is reputed to have said, liberal-democracy is the worst form of government ever invented – except for all other types yet tried. A brief assessment of the liberal-democratic nature of the current Canadian polity will provide the basis for a few suggested reforms.

THE LIBERAL-DEMOCRATIC NATURE OF THE CANADIAN POLITY: PROSPECTS FOR REFORM

In discussing political reform, we are going to use a very different type of comparison: instead of comparing three existing systems with each other, we will compare one existing polity – in this case, the Canadian system – with an ideal system, that of "classical democracy." The purposes or goals of comparison remain the same; the focus is simply altered. However, it is well to keep in mind the remark of George Bernard Shaw that reformers mistakenly believe that "change can be achieved by brute sanity." Rather than sanity, the political context typically constrains and circumscribes the nature and extent of political change.

Few people would disagree that because of its "long experience of competitive politics and free elections, Canada has one of the oldest continuously functioning democratic political systems in the world" (Cairns, 1981: 1). Certainly with comparison to most existing systems, such an assessment is accurate. However, in relation to the democratic ideal, the Canadian polity remains deficient. In the political world of the classical democratic theorists, the individual citizen was concerned, interested, and knowledgeable about the polity, with active political participation a natural outgrowth of such characteristics. Political elites were responsive to the mass public, with elections conferring mandates for the implementation of public priorities. The electoral process was competitive and open, and political dissent was a fundamental ingredient of the political system.

The Canadian political world of the 1980s is very far from this romanticized picture of a democratic utopia: "... with respect to the democrats' requirements that political man be imbued with a developed sense of civic activism, research in Canada has confirmed what long had been suspected, that the interests of the average citizen range from crabgrass to hockey but rarely to politics" (Mishler, 1979: 6). In our view, it is in its participative aspects that the democratic nature of the Canadian political process is weakest. The structural organization of the polity is democratic in form, but often lacking in the substance of active and widespread political involvement. Thus, our suggestions for political reform will largely centre on increasing and making more viable the role of the citizen in the political affairs of the nation.

With respect to the Constitution, several significant changes would be desirable, even if, for political reasons, their adoption seems unlikely. First, once the Constitution Act has been in place for a few years, the override provision in relation to Sections 2 and 7 through 15 should be deleted. Fundamental rights should be recognized as fundamental in fact, or, at least, be restricted only under carefully defined conditions. On either criteria, the general override power of the federal and provincial governments is unacceptable on democratic grounds. Second, citizens should be incorporated into the process of constitutional reform by requiring a national referendum on any such changes before they are proclaimed by the governor general. If nothing else, this change in procedure would increase the legitimacy of the final product. Third, the Canadian Constitution should be consolidated into a single document, instead of being parceled out into a series of constitutional statutes. Such a revision would allow easier understanding of the Constitution by the ordinary citizen. Moreover, we should require a constitution written in plain English or French, as the case may be.

While the principle of federalism is likely to remain in place, the way it operates is open to reform. As a process, federalism can only be effective if the political elites at the federal and provincial levels want it to work: too often, the other level of government serves as a political scapegoat for any problems, which in turn reduces the accountability and the responsibility of both levels of government. Unfortunately, one cannot constitutionally require either good judgment or common sense from the political leaders of the federal and provincial levels of government. Moreover, competent leadership cannot be electorally guaranteed. However, one way of increasing the political sensitivity of leaders is to remove the impediments to office that have tended to limit political careers to one or the other levels of government. A broader mixture of leaders electorally experienced in both political arenas could greatly facilitate the adaptability and flexibility of the federal system. One of the most disturbing trends of recent years has been the inability, as well as the apparent unwillingness, of federal and provincial leaders to empathize with each other – the result has been a confrontation style of politics. The intermingling of federal and provincial political career patterns would be a start in removing some of the obstacles to a more cooperative brand of federalism.

In relation to the pattern of executive federalism, which has removed so much that is vital in federalism from the purview of the electorate, we would suggest that any agreements between the two levels of government be ratified by a resolution of their respective legislatures. These resolutions would either accept or reject the agreements as negotiated; however, such a process would inform the public – or, at least, a segment of it – of what important issues were being decided behind closed doors. Such a change would also have the desirable effect of bringing the legislative branch of government back into the daily workings of the federal system, even if only in a minimal way.

It is unlikely that any reforms could be designed that would effectively involve the mass public in the normal workings and decision-making processes of the executive and legislative branches of government. Instead, we would propose means by which governmental personnel would be made more responsible and thus more responsive to the concerns of the citizenry.

We propose, therefore, that governments, as well as specific elected officials, be subject to a recall procedure, which might work as follows. If a given percentage (say about 40 percent) of the eligible electorate signed a petition requesting the recall of the government, the formal executive would be required to dismiss that government from office and to order new elections. While the actual details of this procedure would have to be carefully specified, it would clearly put a government in continual fear of electoral retribution – not necessarily at the election four or five years hence, but much sooner. Nothing is more apt to make a government responsive than possible loss of office. The major flaw in the electoral process is that elections are too infrequent and usually at the discretion of the government. Under the recall procedure, they need not be.

A similar procedure might also be adopted for individual members of the legislature. If 40 percent of the eligible electorate in a constituency signed a recall petition, the MP would be dismissed from office and a by-election called. For the bureaucracy, a slightly different version of the recall process might be utilized. Only certain important positions would be subject to recall – deputy ministers, heads of crown corporations, members of key regulatory agencies such as the CRTC (Canadian Radio and Television Commission). A given percentage of the respective national or provincial electorate that they serve would be required to sign a recall petition before the procedure would be carried out against a civil servant. Any appointed official who was recalled could not be reappointed to that same position or same department or agency for a specified number of years. Restrictions on how often a recall petition could be used might be necessary to prevent undue harrassment of political leaders. For example, an individual MP might only be recalled once between general elections.

A major problem in relation to the judicial branch of government is the enforcement of individual civil and political liberties. Freedoms are only as good as their application in practice; they are not self-enforcing mechanisms. While the Charter of Rights guarantees many basic freedoms, it may take years and cost thousands of dollars for a citizen to use the judicial alternative for a redress of grievances all the way up to a Supreme Court judgment. One reform would be to require an immediate hearing before a special provincial court on any case involving the Charter of Rights and a possible procedure for sending such a case to the Supreme Court for an immediate appeal. More judges and more courts would be required for any such change in the judicial structure to be effective.

Two significant reforms should be considered in relation to the election process: complete public funding of election campaigns at the consituency level and regularization of the political nomination process. Having legally recognized the existence of political parties and their role in the electoral process, the public now needs to be encouraged to participate in that most vital of party functions, the political recruitment process. Nomination of candidates for public office is too important a democratic task to be left entirely in the hands of the party elites. Rules covering the holding of and procedures utilized in constituency nomination meetings by the parties should be incorporated into the Canada Elections Act. Meetings should be publicly advertised well in advance, membership requirements at the local level should be clearly defined, and the vote conducted by the Chief Returning Officer in that constituency. Eligibility requirements to vote at nomination meetings should be the same as those to be an elector in the general election, plus both party membership and residency in the constituency. These kinds of changes would create the potential for more widespread participation in the nomination process, while at the same time it would limit a party role to party members resident in that constituency who can vote in the general election.

To encourage a more representative cross-section of Canadian society to stand for election to public office, the full cost of campaigns at the constituency level should be paid for from the public treasury. Under current law, about one-third of a candidate's expenses are reimbursed, but given the cost of modern campaigns – even with the limits on constituency expenses – most citizens cannot afford to compete in the electoral process. The salaries of MPs are now quite generous, but most people are not wealthy enough to become serious contenders for public office. The problem is not the remuneration for holding public office, but the cost of getting there.

Although numerous other reforms might be proposed, a final consideration must be dealt with. If it is in the interest of the political elites to keep the nature and extent of mass participation limited and if current mass political beliefs are generally deferential in nature, how can political change be achieved? This paradox is the Catch-22 of Canadian politics. The answer is simply an unrelenting demand from the public for political change. The constitutional review process might be instructive in this regard. The political elites were not only willing to ignore the public's role in the process, but to negotiate away fundamental freedoms such as sexual equality and native rights. However, it was public protest that forced the reinsertion of those provisions back into the Canada Act, because of the political elites' fear of possible electoral retribution. Fear is a great motivator of people and governments. Agnes McPhail (quoted in McPhee, 1980: 149), the first woman elected to the Canadian House of Commons, put it rather succinctly: ''the way to get things out of a government is to back them to the wall, put your hands to their throats, and you will get all they have.''

In addition, it is often assumed that the Canadian elite is a cohesive and unified group, which it is not. Political reform has been achieved, as in the case of the extension of the suffrage, when a segment of the political elite realized that it was in its own political interest to act. It is this combination of changing public perceptions about the nature of the political process and the self-interest of a segment of the political elite that can bring about substantial movements of political reform. Change may be slow, incremental, and infrequent in liberal-democracies, but it does occur and at a faster pace than most critics are willing to admit. Such reforms, intended to increase the participation of the average citizen in the political process will, if adopted, have the effect of encouraging more reform, at a faster rate, in the future.

BIBLIOGRAPHY

ALFORD, ROBERT R. (1963) *Party and Society: The Anglo-American Democracies*. Chicago: Rand McNally.

ALMOND, GABRIEL A. and SIDNEY VERBA (1965) *The Civic Culture: Political Attitudes and Democracy in Five Nations*. Boston: Little, Brown and Co.

BAGEHOT, WALTER (1867, 1963) *The English Constitution*. London: Collins, The Fontana Library.

BANFIELD, EDWARD C. (1980) "In Defense of the American Party System," in Robert A. Goldwin, ed., *Political Parties in the Eighties*. Washington, D.C.: American Enterprise Institute for Public Policy Research, pp. 133-149.

BARKER, ERNEST, ed. (1962) *The Politics of Aristotle*. New York: Oxford University Press.

BECK, J. M. (1968) *Pendulum of Power: Canada's Federal Elections*. Scarborough, Ont.: Prentice-Hall Canada Inc.

_____ (1977) "The Maritimes: A Region or Three Provinces?" Paper presented at the annual meeting of The Royal Society of Canada, Fredericton, New Brunswick.

BEER, SAMUEL H. (1973) "The British Political System," in Samuel H. Beer et al., eds., *Patterns of Government: The Major Political Systems of Europe*. New York: Random House, 3rd ed., pp. 119-329.

BELL, DAVID V. J. (1975) *Power, Influence and Authority: An Essay in Political Linguistics*. New York: Oxford University Press.

_____ and LORNE TEPPERMAN (1979) *The Roots of Disunity: A Look at the Canadian Political Culture*. Toronto: McClelland and Stewart.

BERRINGTON, HUGH (1974) "Review Article: The Fiery Chariot: British Prime Ministers and the Search for Love," *British Journal of Political Science*, Vol. 4, No. 3 (July), pp. 345-370.

BIRCH, ANTHONY H. (1980) *The British System of Government*. London: George Allen and Unwin, 4th ed.

BLACK, CHARLES (1963) *Perspectives in Constitutional Law*. Englewood Cliffs, N.J.: Prentice-Hall.

BLACK, EDWIN R. (1979) "Federal Strains Within a Canadian Party," in Hugh Thorburn, ed., *Party Politics in Canada*. Scarborough, Ont. Prentice-Hall Canada Inc., 4th ed., pp. 89-99.

427

BLANK, ROBERT H. (1980) *Political Parties: An Introduction*. Englewood Cliffs, N.J.: Prentice-Hall.

BLONDEL, J. (1973) *Comparative Legislatures*. Englewood Cliffs, N.J.: Prentice-Hall.

BRADSHAW, KENNETH and DAVID PRING (1972) *Parliament and Congress*. London: Quartet Books.

BRADY, ALEXANDER (1947) *Democracy in the Dominions: A Comparative Study in Institutions*. Toronto: University of Toronto Press.

BROADBENT, EDWARD (1978) "Opening Statement" to the Joint Senate-House of Commons Committee on the Constitution (August 15). Ottawa: New Democratic Party of Canada.

_____ (1980) "Statement on Electoral Reform." Ottawa: New Democratic Party of Canada.

BRODIE, M. JANINE and JILL VICKERS (1981) "The More Things Change ... Women in the 1979 Federal Campaign," in Howard R. Penniman, ed., *Canada At the Polls, 1979 and 1980: A Study of the General Elections*. Washington, D.C.: American Enterprise Institute for Public Policy Research, pp. 322-336.

_____ (1921) *Canada: An Actual Democracy*. Toronto: Macmillan Co. of Canada.

BRYCE, JAMES (1888, 1959) *The American Commonwealth, Volume One*, Lewis M. Hacker, ed. New York: G. P. Putnam's Sons.

BUCHANAN, JAMES M. (1977) "Why Does Government Grow?" in Thomas E. Borcherding, ed., *Budgets and Bureaucrats: The Sources of Government Growth*. Durham, N.C.: Duke University Press, pp. 3-18.

BURKETT, TONY (1975) *Parties and Elections in West Germany*. New York: St. Martin's Press.

BURNS, JAMES MACGREGOR et al. (1981) *Government by the People*. Englewood Cliffs, N.J.: Prentice-Hall, 11th ed.

BUTLER, DAN and BRUCE D. MACNAUGHTON (1981) "Public Sector Growth in Canada: Issues, Explanations and Implications," in Michael S. Whittington and Glen Williams, ed., *Canadian Politics in the 1980s*. Toronto: Metheun, pp. 84-107.

BUTLER, DAVID and DONALD STOKES (1976) *Political Change in Britain*. New York: St. Martin's Press, 2nd college ed.

CAIRNS, ALAN C. (1968) "The Electoral System and the Party System in Canada, 1921-1965," *Canadian Journal of Political Science*, Vol. 1, No. 1 (March), pp. 55-80.

_____ (1970) "The Living Canadian Constitution," *Queen's Quarterly*, Vol. LXXVII, No. 4 (Winter), pp. 483-498.

_____ (1981) "The Constitutional, Legal, and Historical Background," in Howard R. Penniman, ed., *Canada at the Polls, 1979 and 1980: A Study of the General Elections*. Washington, D.C.: American Enterprise Institute for Public Policy Research, pp. 1-23.

CAMERON, DAVID M. (1971) "Regional Integration in the Maritime Provinces," *Canadian Journal of Political Science*, Vol. 4, No. 1 (March), pp. 24-25.

CAMP, DALTON (1979) *Points of Departure*. Ottawa: Deneau and Greenberg.

CAMPBELL, COLIN (1977) "Interplay of Institutionalization and Assignment of Tasks in Parliamentary and Congressional Systems: House of Commons and House of Representatives," *International Journal of Comparative Sociology*, Vol. XVIII, Nos. 1-2 (March-June), pp. 127-153.

_____ (1978) *The Canadian Senate: A Lobby from Within*. Toronto: Macmillan of Canada.

_____ and GEORGE J. SZABLOWSKI (1979) *The Superbureaucrats: Structure and Behaviour in Central Agencies*. Toronto: Macmillan of Canada.

CASSIRER, ERNST (1946) *The Myth of the State*. New Haven: Yale University Press.

CHANDLER, MARSHA A. and WILLIAM M. CHANDLER (1979) *Public Policy and Provincial Politics*. Toronto: McGraw-Hill Ryerson Ltd.

CHEFFINS, R.I. and R.N. TUCKER (1976) *The Constitutional Process in Canada*. Toronto: McGraw-Hill Ryerson, 2nd ed.

CHRISTIAN, WILLIAM and COLIN CAMPBELL (1974) *Political Parties and Ideologies in Canada*. Toronto: McGraw-Hill Ryerson.

CLARKE, HAROLD D. et al. (1979) *Political Choice in Canada*. Toronto: McGraw-Hill Ryerson.

CONWAY, MARGARET M. et al. (1981) "The News Media in Children's Political Socialization," *Public Opinion Quarterly*, Vol. 45, No. 2 (Summer), pp. 164-178.

CORRY, J. A. (1947) *Democratic Government and Politics*. Toronto: University of Toronto Press.

COURTNEY, JOHN C. (1973) *The Selection of National Party Leaders in Canada*. Toronto: Macmillan of Canada.

CRICK, BERNARD (1964) *In Defence of Politics*. Baltimore, Maryland: Penguin Books.

_____ (1973) *Basic Forms of Government: A Sketch and a Model*. London: Macmillan Press.

CROSSMAN, RICHARD H.S. (1972) *The Myths of Cabinet Government*. Cambridge, Mass.: Harvard University Press.

CURTIS, MICHAEL (1978) *Comparative Government and Politics: An Introductory Essay in Political Science*. New York: Harper and Row, 2nd ed.

DAHL, ROBERT A. (1961) *Who Governs? Democracy and Power in an American City*. New Haven: Yale University Press.

_____ (1976) *Modern Political Analysis*. Englewood Cliffs, N.J.: Prentice-Hall, 3rd ed.

DAWSON, RICHARD E. et al. (1977) *Political Socialization*. Boston: Little, Brown, and Co, 2nd ed.

DAWSON, R. MACGREGOR (1970) *The Government of Canada*, rev. by Norman Ward. Toronto: University of Toronto Press, 5th ed.

DE JOUVENEL, BERTRAND (1962) *On Power: Its Nature and the History of Its Growth*. Boston: Beacon Press.

DE TOCQUEVILLE, ALEXIS (1835, 1945) *Democracy in America*, Phillips Bradley, ed. New York: Vintage Books.

DEL GUIDICE, DOMINIC and STEPHEN M. ZACHS (1976) "The 101 Governments of Metro Toronto," in Lionel D. Feldman and Michael M. Goldrick, eds., *Politics and Government of Urban Canada: Selected Readings*. Toronto: Methuen, 3rd ed., pp. 285-295.

DEUTSCH, KARL W. (1968) *The Analysis of International Relations*. Englewood Cliffs, N.J.: Prentice-Hall.

DJILAS, MILOVAN (1957) *The New Class: An Analysis of the Communist System*. New York: Praeger Publishers.

DOWNS, ANTHONY (1957) *An Economic Theory of Democracy*. New York: Harper and Row.

DRUCKER, H. M., ed. (1979) *Multi-Party Britain*. London: Macmillan Press.

DUCHACEK, IVO (1973) *Rights and Liberties in the World Today: Constitutional Promise and Reality*. Santa Barbara, Calif.: ABC-CLIO Press.

DUVERGER, MAURICE (1951) "The Influence of the Electoral System on Political Life," *International Social Science Bulletin*, Vol. 3, No. 2 (Summer), pp. 314-365.

_____ (1964) *Political Parties: Their Organization and Activity in the Modern State*. London: Methuen and Co.

_____ (1972) *Party Politics and Pressure Groups: A Comparative Introduction*. New York: Thomas Y. Crowell.

_____ (1974) *Modern Democracies: Economic Power versus Political Power*. Hinsdale, Ill.: The Dryden Press.

DYE, THOMAS R. (1977) *Politics in States and Communities*. Englewood Cliffs, N.J.: Prentice-Hall, 3rd ed.

Economic Council of Canada (1977) *Living Together: A Study of Regional Disparities*. Ottawa: Supply and Services Canada.

ELLUL, JACQUES (1972) *The Political Illusion*. New York: Vintage.

EPSTEIN, LEON D. (1967) *Political Parties in Western Democracies*. New York: Praeger Publishers.

EULAU, HEINZ (1963) *The Behavioural Persuasion in Politics*. New York: Random House.

FINER, S. E. (1980) *The Changing British Party System, 1945-1979*. Washington, D.C.: American Enterprise Institute for Public Policy Research.

_____ and MICHAEL STEED (1978) "Politics of Great Britain," in Roy C. Macridis, ed., *Modern Political Systems: Europe*. Englewood Cliffs, N.J.: Prentice-Hall, 4th ed., pp. 27-92.

FLETCHER, MARTHA (1977) "Judicial Review and the Division of Powers in Canada," in J. Peter Meekison, ed., *Canadian Federalism: Myth or Reality*. Toronto: Methuen, 3rd ed., pp. 100-123.

FORBES, H.D. (1976) "Conflicting National Identities Among Canadian Youth," in Jon H. Pammett and Michael S. Whittington, ed., *Foundations of Political Culture: Political Socialization in Canada*. Toronto: Macmillan, pp. 288-315.

FORCESE, DENNIS (1978) "Elites and Power in Canada," in John H. Redekop, ed., *Approaches to Canadian Politics*. Scarborough, Ont.: Prentice-Hall Canada Inc., pp. 302-322.

FORSEY, EUGENE (1974) *Freedom and Order: Collected Essays*. Toronto: McClelland and Stewart.

FORSTER, E. M. (1910, 1955) *Howards End*. Harmondsworth, England: Penguin Books.

FOTHERINGHAM, ALLAN (1981) "On Mangling Language," *Maclean's*, Vol. 94, No. 6 (February 9), p. 60.

FRANKFORT, HENRI et al. (1949) *Before Philosophy*. Baltimore: Penguin Books.

FRIEDENBERG, EDGAR Z. (1980) *Defence to Authority: The Case of Canada*. White Plains, N.Y.: M. E. Sharpe, Inc.

FRIEDRICH, CARL J. (1968) *Constitutional Government and Democracy: Theory and Practice in Europe and America*. Waltham, Mass.: Blaisdell Publishing Co., 4th ed.

_____ (1974) *Limited Government: A Comparison*. Englewood Cliffs, N.J.: Prentice-Hall.

GAMBLE, ANDREW (1980) "The Conservative Party," in H. M. Drucker, ed., *Multi-Party Britain*. London: Macmillan Press, pp. 25-53.

GERTH, H. H. and C. WRIGHT MILLS, eds. (1958) *From Max Weber: Essays in Sociology*. New York: Oxford University Press.

GIBBINS, ROGER (1982) *Regionalism: Territorial Politics in Canada and the United States*. Toronto: Butterworths.

GREEN, MARK J. et al. (1972) *Who Runs Congress?* Toronto: Bantam Books.

GREER, DAVID M. (1978) "Redistribution of Seats in the British Columbia Legislature, 1952-1978," *BC Studies*, No. 38 (Summer), pp. 24-46.

GREGG, ALLAN and MICHAEL S. WHITTINGTON (1976) "Regional Variation in Children's Political Attitudes," in David J. Bellamy et al., eds., *The Provincial Political Systems: Comparative Essays*. Toronto: Methuen, pp. 76-85.

GWYN, RICHARD (1980) *The Northern Magus: Pierre Trudeau and Canadians*. Toronto: McClelland and Stewart.

HALL, RON (1969) "The Family Background of Etonians," in Richard Rose, ed., *Studies in British Politics*. London: Macmillan, 2nd ed., pp. 67-77.

HAMILTON, WILLIE (1975) *My Queen and I*. Don Mills, Ont.: Paperjacks.

HILL, DAVID B. and NORMAN R. LUTTBERG (1980) *Trends in American Electoral Behaviour*. Itasca, Ill.: F.E. Peacock Publishers.

HILSMAN, ROGER (1979) *To Govern America*. New York: Harper and Row.

HINCKLEY, BARBARA (1978) *Stability and Change in Congress*. New York: Harper and Row.

HOCKIN, THOMAS A. (1973) "Adversary Politics and the Functions of Canada's House of Commons," in Orest M. Kruhlak et al., eds., *The Canadian Political Process: A Reader*. Toronto: Holt, Rinehart and Winston, rev. ed., pp. 361-381.

_____ (1976) *Government in Canada*. Toronto: McGraw-Hill Ryerson Ltd.

HOFSTADTER, RICHARD (1972) *The Idea of a Party System: The Rise of Legitimate Opposition in the United States, 1780-1840*. Berkeley: University of California Press.

HOROWITZ, GAD (1968) *Canadian Labour in Politics*. Toronto: University of Toronto Press.

HUCKSHORN, ROBERT J. (1980) *Political Parties in America*. North Scituate, Mass.: Duxbury Press.

HURTIG, MEL (1975) *Never Heard of Them ... They must be Canadian*. Toronto: Canadabooks.

IONESCU, GHITA and ISABEL DE MADARIAGA (1972) *Opposition: Past and Present of a Political Institution*. London: Penguin Books.

IREMONGER, LUCILLE (1970) *The Fiery Chariot: A Study of British Prime Ministers and the Search for Love*. London: Secker and Warburg.

IRVINE, WILLIAM P. (1979) *Does Canada Need a New Electoral System?* Kingston, Ont.: Institute of Intergovernmental Relations, Queen's University.

_____ (1980) "Librl, Pcons, Ndpty, Pcred, Rhino," *Report* (July/August), p. 22.

JAROS, DEAN (1973) *Socialization to Politics*. New York: Praeger Publishers.

JOHNSTONE, JOHN C. (1969) *Young People's Images of Canadian Society*. Ottawa: Queen's Printer.

JOY, RICHARD J. (1972) *Languages in Conflict: The Canadian Experience*. Toronto: McClelland and Stewart.

KAVANAGH, DENNIS (1972) *Political Culture*. London: Macmillan.

_____ (1980) "Political Culture in Great Britain: The Decline of the Civic Culture," in Gabriel A. Almond and Sidney Verba, eds., *The Civic Culture Revisited*. Boston: Little, Brown and Co., pp. 124-176.

KEY, V. O., JR. (1956) *American State Politics: An Introduction*. New York: Alfred A. Knopf.

_____ (1964) *Politics, Parties, and Pressure Groups*. New York: Thomas Y. Crowell, 5th ed.

KORNBERG, ALLAN and WILLIAM MISHLER (1976) *Influence in Parliament: Canada*. Durham, N.C.: Duke University Press.

_____ et al. (1979) *Citizen Politicians – Canada: Party Officials in a Democratic Society*. Durham, N.C.: Carolina Academic Press.

_____ et al. (1980) "Parliament and the Representational Process in Contemporary Canada," in Harold D. Clarke et al., eds., *Parliament, Policy and Representation*. Toronto: Methuen, pp. 1-24.

KOUSSER, J. MORGAN (1974) *The Shaping of Southern Politics*. New Haven: Yale University Press.

LAMY, PAUL G. (1975) "Political Socialization of French and English Canadian Youth: Socialization into Discord," in Elia Zureik and Robert M. Pike, eds., *Socialization and Values in Canadian Society: Volume One – Political Socialization*. Toronto: McClelland and Stewart, pp. 263-280.

LANDES, RONALD G. (1976) "The Use of Role Theory in Political Socialization Research: A Review, Critique, and Modest Proposal," *International Journal of Comparative Sociology*, Vol. 17, Nos. 1-2, (March-June), pp. 59-72.

_____ (1977) "Political Socialization Among Youth: A Comparative Study of English-Canadian and American School Children," *International Journal of Comparative Sociology*, Vol. 18, Nos. 1-2, pp. 63-80.

_____ (1979) "The Federal Political Culture in Canada." Paper presented to the annual meeting of the Canadian Political Science Association, Saskatoon, Saskatchewan.

_____ (1980) "Alternative Electoral Systems for Canada." Paper presented to the annual meeting of the Canadian Political Science Association, Montreal, Quebec.

_____ (1981) "The Canadian General Election of 1980," *Parliamentary Affairs*, Vol. XXXIV, No. 1, pp. 95-109.

LAPALOMBARA, JOSEPH (1974) *Politics Within Nations*. Englewood Cliffs, N.J.: Prentice-Hall.

_____ and MYRON WEINER, eds. (1966) *Political Parties and Political Development*. Princeton, N.J.: Princeton University Press.

LAPONCE, J. A. (1969) *People vs Politics*. Toronto: University of Toronto Press.

_____ (1972) "Post-dicting Electoral Cleavages in Canadian Federal Elections, 1949-68: Material for a Footnote," *Canadian Journal of Political Science*, Vol. 5, No. 2, (June), pp. 270-286.

LASKI, HAROLD J. (1940) *The American Presidency*. New York: Grosset and Dunlap.

LASKIN, BORA (1959) "An Inquiry into the Diefenbaker Bill of Rights," *Canadian Bar Review*, Vol. 37, pp. 77-134.

LASSWELL, HAROLD D. and ABRAHAM KAPLAN (1950) *Power and Society: A Framework for Political Inquiry.* New Haven: Yale University Press.

LAWSON, KAY, ed. (1980) *Political Parties and Linkage: A Comparative Perspective.* New Haven: Yale University Press.

LIPSET, SEYMOUR MARTIN (1970) *Revolution and Counterrevolution: Change and Persistence in Social Structures.* New York: Anchor Books.

LOEWENBERG, GERHARD and SAMUEL C. PATTERSON (1979) *Comparing Legislatures.* Boston: Little, Brown and Co.

MACIVER, R.M. (1965) *The Web of Government.* New York: The Free Press, rev. ed.

MACKAY, WAYNE (1981) "Reflections on the Canadian Supreme Court." Lecture given to the Saint Mary's University Law Society, Halifax, Nova Scotia.

MACKINNON, FRANK (1973) *Postures and Politics: Some Observations on Participatory Democracy.* Toronto: University of Toronto Press.

——— (1976) *The Crown in Canada.* Calgary, Alta.: McClelland and Stewart West, Glenbow-Alberta Institute.

MACRIDIS, ROY C. (1955) *The Study of Comparative Government.* New York: Random House.

——— (1980) *Contemporary Political Ideologies: Movements and Regimes.* Cambridge, Mass.: Winthrop Publishers.

MALLORY, J. R. (1954) *Social Credit and the Federal Power in Canada.* Toronto: University of Toronto Press.

——— (1971) *The Structure of Canadian Government.* Toronto: Macmillan of Canada.

MARCH, ROMAN R. (1974) *The Myth of Parliament.* Scarborough, Ont.: Prentice-Hall Canada Inc.

MATHESON, W. A. (1976) *The Prime Minister and the Cabinet.* Toronto: Methuen.

MAYO, HENRY B. (1960) *An Introduction to Democratic Theory.* New York: Oxford University Press.

MCKENZIE, ROBERT (1967) *British Political Parties: The Distribution of Power Within the Conservative and Labour Parties.* London: Heinemann Educational Books, 2nd rev. ed.

MCMENEMY, JOHN (1980) *The Language of Canadian Politics.* Toronto: John Wiley and Sons Canada.

MCNAUGHT, KENNETH (1975) "Political Trials and the Canadian Political Tradition," in Martin L. Friedland, ed., *Courts and Trials.* Toronto: University of Toronto Press, pp. 137-161.

——— (1978) "History and the Perception of Politics," in John H. Redekop, ed., *Approaches to Canadian Politics.* Scarborough, Ont.: Prentice-Hall Canada Inc., pp. 103-112.

MCPHEE, NANCY, ed. (1980) *The Book of Insults: Ancient and Modern.* Markham, Ont.: Penguin Books of Canada.

MCRAE, KENNETH, ed., (1974) *Consociational Democracy: Political Accommodation in Segmented Societies.* Toronto: McClelland and Stewart.

MCROBERTS, KENNETH and DALE POSGATE (1980) *Quebec: Social Change and Political Crisis.* Toronto: McClelland and Stewart, rev. ed.

MCWHINNEY, EDWARD (1979) *Quebec and the Constitition 1960-1978.* Toronto: University of Toronto Press.

_____ (1982) "Giving the Governor-General a more active role to play," *The Globe and Mail* (February 6).

MCWILLIAMS, WILSON CAREY (1981) "The Meaning of the Election," in Gerald M. Pomper, ed., *The Election of 1980: Reports and Interpretations.* Chatham, New Jersey: Chatham House Publishers, pp. 170-188.

MEISEL, JOHN (1979) "The Decline of Party in Canada," in Hugh G. Thorburn, ed., *Party Politics in Canada.* Scarborough, Ont.: Prentice-Hall Canada Inc., 4th ed.

MERRIAM, CHARLES E. (1934, 1964) *Political Power.* New York: Collier Books.

MILBRATH, LESTER W. and M. L. GOEL (1977) *Political Participation: How and Why Do People Get Involved in Politics?* Chicago: Rand McNally, 2nd ed.

MILL, J. S. (1861, 1948) *On Liberty and Considerations on Representative Government*, R.B. McCallum, ed. Oxford: Basil Blackwell.

MILNOR, A. J. (1969) *Elections and Political Stability.* Boston: Little, Brown and Co.

MISHLER, WILLIAM (1979) *Political Participation in Canada: Prospects for Democratic Citizenship.* Toronto: Macmillan of Canada.

_____ (1981) "Political Participation and Democracy," in Michael S. Whittington and Glen Williams, eds., *Canadian Politics in the 1980's.* Toronto: Methuen, pp. 126-141.

MITCHELL, WILLIAM C. (1970) *The American Polity: A Social and Cultural Interpretation.* New York: The Free Press.

MORTON, DESMOND (1974) *NDP: The Dream of Power.* Toronto: Hakkert.

MORTON, W. L. (1950) *The Progressive Party in Canada.* Toronto: University of Toronto Press.

MUELLER, CLAUS (1973) *The Politics of Communication: A Study in the Political Sociology of Language, Socialization, and Legitimation.* New York: Oxford University Press.

NEUSTADT, RICHARD E. (1980) *Presidential Power: The Politics of Leadership from FDR to Carter.* New York: John Wiley and Sons.

NEWMAN, PETER C. (1972) "How to Tell the Grits from the Tories," in Peter C. Newman and Stan Fillmore, eds., *Their Turn to Curtsy – Your Turn to Bow*. Toronto: Maclean-Hunter.

_____ (1973) *Renegade in Power: The Diefenbaker Years*. Toronto: McClelland and Stewart.

_____ (1979) *Bronfman Dynasty: The Rothchilds of the New World*. Toronto: Seal Books.

_____ (1979) "Three Remedies for a Liberal Party that can never again win with Pierre Trudeau," *Maclean's*, Vol. 92, No. 49 (November 26), p. 3.

NIE, NORMAN H. et al. (1979) *The Changing American Voter*. Cambridge, Mass.: Harvard University Press, enlarged ed.

NIEMI, RICHARD G. (1973) "Political Socialization," in Jeanne N. Knutson, ed., *Handbook of Political Psychology*. San Francisco: Jossey-Bass Publishers, pp. 117-138.

NUTTER, G. WARREN (1978) *Growth of Government in the West*. Washington, D.C.: American Enterprise Institute for Public Policy Research.

OAKESHOTT, MICHAEL (1962) *Rationalism in Politics and Other Essays*. London: Methuen and Co.

OBLER, JEFFREY (1981) "Legislatures and the Survival of Political Systems: A Review Article," *Political Science Quarterly*, Vol. 96, No. 1 (Spring), pp. 127-139.

ODDO, GILBERT L. (1979) *Freedom and Equality: Civil Liberties and the Supreme Court*. Santa Monica, Calif.: Goodyear Publishing.

OGMUNDSON, RICK (1976) "The Sociology of Power and Politics: An Introduction to the Canadian Polity," in G. N. Ramn and Stuart D. Johnson, eds., *Introduction to Canadian Society: A Sociological Analysis*. Toronto: Macmillan, pp. 157-211.

OLESZEK, WALTER J. (1978) *Congressional Procedures and the Policy Process*. Washington, D.C.: Congressional Quarterly Press.

OSTROGORSKI, MOISEI (1902, 1964) *Democracy and the Organization of Political Parties*, Seymour Martin Lipset, ed. New York: Anchor Books.

PALTIEL, K. Z. (1970) *Political Party Financing in Canada*. Toronto: McGraw-Hill.

_____ (1975) "Campaign Financing in Canada and Its Reform," in Howard R. Penniman, ed., *Canada At the Polls: The General Election of 1974*. Washington, D.C.: American Enterprise Institute for Public Policy Research, pp. 181-208.

PANITCH, LEO V. (1981) "Elites, Classes and Power in Canada," in Michael S. Whittington and Glen Williams, eds., *Canadian Politics in the 1980's*. Toronto: Methuen, pp. 167-188.

PATEMAN, CAROL (1970) *Participation and Democratic Theory*. London: Cambridge University Press.

PATTERSON, C. A. (1979) "Trudeau was great prime minister and leader," *The*

Mail Star (Halifax), December 15.

PEARSON, LESTER B. (1973) *Mike: The Memoirs of the Rt. Hon. Lester B. Pearson, Volume I,* John A. Munro and Alex I. Inglis, eds. Scarborough, Ont.: Signet Books.

PELTASON, J. W. (1979) *Corwin and Peltason's Understanding the Constitution.* New York: Holt, Rinehart and Winston, 8th ed.

PERLIN, GEORGE C. (1980) *The Tory Syndrome: Leadership Politics in the Progressive Conservative Party.* Montreal: McGill-Queen's University Press.

PETERSON, THOMAS (1978) "Manitoba: Ethnic and Class Politics," in Martin Robin, ed., *Canadian Provincial Politics.* Scarborough, Ont.: Prentice-Hall Canada Inc., 2nd ed.

PIOUS, RICHARD M. (1979) *The American Presidency.* New York: Basic Books.

PIPES, SALLY and MICHAEL WALKER (1982) *Tax Facts 3: The Canadian Consumer Tax Index and You.* Vancouver: The Fraser Institute.

PIRAGES, DENNIS (1976) *Managing Political Conflict.* New York: Praeger Publishers.

POMPER, GERALD M. (1968) *Elections in America: Control and Influence in Democratic Politics.* New York: Dodd, Mead and Co.

PRESTHUS, ROBERT (1973) *Elite Accommodation in Canadian Politics.* Toronto: Macmillan of Canada.

_____ (1981) "Mrs. Thatcher Stalks the Quango: A Note on Patronage and Justice in Britain," *Public Administration Review,* Vol. 41, No. 3 (May/June), pp. 312-317.

PULZER, PETER G. (1972) *Political Representation and Elections in Britain.* London: George Allen and Unwin, 2nd ed.

PUNNETT, R. M. (1980) *British Government and Politics.* London: Heinemann, 4th ed.

PUTNAM, ROBERT D. (1976) *The Comparative Study of Political Elites.* Englewood Cliffs, N.J.: Prentice-Hall.

QUALTER, TERENCE H. (1970) *The Election Process in Canada.* Toronto: McGraw-Hill of Canada.

Quebec Liberal Party (1980) *A New Canadian Confederation.* Montreal: The Quebec Liberal Party.

RADWANSKI, GEORGE (1978) *Trudeau.* Scarborough, Ont.: Signet.

RAE, DOUGLAS W. (1971) *The Political Consequences of Electoral Laws.* New Haven: Yale University Press, rev. ed.

RANNEY, AUSTIN (1965) *Pathways to Parliament: Candidate Selection in Britain.* Madison, Wisc.: University of Wisconsin Press.

_____ (1975) "Selecting the Candidates," in Howard R. Penniman, ed., *Britain At the Polls: The Parliamentary Elections of 1974.* Washington, D.C.: American Enterprise Institute for Public Policy Research, pp. 33-60.

REDEKOP, JOHN H. ed. (1978) *Approaches to Canadian Politics*. Scarborough, Ont.: Prentice-Hall Canada Inc.

_____ (1978) "Continentalism: The Key to Canadian Politics," in Redekop, ed., *Approaches to Canadian Politics*. Scarborough, Ont.: Prentice-Hall Canada Inc., pp. 28-57.

REID, ESCOTT (1979) "The Rise of National Parties in Canada," in Hugh G. Thorburn, ed., *Party Politics in Canada*. Scarborough, Ont.: Prentice-Hall Canada Inc., 4th ed., pp. 12-20.

ROSE, RICHARD (1980) *Politics: England*. Boston: Little, Brown and Co., 3rd ed.

_____ and GUY PETERS (1978) *Can Government Go Bankrupt?* New York: Basic Books.

ROSENBAUM, WALTER A. (1975) *Political Culture*. New York: Praeger Publishers.

ROTH, DAVID F. and FRANK L. WILSON (1980) *The Comparative Study of Politics*. Englewood Cliffs, N.J.: Prentice-Hall, 2nd ed.

RUSSELL, PETER (1975) "Judicial Power in Canada's Political Culture," in Martin L. Friedland, ed., *Courts and Trials*. Toronto: University of Toronto Press, pp. 75-88.

SAFIRE, WILLIAM (1980) *On Language*. New York: Times Books.

SARTORI, GIOVANNI (1976) *Parties and Party Systems: A Framework for Analysis*. London: Cambridge University Press.

SCAMMON, RICHARD N. (1975) "The Election and the Future of British Electoral Reform," in Howard R. Penniman, ed., *Britain At the Polls: The Parliamentary Elections of 1974*. Washington, D.C.: American Enterprise Institute for Public Policy Research, pp. 163-176.

SCARROW, HOWARD A. (1969) *Comparative Political Analysis: An Introduction*. New York: Harper and Row.

SCHATTSCHNEIDER, E. E. (1942) *Party Government*. New York: Holt, Rinehart and Winston.

_____ (1969) *Two Hundred Million Americans in Search of a Government*. New York: Holt, Rinehart and Winston.

SCHLESINGER, ARTHUR M., JR. (1974) *The Imperial Presidency*. Toronto: Popular Library.

SCHULTZ, RICHARD (1981) "Regulatory Agencies," in Michael S. Whittington and Glen Williams, eds., *Canadian Politics in the 1980's*. Toronto: Methuen, pp. 313-324.

SCHWARTZ, MILDRED A. (1974) *Politics and Territory: The Sociology of Regional Persistence in Canada*. Montreal: McGill-Queen's University Press.

SCOTT, FRANK R. (1977) *Essays on the Constitution: Aspects of Canadian Law and Politics*. Toronto: University of Toronto Press.

SEIDLE, F. LESLIE and KHAYYAM ZEV PALTIEL (1981) "Party Finance, The Election Expenses Act, and Campaign Spending in 1979 and 1980," in

Howard R. Penniman, ed., *Canada at the Polls, 1979 and 1980: A Study of the General Elections*. Washington, D.C.: American Enterprise Institute for Public Policy Research, pp. 226-279.

SIMEON, RICHARD and DAVID J. ELKINS (1974) "Regional Political Cultures in Canada," *Canadian Journal of Political Science*, Vol. 7, No. 3 (September), pp. 397-437.

SIMPSON, JEFFREY (1980) *Discipline of Power: The Conservative Interlude and the Liberal Restoration*. Toronto: Personal Library.

SMALLWOOD, JOSEPH R. (1975) *I Chose Canada, Volume II: The Premiership*. Scarborough, Ont.: Signet Books.

SMILEY, DONALD V. (1968) "The National Party Leadership Convention in Canada: A Preliminary Analysis," *Canadian Journal of Political Science*, Vol. 1. No. 4 pp. 379-397.

_____ (1978) "Federalism and the Legislative Process in Canada," in W. A. W. Neilson and J. C. MacPherson, eds., *The Legislative Process in Canada*. Montreal: Institute for Research on Public Policy, pp. 73-87.

_____ (1980) *Canada in Question: Federalism in the Eighties*. Toronto: McGraw-Hill Ryerson, 3rd ed.

SMITH, GORDON (1980) *Politics in Western Europe: A Comparative Analysis*. London: Heinemann Educational Books, 3rd ed.

STEVENS, GEOFFREY (1979) "The Word is 'mess'," *The Globe and Mail*, November 30.

STEVENSON, GARTH (1979) *Unfulfilled Union: Canadian Federalism and National Unity*. Toronto: Macmillan of Canada.

STEWART, WALTER (1971) *Shrug: Trudeau in Power*. Toronto: New Press.

SYMONS, THOMAS H. B. (1978) *The Symons Report*. Toronto: The Book and Periodical Development Council.

Task Force on National Unity (1979) *A Future Together*. Ottawa: Minister of Supply and Services.

THORBURN, HUGH G. (1979) "The Development of Political Parties in Canada," and "Interpretations of the Canadian Party System," in Thorburn, ed., *Party Politics In Canada*. Scarborough, Ont.: Prentice-Hall Canada Inc., 4th ed., pp. 2-11 and 34-56.

TRUDEAU, PIERRE ELLIOTT (1968) *Federalism and the French Canadians*. Toronto: Macmillan of Canada.

TRUDEL, MARCEL and GENEVIEVE JAIN (1970) *Canadian History Textbooks*. Ottawa: Queen's Printer.

TRUMAN, TOM (1971) "A Critique of Seymour M. Lipset's Article, 'Value Differences, Absolute or Relative: The English-Speaking Democracies'," *Canadian Journal of Political Science*, Vol. 4, No. 4 (December), pp. 497-525.

TUFTE, EDWARD R. (1978) *Political Control of the Economy*. Princeton, N.J.: Princeton University Press.

UNDERHILL, FRANK H. (1960) *In Search of Canadian Liberalism*. Toronto:

Macmillan of Canada.

VALPY, MICHAEL (1981) "Above and Beyond the Hurly Burly," *The Globe and Mail*, December 12, p. 10.

VAN LOON, RICK (1970) "Political Participation in Canada: The 1965 Election," *Canadian Journal of Political Science*, Vol. 3, No. 3 (September), pp. 376-399.

VERBA, SIDNEY et al., (1978) *Participation and Political Equality: A Seven-Nation Comparison*. London: Cambridge University Press.

_____ and NORMAN H. NIE (1972) *Participation in America: Political Democracy and Social Equality*. New York: Harper and Row.

VERNEY, DOUGLAS V. (1976) *British Government and Politics: Life Without a Declaration of Independence*. New York: Harper and Row, 3rd ed.

WEARING, JOSEPH (1981) *The L-Shaped Party: The Liberal Party of Canada 1958-1980*. Toronto: McGraw-Hill Ryerson.

Weekend Magazine (1977) "Canadians Think the Queen is Just Fine," October 22.

WELCH, SUSAN (1975) "Dimensions of Political Participation in a Canadian Sample," *Canadian Journal of Political Science*, Vol. 8, No. 4 (December), pp. 553-559.

WHITAKER, REGINALD (1977) *The Government Party: Organizing and Financing the Liberal Party of Canada 1930-58*. Toronto: University of Toronto Press.

WHITE, THEODORE H. (1975) *Breach of Faith: The Fall of Richard Nixon*. New York: Dell Publishers.

_____ (1978) *In Search of History*. New York: Warner Books.

WHITE, W. L. et al. (1972) *Introduction to Canadian Politics and Government*. Toronto: Holt, Rinehart and Winston.

WILSON, HAROLD (1977) *The Governance of Britain*. London: Sphere Books Ltd.

WILSON, JOHN (1974) "The Canadian Political Cultures: Towards a Redefinition of the Nature of the Canadian Political System," *Canadian Journal of Political Science*, Vol. 7, No. 3 (September), pp. 438-483.

WINN, C. and J. MCMENEMY, eds. (1976) *Political Parties in Canada*. Toronto: McGraw-Hill Ryerson.

WOLIN, SHELDON S. (1960) *Politics and Vision*: Continuity and Innovation in Western Political Thought. Boston: Little, Brown and Co.

WRIGHT, F. J. (1973) *British Constitution and Government*. London: MacDonald and Evans, 2nd ed.

YOUNG, WALTER D. (1969) *The Anatomy of a Party: The National CCF 1932-1961*. Toronto: University of Toronto Press.

_____ (1978) "Leadership and Canadian Politics," in John H. Redekop, ed., *Approaches to Canadian Politics*. Scarborough, Ont.: Prentice-Hall Canada Inc., pp. 282-301.

Subject Index

Name Index

A

Agnew, Spiro, 141
Alford, Robert R., 269
Almond, Gabriel A., 68, 225, 251
Anderson, John, 50, 258, 293
Argue, Hazen, 173
Aristotle, 2, 37, 38, 39
Armstrong, Scott, 221
Atkinson, Michael M., 195
Axworthy, Lloyd, 123

B

Bagehot, Walter, 25, 106, 116, 244, 251, 283
Baker, Howard, 185
Banfield, Edward C., 416
Barker, Ernest, 38, 67
Beck, Murray, 233, 312, 330, 333
Beer, Samuel H., 182, 183, 244
Bell, David V.J., 51, 68, 225, 251
Benson, Edgar, 123
Berger, Thomas, 206, 220
Berrington, Hugh, 365
Birch, Anthony H., 136, 181, 212, 290, 324, 373
Black, Charles, 71, 107
Black, Edwin R., 267
Blakeney, Allan, 413
Blank, Robert H., 291, 303
Blondel, J., 193, 195
Boorstin, Daniel, 251
Bourassa, Robert, 3
Bradshaw, Kenneth, 178, 180, 181, 195
Brady, Alexander, 29
Brezhnev, Leonid, 22
Broadbent, Ed, 255, 344, 411
Brodie, M. Janine, 314
Bronfenbrenner, Urie, 380
Bronfman, Sam, 172
Brown, George, 260
Bryce, James, 29, 63
Buchanan, James M., 13
Burkett, Tony, 335
Burns, James MacGregor, 101, 102

Butler, Dan, 13
Butler, David, 287, 330, 365, 381
Butler, R.A., 136
Butt, R., 195
Byng, Lord, 119

C

Cairns, Alan C., 342, 356, 384, 422
Callaghan, James, 63, 288, 323
Cameron, David M., 233
Camp, Dalton, 282, 304, 331, 384
Campbell, Colin, 416
Campbell, Colin, 129, 148, 162, 175, 195
Caouette, Réal, 49
Cardozo, Benjamin, 220
Carter, Jimmy, 140, 214, 297, 325, 350
Cassirer, Ernst, 51
Ceaser, James W., 149
Chandler, Marsha A., 15
Chandler, William M., 15
Cheffins, R.I., 203
Chouinard, Julien, 204
Chrétien, Jean, 127, 396, 397, 410, 411
Christian, William, 416
Churchill, Winston, 108, 422
Clark, Joe, 3, 4, 11, 34, 54, 119, 122, 124, 130, 134, 158, 166, 176, 204, 255, 272, 274, 276, 277, 313, 317, 399, 411, 412, 413
Clarke, Harold D., 195, 235, 331, 370, 381
Conway, Margaret M., 366
Cools, Ann, 312
Corry, J.A., 29
Courtney, John C., 277, 302, 356
Coutts, Jim, 172, 310, 311
Cox, Archibald, 221
Crick, Bernard, 20, 21, 22, 31, 41, 42, 195
Croll, David, 175

447